AF762903

Contemporary China

Contemporary China: A New Superpower? is a unique textbook introducing the complexity and diversity of China's society, politics, economics, and international affairs, and the multiple ways in which their dynamics corroborate to simultaneously construct and challenge perceptions of China.

Structured thematically in three sections – History, Society and Culture; Politics and Economy; and International Relations – this textbook provides answers to one of the most frequently asked general questions in relation to China. Will it become a new superpower and equal the international power and influence of the United States? Chapters written by some of the most recognized commentators and researchers of China cover a broad range of topics and offer an in-depth analysis of issues in contemporary China, such as the impact of the Tiananmen 1989 events, the economic development of the country, the environmental and demographic crises, social control and propaganda, and the role of China in the region and the world.

Introducing students comprehensively to the domestic context and international affairs of China, the book will be particularly useful for undergraduate-level courses in Asian Studies and courses on the history, politics, and international affairs of China and Chinese Studies.

Kristina Kironska is an academic researcher who worked in Taiwan for many years, where she lectured at the University of Taipei and organized human rights lectures at Amnesty International. She currently works as an assistant professor at Palacký University Olomouc, Czech Republic, and advocacy director at the Central European Institute of Asian Studies, Slovakia.

Richard Q. Turcsanyi is the program director of the Central European Institute of Asian Studies, Slovakia, and an assistant professor at Mendel University in Brno and Palacký University Olomouc, both in the Czech Republic. He is an author of *Chinese Assertiveness in the South China Sea* (2017) and a number of other publications dealing with Chinese foreign policy.

Routledge Studies on Think Asia

Edited by Jagannath P. Panda, Institute for Defence Studies and Analyses, India

This series addresses the current strategic complexities of Asia and forecasts how these current complexities will shape Asia's future. Bringing together empirical and conceptual analysis, the series examines critical aspects of Asian politics, with a particular focus on the current security and strategic complexities. The series includes academic studies from universities, research institutes and think-tanks and policy oriented studies. Focusing on security and strategic analysis on Asia's current and future trajectory, this series welcomes submissions on relationship patterns (bilateral, trilateral and multilateral) in Indo-Pacific, regional and sub-regional institutions and mechanisms, corridors and connectivity, maritime security, infrastructure politics, trade and economic models, and critical frontiers (boundaries, borders, bordering provinces) that are crucial to Asia's future.

https://www.routledge.com/Routledge-Studies-on-Think-Asia/book-series/TA

18. Multilateralism in the Indo-Pacific
Conceptual and Operational Challenges
Edited by Swaran Singh and Reena Marwah

19. Contemporary China in Anglo-American and Chinese Perspectives
Making Sense of a Rising China
Emre Demir

20. Indo-Pacific Strategies and Foreign Policy Challenges
The US-China Strategic Competition
Edited by Hyun Ji Rim and James E. Platte

21. South Korea and Foreign Direct Investment
Policy Dynamics and the Aftercare Ombudsman
Choong Yong Ahn

22. Contemporary China
A New Superpower?
Edited by Kristina Kironska and Richard Q. Turcsanyi

23. The United Nations, Indo-Pacific and Korean Peninsula
An Emerging Security Architecture
Edited by Shin-wha Lee and Jagannath Panda

Contemporary China

A New Superpower?

Edited by Kristina Kironska and Richard Q. Turcsanyi

Routledge
Taylor & Francis Group
LONDON AND NEW YORK

Cover image: ©Pavel Dvořák, www.pavel.photos

First published 2024
by Routledge
4 Park Square, Milton Park, Abingdon, Oxon OX14 4RN

and by Routledge
605 Third Avenue, New York, NY 10158

Routledge is an imprint of the Taylor & Francis Group, an informa business

© 2024 selection and editorial matter, Kristina Kironska and Richard Q. Turcsanyi; individual chapters, the contributors

The right of Kristina Kironska and Richard Q. Turcsanyi to be identified as the authors of the editorial material, and of the authors for their individual chapters, has been asserted in accordance with sections 77 and 78 of the Copyright, Designs and Patents Act 1988.

All rights reserved. No part of this book may be reprinted or reproduced or utilised in any form or by any electronic, mechanical, or other means, now known or hereafter invented, including photocopying and recording, or in any information storage or retrieval system, without permission in writing from the publishers.

Trademark notice: Product or corporate names may be trademarks or registered trademarks, and are used only for identification and explanation without intent to infringe.

British Library Cataloguing-in-Publication Data
A catalogue record for this book is available from the British Library

ISBN: 978-1-032-39509-8 (hbk)
ISBN: 978-1-032-39508-1 (pbk)
ISBN: 978-1-003-35006-4 (ebk)

DOI: 10.4324/9781003350064

Typeset in Times New Roman
by Deanta Global Publishing Services, Chennai, India

Contents

List of illustrations viii
List of contributors x
Acknowledgments xii
Note on the transcription of Asian names and nomenclatures xiii

Introduction: A new superpower? 1
RICHARD Q. TURCSANYI

PART I
History, society, and culture 13

1 **Historical legacy: A humiliated 5000-year-old civilization?** 15
FILIP ŠEBOK

2 **Mao Zedong: Why does the revolutionary leader "live forever"?** 29
FILIP ŠEBOK

3 **Tiananmen 1989: How did the massacre change China?** 40
BARBARA KELEMEN

4 **Religion, traditions, and values: What do the Chinese believe in?** 47
KLÁRA DUBRAVČÍKOVÁ

5 **Living standards and social issues: What is it like to live in China?** 58
KLÁRA DUBRAVČÍKOVÁ

PART II
Politics and economy 71

6 **China's political system: How does the Communist Party rule China?** 73
FILIP ŠEBOK

7 **Chinese economic miracle: How did an underdeveloped country change into a world leader?** 89
MARTIN ŠEBEŇA

8 **Social control and propaganda: What is "social credit" and how has China handled COVID-19?** 99
FILIP ŠEBOK

9 **Rule by law: Is there justice in China?** 114
MATEJ ŠIMALČÍK

10 **Technological power: Can China innovate?** 128
MARTIN ŠEBEŇA

11 **Environment: Does China care about it?** 136
KLÁRA DUBRAVČÍKOVÁ

12 **Xinjiang: Why has China imprisoned more than a million Uyghurs in re-education camps?** 147
BARBARA KELEMEN

13 **Tibet: Why is the mysterious "snowy kingdom" part of China today?** 156
LUBOŠ BĚLKA

14 **Hong Kong: How did the "pearl of the Orient" become a city of protests?** 166
MARTIN ŠEBEŇA

15 **Taiwan: Why does China consider it its own and what does it mean for Taiwan?** 177
KRISTINA KIRONSKA

PART III
International relations 191

16 **China in the world: A New Silk Road to world dominance?** 193
MATEJ ŠIMALČÍK

17 **China in its immediate neighborhood: A benevolent power or a hegemon?** 205
ALFRED GERSTL

18 Territorial disputes: Will China go to war? 218
DENISA HILBERTOVÁ

19 Relations with the United States: Are the two great powers headed for a collision? 227
RICHARD Q. TURCSANYI

20 Relations with Europe and Russia: Partners or competitors? 240
RICHARD Q. TURCSANYI

21 China's relations with the Global South: On the rise or past their peak? 252
JOSHUA EISENMAN AND ERIC HEGINBOTHAM

Index *263*

Illustrations

Figures

0.1	A Chinese proverb	xiii
1.1	Yellow and Long/Yangtze Rivers	16
2.1	Statues of Mao Zedong in the Shanghai Propaganda Museum	30
3.1	The tank man – a well-known photo from the 5 May 1989 protests	41
4.1	Lingguang Buddhist Temple in Badachu Park, Beijing	49
4.2	Falun Gong practitioners in Taiwan in 2020	53
5.1	Chinese migrants inside China in 2010	60
6.1	China's administrative division	75
6.2	CCP and its lead authorities	77
6.3	Xi Jinping's book in various languages	87
7.1	Fathers of the Chinese economic miracle – Deng Xiaoping and Zhao Ziyang	90
7.2	Zhu Rongji in 1999	93
8.1	Nobel Peace Prize laureate Liu Xiaobo	101
8.2	Cameras on Tiananmen Square in Beijing	105
9.1	Sima Qian depicted in a Ming dynasty portrait	116
10.1	Shenzhen – the capital of hardware	133
11.1	Water supply per person for one year	139
12.1	Kashgar; old and new parts of the city	151
12.2	Linxia (Gansu), one of the main religious, cultural, and trade centers of the Chinese Muslim population	153
13.1	Map of Tibet	157
13.2	The Tibetan alphabet	158
14.1	Victoria Harbour	167
14.2	Protests in Hong Kong in 2018	174
15.1	Political map of Taiwan	179
15.2	Pride 2022 in Taipei	183
15.3	Gigantic loudspeakers built in 1967 in Kinmen	185
15.4	President Tsai Ing-wen during a protest against nuclear energy in Taipei in 2019	188
15.5	Taiwanese people's perception of cross-strait relations, May–June 2022	189
16.1	Chinese highways and bridges in Shanghai	199

16.2 Malacca Strait in Southeast Asia 200
17.1 South Korean people's perception of China 209
17.2 String of pearls 213
17.3 Pakistani people's perception of China 214
18.1 Sino–Indian border 220
18.2 Chinese claims in South China Sea 224
19.1 Eleanor Roosevelt and Song Meiling in front of the White House 230
20.1 Vladimir Putin and Xi Jinping 249

Table

1.1 One of the possible periodizations of Chinese dynasties 22

Contributors

Luboš Bělka works at the Department for the Study of Religions, Faculty of Arts, Masaryk University, Czech Republic, where he focuses mainly on Tibetan Buddhism. From the early 1990s, he repeatedly visited Buryatia, the landscape around Lake Baikal, and studied the renewal of local forms of Buddhism after the fall of the Soviet regime and its official atheism.

Klára Dubravčíková studied sinology and political science in the Czech Republic, Taiwan, China, and Germany. She currently works as a research fellow at the Central European Institute of Asian Studies, Slovakia, and a data analyst at the Palacký University Olomouc, Czech Republic.

Joshua Eisenman is an associate professor at Notre Dame University, IN, USA, and senior fellow for China at the American Foreign Policy Council, Washington, DC, USA. Besides other publications, he is a co-editor of *China Steps Out. Beijing's Major Power Engagement with the Developing World* and author of *Red China's Green Revolution: Technological Innovation, Institutional Change, and Economic Development Under the Commune.*

Alfred Gerstl is an associate professor at the Palacký University Olomouc, Czech Republic, and president of the Central European Institute of Asian Studies, Slovakia. Previously, he was a lecturer and researcher at the University of Vienna, Austria, and Macquarie University, Sydney, Australia, and associate professor at the Higher School of Economics in St. Petersburg and Novosibirsk State University, Russia. He specializes in international relations in the Indo-Pacific, particularly in Southeast Asia, as well as Central Eastern Europe's relations with China.

Eric Heginbotham is a principal research scientist at MIT's Center for International Studies, MA, USA, and a specialist in Asian security issues. Before joining MIT, he was a senior political scientist at the RAND Corporation, CA, USA, and a senior fellow of Asian Studies at the Council on Foreign Relations, New York, USA. After graduating from Swarthmore College, PA, USA, Heginbotham earned his PhD in political science from MIT.

Denisa Hilbertová is a lecturer at the Chinese Studies Seminar at Masaryk University in Brno, Czech Republic. Her focus is modern Chinese history and contemporary politics. She studied history at Charles University in Prague, Czech Republic; Asia Pacific studies at National Chengchi University in Taipei, Taiwan; and international relations at Metropolitan University in Prague, and is a member of the European Association of Taiwan Studies.

Barbara Kelemen is an intelligence analyst working for a security consulting company in London. She studied in London, China, and Hong Kong, and works as a research fellow at the Central European Institute of Asian Studies.

Kristina Kironska is a socially engaged academic who lived and worked in Taiwan for many years – she lectured at the University of Taipei and organized human rights lectures at Amnesty International. She currently works as an assistant professor at the Palacký University Olomouc, Czech Republic, and is also advocacy director at the Central European Institute of Asian Studies, Slovakia.

Martin Šebeňa works as a consultant at an international accounting firm and is the chief economist at the Central European Institute of Asian Studies, Slovakia. He holds a Ph.D. in political science from the University of Hong Kong, and master's degrees in finance from Curtin University, Perth, Australia, and in politics and sinology from Charles University in Prague, Czech Republic.

Filip Šebok is a sinologist who studied Chinese and international relations in the Czech Republic and China, and is currently working as a research fellow at the Association for International Affairs in Prague, Czech Republic.

Matej Šimalčík is the executive director of the Central European Institute of Asian Studies, Slovakia. He focuses on China–EU relations, as well as on the issues related to strategic corruption and corrosive capital. In 2021, he was listed on the Forbes 30 Under 30 list (Slovak edition) in the governance and social innovation category. He is also a member of the Expert Pool at the European Center of Excellence for Countering Hybrid Threats, Helsinki, Finland. He has a background in international relations and law, which he is also actively practicing in Slovakia. Previously, he worked as legal counsel to the Slovak branch of Transparency International.

Richard Q. Turcsanyi is the program director of the Central European Institute of Asian Studies, Slovakia, assistant professor at the Palacký University Olomouc, Czech Republic, and assistant professor at Mendel University in Brno, Czech Republic. In the past, he completed research stays at institutions such as the University of Toronto, Canada; National Chengchi University in Taipei, Taiwan; Peking University, China and the European Institute of Asian Studies in Brussels, Belgium. He is an author of *Chinese Assertiveness in the South China Sea* and several other publications dealing with China's international relations.

Acknowledgments

This book builds on previously published books in Slovak and Czech languages by Hadart and Epocha. This English-language book is adjusted, updated, and includes new chapters. We would like to thank Jakub Drabik and Josef Hirja from Hadart for agreeing to publish this book. We would also like to express our gratitude to Dr. Jagannath P. Panda, the series editor of the Routledge Studies on Think Asia, as well as to Dorothea Schaefter, Routledge Area Studies editor. This book would not be possible without their support, and their suggestions have made it better (while any mistakes are naturally ours). We also want to thank Runya Qiaoan for creating a calligraphy showing the differences and similarities between simplified and traditional Chinese characters in a specific example. We extend our thanks to Vladimíra Ličková and Nela Valchářová for their help in preparing this book and to Robert Barca, Pavel Dvořák, Michal Dančišin, and Zdeněk Horníček for providing photographs.

Note on the transcription of Asian names and nomenclatures

Chinese language names and nomenclatures are listed in English according to how they are officially transcribed in the respective country. In Mainland China, the official way of transcribing Chinese characters into Latin letters is *pinyin.* In the rest of the Chinese-speaking world – for example in Taiwan, Hong Kong, or Singapore – there are multiple ways of transcribing Chinese into English. In all these places, however, each name has an official transcription under which the person appears internationally. For example, the name of the Taiwanese president is listed in the book as the name she goes by officially – Tsai Ing-wen – and not, for instance, as her name would appear in pinyin (*Cai Yingwen*).

The transcription of Tibetan, which also appears in the book, does not have an analogy of pinyin, and there is no unified form of its transcription (as opposed to transliteration). A distinction is to be made between transcription, which approximates the phonetic notation of a language, and transliteration, which requires knowledge of the Tibetan transcription rules (called Wylie).

In transliteration, each Tibetan character has its equivalent in Latin letters; however, just like in English, some words are spelled differently from how they are

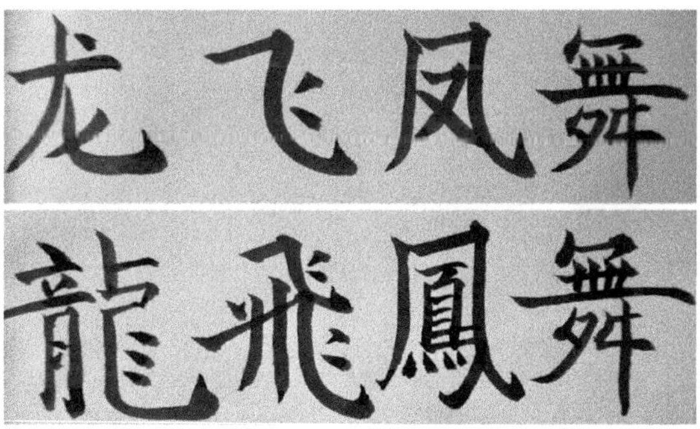

Figure 0.1 A Chinese proverb (*long fei feng wu*, literally "dragon flies, phoenix dances") is often used to describe elaborate calligraphy. The picture above shows the phrases in the simplified characters used in Mainland China, below in the traditional characters used for example in Taiwan, Hong Kong, and Macao. The first three characters differ, but the fourth is the same in both simplified and traditional Chinese (source: Runya Qiaoan).

pronounced. So, for example, the expression དབུས་གཙང is transcribed into English as *U-tsang* but transliterated as *dbus gtsang*. Transliterations are usually only used in scholarly articles, as in other texts they could disturb the reader without adding much value. This book only uses transcriptions.

Introduction

A new superpower?

Richard Q. Turcsanyi

From around the beginning of the new millennium, international media began to be filled up with headlines proclaiming 'China's rise' and the advent of the 'Asian century', in which China would 'rule the world' by taking over from the United States. These moods are understandable: China is unknown to many – a huge, fast-growing country ruled by a communist party on the other side of the world, communicating in a unique writing system entirely unrecognizable to anyone who has not studied it. As such, China remains a symbol of difference and a quintessential 'Other' for many casual onlookers. In such a context, the perceptions of China often derive from general categories – and these seem unambiguous at first glance. However, China also faces several limitations at various levels, which may undermine its future power growth. This book addresses the big question of China's role in the world and its prospects by looking comprehensively at China's domestic situation as well as international engagement. ***Is China a superpower or will it become one? Will it overtake the United States and become the global hegemon?*** *This introduction chapter sums up the main themes of the book to argue that China is still short of being classified as a full-fledged superpower – and the challenges it faces might prevent it from becoming one in the future.*

Will China overtake the United States?

China's economic growth between 1980 and 2020 is historically unprecedented in many ways. Never in human history has such a large population (today about 1.4 billion inhabitants) and such a large part of the world's population (about one-fifth) developed so rapidly. For 40 years, China's gross domestic product (GDP) growth averaged almost 10% a year, making China's economic growth one of the fastest in the world throughout the whole period. China's GDP in 2020 was about 70 times larger than in 1980. While in 1980 China was economically (measured by GDP per capita) at the level of the world's poorest countries and its GDP represented about 2% of the entire world's production, in 2020 its GDP per capita was already at about the level of Bulgaria (an EU member), and its share in the world economy is about 20%. As China's economy grows, so does its military strength and its overall influence and presence in the world.

DOI: 10.4324/9781003350064-1

These statistics are astonishing – and there are many more conveying a similar message. Yet China watchers are generally cautious in assessing China's power and ability to dominate the world. Susan Shirk, in 2007, called China a 'fragile superpower' that often appears to be economically and politically powerful abroad but faces many existential challenges and problems at home.[1] It is the ability of the Chinese government [2] – or the Communist Party – to address domestic problems effectively that is one of the key factors that will influence whether or not China eventually becomes a superpower. In our book, we devote a significant part to analyzing these domestic challenges to understand why maintaining stability in China is so difficult and also consequential for China's international role.

One of the basic characteristics of contemporary China is, of course, its political regime ruled by the Chinese Communist Party (CCP). At first glance, the Chinese government may look stable – especially when compared to how often and unpredictably the governments change in Western democracies. However, this government stability does not necessarily mean the stability of the regime. While governments in liberal democracies have limited powers, take turns in power, and sometimes collapse unexpectedly, their fall does not mean the collapse of the democratic regime. In China, the situation is exactly the opposite – the stability of the regime practically equals the strength of the government. The unexpected fall of the government in such a system could indeed mean the collapse of the whole regime. That is why the Chinese Communist leadership is anxiously trying to maintain domestic stability, and sometimes their exaggerated reactions to various perceived threats seem paranoic. This inherent instability of authoritarian regimes may be an obstacle to China's 'superpower' ambitions in the future if the Chinese government took steps to appeal to the domestic environment even though doing so would undermine its international standing. The phenomenon of the 'wolf warrior' diplomacy, when Chinese officials take confrontational steps against their international partners, is a recent example of this issue: although their steps seem contradictory to China's international goals, they make sense within the domestic political context.[3]

David Shambaugh in 2013 also questioned China's international power, and he argued that China is at most a 'partial power', as in many areas of world politics Chinese influence is not yet very manifested.[4] One of the biggest problems for China is the lack of partners: while the United States has a network of alliances, military bases, and friendly relations around the world (though not only those, of course), China currently has only one base abroad (in Djibouti), and its partners are often states whose contribution and commitment are questionable – think of Pakistan, Iran, Venezuela, Cuba, Zimbabwe, North Korea, and Russia. Although China is increasingly succeeding in gaining support from countries around the world, especially from among developing and authoritarian states, this can still not be likened to the long list of powerful states that have a long history of close cooperation with the United States, including the world's richest democracies such as Japan, South Korea, Canada, Australia, and the European Union. Moreover, although China is seen relatively positively in some parts of the world, such as in Asia, Africa, and Latin America, the United States (and the West, more generally) is still seen more positively and as the preferred partner.[5] The ability to win over key international partners to one's side may prove to be one of the most important factors in the escalating rivalry between China and the United States – and despite some of China's success in recent years, the United States still has a huge advantage in this regard.

Although the role – and behavior – of China in the world has been changing in recent years, many respected China watchers continue stressing similar limitations to China's international power. In 2017, Hung Ho-fung argued that 'China will not rule the world', emphasizing various domestic issues within China which will limit its international standing, not least by making it difficult for China to make friends.[6] In 2021, Ryan Hass published a book, *Stronger*, outlining how the United States can continue to utilize its advantages in the competition with China and preserve the upper hand.[7] Susan Shirk in her recent book argues that China has actually overreached its power: by abandoning 'low profile' diplomacy and engaging in more confrontational relations with the United States, it is undermining its future rise.[8]

In this book, we offer a comprehensive picture of China as a country that is by all means one of the world's great powers and which has become the second most powerful country in the world – after the United States – at the beginning of the 21st century. At the same time, however, we take the position that China has still not achieved 'superpower' status, which we understand as having significant strategic interests – and the ability to protect them – across all the world's geographical regions and topical dimensions (similar to the United States today or the Soviet Union during the Cold War). Moreover, we suggest that it even remains questionable whether China will succeed in becoming a 'superpower' in the future. China's power is most often discussed in the media using simple indicators such as staggering economic growth, the military budget, or rising influence in the world. However, to understand China's current position and prospects, it is necessary to analyze the complex international context and challenging domestic situation. These two dimensions will act as significant limitations to China's future ability to increase its international influence. At the same time, the question of whether China will replace the United States as the world's most powerful country depends to a large extent on how the United States will behave internationally and how it will cope with its own internal problems. However, in this book, we will focus on China.

What is China?[9]

The natural answer to this question is that it is a country in Asia with the world's second largest population (overtaken by India in 2023), first or second largest GDP (depending on whether measured by purchasing power or nominal value), third or fourth largest geographical size (depending on the source), and territorially spanning five time zones (yet with one official time). Another answer may emphasize Chinese people and the historical existence of Chinese civilization with a specific culture, unique scripture, and other distinctive features of 'Chineseness'.

However, the terms China and Chinese are far from unambiguous. There are heated debates – and real-world armed conflicts – about what territory is or should be considered as 'China'. It is not entirely clear who and on what criteria is considered 'Chinese'. China's millennia-long history and traditional culture fascinate many people around the world, but their perceptions are driven by current political, social, and economic realities. These ambiguities are not 'only' academic problems but have concrete implications for the daily lives of billions of people who come into contact with China – which today is basically everyone in the world.

Are you interested in 'Chinese' culture, and would you like to experience it first-hand? You have various options of where to go: Beijing, Taipei, Hong Kong, and Singapore, but also one of the numerous 'Chinatowns' in Northern or Southern America, Europe, and other parts of the world. Each of these places offers a different picture of Chinese people, culture, history, and language – and would probably give a different answer on what it means to be Chinese. These places are also ruled by various governments and have different visa rules that you would have to follow in order to pay a visit. Or would you like to do business with a 'Chinese' company? Prepare for different political, economic, and legal systems, as well as different scripts. Mainland China, for instance, uses 'simplified' Chinese characters while Taiwan and Hong Kong use 'traditional' ones, so you will need multilingual versions of your promotional materials. On the other hand, you need to be careful how you communicate these differences. If you list Taiwan as an independent country on your website, you may face a public boycott in the People's Republic of China (PRC) or even a denial of market entry, as Taiwan is very strongly and emotionally perceived as an inherent part of China. However, if you do mention Taiwan as part of China, public criticism may await you not only on the island of Taiwan, but also in other parts of the world.

The language situation is no clearer. The language of China is commonly called 'Chinese', but in reality, it is more accurate to speak of Chinese languages in the plural. What is known as Chinese – i.e., Standard Chinese, or also Mandarin Chinese – is just one variant of a wide range of dialects, many of which are mutually intelligible and from a linguistic point of view can be considered separate languages. Standard Chinese is the most common variant of the Chinese language and is based on a dialect from the vicinity of the capital, Beijing, that has been spoken at the imperial court for the last centuries (hence the name 'Mandarin'). This variant is today a *lingua franca* in Mainland China (as *putonghua*, or 'standard language') but also in Taiwan (as *guoyu*, or 'state language') and increasingly among the ethnic Chinese in Singapore (as *huayu*, or 'language of the Chinese'). On the other hand, most of the overseas Chinese communities speak other Chinese dialects or languages, as historically most Chinese emigrants came from the coastal areas, where Cantonese, Hakka, Min, and other languages are spoken. In Mainland China, however, the dominance of Standard Chinese has grown in recent decades, gradually displacing other variants, which have been labeled in the process as 'dialects' to underline the political and cultural unity of the Chinese nation and state.

How many Chinas are there?

According to the PRC's official position, there is just one China in the world. However, as we have just seen, the reality might be a bit more complicated. Taiwan (whose regime's official name is the Republic of China) is sometimes still referred to as the 'second China', although many Taiwanese abandoned this idea years if not decades ago. With an even looser interpretation, Singapore, whose majority is ethnic Chinese, can be considered the 'third China'. Hong Kong and Macau are also specific: although they are under the control of the Beijing government, as former colonies of European countries they have a high degree of autonomy, including their own currency and borders. Mainland China, Hong Kong, Macau, Taiwan, and Singapore are sometimes referred to collectively as *Greater China* – which, together with about 40 million overseas Chinese, constitute a Chinese cultural and linguistic world.[10] In many countries, the Chinese diaspora has become quite influential due to its economic success – especially in Southeast Asia and Western countries, but ethnic Chinese communities have existed in Latin America and Europe since the 19th century. It should be mentioned that the overseas Chinese have been often persecuted – anti-Chinese pogroms have taken place in Southeast Asia and elsewhere, with the most recent of these tragic events taking place in Indonesia in 1998 when over a thousand ethnic Chinese were murdered.

In this book, we will devote a separate chapter to Taiwan, whose current specific status and relationship with Mainland China is a direct result of the Chinese Civil War (see Chapter 15). In 1949, after the Communist victory, Mao Zedong declared the People's Republic of China, which is now considered 'China' by default – and this will also be the case in this book unless stated otherwise. The defeated Chinese Nationalist Party *Kuomintang* (KMT), under the leadership of Chiang Kai-shek, withdrew to the island of Taiwan, where they managed to defend against Communist forces. Ever since, the island has operated separately from Mainland China and still bears the official name of the Republic of China, thus directly following the political entity that was established in China in 1912 after the fall of the Qing Empire. However, since the 1990s, the Taipei government has renounced its claim to represent the whole of China and has sought to strengthen, or at least maintain, its *de facto* independence and control over Taiwan and a few remote islands. However, the PRC continues to consider Taiwan to be its province and expects a final (re-)unification that would, in its eyes, finally end the Civil War and the so-called 'century of humiliation' (see Chapter 1). Yet the majority of Taiwan's population seems to be opposed to such a scenario and increasingly feels more 'Taiwanese' and less 'Chinese'. In addition, the Taipei government relies to a significant extent on Washington's help, which has long signaled that it could intervene in the event of a Chinese military attack. Cross-strait relations are not 'just' about the question of 'what China is' and 'who the Chinese are'. Taiwan also remains an unresolved international issue with major implications, including a possible US–China military conflict.

Another chapter will focus on Hong Kong (Chapter 14), which is also not part of Mainland China but has been under the PRC's control and sovereignty as a

'Special Administrative Region' since 1997. The island of Hong Kong was part of the United Kingdom after the Chinese imperial troops of the Qing dynasty were defeated in the First Opium War in 1842. Later on, the so-called 'New Territories' were leased in 1898 to the United Kingdom for a period of 99 years. All British territories within Hong Kong were eventually returned to China under an intergovernmental agreement in 1997, which included an arrangement on the so-called 'one country, two systems'. Accordingly, Hong Kong was granted rights to its own legal and political system for 50 years. In recent years, however, this arrangement has been fading away, tensions have risen, and many people in Hong Kong have protested the actions of Beijing and local authorities, arguing that the government is not abiding by the agreement. Developments in Hong Kong are important because, among other things, the 'one country, two systems' formula has been the way in which Beijing wants to annex Taiwan.

Apart from Taiwan and Hong Kong, separate chapters will be devoted to Tibet (Chapter 13) and Xinjiang (Chapter 12), which are often considered 'problematic' regions, spreading to the far west of the PRC and occupying about a third of the country's total territory, making them important strategic areas, among other things. The majority of China's population – over 90% – is made up of the Han ethnicity, who live in very high concentrations, especially in the eastern and southern parts of the country. Tibet and Xinjiang are inhabited mainly by ethnic Tibetan and Uyghur populations, which differ from the Han people in many respects, including appearance, language, scripts, religion, and culture. Officially, Tibet and Xinjiang are called 'autonomous regions' within the PRC, but in practice, it is difficult to speak of any local autonomy whatsoever. On the contrary, the Chinese government is often criticized abroad for strict central control and human rights abuses in these regions. Recently, international criticism has focused mainly on Xinjiang, where since 2017 the Chinese government has introduced strict social management of the population, which utilizes an extremely high level of online and offline police control. Moreover, according to various estimates, more than a million people, mainly of Uyghur origin, were imprisoned in the so-called 're-education camps' under constant supervision. Several international experts and bodies even call this a 'genocide'.

The relationship between the Han, Tibetan, and Uyghur populations – and at the same time the people in Taiwan and Hong Kong, and the overseas Chinese – represents the ambiguity of what is meant by the term 'Chinese' and who belongs to this designation. These differences are in part the product of certain inconsistencies in the translation. In the Chinese language, the concept of *huaren* exists to represent an ethnic-cultural designation for the Chinese – mainly the Han, who have been historically the bearer of the (dominant) Chinese civilization. As such, this term would include also people from Taiwan and Hong Kong, Chinese Singaporeans, and representatives of the Chinese diaspora, but not necessarily Tibetans and Uyghurs. Another Chinese-language word, *zhongguoren*, is used to denote the citizens of China, in which the Tibetan and Uyghur populations are embedded, while the Chinese diaspora in the world is not. The positions of the people in Taiwan and Hong Kong are disputed in this respect, as the issue of political identity is sensitive in these places. We write about this in the relevant chapters of this book. In any case, the fact that terms such as *huaren*, *zhongguoren*, and often also *Han* are usually translated into English simply as 'Chinese' creates some confusion which is difficult to clarify without reference to the original Chinese concepts.

Unclear heritage of history

The relationship between China's many ethnic groups and the question of what constitutes the territory of the Chinese state is, of course, related to historical developments, which we will address in several chapters of the book. Chinese history consists of the eras of imperial dynasties that ruled China for thousands of years. Xia is mentioned as the first mythical Chinese dynasty, which is thought to have been in power from about 2100 BC. Subsequently, the dynasty that unified China for the first time is Qin, ruling for a relatively short time in the years 221–206 BC. Dynasties that are considered 'Golden Eras' of Ancient China include Han (206 BC–220 AC) and Tang (618–906). During their reign, China was the cultural and civilizational center of the wider East Asian region and was respected as the 'Middle Kingdom' in Japan and Korea, which received many elements of its traditional culture. However, after the Song Dynasty (960–1279), this 'hegemonic' position of China began to change. The territory of what was then China was conquered twice – first by the Mongol Yuan dynasty, which ruled from 1279 to 1368; and second by the Manchurian Qing dynasty, which ruled as the last imperial Chinese dynasty from 1644–1911. Perhaps somewhat paradoxically, during the reign of the 'non-Chinese' Qing, the Chinese state grew to its historical maximum and incorporated (to a much greater extent than before) territories that were inhabited by ethnic groups other than Han. After the fall of the empire in 1912, these territories were inherited by the Republic of China and, since 1949, the People's Republic of China. In addition to the specific status and relationship of regions such as Tibet and Xinjiang, the history of numerous territorial disputes that China has had in the past with almost all of its neighbors is a legacy of this history. Some of them have remained unresolved to this day and present a potential for wider conflicts with India, Japan (for the East China Sea), and the countries of Southeast Asia (for the South China Sea).

As already mentioned, culture has played a key role in history as a unifying element of China – and even as a legitimizing factor for the ruling dynasty. One of the characteristic elements of Chinese civilization is the fact that, compared to Europe, the Middle East, or India, religion has played a much smaller role. The function of religion in China is represented by a combination of Confucianism, Taoism, and other traditional concepts, such as Yin and Yang, which can be characterized more as holistic philosophies and doctrines of life rather than as complete religions. The state power in China has maintained a dominant position throughout history and ruled in a secular manner. An example is Buddhism, which came to China from India and was eventually more or less accepted by society and political powers as part of Chinese culture, but in a subordinate position and adapted to local conditions. Other religions such as Islam and Christianity have not yet found a such stable form of co-existence in the Chinese social and political system and in recent years have witnessed growing persecution. The Chinese government's efforts are to prevent the emergence of any alternative and autonomous form of authority. In the chapter on Chinese culture, philosophy, and religion (Chapter 4), we will provide an answer in the limited space to the question of what effects this specific Chinese 'secular' mix has on today's Chinese society, and subsequently on its politics, economics, and other aspects of public life. In addition, in a separate chapter, we will try to present a picture of what everyday life for people in China looks like, how is it influenced by the legacy of history, and the reality of the communist political system, combined with tremendous economic growth (Chapter 5).

Politics and economics

The People's Republic of China is officially one of five communist regimes (along with North Korea, Vietnam, Laos, and Cuba) that have survived to the present day. In this context, the question arises as to how Chinese communists have managed to stay in power, while most of their comrades in other parts of the world were removed at the end of the Cold War. Several chapters of the book will provide a partial answer to this question. In the first place, China has never entirely rejected an entire era of its own communist history, as was, for instance, the case in the Soviet Union after Stalin's death. A separate chapter will address the controversial legacy of Mao Zedong, who is still revered in China as a unifier and liberator, all while much of society refuses to return to the radical policies that characterized his era (Chapter 2).

The question of the survival of the Chinese communist regime immediately confronts us with the events of 1989 in Beijing's Tiananmen Square, which posed the most serious crisis for the communist government in China in recent decades (Chapter 3). While communist regimes in other parts of the world facing similar challenges opted for a strategy of concessions, negotiations, or reforms against growing protests, the Chinese leadership decided to call in the military, resulting in thousands of casualties. In Mainland China, this part of history is still extremely politically sensitive, it is not discussed publicly, and any related information is censored. In Hong Kong, on the other hand, the anniversary of the massacre was a traditional occasion for a public vigil, attended by more than 100,000 people in 2019, for example (although future vigils are doubtful due to recent changes in the politics of the region). Among other things, the events of 1989 marked the end of the limited political reforms initiated by the party leadership in the 1980s. To this day, the Leninist system of the dominant party – which controls the state apparatus and the army – survives and thrives. Since the 1990s, power over these three components of power (party, army, state) has been centralized in one person – first Jiang Zemin, then Hu Jintao, and since 2012 the current Chinese leader Xi Jinping, who has further strengthened the party's position – and his own. Another significant change brought by Xi is that he remains in power for more than ten years, thus disrupting the unwritten custom of the last three decades. It has been widely believed internationally that Xi's steps will make China less stable in the medium- to long-term, especially when his succession will become an issue.

Two chapters will address some other specific issues of the relationship between state power and the population in China. In Chapter 6, we will discuss the techniques the Communist Party uses to keep itself in power. A key role here is played by the sophisticated system of state propaganda, which aims to maintain the support of the population for the government of one party. Recently, the issue has been so-called 'social credit', which seeks to use the latest technologies (including people's online behavior and their general monitoring) to pool information on the population. Thanks to the high effectiveness of these and other means, the Communist Party largely manages to prevent open threats to its government. In Chapter 9, we will look at how the law works in an authoritarian country. On the one hand, the Communist Party is 'above the law', but on the other, its rule relies heavily on laws and adhering to them – often with the help of the latest technologies, including artificial intelligence, face recognition, and others.

While political reforms in China have been largely frozen since 1989, the same cannot be said of the economy. Shortly after the death of Mao Zedong, Deng Xiaoping came to power and almost immediately began the process of 'reforms and opening up' to the world. This was followed by four decades of growth at around 10% of GDP per year, which is one of the most successful economic performances in human history, given its scale and speed. The impressive improvement in the material security and living standards of the vast majority of Chinese people is a key factor in why the CCP still has great support from ordinary people and why it remains in power. However, with the economic growth slowing down, the question emerges whether dissatisfaction might spread in China – and how the government would respond to such a scenario. The dynamics during COVID-19 might already give a hint of what may await China – more intrusive state control. In Chapter 7, in addition to these political implications, we will look at the unorthodox approach to Chinese economic policies. In Chapter 10, we will try to predict future developments and offer an answer to whether an innovative economy can be built in an authoritarian regime that suppresses the critical thinking of its population.

The downside – and another limitation – of China's tremendous economic growth is environmental problems. For a long time, political interest was practically singularly focused on the exploitation of available resources and production growth. Over time, however, the situation of the environment has reached a critical stage and has begun to significantly affect the lives of ordinary people – for example, in terms of air pollution but also contamination of soil and water. Environmental problems have eventually become one of the most visible areas of public life in China, where citizens have actively asked the state for change. However, there is a fundamental dilemma for the government in this regard: on the one hand, there is the dissatisfaction of the population with pollution, but on the other hand, there are also related economic and social aspects – closing a polluting factory could jeopardize a region's economy and affect public satisfaction as well. In a separate chapter, we will look at how the Chinese government is trying to address this dilemma, albeit with unclear results so far (Chapter 11).

International relations

The domestic political development and the enormous growth of China's economic power are directly related to China's foreign relations, which are often the most interesting for most people living outside China, as they directly affect them. Part III of this book therefore addresses this topic, beginning with a more general Chapter 16, in which we present the starting points of current Chinese foreign policy, its 'core interests', and strategic culture, which influence the decisions of the Chinese leadership. It may be surprising to argue that although we are going to talk about foreign policy, the domestic political reality and the effort to maintain the power monopoly of the Communist Party still come first in the Chinese leaders' minds. Subsequently, we will address a specific topic that defines China's foreign policy in recent years – the Belt and Road Initiative (the official Chinese name for the initiative is *yi dai yi lu*, or literally 'One Belt, One Road').

China cannot escape its geography, and its international relations start at its borders. In fact, China's neighborhood is highly challenging – China is part of at least four subregions (Northeast Asia, Southeast Asia, South Asia, and Central Asia) and has the most neighbors (14) of any country worldwide. Moreover, China's neighbors include great powers in their own rights, some of them armed with nuclear weapons (Russia, Pakistan, India, North Korea), members of the G20 (Russia, Japan, South Korea, Indonesia, India), or countries who have long traditions of opposing China (Vietnam) and preserving treaty links with the United States (Japan, South Korea, Philippines). One could even conclude that China has bad luck to find itself in such a challenging environment – especially when compared to, for instance, the United States, which only borders two countries, neither of which poses a real security threat or significant challenge. To become even a regional hegemon in this context seems like an uphill struggle for China. Chapter 17 will analyze the complex relationships and policies of China toward its immediate neighbors.

The next chapter will analyze another topic on the border of domestic and foreign policy. As mentioned in this introduction already, for complex historical and other reasons, China is now arguing over a border with several neighboring countries. In Chapter 18, we address two of these territorial conflicts – the border dispute with India and the complex situation in the South China Sea. Both conflicts will be almost impossible to resolve in the future to the satisfaction of all parties involved. At the same time, they represent situations that have the potential to escalate into an open military confrontation between great powers.

The most important foreign actor for China has long been the United States, and in recent years their relationship has also been described as 'the world's most important bilateral relationship' (Chapter 19). The history of Sino–US relations has undergone surprising changes over the last 100 years, which also illustrates well the dynamics of China's contact with the world from the end of the 19th century to the beginning of the 21st century – and into the future. China and the United States have found themselves as partners or even allies on several occasions, but their armies have also fought against each other several times in bloody conflicts. With the knowledge of this historical legacy, we will also discuss in the chapter the key issues that plague us now – should we be afraid of military conflict, is there a threat of a new Cold War, and will China become a new world hegemon?

In Chapter 20, on China's relations with Europe, we will address two narrower topics. First of all, we will focus on the EU's relations with China, which are sometimes underestimated as they do not really reach the strategic importance of those with the United States but are still one of the key foreign issues for both parties. The EU and China are each other's largest trading partner, while the EU has also been China's critical source of technology (although that may be changing with China's development of its own technology). The two sides have very different ideological bases, and their relationship has been increasingly tense in recent years, yet they are still trying to work together on many global issues. Second, we will also address Russian–Chinese relations as part of broader European–Chinese relations. Russia is, of course, a specific 'European actor', whose size extends deep into the Far East and shares more than 4,000 kilometers of border with China. While Russia and China are currently close international partners, their historical relationship is much more problematic, and it is possible that the future will bring surprising turns to today's warm relationship.

Finally, in Chapter 21 we will look at China's relations with the Global South. While often overlooked and underestimated in the West (and at some points also in China), the Global South is an important partner of China for various reasons. Importantly, there has been a common ideology-historical basis of the China–Global South link, drawing on anti-colonial, anti-Western, and anti-imperial themes. China has long presented itself as the largest developing country and the leader of the Global South. Economically speaking, China has increased its presence in the Global South to the extent that it is now the major trading partner and provider of finances, while the reverse – the role of developing countries contributing to China – is more limited, especially when compared to the role of the West in China's economic development. Still, China has invested a lot of effort in developing a comprehensive network of relations spanning all regions of the Global South and thus creating a potential alternative to the current Western-led international system.

Notes

1 S. Shirk, *China: Fragile Superpower*, New York: Oxford University Press, 2007.
2 Unless stated otherwise, we will refer to the "Chinese government" in a broad sense to represent the leadership of the People's Republic of China.
3 P. Martin, *China's Civilian Army: The Making of Wolf Warrior Diplomacy*, New York: Oxford University Press, 2021.
4 D. Shambaugh, *China Goes Global: The Partial Power*, New York: Oxford University Press, 2013.
5 R. Q. Turcsanyi et al., "US-China rivalry in the Global South? Insights from a public opinion survey," CEIAS, 2022; R. Q. Turcsanyi et al., "Public opinion in the Indo-Pacific: Divided on China, cheering for US & EU," CEIAS, 2022.
6 H. Hung, *The China Boom: Why China Will Not Rule the World*, New York: Columbia University Press, 2017.

7 R. Hass, *Stronger: Adapting America's China Strategy in an Age of Competitive Interdependence*, New Haven: Yale University Press, 2021.
8 S. Shirk, *Overreach: How China Derailed Its Peaceful Rise*, New York: Oxford University Press, 2022.
9 The same question is asked in the title of Ge Zhaoguang, *What Is China? Territory, Ethnicity, Culture, and History*, Cambridge: Harvard University Press, 2018.
10 D. L. Poston & J. H. Wong, "The Chinese diaspora: The current distribution of the overseas Chinese population," *Chinese Journal of Sociology*, 2 (3), 2016, 348–373.

Part I

History, society, and culture

1 Historical legacy

A humiliated 5000-year-old civilization?

Filip Šebok

If we want to understand today's China, it is impossible to ignore the twists and turns of the country's long and complicated history. However, the aim of this chapter is not to provide a detailed historical excursion – other books will serve better in this respect – but to look at the past from a contemporary perspective and reveal what heritage the past has left for the China of the 21st century and how its history is perceived in China today. This chapter, therefore, looks at some of the key "themes" of Chinese history that we often come across when discussing China. ***What is behind the narrative of China as the oldest civilization in the world with a history of 5000 years, as many Chinese official sources claim? What was behind the emergence of the modern Chinese national identity? How to explain the paradoxical fact that China simultaneously sees itself as an heir to an ancient powerful civilization and as a humiliated victim of foreign oppression?***

The myths of Chinese history

The narratives about China as a country with 5000 years of uninterrupted history do not appear only in the speeches of Chinese officials but have been encountered probably by about everyone who has had more than fleeting contact with China. In China, this statement is expressed with ease as a natural fact, such as in Xi Jinping's first public address following his election as General Secretary of the Central Committee of the Chinese Communist Party (CCP) in 2012:

> Our nation is a great nation. During more than five thousand years of civilizational development, the Chinese nation has made indisputable contributions to the civilizational progress of mankind. In modern history, the Chinese nation has gone through many hardships and found itself in the most dangerous period. Since then, many people with noble ideals rose up to fight for the great rejuvenation of the Chinese nation but failed one by one. After its inception, the Chinese Communist Party united the people and led them steadily forward, struggling relentlessly to turn poor and backward China into a new China, closer and closer to prosperity and strength; the prospects for the great rejuvenation of the Chinese nation were unprecedentedly bright.

For many Chinese, this is also a source of national pride – because it suggests that their country is somehow different and exceptional. In a political context, the

DOI: 10.4324/9781003350064-3

argument has been employed as a universal tool to defend the Chinese Government's stances – Chinese officials, for example, like to ridicule in this respect the "short" history of the United States in response to criticism from Washington.

The notion of China's unique longevity predisposes several other interconnected claims, for example, that China has maintained the basic organizational structure of society, its identity, cultural patterns, or even territory from the early foundations of civilization to this day – and is older than other surviving civilizations. In reality, the oldest confirmed written records in Chinese history date back to the Shang dynasty (1600–1050 BC). Everything before can be considered myth, including the figures of the legendary Yellow Emperor and the Flame Emperor or the "first" Xia dynasty (2100–1600 BC). Moreover, what we now call "China" as a single concept began to be perceived as such only after the unification by the first emperor of the Qin dynasty, Qin Shi Huang, in 221 BC, who is now known all over the world for building the so-called Terracotta Army to protect his mausoleum. Prior to the first emperor, the territory of what is today's China was divided into several separate states without a common identity – a state of affairs that was also to be repeated several times in subsequent history.

The very concept of China (in Chinese, *Zhongguo*, i.e., literally the Middle Country/Kingdom) was used as a designation for a sovereign political unit with clear boundaries only under the rule of the last Qing dynasty. In its original, significantly older meaning, which appeared in the Zhou dynasty, it referred to the states of the "central plain", the "cradle" of the Chinese civilization between the Yellow River (in Chinese, *Huanghe*) and the Long River (in Chinese, *Chang Jiang*, or in some areas also *Yangzi Jiang*, from which the English name *Yangzi* is derived).[1]

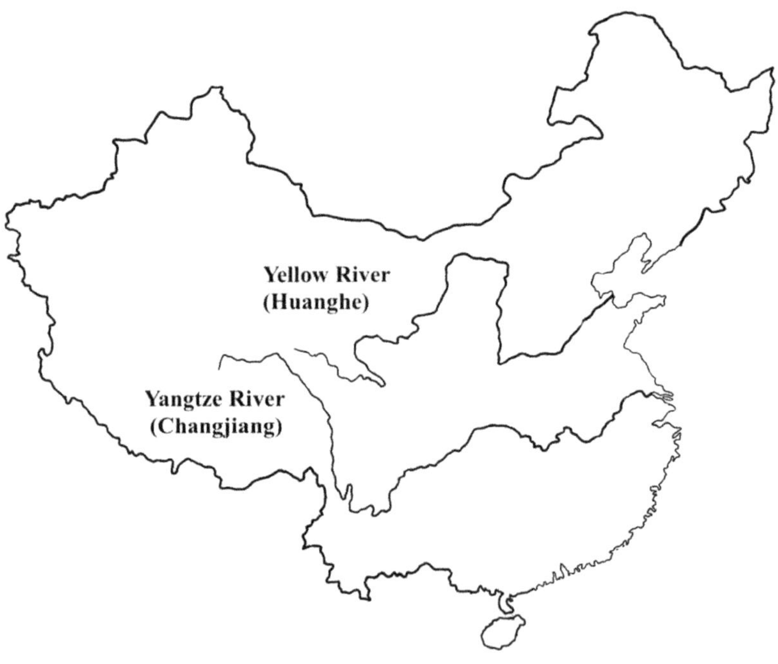

Figure 1.1 Yellow and Long/Yangtze Rivers (source: CEIAS).

Historical Chinese political entities were instead named after the ruling dynasties – such as Qing, Ming, and others. Moreover, the territory controlled by these dynasties has varied significantly – and was mostly smaller, but sometimes also larger, than that of today's China. In times of the greatest territorial expansion, for example, the last imperial Qing dynasty ruled over a territory twice as big as the previous Ming dynasty. Although unity has been one of the key themes of Chinese history, China has in fact been divided into several entities for much of its historical development. The famous Chinese novel *The Romance of the Three Kingdoms* begins with a sentence that captures the prevailing concept of the cyclical nature of Chinese history: "Long united must divide, long divided must unite".

When discussing the notion of the unbroken thread of China's existence as a cultural and political entity, it is also important to realize that for much of history, contemporary concepts of clearly defined borders and state entities mutually recognizing their sovereignty did not exist. While in Europe these principles began to be widely accepted from the 17th century onwards, in Asia this was only at the end of the 19th century or even later. It is problematic to use modern concepts (such as borders) retrospectively to assess under whose jurisdiction a particular territory was, and therefore what could be considered as part of "China" or of another country. That is why the statements of the Chinese Government about the territories that have allegedly belonged to China "since time immemorial" have to be taken with caution. A good example would be the island of Taiwan (see Chapter 15), which came under Chinese domination only during the Qing dynasty, as well as Tibet (see Chapter 13), Xinjiang (see Chapter 12), and other territories, which are today subjects of territorial or political disputes.

Throughout history, the individual Chinese dynasties, which have often exhibited control over different territories inhabited by various ethnicities, have been united by their claim to political legitimacy – the so-called "mandate of heaven", serving as a moral and political basis for their power. The history of the previous dynasties was then interpreted by the new ruling dynasties in line with their interests. It is believed that the very concept of the mandate of heaven arose as an attempt to justify the coming to power of the Zhou dynasty, which retrospectively painted the last kings of the Shang dynasty as immoral and unworthy to rule. As a result, whether a particular dynasty was legitimate or not was subject to retrospective judgment by its successors, and the very fact that a given dynasty lost political power was subsequently (quite tautologically) interpreted as the loss of the mandate of heaven – which was transferred to the new dynasty. Emperors would task scholars to compile the officially sanctioned account of the past in the so-called dynastic histories, which helped to create an impression of political continuity. From the *Records of the Grand Historian* by Sima Qian (145–86 BC), which described the entire history known until then, to the official history of the Ming dynasty, written by its successor the Qing dynasty, altogether 24 official dynastic histories were compiled.

Moving to other persistent myths, it can hardly be accepted as a fact that the inhabitants of today's China have always considered themselves Chinese and are linked by "blood ties", motives that often appear in Chinese propaganda.[2] Different ethnicities have always intermingled on the territory of today's China – as in Europe and most other parts of the world. Several originally nomadic "non-Chinese" (non-Han) tribes mingled with indigenous peoples and even controlled China politically for a significant period of its history. Two of the major Chinese dynasties – the Mongolian Yuan dynasty (1279–1368) and the Manchurian Qing dynasty (1644–1912) – originated from territories originally outside what was then considered traditional Chinese territory and were ruled by non-Han elites.

Along with the mixing of ethnicity and "foreign" domination, different cultures have also influenced each other. Thus, "Chinese" culture has been subject to constant development and transformation when it absorbed "foreign" aspects, and has never been an unchanging concept, as an essentialist perspective would have us believe. It is paradoxically in this aspect that Chinese culture has proved to be quite unique – it has been able to integrate various, often very distinct influences and make them a part of the whole. An example is the integration of Buddhism, now seen as an integral part of Chinese culture, which came to China from India through Central Asia in the first century AD. The Manchus of the Qing dynasty, who, after gaining military control of China, accepted many aspects of Chinese culture and gradually assimilated with the majority of Chinese society, are another example. A historically more recent case, with no less significant impact, is of course the "Sinification" of Marxism and communism in the 20th century.

Throughout most of history, belonging to Chinese civilization was not primarily a question of ethnic origin, but of the degree of acceptance of Chinese culture, which traditionally divided the world into "civilized" and "barbaric" people. Chinese civilization and the state units that emerged from it perceived themselves as the center of the "(all) under the heaven" (from the Chinese term *tianxia*) ruled by the emperor, the Son of Heaven. The further away from the center, the more the emperor's political power weakened, and the "level of civilization" decreased.[3] In this understanding, Chinese civilization, Chinese dynasties, and Chinese emperors did not have their equals in the world. Yet even those from the outskirts outside the civilized realm could become civilized if they accepted Chinese culture and the emperor's rule.

Construction of Chinese identity

The emergence of modern Chinese national identity did not take place until the 19th century, with a great contribution of ideas that flowed to China from the West. To a significant degree, the construction of this identity stemmed from an effort to negatively identify themselves against the "non-Chinese" Qing dynasty among revolutionary circles.[4] In this original understanding, the Chinese identity was associated mainly with the dominant Han ethnicity. However, many Chinese nationalist thinkers, among whom Liang Qichao was probably the most prominent, considered such a definition to be too restrictive. In political terms, it could mean that China would lose the "peripheral" territories of the empire without dominant Han settlement – including Tibet, Xinjiang, Mongolia, or Manchuria, which, in fact, made up most of the Qing dynasty's territory.[5] Following this intellectual debate, the Republic of China, founded after the fall of the empire in 1912 by Sun Yat-sen, was already established on the principle of the "union of five races" – Han, Manchurian, Mongolian, Tibetan, and Hui, under the roof of a single Chinese nation (*zhonghua minzu*).[6] Following the establishment of the People's Republic of China (PRC), the Chinese Communist government extended the official number of ethnicities constituting the "Chinese nation" to 56, of which 55 (i.e., excluding the Han) are perceived as minorities.

One aspect of the "construction" of the Chinese nation, serving the purpose of transforming the Chinese empire into a modern nation-state, was the accentuation of the common origin of all Chinese ethnicities. One aspect of this effort is the promotion of myth that all these ethnicities are descendants of the Flame and Yellow Emperors (in Chinese *Yandi* and *Huangdi*), the common mythical ancestors who supposedly ruled China in the third millennium BC. The position of the forefather of the Chinese nation belongs primarily to the Yellow Emperor, whose significance was reinterpreted in the ethnic sense by Chinese nationalists at the beginning of the 20th century.[7] The cult of the Yellow Emperor was banned by the communists after taking power, but in recent decades it has been restored and has even gained the official support of the Communist Party.[8] The state propaganda also uses the Yellow Emperor to emphasize the bond between the people of mainland China and Taiwan, as well as between all the people of Chinese origin in the world, regardless of their citizenship. In its messaging, the Communist Party often works with the metaphorical concept of the family, which emphasizes the unbreakable ties between all Chinese people but also implies the expectation of devotion and obedience to the motherland.

Overall, the notion of the historical continuity of today's China and its predecessors is questionable. Today's China is radically different from the China of 200 years ago – and it can be argued that the country has made more of a clean break with its history than most Western countries have. However, in some ways, the durable aspects of Chinese civilization are indeed truly unique compared to other countries. The best example is the Chinese writing system. Despite several changes, it still maintains the basic characteristics acquired after the unification of various writing systems by the first emperor Qin Shi Huang in the 3rd century BC. The shared ability to read and write Chinese characters was also the basis for the political regime and shared culture, literature, and art throughout Chinese history. Different variants of spoken Chinese are so different from each other that they could easily be considered different languages in a different political context. However, their written form – and centralized political power – was able to bring them together. For centuries, the use of classical Chinese as a common written language was widespread throughout the sphere of influence of Chinese civilization, including Japan, Korea, and Vietnam. In some ways, classical Chinese in East Asia resembled Latin as the *lingua franca* of medieval Europe.

There are also some aspects of China's political and administrative establishment that have persisted through the millennia, even if their form has changed significantly. Perhaps the most famous one is the system of imperial examinations, which appeared in its original form already during the Han dynasty (3rd century

BC–3rd century AD) and was further developed during the Sui and Tang dynasties (581–908).[9] National examinations have led to the establishment of an extensive bureaucratic apparatus, built on education in the officially sanctioned Confucian learning. Imperial examinations were abolished only in 1905, but to this day, their legacy can be recognized in the civil service examinations in the PRC and Taiwan.

Pitfalls of orientalism

It is not just China that creates persisting myths about itself. In fact, many of the misconceptions are related also to the (predominantly) Western perspectives on China from the 19th century onward. Shackled by the mental confines of "orientalism", as described by Edward Said, the West has traditionally perceived China as a radically different, exotic, and unique entity that supposedly escapes rational understanding.[10] In particular, several other dubious claims are associated with the perception of China as a uniquely ancient civilization – the notion that the Chinese people think in terms of centuries, that Chinese culture and society are still mainly influenced by Confucian learning, that it is uniquely spiritual (vs. the materialistic West), etc. Whether these stereotypes are positive or negative, they can lead to a distorted picture of China. To put it in perspective, reading the *Analects* by Confucius will be probably of no better use for understanding the mindset of the contemporary Chinese people than it would be to read the philosophical treatises of Plato in the case of modern Europeans.

In line with the orientalist mental framework, some aspects of contemporary China are ultimately perceived as "essential", given, and historically unchanging, which carries fundamental political implications. One example is the view of China as a traditional model of "Eastern (oriental) despotism", where the government enjoys almost unchallenged power over its citizens. We often hear arguments that China is a unique country, whether because of population size, culture, or historical legacy, which should persuade us that democracy or universal values cannot function in China. Such arguments are of course promoted also by the Chinese Communist Party to justify certain "Chinese characteristics" of the authoritarian regime. However, the modern history of Taiwan, South Korea, and Japan shows that even societies that share a broadly common cultural basis with China can build a fully-fledged and functional democratic polity that is not fundamentally different from the standards of Western liberal democracy. Ultimately, in understanding China, as well as other countries, it is appropriate to find a balance between understanding its "uniqueness" and identifying processes that find their comparison elsewhere.

From the center of all under heaven to the century of humiliation

While the glorious imperial history is a source of pride in China, the modern Chinese historical outlook is also coupled with a distinct sense of shame and humiliation. This aspect of collective memory stems from the contrast between the glory of imperial China and its dramatic decline in the 19th and 20th centuries. Only the combination of these two seemingly conflicting perspectives allows us to understand today's Chinese perception of history and how it is used for political purposes.

During the northern Song dynasty in the 10th–13th centuries, China was the richest country in the world measured by GDP per capita, even with its vast population.[11] Until the 18th century, China was the largest economy in the world in absolute terms, although it started to lag behind Europe in per capita terms already before the Industrial Revolution.[12] The Chinese Empire had a strong internal market and engaged in vigorous trade relations with neighboring countries. In the wider East Asian region, China maintained a hegemonic position at the top of the system of relations, which were organized hierarchically and, in some ways, resembled medieval vassal relations in Europe. In this context, Chinese civilization was perceived as the economic and cultural peak, with its influence leading to the wide adaption of Chinese cultural and political norms across the region.

Nevertheless, the Chinese empire suffered a significant decline starting from the 18th century during the Qing dynasty, while at the same time, the European powers were growing stronger and gradually expanded their influence around the world. It took the Qing dynasty a long time to realize that it could not keep up with the Western powers. Macartney's mission serves as a telling example of China's perception of the world at the time.[13] In 1793, the British East India Company sent a diplomatic mission to China in order to achieve a greater opening of the Chinese market to British trade and the establishment of a diplomatic representation of the British Crown in Beijing. The leader of the British mission George Macartney was indeed received by Emperor Qianlong, who perceived the mission as yet another of many traditional "vassal" visits and rejected all the British demands. In a letter to the then British King George III, Qianlong made it clear that he did not perceive him to be equal, and that China was not interested in commerce with Great Britain:

> Yesterday your Ambassador petitioned my Ministers to memorialize me regarding your trade with China, but his proposal is not consistent with our dynastic usage and cannot be entertained. Hitherto, all European nations, including your own country's barbarian merchants, have carried on their trade with our Celestial Empire at Canton. Such has been the procedure for many years, although our Celestial Empire possesses all things in prolific abundance and lacks no product within its own borders. There was therefore no need to import the manufactures of outside barbarians in exchange for our own produce.[14]

However, this notion of superiority came to pass in the face of reality. Great Britain, through the East India Company, had been operating a lucrative opium trade since the end of the 18th century, importing the drug to China from India. Opium proved to be the most suitable commodity of interest in China that Great Britain could use to address its trade imbalance. When in 1839, Emperor Daoguang, Qianlong's grandson, decided to put an end to the illegal opium trade that robbed China of silver and had a detrimental impact on Chinese society, the United Kingdom responded with military force. The obsolete Chinese army

Table 1.1 One of the possible periodizations of Chinese dynasties

Name of the dynasty			*Period of rule*
Xia dynasty			2100 BC–1600 BC
Shang dynasty			1600 BC–1050 BC
Zhou dynasty	Western Zhou dynasty		1046 BC–771 BC
	Eastern Zhou dynasty	The Spring and Autumn Period	770 BC–475 BC
		Warring States Period	475 BC–221 BC
Qin dynasty			221 BC–206 BC
Han dynasty	Western Han dynasty		206 BC–9
	Eastern Han dynasty		25–220
Three Kingdoms Period			220–280
Jin dynasty			266–420
Northern and Southern dynasties			386–589
Sui dynasty			581–618
Tang dynasty			618–906
Five Dynasties and Ten Kingdoms Period			907–979
Liao dynasty			916–1125
Western Liao dynasty			1124–1218
Song dynasty	Northern Song dynasty		960–1127
	Southern Song dynasty		1127–1279
Western Xia dynasty			1038–1227
Jin dynasty			1115–1234
Yuan dynasty			1279–1368
Ming dynasty			1368–1644
Qing dynasty			1644–1912
Republic of China			1912–1949/present (Taiwan)
People's Republic of China			1949–present

was not ready to face modern European weapons and combat tactics and suffered a crushing defeat. In 1842, the emperor was forced to accept the terms of the Nanjing Treaty, which ended the so-called First Opium War. The treaty opened up new ports for foreign trade, provided for a payment of reparations by China, and ceded Hong Kong Island to the United Kingdom. The Nanjing Treaty became the first in a series of so-called unequal treaties that China was forced to sign by foreign powers in the coming decades.

The defeat in the First Opium War marked the beginning of the so-called century of humiliation, when China, with its weak central government, was left at the mercy of foreign influence while struggling with internal unrest. While the Qing dynasty remained formally in power, it was steadily losing control over the country. Following the example of the United Kingdom, other colonial powers tried to reap benefits in China, leading to a full-blown race for gaining a foothold in China in the second half of the 19th century. Gradually, Russia, France, the United States, and other Western powers asserted their interests. Japan joined the race as well after its modernization reforms in the 1860s.

Although China has never been directly colonized, as many other parts of Asia and the world have, it gradually lost territory, either permanently or in the form of territorial concessions administered by foreign powers. China has lost control of Outer Manchuria with today's city of Vladivostok and large territories in Central Asia around Lake Baikal to Russia, northern Vietnam (a vassal state) to France, and Korea (a vassal state) and Taiwan to Japan. Some of the territories where the imperial power weakened were later reclaimed (e.g., Xinjiang, Tibet, Hong Kong – see Chapters 12, 13, and 14), while others managed to gain independence fully or in part (e.g. Mongolia, Vietnam, and Korea) or remained part of another state, especially in the case of territories lost to Russia.

Adding to the troubles of the Chinese emperors, China was rocked by an enormous wave of internal unrest. In 1850 the Taiping Rebellion started, led by a South Chinese religious sect inspired by some Christian elements (their leader Hong Xiuquan claimed to be Jesus' brother). The sect managed to gain control over a large territory with the capital in Nanjing, establishing the Taiping Heavenly Kingdom that lasted for several years until it was defeated by the Qing armies aided by the UK and France in 1864. The Taiping Rebellion was one of the most destructive conflicts in the history of mankind and claimed 20 to 30 million victims.

In response to the external and internal turmoil, there have been intensive debates in China on how to get the country back on its feet.[15] The conservative wing believed that China must continue to rely on its own tradition, which, in their view, was still superior to the West. Others, on the other hand, were convinced that the only salvation for China would be to copy Western countries as faithfully as possible, following the example of Japan. Concluding the tumultuous century, between 1899 and 1901, the Boxer Rebellion motivated by anti-colonial and anti-foreign sentiments erupted. In the end, the revolt was suppressed by the Eight-Nation Alliance of colonial powers, leaving China humiliated once again and forced to pay reparations (see Chapters 19 and 20).

Facing internal and external turmoil, the Imperial Court, headed by Empress Dowager Cixi, finally decided to undertake fundamental reforms toward constitutionalism. However, they came too late to be able to save the imperial dynasty. The nationalist movement regarded the Manchu Qing dynasty as the main source of Chinese weakness, seeking its demise and the establishment of a republican regime. This was finally achieved in 1911 when local troops rebelled in Wuchang, now part of the city of Wuhan in central China's Hubei province. The revolution spread to other parts of China as well, and on February 12, 1912, the six-year-old Emperor Puyi formally abdicated the throne, bringing the long imperial history of China to a close.

However, China remained weak and fragmented for decades to come. In May 1919, the republican government, despite China's involvement in the war on the side of the Entente Powers, was forced to accept the terms of the Treaty of Versailles, which led to the transfer of the Shandong Peninsula from Germany to Japan. This provoked a radical response in China and led to the so-called May Fourth Movement with the aim of combating imperialism, modernizing the Chinese state and its culture, and rejuvenating the Chinese nation. The activists of the time wanted to bring democracy and science to China, and radically rejected Chinese traditions. Despite the fact that the movement did not achieve its immediate goals, it has significantly influenced subsequent intellectual development and political activism, including the early Chinese communists. To this day, the legacy of the May Fourth Movement is claimed by not only the Communist Party but also its critics, with each having a different understanding of the movement and its importance.

As the episode from the Versailles Peace Conference indicates, the weakening of the influence of Western powers in China in the first half of the 20th century led to the strengthening of Japan's position, which gradually expanded its territorial control in northeast China and eventually unleashed an open war of conquest in 1937. China was to become the heart of the Japanese Empire in Asia and the Pacific, built under the slogan "Asia for the Asians", but in reality, it was just another form of colonialism that emphasized the racial superiority of the Japanese. Hence, China had already become one of the major battlefields of the Second World War two years before the war broke out in Europe. The final expulsion of foreign influence and the establishment of a strong central government came only after the defeat of Japan and the end of the Chinese Civil War in 1949 when the communist forces – to some extent surprisingly – managed to gain control of the whole fragmented country after the Kuomintang government of the Republic of China escaped to the island of Taiwan (see Chapter 15).

A number of tragic moments are associated with the "century of humiliation", which has become a symbol of China's national trauma. At the end of the so-called Second Opium War in 1860, French and British troops, in retaliation for the detention and torture of Western prisoners by Chinese troops, looted and destroyed the Imperial Summer Palace in the north of Beijing. Only a pile of ruins remains from the extensive complex, now turned into a tangible reminder of China's humiliation and frequented by Chinese (and other countries') tourists. Another tragic symbol of China's "century of humiliation" is the Nanjing massacre of 1937 and 1938. After the occupation of the Republic of China's capital, Nanjing, Japanese troops unleashed murderous rampages, rapes, and looting. According to official figures from the Chinese Government, the Nanjing massacre claimed up to 300,000 victims, and although international estimates indicate lower estimates, it does not change the fact that it was one of the most terrible moments of the entire war. Moreover, Japan has not taken full responsibility for the Nanjing massacre and other war crimes committed in China (and elsewhere in Asia) during the war. As a result, the relationship with Japan is still perceived very sensitively in China today (and also in Korea).[16]

Who does history serve in China?

History is not a purely objective retelling of the past anywhere in the world, and its perception is subject to various distortions, whether intentional or unintentional. In particular, history is often abused for political purposes in regimes like today's China, where political power sets the boundaries of free debate and scientific research and employs various tools to shape and control the thinking of the population. The CCP uses history, which it modifies according to its own needs, as one of the most powerful legitimizing tools by which it justifies and strengthens its position in power. From this point of view, the Communist Party follows in the footsteps of the historical dynasties of imperial China, creating a historical justification for its rule.

The vision of a return to the glorious history of China and the rejuvenation of the Chinese nation is at the heart of the concept of the "Chinese dream" of China's current leader, Xi Jinping. According to him, China is bound to return to the main stage of world history and become a superpower again, i.e., to regain the status that belonged to it for centuries. Hence, from this point of view, China's rise today is only a redressing of a short-term anomaly in world history caused by the "century of humiliation". The Communist Party even has a specific timeline for this goal – China is to become a "rich and strong, democratic, civilized, harmonious and beautiful socialist modern power" by 2049 – the centenary of the establishment of the PRC.[17] Pride in the Chinese nation, its history, and culture among the Chinese populace is then often naturally linked to the support for the regime that has secured this historic reversal, and the Communist Party makes sure to stress such a historical feat could only happen with it at the helm.

However, the notion of the continuity of China's historical development, of which the CCP is to be the new representative, has not always been present. Although the Communist Party was a nationalist movement from the very beginning, in the first decades of its rule over China after 1949 it brought about a sharp break with Chinese history and traditional culture. Marxist ideas, albeit adapted to the Chinese context, constituted a foreign and hostile element to the traditional structure of Chinese society. During the Cultural Revolution, Mao Zedong and his fanatical supporters even tried to destroy Chinese culture and history completely, including both its physical and intangible elements (more in Chapter 2). The so-called old society, which in the eyes of Communists represented feudal backwardness, was to disappear and be replaced by the utopian ideal of a classless society. In fact, it can be argued that modern Chinese society is uniquely historically uprooted because of the decades of communist rule.

After Mao Zedong's death, the Communist Party abandoned these radical views, but it was only the shock of the 1989 protests that brought about a fundamental change in its attitude (more in Chapter 3). At that time, the Communist Party realized that after the gloss of the communist ideology had worn off, it needed a new foundation on which to establish its legitimacy among the Chinese population and thus maintain its hold on power. In addition to the promise of improving the standard of living, i.e., a highly pragmatic source of popular support, the Communist Party has opted for nationalism and the use of history, which, on the contrary, are elements largely based on emotions. In the 1990s, the Party launched a campaign for "patriotic education", which highlighted the Communist Party's historic mission.[18] The Party claimed it was the representative of the interests of the entire Chinese nation, and support of it was interpreted as the most patriotic duty of every Chinese person.

Ironically, an important aspect of this new appeal to national pride was to emphasize the history of the "century of humiliation" as part of the collective memory of the Chinese nation. While in the first decades of Communist China, the aspect of glorious victory was emphasized in the narratives about history, the self-stylization of China as a humiliated victim has now gained momentum. In its domestic and foreign propaganda, the CCP points to the wrongs China has suffered from foreign powers and claims that it was only the victory of the Communist Party that ensured that China was no longer to be humiliated.[19] Likewise, it is the only guarantee that China will not be humiliated in the future.

Because of the appeal of the "century of humiliation" concept, whether as an element of collective historical memory or as a useful political instrument, China also responds very strongly to any foreign statements and actions on Tibet, Hong Kong, or Taiwan. These sensitive issues of territorial integrity and sovereignty for China are interpreted as remnants of a time when China was weak and fragmented. For many Chinese people sharing this outlook on history, historical traumas will not be resolved until China rules Taiwan and is finally "united".

The coexisting Chinese self-perceptions of strength and vulnerability, of glorious history and humiliation, which British academic William A. Callahan aptly called "pessoptimism", is an explosive mix supporting nationalist sentiments.[20] The Chinese Government is able to skillfully use these sentiments and emphasize or, conversely, suppress those aspects of history that are deemed suitable at a given moment. For example, while Chinese state media often points to the Japanese crimes against China, there is hardly any mention of the fact that China has historically lost most of its territory to Russia, now one of China's most important international partners.

However, even the Communist Party cannot fully subordinate history to its interests, and historical awareness also develops outside the limits set by the regime. The Internet has also made it possible to give visibility to radical nationalist views, which are harder for the state to censor than voices coming from the liberal spectrum. Even Chinese diplomacy is sometimes under pressure from the ultra-nationalists, who criticize every perceived concession in foreign policy as a sign of weakness. Nationalism can thus be perceived as a double-edged sword – on the one hand, it allows the Communist Party to build its legitimacy using other than pragmatic material foundations, but on the other hand, it leaves the Party vulnerable to nationalist criticism.

Even though historical opportunism is characteristic of the Communist Party, it is important to note that many of the ideas about the Chinese past had originated before the current regime and thus should not be simply rejected as fabrications of "communist propaganda". The dilemma of how to achieve "rejuvenation" of the Chinese nation in the face of the humiliation inflicted by foreign powers was already discussed by Chinese intellectuals in the 19th century and was a leading motive of the May Fourth Movement as well. The commemorative "National Humiliation Day" was already introduced by the then Republic of China's government of Kuomintang.[21] However, the Communist Party managed to adopt these notions and effectively use them for its own needs. In the context of China's growing power in international relations, including its military potential, extreme nationalism stemming from the perceptions of historical grievances can lead to very dangerous results.

Shared ideas about the national past are a very powerful building block of the identity of today's Chinese nation and state. One should keep in mind that these notions are based on a selective perception of the past and not on objective knowledge based on impartial scientific research. However, in their real-world effects, they are no less real and should be properly understood rather than automatically dismissed.

Notes

1 L. S. Kwong, "What's in a name: Zhongguo (Or 'Middle Kingdom') reconsidered", *The Historical Journal* 58(3), 2015, 781–804.
2 "Yellow Emperor still a unifying force", *China.org*, 3 April 2017.
3 Z. Ge, *What Is China? Territory, Ethnicity, Culture, and History*, Cambridge: Harvard University Press, 2018.
4 S. Zhao, *A Nation-State by Construction: Dynamics of Modern Chinese Nationalism*, Stanford University Press, 2004.
5 D. Zheng, "Modern Chinese nationalism and the awakening of self-consciousness of the Chinese Nation", *International Journal of Anthropology and Ethnology* 3(1), 2019, 1–25.
6 Ibid.
7 L. Liu, "Who were the ancestors? The origins of Chinese ancestral culture and racial myths", *Antiquity* 73(281), 1999, 602–613.
8 F. Dikötter (ed.), *The Construction of Racial Identities in China and Japan: Historical and Contemporary Perspectives*, Honolulu: University of Hawai'i Press, 1997.
9 H. Liu, "The origin of the system of imperial examinations and the start of the Jinshi ke (Examination for Selecting Talented Individuals)", *Historical Research* 6, 2000.
10 E. Said, *Orientalism*, New Delhi: Penguin Books, 1978.
11 S. N. Broadberry, H. Guan, & D. Li, "China, Europe and the great divergence: A study in historical national accounting", *The Journal of Economic History* 78(4), 2017, 1–46.
12 Ibid.
13 J. K. Fairbank & M. Goldman, *China: A New History*, Cambridge: Harvard University Press, 2006.
14 E. Backhouse & J. O. P. Bland, *Annals and Memoirs of the Court of Beijing*, Boston: Houghton Mifflin, 1914.
15 Fairbank & Goldman, *China: A New History*.
16 K. Kironska, Y. Chen, & R. Q. Turcsanyi, "What do Chinese people really think about some of China's important partners?", *The Diplomat*, 28 July 2022.
17 "China a step closer to centenary goals", *Xinhua*, 9 October 2017.
18 S. Zhao, "A state-led nationalism: The patriotic education campaign in post Tiananmen China", *Communist and Post-Communist Studies* 31(3), 1998, 287–302.

19 Z. Wang, *Never Forget National Humiliation: Historical Memory in Chinese Politics and Foreign Relations*, New York: Columbia University Press, 2014.
20 W. A. Callahan, *China: The Pessoptimist Nation*, New York: Oxford University Press, 2009.
21 W.A. Callahan, "National insecurities: Humiliation, salvation, and Chinese Nationalism", *Alternatives: Global, Local, Political* 29(2), 2004, 199–218.

2 Mao Zedong

Why does the revolutionary leader "live forever"?

Filip Šebok

A revolutionary hero or a mass murderer? These are some of the common labels attached to Mao Zedong, one of the most prominent political figures of the 20th century. No matter how we view Mao, it is impossible to deny that without him, China's modern history could have developed quite differently. However, Mao is far from being just a historical figure. He is at the center of many debates on the present and future direction of China. It is therefore essential to continue to try to understand Mao, both as a historical figure and a political symbol. ***So, who was Mao Zedong and how did he become the leader of the communist revolution that led to the creation of "new China"? How did Mao's rule lead to the unprecedented disasters of the Great Leap Forward and the Cultural Revolution? Why did the Chinese Communist Party, despite all his catastrophic mistakes, refuse to abandon Mao's legacy and still cherishes him as one of its main symbols? Finally, how is Mao's legacy reflected in today's Chinese politics and society?***

Father of "new China"

Mao Zedong was born in 1893 in Hunan Province in a rich peasant family. From an early age, he was interested in political developments, influenced by the contemporary ideas that flowed to China from the West and from Japan. What united Chinese progressive intellectuals and activists at the time was the goal to overthrow the empire, modernize China, and make it a strong and united country free from the influence of foreign powers. Mao was not a convinced communist initially – his ideology framework was more of a nationalist one. It is also often argued that he had a poor understanding of key features of Marxism, engaging with the significant body of the literature only later. At the beginning of the communist movement in China, the leading promoters of communist ideas in China were Chen Duxiu and Li Dazhao, now relatively little-known figures. Mao, however, was already among the attendees of the first Congress of the Communist Party in 1921 in Shanghai and led a Party cell in the capital of Hunan Province, Changsha.

In its early days, the Chinese Communist Party (CCP) cooperated with the nationalist Kuomintang (KMT) in the so-called "unified front", with the aim of unifying China, which was then divided among regional military warlords in shifting

DOI: 10.4324/9781003350064-4

Figure 2.1 Statues of Mao Zedong in the Shanghai Propaganda Museum (source: Robert Barca).

alliances. In 1927, however, the KMT, under Chiang Kai-shek's leadership, turned against the Communist Party, killing thousands of Communist sympathizers in Shanghai. It was the end of this alliance that marked the beginning of the growth of Mao Zedong's power. Mao led the Communist troops and settled in the mountains of Jiangxi Province, where he attempted to establish the first communist quasi-state in China. This "Soviet republic" was gradually surrounded by the nationalist troops that sought to exterminate the communist movement. In 1934, under the pressure of the KMT, the Communists were forced to embark upon what was later called the Long March, which became one of the key aspects of the early communist mythology. During the Long March, Mao managed to accede to the leading role in the Party, the position he maintained until his death four decades later. After the Long March, during which the Communists suffered enormous losses, the northern province of Shaanxi and the city of Yan'an became their new revolutionary bases.

Meanwhile, China had been facing an increasingly expansionary Japan since the early 1930s. In 1936, therefore, the CCP and KMT joined forces again in a second united front against the common Japanese enemy. From 1937, China was fighting for its survival in a full-scale war against the invading Japanese. In addition to the fight against the invaders, Mao focused on further strengthening his power in the Party and in the communist-controlled areas. It was at that time that he instigated radical campaigns and purges against Party and personal enemies, which he later applied on a much larger scale throughout China. The contribution of the Communist Party and its military forces in the fight against Japanese forces is now heroized by the official account of history. However, a significant number of independent historians claim that the main burden of the war against Japan was born by the KMT, while the Communist Party took advantage of the situation to bolster its own position.

The formal alliance of the CCP with the KMT did not survive the victory over Japan, and in 1945, the civil war broke out again. In 1949, the Communists finally, with the significant help of the Soviet Union, achieved victory; and Mao Zedong thus could declare the People's Republic of China (PRC) from the Tiananmen Gate in Beijing. Chiang Kai-shek and the KMT withdrew to Taiwan after their defeat, where they managed to defend themselves, and the original authoritarian regime was gradually transformed into today's full-fledged democracy, still bearing the official name Republic of China (see Chapter 15).

Mao's life left an indelible mark on Chinese modern history. He adapted Marxism, "imported" from Europe (through Russia) to the conditions of China, which in his assessment, was a half-feudal, half-colonial society. Instead of the urban proletariat, which was supposed to lead the revolution according to Marx, Mao put Chinese peasants at the forefront, in accordance with the reality of China in those days. Unlike Lenin's idea of a revolution where the Communist Party played the main role as the revolutionary avant-garde, Mao put more emphasis on the direct involvement of the popular masses in the political struggle. Mao also developed the theory (and practice) of the so-called "people's war" of guerrilla warfare, used against the KMT and Japan. Mao is therefore also considered an important military strategist, with the doctrines that he developed studied and later also replicated worldwide. The set of Mao's thinking called "Mao Zedong's Thought" is still one of the ideological foundations of the Communist Party.

At the same time, Mao proved to be an uncompromising technician of power during his journey to power, who did not hesitate to use the harshest means against his (real or imagined) enemies. Gradually, Mao built a cult of personality around himself and usurped almost unlimited personal power. For Mao, mass loss of life was at best a necessary cost to achieve the noble goals of the revolution. Mao's rule over the "new China" was thus accompanied by unprecedented human disasters, of which he was personally the main instigator.

Permanent revolution

After the Communists took power in China in 1949, they found themselves ruling over a 500-million behemoth of a largely rural and backward country ravaged by wars. In some areas, the Communist regime brought undeniable progress. The country started massive industrialization and land reform along the lines of the Soviet Union. Progress has also been made in social issues, for example through campaigns to increase literacy, expand and improve health care, or broaden women's rights (more in Chapter 5), where the traditional practice of foot binding, for example, was banned. After many years, China once again became a fully sovereign and united country (except for Taiwan, which was and still is perceived as "unfinished business" by the Communists), a dream of Chinese nationalists since the end of the 19th century.

However, Mao was convinced that the revolution had not ended with the establishment of the PRC and that it had to continue continuously to preserve its fruits. Mao ruled through a never-ending succession of campaigns in which he relied on his charismatic authority and ability to mobilize the masses. Massive campaigns, such as the late 1950s' "anti-rightist campaign", were accompanied by systematic violence and mass murder. However, according to Mao, it was necessary to move vigorously and uncompromisingly against the enemies of the revolution.

Mao gradually became impatient because of what he deemed a slow pace of progress and decided that China would no longer follow the example of the Soviet Union in the economic sphere. In 1958, therefore, Mao initiated the so-called Great Leap Forward, a program of accelerated economic development, built on the industrialization of rural areas, collectivization, and organization of society into production units, the so-called communes.

The Great Leap Forward was accompanied by the adoption of a number of unscientific and harmful practices. One of them was the increased sowing density in the fields, which led to a significant reduction in the harvest. Under pressure from above, local authorities often concealed the actual number of supplies. These were then centrally collected and further redistributed away from the areas where they were in fact direly needed. Instead of working in the fields, peasants and other workers were sent to produce steel in domestic furnaces to achieve Mao's dream of catching up with the steel production of developed Western countries. In reality, however, most of the produced steel was of low quality and essentially of no economic value.

These factors led to enormous inefficiencies and, consequently, to poor harvests, exacerbated by natural disasters such as drought and massive floods on the Yellow River. The resulting famine, according to various estimates, caused the deaths of 20 to 50 million people, and millions more died as a result of violence accompanying forced collectivization, local revolts, or refusals to hand over crops. The Great Leap Forward turned out to be the greatest famine in human history and one of the greatest man-made tragedies ever.

It is still unclear to what extent Mao himself was aware of the gravity of the situation. His subordinates were often afraid to provide accurate information to Mao that would testify to the failure of his policy. While the official line blamed natural disasters as the main cause of the famine, Mao's personal responsibility was undeniable. After the end of the Great Leap Forward, Mao even underwent self-criticism and temporarily retreated into the background. More pragmatic-minded politicians took control over the economy, including the future leader Deng Xiaoping, who began to return the country to a relatively normal state.

In fact, however, Mao used his step away from the limelight as a tactical retreat and began to plan his return and revenge against those who undermined his position. Gradually, he became convinced that the greatest danger to the success of the revolution was posed by the "capitalist", and "revisionist" forces that supposedly still existed within the Party, seeking a return to old ways. Seeking to realize his ideal of a never-ending revolution and undermining rivals in the Party, Mao unleashed the so-called Cultural Revolution.

The Cultural Revolution brought chaos and the virtual collapse of the social fabric of China. The main perpetrators of the revolutionary rage were the so-called Red Guards from the ranks of radical students, whom Mao called upon to revolt against the authorities under the slogan "to rebel is justified". Millions of people were accused of being revisionists or enemies of the revolution and ended up in re-education camps, were sentenced to death by makeshift revolutionary tribunals, or were murdered or maimed in public lynchings. Mao's opponents within the highest circles of the Communist Party, including President Liu Shaoqi (who eventually died in 1969) and Deng Xiaoping, but also Xi Zhongxun, the father of Xi Jinping, were also targeted in purges. Moreover, the Red Guards were determined to destroy everything that represented the so-called old society. Countless temples and other historical monuments, archives, furniture, and works of art have been irretrievably destroyed.

Mao's cult of personality reached its peak in this period. "Little Red Books" with Mao quotes became a must-have for every Chinese. The Chinese leader was referred to as the "great red sun in our hearts", the perfect and all-powerful leader of widespread admiration and even deep personal emotional relationships. Mao's portraits were everywhere – it is estimated that up to 90% of people in China wore a badge with Mao's portrait on it.[1]

The general anarchy of the Cultural Revolution brought China to the brink of civil war when various groups of the Red Guards and the People's Liberation Army (PLA) began to fight each other over who was more loyal to Mao and the ideal of the revolution. Under the pretext of a revolutionary struggle, many people moved against their personal enemies or simply used the situation to gain power. At that time, Mao also realized that the decay caused by the Cultural Revolution must be limited before it spun out of control. In 1969, Mao declared the revolution officially over, and the Red Guards were sent from the cities to the countryside to "learn" from simple peasants. However, the real end of the Cultural Revolution came only after Mao's death in September 1976.

(Not) dealing with the legacy of Mao

After Mao's death, there was a power struggle for succession in China. Before his death, Mao chose the relatively unknown Hua Guofeng as his successor (after the two previously appointed successors were accused of treason), who, allied with several leading figures in the Party and the PLA, managed to overthrow the so-called "Gang of Four" (leading figures of the Cultural Revolution, including Mao's wife Jiang Qing). Yet, by 1978, Deng Xiaoping side-lined Hua Guofeng and became the *de facto* leader of the Party, maintaining his grip over Chinese politics almost until his death in 1997.

One of the key challenges facing Deng was how to deal with the legacy of Mao Zedong. Deng himself had been the victim of Mao's political cleanses on several occasions during his career (while previously also participating in several of the brutal campaigns) and saw the Great Leap Forward and the Cultural Revolution as disasters for China. In fact, the Cultural Revolution led to a weakening of the authority of the Communist Party, which threatened its hold on power. Nevertheless, Deng was aware that the Communist Party could not completely distance itself from Mao and would need him further as a symbol of its legitimacy.

Unwillingness to abandon Mao Zedong was evidenced already by the first steps made after his death. Instead of the cremation that Mao himself wished for, a mausoleum was built for him in the very political heart of China on Tiananmen Square. Following the example of Lenin, Mao's embalmed remains were deposited in the mausoleum on public display. Another signal was the dealing with the "Gang of Four", who were blamed – together with Lin Biao (Mao's original chosen successor) – for most of the excesses of the Cultural Revolution. The public trials of the Gang of Four were followed closely by the Chinese public and served as a reckoning with the decade of chaos. The main culprit of the Cultural Revolution, however, was not acknowledged.

After seizing power, Deng worked hard to bring the country back to normal after years of revolutionary disintegration. Gradually, many of the victims of persecution during the Cultural Revolution were rehabilitated, including Liu Shaoqi (another of the previously preferred Mao's successors) who was given a proper burial. The Communist Party officially resigned upon class struggle, replacing it with modernization and economic development as the new slogan. A process of "de-Maoization" started in the country, the most visible part of which was the gradual disappearance of Mao's previously ubiquitous images and sculptures from public spaces. More consequentially, Deng initiated limited political reforms (see more in Chapter 6) motivated by efforts to prevent a replay of the disasters resulting from the excessive concentration of power in the hands of one person.

However, Deng made it clear that Mao's death did not mean the end of the Communist Party's dictatorship. After a short period of political relaxation following Mao's death, Deng intervened harshly against the voices calling for democratic change, epitomized by the so-called "Democracy Wall" in Beijing, where ordinary people put up posters demanding political reforms. Deng proclaimed in 1979 the so-called "Four Cardinal Principles", which delineated what is not allowed to be questioned politically – socialism, the dictatorship of the proletariat, the leading role of the Communist Party, and the ideology of Mao Zedong's Thought and Marxism-Leninism.

In 1981, after more than a year of a complicated drafting process, the CCP adopted an official Resolution "on some issues in the party's history since the establishment of the PRC".[2] Since the Party's history was closely tied to Mao Zedong, it was largely about reckoning with his legacy. The Resolution remains the official position of the Party on historical issues, and Chinese censorship restricts free historical research on the topics contained therein.

As the Resolution claims, "if we evaluate [Mao's] activities as a whole, his contribution to the Chinese revolution goes far beyond his mistakes. Its merits are primary and its errors secondary".[3] While the Resolution positively assesses the conduct of Mao as a revolutionary leader, anti-Japanese military leader, and founder and leader of China in its early years, it particularly critically assesses his role after 1958. However, it is worth noting, that, for example, the drastic

"Anti-Rightist Campaign" of the late 1950s and other radical political crackdowns are described as correct by the Resolution. Still, the Great Leap Forward and the Cultural Revolution are already perceived as the result of increasing "leftist tendencies", growing arrogance, the cult of personality, and the usurpation of absolute power in Mao's hands. The Cultural Revolution itself is described by the Resolution as the greatest failure in the history of the Party and the state.

Paradoxically, the Resolution argues that Mao Zedong made mistakes by deviating from Mao Zedong's teachings. In this way, the Party "cleverly" separated Mao as a person from his ideological canon. As for those parts of Mao's legacy that did not suit the Party, the Communist Party retrospectively declared that they were in conflict with the ideological orthodoxy and thus relieved itself of the unwanted burden. In this way, the Party managed to avoid jeopardizing the whole ideological system on which it based its legitimacy. In doing so, the Party followed the warning of Mao himself, who previously criticized de-Stalinization in the Soviet Union out of similar concerns.

Origins of "neo-Maoism"

Deng's treatment of Mao's legacy was built on several contradictions. These became more and more pronounced as Deng and his followers pushed China further on the track of the "reform and opening up" policies, moving away from Mao's original ideals. China gradually opened the door to Western capital, the state-planned economy was increasingly replaced by market forces, and the elements of the socialist welfare state were dismantled. The reform of state-owned enterprises in the second half of the 1990s led to unemployment for tens of millions of people. Many Chinese found themselves not only without work but also without health or social insurance. While economic growth has benefited the whole country, the distribution of its benefits has been significantly uneven. The new capitalist class in the formally communist state was striking with its luxury and boundless materialism. Moreover, the business class and private entrepreneurs became a new recruitment base for the Communist Party after 2001 under Jiang Zemin.

These changes amplified voices critical of China's direction. For left-wing critics, Mao Zedong has become a frequently used symbol, representing nostalgia for the idealized pre-reform times. The critics also hoped that if they dressed their views in reverence for Mao, they would avoid a harsh reaction from the authorities – who would dare to go against Mao, whose party still recognized him as the most important figure in its history?[4] After 2000, the so-called neo-Maoist movement began to grow in China. It found support not only among the masses, nostalgic for the old times but also in influential intellectual circles. Left-wing activists were increasingly able to organize themselves thanks to the Internet and set up websites to communicate their views. The influential Utopia portal (in Chinese, *wuyouzhixiang*), for instance, also operated in the "offline" world and organized various events and campaigns.[5]

From the neo-Maoist circles came some very radical proposals. For example, Ma Bin's book *Remembering Mao Zedong* criticizes the "dismantling" of the path of socialism and argues that China would need to unleash a new Cultural Revolution every seven to eight years in order to rid the country of counter-revolutionary elements.[6] There is also a connection between left-wing ideas and ultra-nationalism – in the eyes of his admirers, Mao was not only the guarantee of authentic socialism but also of a strong "anti-imperialist" policy.[7] Nationalists were convinced that China was humiliated in becoming part of the world capitalist establishment under the leadership of the United States. Nationalist sentiments were stirred up by the 1999 incident, when a US aircraft accidentally bombed the Chinese embassy in Belgrade during NATO's operation against then Yugoslavia, which claimed three Chinese victims. Most Chinese still believe that the attack was deliberate.[8]

The Party has always been very sensitive to criticism from the "left", as it was able to pinpoint the striking conflict between the official ideology and reality. Deng Xiaoping himself warned that the Party must be warier of the left than the right. On the one hand, the Communist Party responded to the growing neo-Maoist movement with repression – a standard response to all "problematic" social forces. On the other hand, however, it began to reflect more the "left-wing" criticism and to adjust its political course. Under President Hu Jintao and Prime Minister Wen Jiabao, for example, the Party began to implement various measures aimed at reducing social disparities and improving the lives of the lowest strata of society. The leadership started to place a greater emphasis on the overall quality of life of the Chinese population, including the environment.

Mao's shadow in China's politics

The Maoist tradition was revived in political terms by Bo Xilai, the former party leader of Chongqing, and a member of Politburo, who was once considered a candidate for the highest echelons of power. During his stint in Southwest China's metropolis of Chongqing from 2007 to 2012, Bo became one of China's most prominent political figures on the national level. Bo abounded with what most of his Party comrades lacked – enormous personal charisma and the ability to speak directly to the masses. In this aspect, he resembled Mao, but the similarities did not end here. Bo's policies led to the creation of the so-called Chongqing model, which represented a set of policies emphasizing the dominant position of the state sector in the economy, maintenance of the public order, social welfare policy with an emphasis on the poorest groups of the population, and left-wing ideology.[9] Bo brought back old ideological campaigns and slogans, including reciting Mao's quotes, building Mao's statues, singing revolutionary songs, and mobilizing popular masses through mass campaigns. Bo also gained popularity by cracking down on the local mafia. The Chongqing leader became a rising star throughout the whole country, especially in neo-Maoist circles, where he was seen as a follower of Mao's tradition.

However, Bo Xilai's career ended abruptly at the beginning of 2012, just a few months before the Communist Party Congress, where he was expected to join the Politburo Standing Committee. Bo was accused of using his power to obstruct an investigation into a murder committed by his wife and of corruption. He was subsequently stripped of his office and his Party membership and was sentenced to life imprisonment for abuse of power and corruption. The fall of Bo Xilai provoked stormy reactions, against which the Communist Party took decisive action.[10] Authorities blocked several influential left-wing Internet portals and censured any criticism of Bo Xilai's removal. Support for the "red culture" and other aspects of the "Chongqing model" was no longer tolerated. Prime Minister Wen Jiabao, in an unusual public statement, suggested that Bo Xilai was trying to bring back the Cultural Revolution, straying far away from the political mainstream.[11] It seemed that with the fall of Bo Xilai, neo-Maoist politics were defeated.

What really happened behind the curtain of the 2012 power struggles is still a mystery. What is certain, however, is that Xi Jinping emerged victorious and became the general secretary of the Communist Party at the autumn congress. However, a look at Xi Jinping's record after taking power suggests that he was in fact inspired by his fallen rival's politics.[12] In the ideological field, Xi brought the return of campaigns at the national level, ideological education, and emphasis on the connection of the Communist Party with the popular masses. The slogan of Xi's efforts was a return to the idealized beginnings of the Communist Party. Xi brought back aspects of the Mao era, such as the public self-criticism of Party members. The new emphasis on returning to the Party's roots unavoidably also resulted in the promotion of Mao Zedong's status and his rehabilitation for current political purposes. However, despite the similarities, Xi is not the second Mao. Unlike the chaos Mao reveled in, Xi prefers stability, order, and an authoritative system that works like a sophisticated machine – any replay of a Cultural Revolution is thus highly unlikely under his rule.

Xi Jinping followed up on Deng and also tried to solve the contradictions that the figure of Mao brings to the Party. Xi has stressed that the two periods of development of Communist China must be understood as one integral whole.[13] Xi warned against anyone questioning China's current course on the basis of the Mao era, but also against those who would question Mao's role in "laying the foundations" of today's Chinese success. The Communist Party under Xi officially describes such "erroneous" thinking as "historical nihilism". Although the Party continues to officially acknowledge Mao's mistakes, it is not in its interest to discuss them too much.

Ultimately, the Party's schizophrenic stance on Mao Zedong's legacy was not resolved by Xi Jinping either and some of its contradictions have been laid bare. One can mention the crackdown on Marxist activists in 2018.[14] At the welding plant in Shenzhen, South China's Guangdong, an all too familiar dispute arose between the company's management and the workers who wanted to establish their own free trade union. The workers were reinforced also by idealistic students from far away Beijing who came to Shenzhen to support the movement. At the protests, the students carried banners with portraits of Mao Zedong and revolutionary slogans. Domestic security forces struck hard against the students, detaining many of them, with several of the students disappearing for a long time without trace. Those who returned to schools faced various disciplinary punishments and reprimands. At Beijing University, the leadership of the student Marxist Association was eventually replaced by "loyal" students. Beijing demonstrated that Mao's slogan "to rebel is justified" is valid only as long as it does not threaten the Party and the mantra of "social stability".

Mao as an immortal symbol

In China, however, Mao does not only survive as a political instrument used by the Communist Party. The first communist leader became the personification of China itself, someone who is practically inseparable from its modern history. The image of Mao still hangs on the Tiananmen Gate in central Beijing and looks at us from the front of every Chinese banknote of all denominations. Mao's birth house in Shaoshan, Hunan, has become a sort of pilgrimage site visited by tens of millions of tourists every year. Mao's quotes and calligraphy have become part of China's cultural heritage. For some Chinese, Mao has even become a kind of god that can be found in peoples' homes next to depictions of Chinese deities, or as a lucky charm in cars.

Under the influence of the official version of history promoted by the Communist Party, many Chinese do not have a complete idea of the extent of Mao's "mistakes". Museums presenting Chinese modern history often dispense with catastrophic Mao excesses such as the Great Leap Forward and the Cultural Revolution only with a brief reference to partial "stumbles" on the way toward today's remarkable achievements. Any mistakes are perceived as secondary, and Mao remains painted in the collective memory mainly as the great revolutionary and father of the new China. Moreover, considering the undeniable successes of China's economic development over the recent decades, many Chinese perceive dwelling on the past as unnecessary – a mentality that also explains the widespread attitudes to the 1989 protests (see Chapter 3).

Despite that, Mao has many critics in China who denounce his legacy completely. However, public criticism of Mao can even end one's career. In 2015, because of the mockery of Mao at a private dinner, Bi Fujian, one of the most popular TV personalities in China, had his career ended overnight.[15] Due to criticism of Mao's role in the Great Leap Forward, a university professor in Shandong Province also lost his position in 2017.[16] Many other public figures who dare to "disparage" Mao's name face fierce anger from neo-Maoist circles.

In conclusion, it is probably safe to say that Mao is associated with the PRC to such an extent that the Communist regime will probably never get over the numerous dilemmas connected to his persona and his legacy. Revisiting his legacy would only be possible if China's regime changed. In effect, the communist propaganda rings true – Mao Zedong, indeed, lives forever.

Notes

1 G. Jian, Y. Song & Y. Zhou, *Historical Dictionary of the Chinese Cultural Revolution*, Oxford: Scarecrow Press, 2006.
2 "Resolution on certain questions in the history of our Party since the founding of the People's Republic of China", Marxists.org, 1981.
3 Ibid.

4 J. Blanchette, *China's New Red Guards: The Return of Radicalism and the Rebirth of Mao Zedong*, New York: Oxford University Press, 2019.
5 K. Brown & S. van Nieuwenhuizen, *China and the New Maoists*, London: Zed Books, 2016.
6 Blanchette, *China's New Red Guards*.
7 Ibid.
8 S. Shen (ed.), *Redefining Nationalism in Modern China*, London: Palgrave Macmillan, 2007.
9 Brown & van Nieuwenhuizen, *China and the New Maoists*.
10 Blanchette, *China's New Red Guards*.
11 W. Lam, "The Maoist revival and the conservative turn in Chinese politics", *China Perspectives* 2, 2012, 5–15.
12 S. Zhao, "Xi Jinping's Maoist revival", *Journal of Democracy* 27(3), 2016, 83–97.
13 X. Jinping习近平, "Zhengque kandai gaige kaifang qianhou liang ge lishi shiqi正确看待改革开放前后两个历史时期", *Renmin Ribao* 人民日报, 8 November 2013.
14 J. C. Herandez, "China's leaders confront an unlikely foe: Ardent young communists", *New York Times*, 28 September 2018.
15 "China TV anchor Bi Fujian to be punished for Mao insult", *BBC*, 10 August 2015.
16 C. Shepherd, "Chinese professor sacked after criticizing Mao online", *Reuters*, 10 January 2017.

3 Tiananmen 1989

How did the massacre change China?

Barbara Kelemen

In 1989, many political observers expected the accelerated fall of the Chinese Communist Party (CCP) and the impending democratization of Chinese society. The gradual collapse of communism in Central and Eastern Europe had seemingly shown that such a model was unsustainable and that a regime change in China, too, would not take long. However, the protests that had spread throughout the country did not ultimately lead to democratization. ***What were the dynamics behind this movement, and what did it want to achieve?*** *At the same time, the Chinese leadership was also divided on how to approach the situation.* ***Who were the main players that became ultimately responsible for the tragic events at Tiananmen?*** *And while the democratization process was ultimately reversed once the protest movement was suppressed, the events remain an important element in understanding China of today.* ***How did this episode reshape the relationship between the state and its population?*** *After initial days of confusion after the massacre, the reaction by the international community came mainly in the form of condemnation and sanctions. China's suppression of the demonstrations has caused almost irreparable damage to its reputation.* ***How do foreign countries perceive the legacy of this event for the Chinese government?***

Timeline of events

The protests on Tiananmen Square (translated as the Gate of Heavenly Peace Square), which were suppressed on the night of 3–4 June 1989, began as a sporadic demonstration by students following the former reformist leader Hu Yaobang's death in April. The demonstrations gradually took hold, and thousands of students went on a hunger strike in the square on 13 May, causing a disruption in the planned state visit of Mikhail Gorbachev. The growing number of activists in Beijing (estimated at around one million people), and the spread of protests to other cities, led to the declaration of martial law on20 May, and to the deployment of the army to the capital. The situation escalated and resulted in military intervention and bloody suppression of the protests in the early hours of 4 June. During the operation, the army shot at protesters and many reportedly died following collisions with tanks and military equipment. The event claimed thousands of lives, although the exact number is unknown. To this day, the "incident", along with the protests, is heavily censored in China, and many, especially among the younger generation, know little

DOI: 10.4324/9781003350064-5

or nothing about the events that unfolded during the period. Indeed, the protest movement and its suppression in Tiananmen Square in 1989 represent the greatest challenge faced by the CCP in recent decades and have fundamentally changed the relationship between the Chinese state and society.

More than 30 years after the massacre, the Communist Party maintains its position of power. Families who lost their members during the protests were either silenced by the Chinese authorities. Meanwhile, public dissatisfaction with the violence used against the protesters did not translate into a widespread opposition movement, and the "incident" remains a sensitive issue. Even more surprising may be the attitude of many Chinese citizens, who over time have begun to agree with the violent repression of protests and perceive government repression at the time as a "necessary evil" to maintain stability in the country.[1] This shift in thinking was mainly due to the dynamic economic growth, which brought growing prosperity to most of the population over the following decades. In this respect, the improving material situation and long-term stability are the two main reasons that have contributed to the legitimacy of the Communist Party in the eyes of the Chinese people, on whom the party relies to this day.[2]

Protest causes

In foreign media, the Tiananmen Square protests were often simplified as a student movement fighting for democracy. However, the reality was more complicated. The reasons that led to the culmination of large-scale protests across the country must be understood in the context of the more complex processes of economic and social liberalization led by Deng Xiaoping.

Figure 3.1 The tank man – a well-known photo from the 5 May 1989 protests (source: Wikimedia Commons).

In the 1980s, the Communist Party embarked on a path of economic reform and decided to gradually open the Chinese economy, which until then had been largely closed to foreign countries and centralized under state leadership. Due to economic stagnation, the party decided to gradually de-collectivize agriculture, allow foreign investment, and partially liberalize private enterprise (more in Chapter 7). One of the most important changes was the partial decentralization of state control, which gave regional governments more freedom to implement new economic regulations. Although the state economy was still the dominant force in larger cities, villages, and remote parts of China, peasant families were once again in a position of control over their own production.[3] This reform led to a change in the central pillar of Chinese economic ideology, which, under Mao Zedong, focused on the class struggle and was now replaced with economic modernization as the new goal of the Chinese regime.[4]

Economic liberalization has led to higher socio-economic dynamism, which has manifested itself on several levels. As the standards of living began to improve, the new business class, along with increasingly independent intellectuals, began to expect further reforms and relaxation. However, growing changes have also led to concerns among those who were comfortable with the old system and feared that liberalization could deprive them of their power or economic benefits. Another factor was the penetration of new ideas, culture, and art from the West – especially among students. One of the main characters demonstrating such a factor was the singer Cui Jian, whose song "Nothing to My Name" became the anthem of the 1989 student protests. Another symbol of this movement was also a popular young poet Haizi (real name *Zha Haisheng*), whose suicide only a few months before the protests added to the symbolism of his poems.

The changes have led to the deepening divides in the previously unitary society of China and the increase of the individual's power. Some frustrations became apparent as early as 1986–1987, during which students organized demonstrations in several cities across China, influenced by intellectuals such as Fang Lizhi and Wang Rowang, both advocating a higher degree of political liberalization that included Western ideals such as freedom of speech, the press, and academic freedom. These ideals were summarized under the auspices of the so-called "fifth modernization", which was to lead to the establishment of democracy. The idea was inspired by an essay that appeared in 1978 on the so-called "wall of democracy" in Beijing. It was authored by Wei Jingsheng, a prominent human rights activist and dissident, who was arrested after its publication. Indeed, the wall of democracy became the center where people were able to express their views on freedom of speech, human rights, and democracy. At the same time, unofficial newspapers and publications discussing China's political direction began to circulate, which became one of the main tools for spreading the ideas of China's growing democratic movement.

Whether it was foreign relations, the availability of information, or the increased mobility of the population, the Communist Party had increasingly less control over the growing number of activities that allowed citizens to engage publicly and express their views on changes happening in Chinese society. At the same time, dissatisfaction with economic development, rising inflation, and its impact on the purchasing power of a large part of the population gradually led to dissatisfaction with the regime.

This interplay of several factors shows that the protests were not just an effort to establish the Western democratic model but primarily an expression of popular dissatisfaction with the current political-economic situation. For the most part, during the 1980s, the movement sought to gradually liberalize and open up the communist regime rather than overthrow it. The majority of protesters in Tiananmen Square tried to get the government to listen to their demands, and only a few called for the fall of the Communist Party, although such calls grew more frequent as the situation escalated.[5] The protesters' demands were discussed during open dialogues between the student representatives and the government delegation. However, the course of these meetings showed that the protesters were not perceived as legitimate, which contributed to the escalation of the conflict.

Internal fight within the CCP

During the protests, the Communist Party was internally divided – an important characteristic of the events of 1989. Such a divide subsequently became a lesson for the party in the future when party unity – especially outwardly – became paramount. The dramatic changes associated with economic and social liberalization under the leadership of Deng Xiaoping led to growing opposition from the conservative ranks of the ruling party.[6] On one side of the spectrum stood Zhao Ziyang, an advocate for reforms and a relaxation of the regime, who had served as the party's secretary-general since 1987 until his dismissal after the crackdown on protests. Zhao was sympathetic to progressive liberalization (more in Chapter 9) and repeatedly tried to communicate and negotiate with student councils during protests, an effort often blocked by his leaders. Zhao replaced in office Hu Yaobang, whose style and openness to liberal thought movements ensured growing hostility among the party's older conservatives, leading to his forced resignation in 1987. His death in April 1989 led to student protests that later grew into the demonstration in Tiananmen Square. However, Zhao shared many of his predecessor's views, so the 1987 exchange did not fundamentally change the trend of reforms and liberalization.

At the other end of the spectrum was Chen Yun, an influential and powerful member of the party due to his political career under Mao Zedong. Although he supported many aspects of Deng's economic reform and agreed to it in principle, the way in which the reforms were implemented conflicted with his belief in the subordination of the market to party ideology. Chen was the head of a conservative wing that believed that the planned economy should be the essence of the Chinese system while the market economy should play only a complementary role. Such beliefs led to his criticism of Deng Xiaoping, who, according to Chen, implemented reforms and disregarded the strict limits that should be set by the state. To this day, Chen is associated with the vision of an economy that should function like a "bird's cage". He believed that the Chinese market should operate as a bird in a cage, which can fly freely only in a predetermined space but can also control it.[7] Similar criticism also came from broader conservative intellectual and artistic circles, who perceived the new reforms as bourgeois liberalization affecting Chinese society.[8]

Party differences were also reflected in how the protests should be handled. While party leader Zhao tried to negotiate with the protesters and find a solution that would satisfy everyone, Prime Minister Li Peng proposed a tough approach and is seen as the chief architect of the massacre. Li Peng was one of the advocates for martial law and the violent suppression of protests, which he said threatened the very existence of the CCP regime. According to Li Peng, Zhao's moderate approach only encouraged student councils and gave them hope that continued protests could lead to political concessions from the Communist Party. These differences escalated after Zhao Ziyang traveled in late April to North Korea for a pre-planned visit. During his absence, under the leadership of Li Peng a critical editorial was published on the front page of People's Daily on 26 April, calling the protests "anti-party rebellions". The tone and content of this article outraged the protesters, who subsequently demanded a change in the interpretation of their movement. Upon his return to the country, Zhao tried to persuade his colleagues to adjust their position to de-escalate the situation. However, he did not succeed, and further development led to the tragedy.

To express their views, the protesters decided to go on a hunger strike during Mikhail Gorbachev's historic visit to China. This was perceived as a mockery and loss of face on the international stage by the Communist Party. Growing pressure on party leaders to calm the situation led to the key Politburo meeting on 17 May. During the meeting, Li Peng and his followers criticized Zhao's strategy and the public outcomes, which were perceived by many as a sign of internal party differences. The final decision on how to handle the situation was ultimately in the hands of Deng Xiaoping, who joined Li Peng and ordered martial law. After the meeting, Zhao went to the square one last time to persuade the protesters to end the hunger strike. However, the students decided to continue, and on 20 May, martial law was officially enacted in the country. Eventually, the government mobilized the army, which began the violent suppression of protests on the night of 3–4 June 1989.

Criticism of how the political leadership reacted to the situation did not take long to emerge. As Deng Xiaoping's position as the central leader was inviolable (even a critic like Chen Yun never directly attacked Deng), Zhao Ziyang became the scapegoat, marking a new era of the Communist Party that ended debates on potential political and social liberalization in China. Zhao was purged and spent the rest of his life under house arrest. During this time, he managed to secretly record his memoirs, which were later smuggled on cassettes abroad and published as a book.[9] Meanwhile, more conservative politicians had come to power.

Tiananmen and its impact on China

Decades after the Tiananmen events, an image appears in which a Chinese society more or less accepts the crackdown supposedly in exchange for social stability and economic prosperity. Indeed, the legitimacy pillars of the Communist Party have shifted from fulfilling the communist ideology to the ability to administer public affairs and provide tangible results. At the same time, the episode showed the leaders of the party the importance of coherence and party unity within the Communist Party.

A stronger emphasis on patriotism and nationalism was another government response to regaining its legitimacy. The crisis of internal legitimacy and communist ideology, highlighted by the protests, led to a stronger emphasis on patriotic education as part of a nationwide campaign to strengthen nationalism. Such reinforcement was intended to ensure the loyalty of the population and, together with improving material living conditions, became a key building block of the party's legitimacy in the subsequent years. The nationalistic campaigns focus, to a large extent, on foreign powers, whose negative influence is portrayed as chiefly responsible for China's historical and contemporary problems (see Chapter 1).

Another apparent change after the events of 4 June 1989 was an increased emphasis on the state's ability to control its population. While at the economic level, the process of reforms and opening up to the world continued (after a short process of freezing), any political liberalization was ruled out. The Chinese government has emphasized internal stability and control over the population through strict laws. All organized movements that could potentially pose a threat (or competition) to the governing party are seen as particularly problematic (e.g., the suppression of Falun Gong at the end of the 1990s). This is associated with a low tolerance for activism, although certain forms, such as environmental initiatives, are tolerated, especially if they are in line with the broader agenda of the Chinese government).[10] Most activism today takes place in the online space, which, despite growing government censorship, remains a platform for expressing different views, to some extent at least.[11] Although the mantles of what is tolerated alternately narrowed and widened (more in Chapter 8), the social and activist scene overall suffered a severe blow in 1989 from which it has not shaken to this day.

Tiananmen's international heritage

The international community was shocked by the bloodshed in China, a country with which it had relatively good ties until then. The main response was the introduction of economic sanctions, the suspension of official visits, and strong criticism. US President George H.W. Bush repeatedly condemned the suppression of protests, and US–Chinese relations immediately cooled after relatively friendly relations over the previous 20 years. Markets in Hong Kong plummeted, and many withdrew their money from local banks in Hong Kong as they prepared to flee.[12] A lot of states also decided to suspend the sale of military and police equipment, a decision that persists to this day in the case of the United States and the European Union as an important symbolic aspect. China has criticized these sanctions, but for the Western countries, they represent a way of expressing their position on the massacre and the overall human rights situation in China.

The bloody suppression of the protests has significantly changed perceptions of China in the world, especially in the West, and has terminated hopes that the

Chinese regime would evolve toward liberal democracy, as has happened in the Central and Eastern European communist states. Public opinion against China deteriorated significantly in Western countries, and the country became partially (though only temporarily) isolated from the international community. Although relations with China have gradually normalized after a few years, China's image, especially in democracies, has remained influenced by the memory of the massacre. China carries the label of a country that attacked its own citizens.

The Chinese government has sought to find a new approach to foreign policy in the aftermath of the protests. Some have called for intensified relations with countries of the Global South and the severance of contacts with the West in response to their criticism of China. In the end, the pragmatic line prevailed, trying to balance between a conservative policy calling for weaker cooperation with the West, and a more reformist line, which in turn argued for more comprehensive cooperation between China and the United States.[13] The result was marked by a pragmatic approach to continue deepening international economic cooperation, combined with a persistent distrust of the United States. In the late 1990s, cooperation with the United States improved, and more radical views in China were pushed to the margins of academic and political debate. For 20 years after the Tiananmen Square protests, Chinese diplomacy was largely guided by the directive of Deng Xiaoping to avoid foreign policy confrontations and focus on domestic issues. Thanks to this position, during the first decade of the new millennium, China's international image started to improve. However, the arrival of Xi Jinping in 2012 and the growth of foreign policy "assertiveness" reversed such trends.

Notes

1 A. J. Nathan, "'China's changing of the guard: Authoritarian resilience", *Journal of Democracy* 14(1), 2013, 6–17.
2 J. Fewsmith, *China Since Tiananmen*, Cambridge: Cambridge University Press, 2008.
3 T. B. Gold, "Tiananmen and beyond: The resurgence of civil society", *Journal of Democracy* 1(1), 1990, 18–31.
4 Fewsmith, *China Since Tiananmen*.
5 C. Calhoun, "Revolution and repression in Tiananmen Square", *Society* 26(6), 1989, 21–38.
6 S. Zhao, "A state-led nationalism: The patriotic education campaign in post-Tiananmen China", *Communist and Post-Communist Studies* 31(3), 1998, 287–302.
7 S. Wudunn, "Patriarch who helped slow, reforms is dead at 89", *The New York Times*, 11 April 1995.
8 Fewsmith, *China Since Tiananmen*.
9 Z. Zhao, *Prisoner of the State: The Secret Journal of Premier Zhao Ziyang*, New York: Simon & Schuster, 2010.
10 F. Wu, "Environmental activism in provincial China", *China's Local Environmental Politics* 1(5), 2013, 45–58.
11 G. Yang, "China since Tiananmen", *Journal of Democracy* 20(3), 2009, 33–36.
12 J. W. Garver, *China's Quest: The History of the Foreign Relations of the People's Republic of China*, New York: Oxford University Press, 2016.
13 H. Harding, "The impact of Tiananmen on China's foreign policy", *NBR Analysis* 1(3), 1990.

4 Religion, traditions, and values

What do the Chinese believe in?

Klára Dubravčíková

In 2015, more than half of all respondents involved in a survey concerning the state of religion in China were classified as non-believers. It is surveys like this that made China to be considered the largest atheist state in the world, followed by countries such as Japan, the Czech Republic, and Spain.[1] *As early as the 19th century, European researchers considered China to be a non-religious entity. Similar views were also held by some Chinese intellectuals who described Chinese society as being essentially philosophical.* ***Is this really the case? What role does religion play in China? What do the Chinese believe in, and how does the Communist Party approach religions in contemporary China? Do traditional Confucian values still have a place in today's Chinese society?***

Religion vs. irreligion

Philosophy has played an important role in shaping Chinese culture. Confucianism, Mohism, Taoism, Legalism, the school of Yin and Yang, and the so-called 'school of names' form six major philosophical schools of China which were classified already 2000 years ago by one of the most important Chinese historians, Sima Qian. All these philosophical schools competed throughout history in the search for the most appropriate method of ending chaos and establishing order and the proper state of society, which is one of the main focus points of Chinese philosophy. At the same time, these schools of thought have also influenced the politics of Chinese states as well as social norms and customs. While some disappeared throughout history, others gradually became major philosophical currents.

During the reign of the Han dynasty, Confucianism became a state ideology, the norm of education, and the condition for a successful career in public administration. It remained at the center of state decision-making until the last phase of the Qing dynasty. Legalism, in turn, laid the foundations of successful administrative reforms in the so-called Warring States period. Nevertheless, philosophical traditions and philosophy *per se* are more of a feature of Chinese elites who have been involved in the management of the Chinese state, rather than of the general population. Thus, it would be inaccurate to claim that philosophy stands at the heart of Chinese culture and that religion has entered "from the outside". As in other cultures, there are ancient numerous religious elements in Chinese society, some of which are still practiced in various forms today.

DOI: 10.4324/9781003350064-6

At the same time, Chinese religious reality is relatively difficult to grasp, especially because Chinese society is syncretized by various popular religions, imported religions (especially Buddhism, Islam, and Christianity), and philosophical currents, some of which also have the characteristics of religions (such as Taoism and Confucianism). Given that Chinese people practice religion, how is it possible that up to 60% of the population is considered atheists according to the 2015 survey?

The answer to this question relates to the way the concept of *religion* is perceived in various parts of the world. The awareness of the difference between religion and philosophy did not emerge in China until the end of the 19th century when modern European concepts were introduced to Chinese society. China encountered these concepts as a result of the expanding influence of Western civilization, its culture, science, technology, and ways of thinking. Until then, the terms "religion" and "philosophy" did not exist in Chinese, and their translations were in fact taken from the Japanese language which adopted many Western concepts by creating neologisms during the Meiji reforms.

For Europeans, religion was referring to their own understanding of religious faith, thus taking mainly the characteristics of Christianity. In their perspective, religion was associated with exclusivity and control exercised by the church or another institution. Moreover, religion was supposed to be based on a codified body of doctrine and a system of comprehensive practices. It was this Eurocentric notion and its application to Chinese reality that led to the belief that China lacked religion.[2]

For this reason, the concept of religion (*zongjiao*) in today's China may be understood mainly as a reference to the officially recognized religions under the control of the state. There are five of them in China, including Buddhism, Islam, the official Protestant and Catholic associations, and the only "domestic" faith that is classified as a religion – Taoism. Followers of one of these five formal religions are thus likely to be considered believers (*xinyang zongjiao*, literally "believing in religion").[3] The way a question is asked in the given survey is therefore crucial, as the answer to it depends on the understanding of the terms used.

Another reason why some respondents in the survey might have stated that they were atheists may be associated with the influence of self-censorship and general skepticism about participating in public opinion polls. Atheism is officially promoted by the Chinese Communist Party (CCP), and some people may therefore tend to conceal their faith and respond in accordance with the government's official position.[4] Due to this factor, the interpretation of various social surveys and polls in China is complicated, and the data obtained must be taken into account in this context. All in all, it may not be accurate to label China as the largest atheist country in the world based solely on the survey results. Chinese religious reality is in fact far more complex.

Faith in China: Fusion of religions and emphasis on pragmatism

In China, people may practice several religions at once, mostly a kind of "fusion" of Taoism, Buddhism, and the folk religion which is usually referred to as the traditional faith (*chuantong xinyang*).[5] While people in the West are aware of a collision between religions and it is uncommon to practice more than one religion, it is not unusual for people in China to worship several gods, goddesses, and spirits, make sacrifices in both Taoist and Buddhist temples, and not doubt own practices in the context of religious affiliation. The concept of religious syncretism can be thus discussed in relation to the state of religion in China that, from a Western point of view, lacks institutionalization and is relatively fragmented. Indeed, many Chinese are not exclusively affiliated with only one faith – their personal beliefs may lie in a combination of faith and practices based on several religions. Hence, what do Chinese people believe in, and in what ways exactly is the traditional faith evinced in society?

China's traditional folk religions are complicated and diversified. One of their basic features is the practice of spirit worshipping and belief in various deities that usually have a human origin, as the religious tradition often revolves around the so-called ancestor veneration. In ancient China, people commonly believed that their deceased relatives had become spirits with whom it was possible to maintain contact by making sacrifices. Worshipped ancestors can include family members, but also common ancestors of a larger community, an entire village, or even

Figure 4.1 Lingguang Buddhist Temple in Badachu Park, Beijing (source: CEIAS).

the ancestors of all Chinese, such as the mythical ruler the Yellow Emperor (see Chapter 1). The founder of "new China" Mao Zedong, whose portraits can sometimes be seen next to statues of deities in smaller or family temples, also enjoys similar treatment of reverence (see Chapter 2).

Chinese traditional religious practices are associated with the idea that the world is full of human spirits, to whom it is necessary to communicate, worship, and pay respect. Deities often arise in such a way that the circle of worshippers evolves over time and exceeds the family or community, as happened in the case of the Yellow Emperor or Confucius who are worshipped by a wide circle of people. At the heart of this process of "deification" stands the idea that powerful figures retain their power and importance even after death. In other words, human spirits are believed to have an impact on people's lives, and therefore it is necessary to take care of them and provide for their needs. These religious practices of worshipping are influenced by Confucian, Taoist, and Buddhist ideas, which complement each other. Confucianism emphasizes mainly family ceremonies and self-cultivation. Taoist ideas, on the other hand, stress the need to establish a proper social order and efforts to influence spirits in such a way that is convenient for the worshippers. Finally, Buddhism is associated mainly with funeral rituals related to the reincarnation process.

Temples are mainly used to communicate with the deities and spirits of the ancestors. People offer sacrifices to them and pay respect by burning incense sticks and various paper imitations of money and other objects. Small family altars, shrines, and sometimes private temples can be often found near traditional houses in rural China, or even in city apartments. They are used to worship family ancestors and various spirits who might protect people in their homes and bring happiness and wealth.

Religion and traditional religious practices are rooted in family and social life in China. One can become a member of certain religious communities at birth and does not have to undergo any initiation rituals to participate in religious activities.[6] In fact, the practices that are often perceived as religious by some in the West may not be related to faith as such in the eyes of the Chinese. Rather they are simply viewed as proper behavior or a way of life. Indeed, for the Chinese, religious practices have mostly been a way to fulfill their obligations to their ancestors and to express respect for them. These practices are part of social life and a reflection of traditional Chinese culture and its values based on Confucianism.[7]

At the same time, traditional religious rituals, as well as rituals taken from other religions, including Buddhism, have always been relevant to the course of daily life in China – people have mastered practices of various religions which they saw useful and practically beneficial. The primary purpose of these practices can be said to rest on the objective of improving one's life instead of focusing on entering heaven and guaranteeing an afterlife in paradise. In temples, Chinese people make sacrifices for their health or success in their studies, careers, and personal lives. Many people also wear various amulets or ornaments to protect them from misfortune or to bring happiness. The style of worship also reflects a pragmatic purpose of religion in Chinese society – it is common to bring food and drinks to the temples, such as fruits and other fresh produce, but also oil and processed food, including sweets and soft drinks. Through these gifts, the worshippers aim to make the lives of the gods as pleasant as possible and thus increase the chances that their prayers will be heard. Likewise, by burning incense, paper "money", imitations of homes, or various modern objects, such as cell phones or cars, people try to ensure that the gods and their deceased loved ones have everything they may desire in the afterlife. At the same time, by providing these sacrifices, people show their respect for their family members and fulfill their duty appropriate to their roles in the family.

In addition to worshipping, Chinese society has also been influenced by the long history of various sects, associations, and religious affiliations that preach different paths of salvation, self-cultivation, and morality through philanthropic deeds.[8] Many such sects were identified as "superstitious groups" (*mixin jiguan*) and were banned already during the republican period (1912–1949). Under Article 300 of the Criminal Law of China, membership or involvement in the activities of "superstitious organizations and secret societies" is punishable by up to seven years of imprisonment. In today's China and in Taiwan, these societies function as underground religious organizations, and they include, for example, the Confucian cult called Holy Way (*Shengdao*) and the religious sect *Xiantiandao* and its branches, which can be linked to the secret Buddhist movement White Lotus, which existed in China until the 19th century. These religious branches are not recognized by the Chinese state and therefore operate unofficially. The same is true of the various Christian churches and sects, which are not officially recognized and therefore operate illegally.

State control: Christianity, Islam, Falun Gong

Although the Chinese people's right to the freedom of religion is formally protected by the Constitution of the People's Republic of China (PRC), in reality such freedoms are limited. According to the law, "*no one may use religion to engage in activities that disrupt public order, harm the health of citizens, and interfere with the education system of the state*", meaning that all religious activities that go beyond the government-controlled scope may be identified as a security threat and thus suppressed.[9] The government requires religious groups to respect the Party's monopoly and to spread the "right" moral values. To this day, the Chinese Communist Party retains control over the appointment of religious dignitaries – until 2018, this was also the case for the appointment of bishops of the Catholic Church, who are routinely appointed by the Pope.[10] Today, bishops in China are appointed by the Pope as well as by the CCP which approves and appoints also imams and interferes in the process of Buddhist rebirth and selection of reincarnate custodians. Moreover, the government also has full control over the funding of officially recognized churches.

According to official figures, there are about 44 million Christians in China who are registered with government-approved Christian groups. These include the Protestant "Three-Self Patriotic Movement" and the Catholic "Chinese Patriotic Catholic Association".[11] Large Christian communities are predominantly located in rural areas, but their representation is also rising in cities, especially among the elderly. In fact, it is estimated that the number of Chinese Christian believers could exceed 100 million, as there is a large number of unregistered or illegal Protestant and Catholic "underground" church groups in China. Catholic "underground" associations (*dixia jiaohui*) include those who refuse to register with the state-controlled church and remain loyal to the Pope. The Vatican itself does not officially recognize the People's Republic of China and maintains diplomatic relations with the Republic of China in Taiwan. It is estimated that such Catholic associations could have up to 12 million followers in China.[12] Protestant independent churches, which are free from state control, are often referred to as home churches (*jiating jiaohui*), as they often function within local communities and thus operate outside physical churches. Between 60 to 80 million Chinese believers may be included in these churches. Under the strict religious control of the state, however, these unofficial churches are referred to as cults, and their followers are persecuted and often face imprisonment.[13] This is one of the reasons why some members of these churches seek asylum abroad.

There are many "cults" and sects in China, and their teachings are not based on the Christian faith alone. The Christian community in China outnumbers the Muslim community of about 23 million believers but does not reach the most represented religion – Buddhism – which, according to official statistics, is followed by more than 200 million people in China, divided into various subgroups and sects.

Falun Gong, which has its roots in the Qigong movement – practicing various meditation and breathing exercises that were popular in China in the 1980s and 1990s and back then even enjoyed the official support of the CCP – is among the most famous ones. Like political activists and followers of unregistered religious churches, Falun Gong practitioners in China face persecution and harsh repression, imprisonment, or brutal conditions in labor camps. The persecution of members of the movement started in the late 1990s when Falun Gong was very popular with the Chinese public. It was the rapid rise in popularity of the movement that led the CCP to perceive it as a threat to its governance.

In 1999, the Chinese government marked Falun Gong as an illegal sect that violated public order. Consequently, a repressive campaign against tens of millions of practitioners was launched.[14] At the end of the first decade of the 21st century, an estimated half a million to one million supporters of the movement were set to be imprisoned and exposed to physical violence, bullying, or, according to some reports, forced organ harvesting in labor camps and prisons.[15]

Today, Falun Gong is one of the taboo topics that are censored in China, similar to the events of 1989 or the uncomfortable activities of prominent dissidents. Currently, Falun Gong is practiced in about 70 countries around the world, with the largest number of followers being in Taiwan and North America, mostly in cities with a large Chinese community, such as New York or Toronto. Outside the PRC, there are various art associations (such as Shen Yun) or media organizations affiliated with the Falun Gong movement (Epoch Times, NTDT TV channel, or Sound of Hope radio station). However, these media are subjects of controversy, as, in addition to reporting on the human rights violations in China, they sometimes also spread unconfirmed information or even conspiracy theories and politically biased articles.[16]

Another group that is denied freedom of religion in China is the Uyghur minority, which largely follows Islam. As the state control of religion has further tightened since about 2012, the religious policy of the CCP was fully reflected in the frequent demolition and reconstruction of not only mosques but also churches. Uyghurs are often subjected to a policy of forced abandoning of religion, sinicization, and re-education in a "socialist" vein that takes place in the so-called re-education camps that began to appear in Xinjiang around 2017 and were legalized in 2018.[17]

For the CCP, sinicization is a political agenda aimed at enforcing the loyalty of religious leaders and institutions to the Party's leadership and embedding state ideology, that is, socialism with Chinese characteristics. In addition to "assimilating foreign religions", the government is also promoting the return of society to "traditional" and "domestic Chinese values" and beliefs, including Taoism, Confucianism, and also Buddhism, although it was brought to China from India.[18] At the same, even though Christianity and Islam have existed in China for a very long time – the spread of Christianity in China dates back to the seventh century – unlike Buddhism, both religions are still perceived as "foreign".

Figure 4.2 Falun Gong practitioners in Taiwan in 2020 (source: CEIAS).

The heritage of Confucianism and social values

It is quite commonly believed in the West that almost everything in contemporary Chinese society is influenced by ancient Confucian philosophy. It is true that Confucianism is deeply rooted in Chinese society, but opinions on it, as well as on other philosophical currents, have been changing throughout history. Confucianism has variably maintained its status as a state ideology from the Han dynasty to the last phase of the Qing dynasty when it was denied, criticized, and accused of causing China's backwardness and decline.

Indeed, when the Chinese empire succumbed to the more technically advanced Western powers in the Opium Wars in the 19th century, Confucian traditions began to appear regressive. Chinese thinkers began to turn away from Confucian traditions and sought to reform China in line with the Western model. Of course, there were those who defended Confucianism as a cultural heritage, praised the "philosophical" nature of the Chinese nation, and opposed the "Westernization" of the country. Confucianism, however, was largely rejected and systematically criticized after the collapse of the empire. Its condemnation then peaked at the time of the Cultural Revolution, initiated by Mao Zedong, who aimed to transform the country in such a way that it would definitively break away from old traditions and values.

In various respects and to varying degrees, Confucianism represents a large part of the cultural heritage of China and other East Asian countries, including Korea, Japan, and Vietnam. Many social rituals and patterns of behavior are based on Confucianism, which emphasizes a harmonious world order, good behavior, obedience, self-cultivation, and constant refinement. These aspects may be observed in today's Chinese and other East Asian societies, for example, in the form of a strong emphasis on education. However, it must be borne in mind that today's understanding of Confucianism and its prominence is relatively distant from the significance it once had during the Han dynasty period.

Today's notion of "Asian values" is a manifestation of this dynamic, believed to be influenced by Confucianism, as it emphasizes family ties, education, discipline, respect for authority, and collective well-being. Yet, social values are not immutable, nor are they based solely on one ancient current of thought. In fact, they are changing the same way as politics, the economy, and the whole of society. For centuries, Chinese society has been influenced by several philosophical and religious movements, including folk religions, Taoism, and Buddhism, which have coexisted with Confucianism.[19] Hence, not all the qualities, virtues, ailments, and patterns of behavior associated with China can be attributed to the Confucian tradition. Given the enormous transformation that Chinese society has undergone, especially (but not only) since the rise of Communism, many Confucianism-embedded values are manifested differently today.

In the last several decades, there has been an apparent departure from the traditional culture in China compared to Taiwan, Singapore, and other Chinese overseas communities. With rapid modernization and economic growth that came with the Open Door Policy, Chinese society relatively quickly adopted materialism and consumerism. Many people in China today associate success with wealth and ownership of expensive cars and modern homes. The pursuit of money and material belongings, as well as a clear departure from some Confucian values, can be observed in Chinese society.[20]

From Confucianism to socialism with Chinese characteristics

During the 20th century, Confucianism was blamed for causing China's decline. Mao Zedong even tried to eradicate it entirely during the Cultural Revolution. However, with the transformation of Communist leadership after his death, a gradual rehabilitation of Confucius and his opinions on the world order and society occurred. Since the rise of Deng Xiaoping, China has been heading for a revival of Confucian values and traditions, the successor and defender of which was to be the CCP itself as it has been looking for solutions to several problems over the last 40 years.

The first was the "moral crisis" of Chinese society, which in pursuit of economic progress and wealth, lost some Confucian traits, such as interest in the well-being of others and confidence in morality.[21] Support for traditional philosophical schools and religions was intended to correct the perceived moral decline of society while slowing the spread of "foreign" religions. Xi Jinping allowed Taoism and Confucianism to flourish, aiming to encourage the inculcation of "traditional Chinese values" back into society. These efforts were reflected in the construction of the 12 "new" fundamental values of socialism (*shehuizhuyi hexin jiazhiguan*) that should reflect the "Chinese characteristics" and emphasize moral values. Among them, harmony, freedom, patriotism, and friendship are all included, which refer to the basics of Confucius' teachings, and it is difficult not to encounter them in China at every corner – on public transport, on billboards, and propaganda posters in residential areas, but also in schools and train stations.

The second problem the CCP wanted to solve was securing its monopoly in an ever-modernizing China. The Confucian emphasis on obedience and the belief in social harmony thus serves the Party as a very useful ideological tool. Confucianism has become a necessary means of uplifting nationalism and has been supported as an essential element of Chinese identity, based on which the Communist leadership seeks to prove its legitimacy as an authority and support the development of a "harmonious socialist society". Harmony is an essential Confucian value that the Chinese government – at least in its rhetoric – uses to its advantage. As the Chinese economic system had shifted from socialism to capitalism, the Party had to find the proper justification for the discrepancy between its actions and the values it claims to profess. Thanks to the Confucian values, the Chinese leadership has been able to justify the building of "socialism with Chinese characteristics", which, according to the CCP, "is based on more than five-thousand-year history of the Chinese nation" and represents the initial phase of the road to prosperity and well-being of the whole society (*xiaokang shehui*, where *xiaokang* is a Confucian term for the ideal state of society).[22]

Confucianism has also become a complementary force in China's international policy, where it represents China's "peaceful side". This is also why China increasingly emphasizes not only the need for a "harmonious society" within its territory but also the importance of "harmonious international cooperation", "peaceful coexistence", and the creation of a "harmonious world of lasting peace and common prosperity" that is said to be reached through a "fairer and more balanced" global partnership – a "community of common destiny for all mankind" (*renlei mingyun gongtongti*). Five related vital principles are upheld by China in its foreign policy, including the principle of non-interference in the affairs of other states, mutual respect for territorial integrity and sovereignty, peaceful coexistence, equality, and the principle of non-aggression.[23]

The transformation of the Party's attitude to Confucian heritage and traditions is hard to overlook. Confucianism has become a tool of the pursuit of Chinese socialism and a dynamic force for modernizing the Chinese state and building a prosperous society headed by the Communist government that claims to be the successor of "five thousand years old Chinese culture". Indeed, the changes of recent decades in China have destroyed part of the Communist Party's prior ideological foundation. To restore some of it, the Party has turned to Confucianism. However, there is a visible contradiction within such a move: whereas the Communist Party had been denouncing Confucianism for many years before, currently, the Chinese leadership aims for its revival to promote patriotism and nationalism and bolster its legitimacy.

Notes

1 "Losing our religion? Two thirds of people still claim to be religious", *Gallup International Center for Public and Political Studies*, 8 June 2015.
2 P. Šindelář, "The concept of religion in modern Chinese society and its scientific reflection", *Religio: A Review for Religion Studies* 20(2), 2012, 233–251.
3 I. Johnson, "A problem of 'religion,' and polling, in China", *The New York Times*, 1 July 2015.
4 J. Geer, *Public Opinion and Polling Around the World: A Historical Encyclopedia*, Santa Barbara: ABC-CLIO, 2004.
5 Johnson, "A problem of 'religion,' and polling, in China".
6 F. Yang & G. Lang, *Social Scientific Study of Religion in China: Methodology, Theories, and Findings*, Leiden: Brill, 2011.
7 V. Goossaert & D. A. Palmer, *The Religious Question in Modern China*, The University of Chicago Press, 2011.
8 Ibid.
9 Guowuyuan zongjiao Shiwa it zhengce faguisi 国务院宗教事务局政策法规司. Zhongguo de zongjiao he zongjiao xinyang ziyou yuangkuang 的 的 宗教 和 宗教信仰 自由 状况. Qinghaisheng minzu zongjiao Shiwa weiyuanhu i青海省民族宗教事务委员会, 30 March 2014.
10 "World report 2019: China and Tibet", Human Rights Watch, 2019.
11 T. Hadano, "China's Christians keep the faith, rattling the country's leaders", *Nikkei Asian Review*, 10 September 2019.
12 Ibid.
13 "World Report 2019: China and Tibet".
14 S. Cook, *The Politburo's Predicament: Confronting the Limitations of the Chinese Communist Party Repression*, New York: Freedom House, 2015.
15 "China: COI compilation", Austrian Center for Country of Origin and Asylum Research and Documentation, 2014.

16 K. Roose, "Epoch Times, punished by Facebook, gets a new megaphone on YouTube", *The New York Times*, 5 February 2020.
17 J. Shi 石建杭, Jiang woguo zongjiao zhongguohua Chix tui Xiang Shenru 将我国宗教中国化持续推向深入, Zhongguo minzu zongjiao Wang 中国民族宗教网,10 January 2019.
18 J. Rudolph, "'Party vs profit in tug of war over Chinese Buddhism"', *China Digital Times*, 27 April 2018.
19 Y. Lee, "Do traditional values still exist in modern Chinese societies?", *Asia Europe Journal* 1, 2003.
20 Ibid.
21 B. Hammer, "Confucian thought and China's moral crisis", *International Communication of Chinese Culture* 4, 2017.
22 D. A. Bell, *China's New Confucianism: Politics and Everyday Life in a Changing Society*, Princeton University Press, 2008.
23 L. Zhang, "China's traditional values and modern foreign policy", *Carnegie-Tsinghua Center for Global Policy*, 15 January 2013.

5 Living standards and social issues

What is it like to live in China?

Klára Dubravčíková

China's GDP has grown on average by almost 10% per year since the late 1970s. In 2019, the average salary in China was about 7,500 Chinese yuan, and the GDP per capita exceeded US$10,000 for the first time.[1] *China is thus symbolically only a step away from surpassing the US$12,000 mark, a level that, according to the World Bank's indicators, would classify China as a high-income country.*

With the growing economy, many aspects of life in China naturally improved – in 2018, the average life expectancy reached 77 years, and access to education also broadened. In 2000, less than a million people earned a university degree in total, and today about three million people complete their university education in China. Infrastructure has improved significantly throughout China – the construction of motorways, railways, and high-speed railways has gradually expanded from the east coast to less developed areas of the country. Today, high-speed railways link most of the major provincial cities, and China has more high-speed railways than the rest of the world combined.

Still, the country faces many social problems. Some of them are related to the large size of the population, the social structure, and the control of population growth. Others are a result of the political situation, cultural values, or the changes in lifestyle and value system following rapid economic growth. This chapter focuses on the social issues the Chinese government and society are facing. ***What is living in Chinese cities and the countryside like? How equal (or unequal) is society? And what are the problems faced by the members of ethnic minorities?***

Life in the factory of the world

The first so-called special economic zones (*jingji tequ*) – the cities of Shantou, Shenzhen, Zhuhai, and Xiamen – opened in the late 1970s and gradually accelerated the development of the entire east coast of China. Over time, large agglomerations were formed in these areas, creating "belts" of economic centers extending from the provinces around the Bohai Sea in the northeast through the city of Shanghai to the southern province of Guangdong. These areas have been the driving force behind China's economic growth. The special zones together with the entire eastern provinces developed gradually over the 1980s and 1990s, while the population of rural areas in central China experienced job losses because of the modernization of agriculture. The inner provinces were not able to compete with

DOI: 10.4324/9781003350064-7

the coastal parts of the country in terms of infrastructure, nor in conditions suitable for the development of industry – they lacked the prerequisites to become economic centers, and their populations had to look for new opportunities in the large cities in the east of the country.

China is characterized by significant disparities between urban and rural areas, as well as between central provinces and coastal regions. According to almost all measurable aspects, it is objectively much better to live in Chinese cities than in the countryside. Not only are average incomes in cities up to twice as high as in rural areas, but access to education or health care is much more difficult in rural areas than in the cities. To date, urban areas are an important source of job opportunities for rural populations, as, in their own regions, stable employment and high earnings are scarce.

Higher incomes and improved quality of life have gradually attracted large numbers of people from the countryside in the inner Chinese provinces such as Hubei, Henan, and Gansu to the more developed urban areas. Simply put, the economic growth, concentrated in several areas, has also caused one of the largest national population movements which is still ongoing – tens of millions of people from poor rural areas move to cities. In 2000, 120 million non-residents lived in cities temporarily – mostly migrants from rural areas looking for job opportunities (*nongmingong*). In 2017, it was more than 240 million.[2] However, these figures do not include migrants who have not obtained the necessary documents and permits to work in cities and thus live there illegally.

In most cases, migrants are laborers from rural areas who are unable or unwilling to find a job in agriculture in their areas of permanent residence and therefore leave for larger towns and cities to work in the manufacturing and construction industries. Some work as small traders and in the service sector, such as taxi drivers, messengers, or restaurant staff. The problem, however, is that even though these people live in cities for years, work there, pay taxes, and in some cases even start families, they often cannot settle permanently and formally become urban residents.

This is due to a restrictive system of registration of households called *hukou*, linking each individual with a certain place of permanent residence. The system requires that every Chinese citizen be assigned either rural or urban status at a given location. *Hukou*, however, is not tied to the place of birth, but rather to the *hukou* of one's parents. The change of status is therefore very difficult for the rural population, as it is often conditioned by higher education or even by a certain value of property or level of income.[3]

Indeed, *hukou* has an impact on the quality of life of people. For example, it determines the place of primary and secondary school attendance and may even affect the number of points obtained during entrance examinations for universities, so-called *gaokao*. Given the size of China's population and the limited number of quality universities, competition between high school applicants is very high. For *gaokao*, each student has only one attempt per year, and the result determines what universities they can be admitted to. That is also why Chinese children are led to discipline: very high demands are placed on them not only by parents but also by the whole society. After all, being admitted to a prestigious university, such as Beijing University, Tsinghua University, or Fudan University, significantly improves one's chances to succeed in a future career – and also improves chances of getting an urban *hukou*.

Moving from the countryside to the cities is not easy. Non-urban populations in China face several obstacles. For example, if a worker with rural *hukou* in the Sichuan province migrates for work to the provincial capital Chengdu, they must first obtain a special permit, which also has to be paid for and then registered in the city. However, the permit does not give its holder the right to settle permanently and to benefit from the social advantages enjoyed by the urban population. These migrant workers are not entitled to a pension, their children are not allowed to attend municipal schools, and it is *not* possible for them to purchase an apartment or other housing in the city without the relevant municipal *hukou*. Thus, millions of laborers remain trapped on the cities' outskirts either in cheap hostels or even illegal housing units. What is more, they do not even enjoy the same labor rights as the urban population. In some cases, migrant workers earn up to 40% less than the local population on average and face many discriminatory practices.[4]

There are other restrictions on the migrant population. For example, if one decides to move to the city for a job, they cannot bring their family with them, so normally, children remain in the area of origin where they attend local schools,

Figure 5.1 Chinese migrants inside China in 2010 (one dot represents 10,000 people) (source: CEIAS).

while their parents work in hundreds and sometimes thousands of kilometers distant agglomerations. It is in fact rather common for families of rural migrant populations to meet only once a year during the celebrations of the Lunar New Year. Rural children are often raised by grandparents and sometimes even left to rely on themselves. The same is true for the elderly, who are often dependent on the income of their children working in cities.

An enormous influx of laborers into large Chinese cities with more than 13 million inhabitants, such as Beijing, Shanghai, Nanjing, Shenzhen, Guangzhou, and Chengdu, has led most of these cities to try to limit the number of migrants by restrictive measures over the last few years. For example, in 2017, the Beijing government launched a campaign to evict migrants from its outskirts and ordered the demolition of dozens of illegal accommodation facilities housing thousands of migrant workers.[5] They were forced to move out and leave the city.

At present, it is very difficult for migrants to move legally to large cities for work. Yet, paradoxically, it is this external labor force that has enabled cities to prosper. People from rural areas are therefore increasingly turning their hopes of working outside the countryside toward medium-sized cities such as Xi'an, Dalian, Qingdao, Ningbo, and Xiamen, which have around 5 million inhabitants. There is a much higher chance of success, since these smaller cities have relaxed their restrictions on immigration in response to a new government policy promoting urbanization and raising the standard of living of rural populations.[6] In 2019, the proportion of the urban population in China reached the level of 60%, but only less than 45% of the Chinese had an urban *hukou*.[7]

The crisis of the Chinese middle class

Living standards have risen significantly in China over the last 40 years, with rapid industrialization and economic transformation. These dynamics have also led to a surge in the number of billionaires and a growing middle class, which is now also acting as a stabilizer of economic growth, as it is an important source of domestic demand for consumer goods. Although many people, especially in the West, have long believed that economic growth and a growing middle class in China would bring about democratic reforms, the opposite is true so far: the opposition to the Communist regime is minimal within the middle class. In fact, from various indicators, we can conclude that the vast majority of middle-class Chinese are satisfied with the Chinese Communist Party (CCP) and credit it for their increased material well-being.[8] It is therefore desirable for the CCP to keep the middle class happy.

It is estimated that China's middle class in 2019 comprised around 400 million people, which is less than a third of China's population but about equal to the population of the European Union.[9] It is mainly the population of large cities in the eastern provinces, whose monthly income is around 5,000 yuan (about 630 euros), who fall into this category. More and more Chinese people travel abroad and can also afford to study at foreign universities. In 2018, almost 150 million people traveled abroad, and more than half a million university students studied abroad.[10] However, the COVID-19 pandemic has abruptly stopped most of the international mobility of the Chinese, and it remains to be seen when – if at all – the foreign exchanges return to their pre-pandemic levels.

Together with the economic growth of China's eastern coast, as well as large inland cities such as Chengdu, Chongqing, Wuhan, and Zhengzhou, demand for consumer goods has been growing very rapidly. However, the growing consumerism in Chinese society also has negative impacts – it contributes to the deterioration of the environment and changes social values.[11]

It is now recognized that China faces a "decline in public morality" among the population. Urban populations are characterized by separation from traditional "moral virtues" such as respect and duty to help others. Many of today's inhabitants of Chinese cities can be characterized by a certain distrust toward others and also by an emphasis on material enrichment. This "moral decay" is visible in several aspects – for example, it is not very common to contribute to charities to help other people, nor do people usually help each other in life-threatening situations, such as traffic accidents. A certain level of apathy and pursuit of one's own interests are largely present in Chinese urban society.[12] This phenomenon is often explained by a very rapid change in lifestyle and the loss of belonging to a certain community, which in turn is typical of the rural population. Rural people live in communities, where they are generally closer to and help each other. However, this sense of belonging has gradually declined with the development of an anonymous urban society and the disappearing emphasis on typical "Confucian virtues" such as kindness and empathy.

This is also why the CCP is currently trying to restore patterns of behavior in society based on traditional thinking, highlighting the influence of Confucianism on the shaping of Chinese culture and describing itself as a promoter and successor of Confucian traditions. However, the goal to remedy the moral crisis in Chinese society is secondary in this case – the primary objective of this policy of returning to the "Confucian roots" is to legitimize CCP's power in the country and justify its ruling position (see Chapter 4).

Population control

One of the other problems that the CCP faces and has been trying to cope with for several decades is the size of the Chinese population. China was the most populous country in the world for centuries (before it was was overta ken by India recently). In 2022, the newest demography research estimated that China's population might be already peaking and would soon start decreasing. By the end of the 21st century, China's population could decrease to about 800 million people.[13]

Initially, during the Mao Zedong era, the government supported population growth, and the size of the Chinese nation almost doubled between 1949 and 1977 – the number rose from about 540 million to 950 million.[14] However, the rapid population growth and the ongoing global debate on the potential consequences of overpopulation of the planet forced the CCP to introduce a policy known as "later, longer, and less" (*wan, xi, shao*). The government encouraged couples to postpone parenthood, to have longer periods between pregnancies, and, in particular, to have fewer children. These measures of 1973 can be seen as the first phase of population control. However, the government recommendations were voluntary and were not enforced or controlled. Although population growth declined sharply after 1973, the Chinese authorities tightened the family planning policy in 1978 and introduced the so-called "one-child policy" (*jihua shengyu zhengce*). This birth-planning policy was fully implemented in 1982, when it was incorporated into the Constitution, and lasted with modifications until 2016.

The one-child policy did not mean a general ban on having more children, so its usual name in English is a little misleading. Rules and their enforcement varied from province to province and depended also on the ethnicity of the parents and *hukou*. The conditions were very strict for the urban population, which in 1980 accounted for about 20% of the total population of China, and for the Han population, the largest ethnic group in China.[15] However, even for these groups, the one-child policy was gradually relaxed, and several exceptions became applicable. For example, if the expecting partners were both only children, they could have two babies. This adjustment came into effect in 2013 after more than 30 years of implementation of the birth-planning policy. Families in some provinces could also apply for permission to have a second child if their first child was a girl. The "modified" plan had a rather degrading name – the policy of one and a half children (*yi hai ban zhengce*). A strict ban on having more than one offspring applied to "only" about 35% of the Chinese, and the modified versions concerned about half of the total population. Some minorities, such as the Tibetan or Uyghur populations, were not affected by the rules and could have three or more children. Conversely, in the case of families that did not benefit from any exemptions, the single-child rule was enforced by very heavy fines and sometimes by forced abortions, sterilization, and other radical practices. However, such draconian steps were not commonly used by the authorities and occurred predominantly at the initial stage of the introduction of population growth control, i.e., in the 1980s and 1990s. Overall, it is estimated that the one-child policy prevented the birth of about 200–400 million people.[16]

Today, each woman in China has on average about 1.6 children, while in 1979 it was up to 2.9.[17] This significant decline in the birth rate is not only a result of the one-child policy but also a side effect of rapid economic growth and growing wealth in society. As living standards rise, the cost-of-living increases, which is especially the case in large cities. Raising children poses a relatively heavy financial burden for many families, which is why many people currently prefer only one offspring even though the regulations have ended.

The phenomenon of low and decreasing birth rates in China is accompanied by a rapid aging of the population, which is not favorable for the future development of the state, its economy, and the social system. The rapidly growing number of retired seniors and the simultaneously declining number of the working population put increasingly heavy pressure on the social and health systems. Population aging is therefore a serious problem and was also one of the main factors for ending the one-child policy. However, the relaxation of the policy has probably been late.

Ironically, the systematic reduction of the birth rate, which lasted almost 40 years in China and led to the initially desired decline in population growth, has not only accelerated the aging of society but has also contributed to other challenges that the current government has to tackle. China is certainly not the only country in the world facing such problems – but its long-term policies on birth control have eventually made the problem worse.

The problem with the "4:2:1" family model

Even though the government first allowed and then started supporting families to have more children, the birth rate in China continues to decrease. Most couples still prefer to raise only one offspring, which exacerbates the demographic inequality that is a direct result of the planned parenting policy and which we can divide into two groups – generational and gender-related.

Generational inequality is usually referred to as a 4:2:1 problem (*si er yi jiating wenti*). This label reflects the changes in the structure of Chinese families that have occurred because of the one-child policy and concerns couples who care for their four parents and one child at the same time.[18] Despite the state-sponsored elderly insurance scheme launched in 2009, most older people, especially those in rural areas, do not receive a sufficiently high pension. These seniors are therefore largely dependent on financial and other assistance from their child(ren) and sometimes grandchild(ren). From the perspective of the "one child" – namely the Chinese millennial generation – the situation is similarly problematic, as they might increasingly deal with a situation where the responsibility for supporting two parents and sometimes all four grandparents in old age is borne by them alone.

Most Chinese in their 40s and younger might hence provide assistance to up to six other people, which, if they still have their own family, represents a significant burden. And if they refuse to aid their parents or do not provide other sufficient care, Chinese laws allow for the option to deduct funds from them for their parents. In addition, under the law on the protection of the rights of seniors, children also have an obligation to visit their parents regularly and to ensure their needs are met.[19] These obligations, included in the law, are based on a particular Confucian virtue known as "filial piety" (*xiao*), which manifests itself in respect for one's parents and care for elderly family members. Traditionally, it was the sons who took care of the parents financially, while the daughters helped the parents and cared for them. Today, this is also changing because of the one-child policy, and children provide assistance to their parents in all directions regardless of gender. Still, it is generally true that daughters visit their parents more often and also pay more attention to their needs.[20]

Disbalance in the gender ratio

In Chinese culture, men have long been preferred, which was related to the Confucian hierarchical order of society. While sons were "preservers" of the family and, unlike daughters, they were able to make sacrifices to the spirits of their ancestors and thus take care of the family line, women left their families after marriage and became members of their husband's families. Having a son was almost a necessity for the Chinese because otherwise, their family line could disappear – in China, traditionally, women do not change surnames after marriage, but children get the surname of the father.

With the introduction of the one-child policy, the preference for sons gradually stood out. This trend became even more pronounced at a time when it was possible to determine the sex of the fetus by ultrasound. Many parents, after finding out they were expecting a girl, decided to undergo an abortion. It is estimated that in the 1990s about 500,000 pregnancies were terminated for this reason each year.[21] Today, determining the gender of unborn children is illegal in China, as it has caused gender-motivated abortions. However, there are still ways to circumvent these rules – for example, by going to Hong Kong or other countries for pregnancy screenings. The preference for sons is still evident in Chinese society, although this mindset is gradually changing. However, the long-term preference for male offspring could not have resulted in anything other than a significant gender imbalance. In China today, for every 100 women born after 1980, there are an average of 118 men, but in some areas, this disproportion reaches as much as 100:140. This means that China "lacks" about 30 million women – and it also makes China the country with the largest gender imbalance in the world, both in absolute numbers and in terms of the ratio.[22]

The "lack" of women not only affects the further development of the population but is the cause of many social problems. These include, for example, the deterioration in the quality of elderly care, mainly in rural areas, as it is mostly the daughters who regularly take care of the elderly family members. Other problems resulting from gender disparities are various criminal activities such as the abduction of women and girls, human trafficking, forced weddings, or slavery.

These problems largely result from the increasing demand for young women, especially from lonely (heterosexual) men who are not able to find a partner in their region. There are cases of Chinese men buying women from other Chinese provinces, but also from abroad, such as Myanmar, Laos, Vietnam, and North Korea, and then forcing them to start a family with them. According to official Chinese statistics, more than 90,000 children and young women were victims of human trafficking between 2000 and 2013, but this figure is estimated to be many times higher.[23] In addition, it is believed that about 70,000 children disappear each year in China, and about 200,000 are sold abroad for adoption.[24] What is more, as a result of the decades-long one-child policy and preferences for male offspring, millions of "unauthorized" children were born, whose existence had to be kept secret by the family. These people do not have a birth certificate and are not registered in the household registration system, which means that they do not have *hukou* and therefore cannot participate in normal work or social life, because they simply do not exist for the state system. For some families, it is more beneficial to sell these children and try to provide them with a better life in such a way.

Gender inequality

Clearly, the one-child policy caused a huge number of social problems. It might also seem that the problem of finding partners concerns exclusively (heterosexual) men, whose number significantly exceeds the number of women. However, such an impression would be wrong, since (heterosexual) women also have similar problems. Women in China are increasingly characterized by quality education, better employment opportunities, and economic self-sufficiency. Sometimes they prefer to build their own professional career before marriage, or simply have higher demands on their life partner. These women are often called "leftover women" in China (*sheng nü*) if they are not married by the age of about 30.

The one-child policy and reduced birth rates have also led to some positive changes, including a decrease in maternal and child mortality. Also, it laid down the foundation for a gradual leveling out of inequalities between men and women. The increase in the number of only-child girls has gradually changed social norms and contributed to an increase in the proportion of girls who have completed secondary or higher education.[25] While in the past education was a boys' privilege, today more than half of university students are women.

Until a few decades ago, Chinese women were subordinate to men, whether within the family or in marriage. After the collapse of the empire, in 1912, the foot-binding practice was banned in China, which marked the beginning of the women's emancipation process in Chinese society. The practice of binding the feet almost disappeared by 1949, but it was only with the advent of Communist leadership that the position of women began to change. The CCP was the first ruling party to "liberate" women, at least symbolically, from "male domination" by introducing a new marital law that promoted free will, prevented arranged marriages, and allowed women to divorce. Mao Zedong also solemnly declared that women hold up half the sky and are thus equal to men in terms of rights and status. Prostitution was outlawed, and women had the opportunity to study and become part of the workforce.

However, as in many other countries, women in China are still subject to different forms of discrimination – for example, part of the jobs are reserved for men only, and the gender pay gap is rather wide (women earn on average 70% of their male counterparts' salaries), and up to half of the Chinese population still believes that the primary role of women is to care for the family.[26] Women's representation in politics also remains very low – no woman has ever been included in the top body of the People's Republic of China (PRC) – the Politburo Standing Committee. Moreover, in 2022, for the first time in decades, no woman was even present in the broader Politburo, symbolizing a setback for women's participation in Chinese politics under Xi Jinping.

Traditional gender roles are thus relatively firmly anchored in Chinese society, which is also reflected in the status of women in the household. Although surveys show that Chinese women are fairly satisfied with their position in the family, almost a quarter of them also report being victims of domestic violence, including restrictions on personal freedom, physical violence, or verbal or sexual abuse.[27] While overall the position of women in China has undoubtedly improved in public life, their position within the family, whether as daughters or wives, is not entirely favorable. This is particularly true for the rural population. To this day, it is common for countryside families to invest more money in their sons' health or education compared to their daughters, and males often have the upper hand even in the case of distribution of wealth or inheritance.

LGBTI community

Just as the position of women in Chinese society is gradually improving (in the long term at least), a similar trend is visible in the case of the position of the LGBTI community. Although legal rights for LGBTI people in China are limited (e.g., no possibility of civil unions or same-sex marriage), the attitude of Chinese society toward this community has become increasingly tolerant.

Still, the government has also repeatedly initiated crackdowns against the LGBTI community and its activism in the public space. In spring 2018, Weibo banned discussions about the LGBTI community as part of the campaign to create a "clean and harmonious cyber-environment". This step, however, provoked a wave of resentment in society and earned criticism from the party newspaper *Renmin Ribao*, which is why the ban was eventually rescinded. Although the state media in this case expressed support for LGBTI people and even supported their rights, this did not result in a fundamental change in the government's stance. On another occasion, the government banned public activities related to the International Day Against Homophobia, Biphobia, and Transphobia in 2018, showing it wants to limit exposure to the issue. First and foremost, it is not in the interest of the government for the rights of the LGBTI community to become a political issue.

Ethnic minorities

The issue of the treatment of ethnic minorities in China has been much more controversial. There are officially 56 ethnic groups recognized by the Chinese government, including the Han, who make up almost 92% of the population. China, despite the ethnic dominance of the Han people, is a multi-ethnic state, which was also reflected in the first Chinese flag used in 1912–1928, which was supposed to denote the coexistence of all the Chinese ethnicities that the government recognized at the time, including the Han, Manchurian, Mongolian, Tibetan, and Uyghur. After the establishment of the PRC, the concept of "Chinese nation" (*zhonghua minzu*) was extended to the Han population and 55 ethnic minorities.

Ethnic minorities in China have a legally guaranteed "significant degree" of autonomy, which is reflected in the creation of autonomous areas such as Xinjiang, Tibet, Inner Mongolia, Ningxia, and Guangxi. Despite their official status and legal protection, most of the non-Han ethnic groups have faced "sinicization", or more accurately, "Hanization". For decades, the government has supported Han people moving *en masse* to regions previously dominated by ethnic minorities, such as Xinjiang, Inner Mongolia, or Tibet, to change the ethnic makeup of the local population.

Moreover, the government has, through various means, pushed the ethnic minorities to abandon their traditional lifestyle and has slowly side-lined many aspects of their culture, including language, promoting instead the mainstream Chinese culture and standard Chinese language. In many cases, the government has presented these efforts as driven by the objective of raising their living standards and promoting overall economic development. While Chinese minorities have faced various forms of oppression and discrimination for decades, it was under Xi Jinping that the Chinese ethnic minorities policy became much more stringent, with a clear goal of outright assimilation. The most extreme assimilation efforts have been undergone in Xinjiang, where the Uyghur population is being "re-educated" in internment camps (see Chapter 12 for more details).

Growing quality of life vs. social problems

With its dynamic economic development over the past decades under an oppressive political regime, Chinese society has faced several difficult social ills. These include poverty, organized crime, prostitution, religious freedom, freedom of expression, corruption, and others. In the world's most populous country, living standards are rising at a high pace – in the last 40 years, the average income of the Chinese population has increased many times, with the urban population now on average enjoying good living standards with access to education and health care. Extreme poverty has been essentially eradicated, too, according to the official statistics of the World Bank.

However, there are also many social groups in the country that have been left behind in economic development. Huge gaps are present in income levels, social benefits, the ratio of the economically active population, level of education, and other aspects. One social issue that is quite specific to China is the gender imbalance, caused by decades of population-planning policies. China is also facing a rapidly aging population, posing a real threat that the country will "become old before it gets rich".

The Chinese government has introduced policies to tackle these issues, with varying success rates. In recent years, the government has moved from limiting population growth to promoting the birth rate, has promoted the social benefits for the elderly, and has mounted a successful campaign against extreme poverty. However, just as the effects of the one-child policy were only fully felt after a few decades, even with the actions of the current government, the results will not be visible immediately, and we will have to wait several years to see whether the reality of life for most of the people in China will be largely defined by rising standards of living or by mounting social problems.

Notes

1 C. Chang, "China still has a wealth gap problem: Economist", *Taiwan News*, 2 June 2020.
2 "Tu 1.18 liudong renkou shuliang, 1982–2017 nian" 《图 1.18 流动人口数量，1982–2017年》, UNICEF China, 2017.

3 Y. Song, “Hukou-based labor market discrimination and ownership structure in urban China”, *Urban Studies 53(8)*, 2015, 1657–1673.
4 M. Maurer-Fazio, R. Connelly & N. Thi Tran, “Do negative native-place stereotypes lead to discriminatory wage penalties in China’s migrant labor markets?”, *IZA*, 2015.
5 B. Haas, “China: ‘Ruthless’ campaign to evict Beijing’s migrant workers condemned”, *The Guardian*, 27 November 2017.
6 Z. Zhang, “China is relaxing Hukou restrictions in small and medium-sized cities”, *China Briefing*, 17 April 2019.
7 X. Shan, “Guojia tongjiju: 2019 nian zhongguo chengzhenhua lü tupo 60% huji chengzhenhua lü” 44.38%《统计 国家： 2019 60% 44.38%, Zhongguo jingji wang, February 28, 2020. 局年中国城镇化率突破 户籍城镇化率》中国经济网.
8 D. Goodman, “Why China’s middle class supports the Communist Party”, *The Christian Science Monitor*, 22 October 2013.
9 M. Cyrill, “China’s middle class in 5 simple questions”, *China Briefing*, 13 February 2019.
10 S. Mathur, “With eye on tourists from China, India revamps policy”, *The Times of India*, 31 December 2019.
11 “How well-off is China’s middle class?”, *China Power*, 26 April 2017.
12 B. Hammer, “Confucian thought and China’s moral crisis”, *Journal of Chinese Humanities*, 2017.
13 Y. Ye, “When will China’s population peak? It depends on who you ask”, *Nature*, 25 August 2022.
14 “Total population, CBR, CDR, NIR and TFR of China (1949–2000)”, *China Daily*, 24 December 2017.
15 Y. Zeng & T. Hesketh, “The effects of China’s universal two-child policy”, *The Lancet*, 2016.
16 Ibid.
17 A. Fensom, “Dangerous demographics: China’s population problem will eclipse its ambitions”, *The National Interest*, 16 September 2019.
18 Zeng & Hesketh, “The effects of China’s universal two-child policy”.
19 “Zhonghua renmin gongheguo laonianren quanyi baozhang fa”《中华人民共和国老年人权益保障法》, Quanguo renmin daibiao dahui, December 29, 2012. 全国人民代表大会.
20 Y. Wang & J. Quan, “Yang nüer bi erzi geng neng fanglao”《养女儿比儿子更能防老》, Renmin wang 人民网, 30 November 2015.
21 I. Attané, “Being a woman in China today: A demography of gender”, *China Perspectives 4*, 2012, 5–15.
22 J. Sun, “Zhongguo nannü bili shiheng xianxianguch 00 hou nanxing meinian duo chu baiwan ren” 《中国男女比例失衡现象突出 00后男性每年多出百万人》, Xinlang caijing, 新浪, 23 January 2019.
23 T. Zheng, “Human trafficking in China”, *Journal of Historical Archaeology & Anthropological Sciences 3(2)*, 2018, 171–178.
24 Ibid.
25 Zeng & Hesketh, “The effects of China’s universal two-child policy”.
26 Attané, “Being a woman in China today”.
27 Ibid.

Part II

Politics and economy

6 China's political system

How does the Communist Party rule China?

Filip Šebok

While most people know that China is an authoritarian regime under the control of the Communist Party of China, the particularities of its functioning often remain shrouded in mystery. Both the media and politicians often create an unrealistic image of China as a unified monolith, where the word of the top leaders in Beijing is the law to which the entire huge country automatically submits. However, when looking closely at the functioning of the Chinese political system, we find that it is more complicated, and implemented rules often diametrically differ across China. The appearance of a monolith evaporates even further when looking at the Chinese Communist Party (CCP) or broader state apparatus, in which there are several rival camps and "interest groups". To a large extent, China functions as a "fragmented authoritarian system" – and this is precisely what Xi Jinping is trying to change.[1]

China itself denies it is an authoritarian state and claims it has its own form of democracy. The Chinese political system is very far removed from the Western vision of liberal democracy, but it is true that the CCP also uses, to a limited extent, decision-making processes in which broader sections of the population are involved. Such popular participation, under the close leadership of the Party, ensures more effective policymaking and maintains the regime's ability to respond to the concerns of the population and various interest groups. Moreover, if we take a closer look, we will find that the CCP has undergone a dynamic reform process over the past decades, which brought optimization and professionalization of processes within the autocratic system. The Communist Party was thus able to maintain its power, even while most other communist regimes in the world gradually collapsed. However, many of these adjustments have been reversed by Xi Jinping, and Chinese politics is currently in flux. ***In which direction is China headed under Xi Jinping?***

Center versus provinces

Even though China is officially a centralized system, this does not mean that everything is decided in Beijing. In such a large country, this would not be realistically possible. It is often difficult for China's central government to get the directives from above through a massive hierarchy to the very lowest levels. This problem was not dissimilar to what was experienced by the Chinese emperors in the past

DOI: 10.4324/9781003350064-9

– as an old Chinese proverb says: "Heaven is high and the emperor is far away" – the local authorities can often do as they please, hidden from the eyes of the central government.

It is not uncommon for local policies to be in conflict with what Beijing prefers. Consider, for example, environmental protection measures – although regulations in China have become relatively strict, local authorities are often circumventing them. That is why one should always be wary of generalizing from a single piece of news coming from China as being representative of the whole country.

However, the fragmentation of authority can also be an advantage for the Communist Party. Beijing often deliberately announces only broad policy contours and leaves it to the local authorities how to implement them. The latter often have significant powers, particularly in the economic and social spheres, and can thus in practice adapt the regulations to local conditions. At the same time, provinces and individual cities are actively competing to achieve better results. The vibrant competitive environment and the possibility to experiment locally with economic and social policies have been, in fact, key factors ensuring the success of economic reforms since the 1970s (see Chapter 7).

In practice, China is often referred to as a quasi-federal system, although officially it is a centralized, unitary state. The administrative division of the country is relatively complicated, consisting of different levels. China is divided into 22 provinces (as the 23rd province China claims Taiwan), five autonomous regions, four directly administered municipalities, and two special administrative regions (Hong Kong and Macao). All these administrative units are then further divided into smaller units, through prefectures and districts down to the level of residential communities and villages.

Directly administered municipalities include Beijing, Shanghai, Chongqing, and Tianjin; these are the metropolises with the strongest position in both the Chinese economy and politics. While Beijing is the political heart of China, Shanghai is the center of China's economy. Chongqing became a directly administered municipality only relatively recently, in 1997, when it was separated from the Sichuan province. The goal was to turn Chongqing into a metropolis of Western China, which has always lagged behind the coastal areas, both economically and politically. Tianjin, on the other hand, has long had a unique position, as it has been one of the main centers of activity of Western powers since the 19th century.

In addition to the urban areas, these four cities also manage large adjacent territories. One might encounter the misleading factoid that Chongqing is the largest city in the world with 30 million inhabitants. In fact, the city of Chongqing itself (as a continuously built-up area) occupies only a small part of its entire designated area – with the rest being other cities and rural areas.

Autonomous regions – Xinjiang, Tibet, Ningxia, Guangxi, and Inner Mongolia – have more powers on paper than provinces or directly administered municipalities. These are the regions where some of the largest ethnic minorities live – the Uyghur minority in Xinjiang, the Tibetan minority in Tibet, the Zhuang minority in Guangxi, the Muslim Hui in Ningxia, and the Mongols in Inner Mongolia. Autonomous regions are often governed by representatives of these minorities.

Figure 6.1 China's administrative division (source: CEIAS).

Apart from the autonomous regions (i.e., the provincial-level units), there are also autonomous administrative units at a lower level. In reality, however, these entities do not have real autonomy and their "autonomous" powers are purely formal. It can be argued that autonomous regions are not fundamentally different from other Chinese provinces – on the contrary, Tibet and Xinjiang are known for greater control by the central government.

Macao (former Portuguese colony) and Hong Kong (former British colony) are the two special administrative regions of China. On paper, they enjoy considerable autonomy under the "one country, two systems" principle, which is supposed to ensure that the existing system is maintained for 50 years after the transfer of sovereignty to China. This applies to political institutions, the economic establishment, the judiciary, the currency, and other areas of domestic policy. Hong Kong and Macao are also special customs territories and are separated from the rest of China by border controls – the citizens of the PRC must even obtain a special visa-like permit for entry. Beijing is primarily responsible for the foreign policy and defense of these territories. In reality, the degree of autonomy of these two regions has been decreasing in recent years. This is especially true for Hong Kong, which lost its relative autonomy in a span of a few years after local protests alarmed Beijing (see Chapter 14).

The chimera of political power – the Party, the state, and the military

China's political institutions operate as a two-track system. From the lowest administrative units to the central authorities, there are state and Party institutions in parallel, with the Party ones being more powerful. Thus, in the hierarchy of power, the governor of Guangdong Province or the mayor of Beijing City only rank after the provincial or municipal Party secretary. Although the state and the Party operate in parallel, in practice they often merge. The mayor of Beijing, which is a state position, also serves as the deputy city Party secretary. The positions of the current leader Xi Jinping serve as a good example. In foreign media, he is most often titled as President, which is a position in the state apparatus. Yet, in terms of actual power, his role as the Party General Secretary is much more important.

Political power in China is vested in the CCP and its governing bodies. Formally, the highest body of the Communist Party is the National Congress. It takes place every five years in autumn. At each National Congress, the Central Committee of the Communist Party is elected, which currently has 205 voting members and 171 non-voting substitutes. The Central Committee then elects the Politburo and the Politburo Standing Committee, headed by the General Secretary of the Party. In the current configuration since 2022, the 20th Politburo has 24 members, with seven of them sitting also on the smaller Standing Committee, but the sizes of these bodies have varied. It is worth noting that in the current Politburo there is no woman, as Sun Chunlan – the only woman in the previous 19th Politburo – retired in 2022. There has never been a single woman in the Politburo Standing Committee.

The selection of the leadership to the highest organs of the CCP is a complicated process. The exact processes are not publicly known, but the nominations are the result of an agreement between the current and former leadership of the CCP and is not limited to formal structures of power. Some places in the Politburo are more or less fixed – for example, the Party Secretaries of Shanghai and Beijing and other major provinces such as Guangdong, as well as representatives of the central government, have practically guaranteed seats in the Politburo. The same applies to two representatives of the Chinese People's Liberation Army (PLA). The purpose of such a composition is to achieve a balance of different interests.

The Politburo Standing Committee is the most powerful body in all of China and the nerve center of the system, but we know very little about its practical functioning. The majority of its members hold key positions in state bodies – General Secretary Xi Jinping is also President and Chairman of the Central Military Commission and combines all three elements of power – the Party, the state, and the military – into one person. Number two is Li Qiang, the Prime Minister of the State Council, i.e., the Chinese government cabinet, the main executive body. The other members are Zhao Leji, the Chairman of the Standing Committee of the National People's Congress (NPC); Wang Huning, who chairs the National Committee of the Chinese People's Political Consultative Conference (CPPCC);

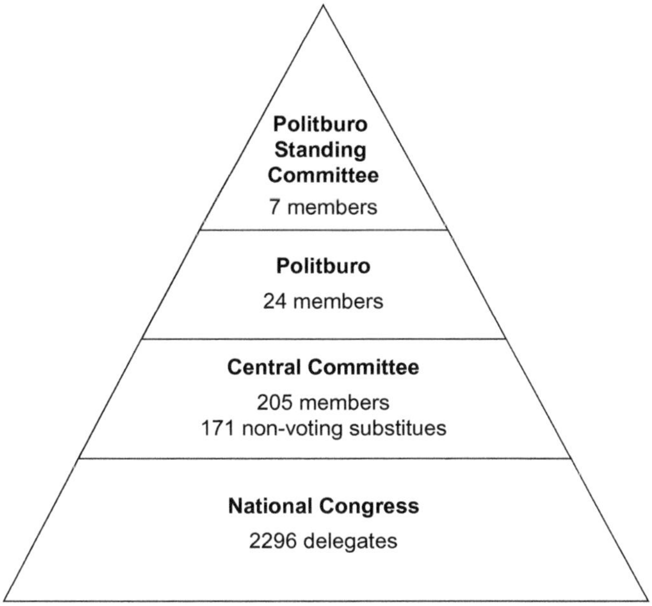

Figure 6.2 CCP and its lead authorities (source: CEIAS).

Cai Qi, who manages Party Secretariat and the powerful General Office; Ding Xuexiang, who serves as an Executive Vice Prime Minister of the State Council and is responsible for Hong Kong and Macao issues; and Li Xi, who is in charge of the anticorruption agenda via his role as a Secretary of the Central Commission for Discipline Inspection.

In terms of making important political decisions, plenary sessions (plenums) of the Central Committee are the most important political events every year. In recent years, the number of plenums during the five-year mandate of the Central Committee has stabilized at seven. The results of plenums are often important decisions that set China's course for the years to come. The third plenum of the 11th Central Committee, for example, is known for launching the "reforms and opening up" of Deng Xiaoping, fundamentally changing the course of China after Mao Zedong's death and making China an economic powerhouse as we know it today.

The state authorities are subject to the Party's decisions. In principle, the state, headed by the State Council, is mainly involved in the implementation of the policies determined by the Party. Therefore, individual ministries are not the highest decision-making bodies in their field and depend on parallel Party institutions. For example, the highest authority in military affairs is the Central Military Commission headed by Xi Jinping, with the top military officials placed higher in the hierarchy than the Minister of Defense. Similarly, the most important authority in China's foreign policy is not the foreign minister but the head of the Party's foreign affairs commission.

Apart from the Party and the state, the third pillar of power in China is the military. From its very beginning, the Communist Party has adhered to the words of Mao Zedong that "political power grows out of the barrel of a gun". Interestingly, the Chinese PLA is not formally the military of the state but is subordinate to the Communist Party. Its primary task is therefore to protect the interests of the Party and not necessarily to protect Chinese citizens. This was demonstrated during the 1989 protests when the PLA cracked down violently against the protesting masses to defend the position of the Communist Party.

The organizational system of the PLA is dual, as is the system of the Chinese state administration, with Party committees present across the hierarchy. In practice, the Party and the military often merge: on one hand, the Communist Party controls the PLA, but the representatives of the military also have their place in the leading Party organizations, including the Politburo. The Party control over the PLA is ensured by the Central Military Commission (attached to the Central Committee of the Communist Party), chaired by Secretary General Xi Jinping. This Commission appoints generals and sets out the most important defense policy decisions, which are then implemented by the Ministry of Defense.

When looking back on history, it was not always easy for the Party to exercise power over the PLA. In the 1990s, when the PLA was allowed to run its own private business, it created a large economic empire and often functioned autonomously. The PLA was involved in illegal businesses such as gambling, prostitution, drug trafficking, and smuggling. Jiang Zemin put an end to this practice and forbade the PLA, with some exceptions, from participating in any business activities.[2] Former General Secretary Hu Jintao, in turn, was considered a leader with weak control over the PLA, which sometimes even acted apparently without his knowledge. However, current General Secretary Xi Jinping has quickly gained authority over the PLA since taking office in 2012, subordinating it closely to the Party and himself personally.

"Representative" bodies: NPC and CPPCC

The regime does, to a certain extent, involve the population in decision-making through quasi-democratic processes. These elements provide the system with the opportunity to optimize policymaking, build consensus, and ensure that some form of feedback loop is present, enabling the CCP to respond adequately to population dissatisfaction that could spin out of control if left unchecked.

One such element is represented by the quasi-parliamentary institutions, which are supposed to represent the entire Chinese society, i.e., not only the CCP – the National People's Congress (NPC) and the Chinese People's Political Consultative Conference (CPPCC). The two bodies meet once a year in the spring, the so-called two sessions.

According to the Chinese Constitution, the NPC is the highest institution in the Chinese political system. The 14th NPC, convened in 2023, has 2977 delegates serving a five-year term. The NPC only meets in full once a year during the two sessions, and its powers are thus mostly delegated to the Standing Committee of 175 members. The NPC formally approves candidates for the highest state positions and amendments to the constitution.

NPC delegates are elected indirectly in a system that resembles a pyramid. The NPC is elected by provincial people's congresses, which in turn are elected by congresses on lower levels. The PLA also elects its own delegates. Only at the grassroots level are the delegates directly elected, in orchestrated elections. Approximately 70% of the delegates in the NPC are members of the Communist Party.

No significant decisions are taken during the annual NPC sessions, as everything is already decided in advance within the Party and in consultation with the relevant authorities. The vote in the NPC is just the final formal step. Most of the proposals are approved by a large majority, often unanimously. For example, in 2018, the NPC approved the amendment to the Constitution, which lifted restrictions on the term of office of the President, with 2,958 votes in favor and only two against.[3] The NPC never vetoed a proposal, so even a significant number of votes against always means that the proposal is very controversial and there is no strong consensus. An example is a vote on the controversial construction of the Three Gorges Dam in 1992, which was approved with the support of "only" just under 70% of the votes.

The situation is a bit different in the NPC Standing Committee – in the past, it even vetoed some laws, such as the Highways Act in 1996, returning it to the government for redrafting. In the case of provincial congresses, some nominees from Beijing were not approved, with local delegates choosing their own. However, such incidents are exceedingly rare and only relate to non-crucial decisions. A unique institution of the Chinese political system is the CPPCC. This institution is sometimes likened to the role of the Senate in some political systems, but this comparison is imperfect, as the CPPCC is not a constitutional body. Like the NPC, this institution has its parallels at local levels. The delegates in CPPCC number 2,158 and come from different constituencies. The role of the CPPCC is primarily advisory, but it serves an important role in helping the CCP exercise control over various spheres of society in the system of the so-called Unified Front. In addition to the CCP, the representatives of which are, in this body, in a minority (about 30%), and there are also representatives of the so-called eight democratic parties in the CPPCC. These parties play a predominantly formal role in the system, and all recognize the leading role of the Communist Party but also represent important interest groups. Youth organizations, trade unions, women's organizations, religious organizations, ethnic minorities, and various other groups of people are also represented in CPPCC. Interestingly, the famous Hong Kong actor Jackie Chan and basketball player Yao Ming have also been members.

Popular involvement in political processes

Other quasi-democratic elements of the Chinese system are elections and consultations. A large part of the electoral process takes place indirectly and only one candidate is nominated for the position. The entire process is under the control of the CCP, which closely controls the selection of candidates and ensures that they receive sufficient support.

However, there are also direct elections at the grassroots level. Since the 1980s, China has introduced direct elections for the heads of village committees. At this level, elections are held with several candidates, who have, in some cases, run an open campaign soliciting votes and even held electoral debates. The decision to give the local population more power in choosing their representatives was motivated by the desire to make the local governments more efficient and to delegate responsibility. In contrast to the higher levels, in villages the residents personally know the candidates and can supposedly evaluate who will be more competent in solving local problems. As the range of powers at the disposal of the local leadership is limited, the risk of endangering the political monopoly of the CCP is not significant. However, if candidates are unacceptable for some reason, the Communist Party can always influence the elections. The results of this democratic experiment vary from region to region and have started to be rolled back as part of the general political tightening under Xi Jinping.

In addition to the elections, various forms of public consultation have been introduced under the principle of so-called deliberative (or consultative) democracy. At the national level, this instrument is represented by the CPPCC. At the local level, consultations complement the limited elections in involving the population in the political process. Local authorities in many localities organize public debates where people can present their views on local issues that directly affect their lives – for example, the construction of a waste incineration plant near their homes. The benefits of consultation vary – while in some places they provide a real opportunity for leaders to be confronted with the concerns of the people, elsewhere they remain as rather a formal instrument. In addition to consultations at the local level, national consultations on government proposals have been launched in China as well. Draft laws are submitted for consultation to the public, which can submit comments. Environmental NGOs, for example, have been involved in the legislative process in this way.

Some of the final draft laws can therefore have a limited impact on the public. This is particularly the case for laws that may cause public outrage but do not fall under areas that would jeopardize the Party's role. An example is the draft law on the relaxation of the rules for "green cards" for foreigners, which was presented at the beginning of 2020. A great deal of resentment rose against the law because of (largely unfounded) fears that the new rules would lead to mass immigration into China. Subsequently, the authorities announced that the changes in the law would reflect public opinion.

All these elements lead to the fact that democracy as a concept is not taboo in China, and the Party itself has often operated with it throughout its history. However, as in many other areas, the Party highlights 'Chinese characteristics'. Eventually, quasi-democratic instruments are only means of strengthening the power of the CCP.

The Party of 96 million

The discussion about the CCP often revolves around its top institutions. However, the CCP is an organization that permeates all layers of Chinese society. Currently, the Party has about 96 million members and is the largest political party in the world. Still, the Party is rather selective in choosing its members. In 2014, for example, two million people were admitted to the Party out of 22 million applicants.[4]

Applicants who want to join the Party must be recommended by at least two other Party members and need to be approved by a committee after careful screening. When joining the Party, the approved member must take an oath before the Party flag, where, among other things, he or she promises to "fight for communism all life, be constantly ready to sacrifice everything for the Party and for the people and never betray the Party".[5] The new members will then have a one-year observation period during which their behavior is monitored and evaluated – if there are no problems they then become full members of the Party.

Membership in the Communist Party is for life. If one is stripped of membership, it is usually a punishment for particularly serious misconduct, such as corruption. Sometimes membership is even taken from deceased people, which is a great disgrace to their legacy. On the other hand, membership has often been reinstated after rehabilitation, especially after the Cultural Revolution.

The motivation for joining the Communist Party varies. Many are undoubtedly true believers in the Party's ideology and see membership as an opportunity to fulfill their patriotic obligation. On the other hand, membership is often a pragmatic decision. For career growth, a Party membership 'card' can be essential, and it is often the most ambitious young people who join the Party. State-owned enterprises, but also private companies, prefer people with a Party membership. According to research, members of the Communist Party earn on average more than non-members under comparable conditions.[6]

The Party maintains control over the entire Chinese society – the members are grouped in more than four and a half million Party cells.[7] All formally registered organizations, including private firms employing more than three Party members, are obliged to establish a Party cell. Their importance varies from one organization to another: while in some places it may be a formality, as in the case of smaller private firms, elsewhere they are directly involved in decision-making.

There is virtually no major organization in China that is not somehow linked to the CCP. For example, all trade unions in China are associated with the national trade union organization, directly subordinate to the CCP. More than a tool for advancing the interests of the working class, they serve as a tool for Party control. Efforts to establish independent trade unions are repressed.

The Party of cadres

A key tool in the hands of the Party is cultivation and selection of cadres. This task is carried out by the Organization Department of the Central Committee and its equivalent bodies on lower levels. These authorities decide not only on leadership positions in Party and state bodies, but also other personnel decisions. This makes them important power brokers in the system. They also select people for leading positions in state-owned companies, state newspapers or television stations, universities, courts, research organizations, and other key organizations. The Organization Department at the central level is directly responsible for the filling of around 5,000 posts, and another around 40,000 nominations are reported to it from the lower levels.[8]

The criteria for advancement in the Party hierarchy have evolved over time. Following reforms in the 1980s, professional competence and performance records began to be valued. Technocrats, often with university education in natural sciences or technical fields, were lifted to the top positions in the Party. This process was guided by Deng Xiaoping's call that it was important that Party members needed to be not only "red" but also experts. The Communist Party has created a system for evaluating officials with several criteria. The most important contribution was initially economic growth. Therefore, local Party leaders were striving to achieve the highest possible GDP growth rates to secure career progression. The maintenance of political stability has been a no less important indicator for officials' prospects. That is why local leadership tries to silence any social unrest already in its infancy before it comes to the attention of the higher levels of government. Partly owing to his effective reaction to the protests in Shanghai in 1989, the then Party Secretary of Shanghai, Jiang Zemin, caught the attention of the center, and Deng Xiaoping chose him as his successor. The evaluation criteria have been gradually changing, placing greater emphasis on compliance with environmental measures and achieving a more balanced growth rather than purely chasing numerical targets.

The experience from different parts of China is also important for promising Party cadres. Usually, higher cadres do not work in their home provinces, and it is rarely the case that a native of a given province serves as its Party secretary or governor. In this way, cadres rotate and gain experience from working in different parts of China. The experience from an economically dynamic and relatively developed Shanghai is quite different from working in the poor province of Guangxi, also home to a significant minority population. For example, Xi Jinping served in Shaanxi, Hebei, Fujian, Zhejiang, and finally Shanghai throughout his career, until he joined the Politburo Standing Committee in 2007.

Chinese cadre selection is sometimes presented as an example of a meritocratic system where the most capable are promoted to increasingly important positions based on their previous performance.[9] However, the reality is that while professional competence plays an important role, it is far from being the only factor in consideration. For promising leaders, it is important to have the right contacts and not to antagonize important people. Sometimes the family background also helps. Finally, in some cases, officials simply bribe their way to promotion.

The Party of factions

The Communist Party is determined to display perfect unity in all circumstances and has been guided by the principle of so-called democratic centralism. Hence, decisions are to be arrived at by consensus, resulting from discussions within the Party. However, after the decision has been made, it is expected that the whole Party will submit to it without question. Only very rarely does the public get a hint of internal Party discord. In reality, however, there are factions within the Party that are competing with each other.

One of the important factions has been the Communist Youth League faction, associated with the organization of the same name. Some of those usually seen as representatives of the faction include Prime Minister Li Keqiang (2012–2022) or former President Hu Jintao (2002–2012). The Communist Youth League faction representatives have often built their position based on their own abilities and have often come from simple backgrounds. This faction is considered populist in the Chinese context – i.e., it stresses the concerns of the lower classes of society and puts great emphasis on the issue of economic equality.

The so-called "princelings" (or also the "second red generation") are often seen as standing on the opposite end of the imagined divide. These are descendants of important communist leaders, whose power stems mainly from their family background. Many princelings possess significant economic power, often through large state-owned enterprises. The current leader Xi Jinping is considered a princeling – his father, Xi Zhongxun, was a revolutionary leader and also one of the engineers of economic reforms in the 1980s. The same applies to Xi's erstwhile rival, Bo Xilai, who was seen as a prospect for top Party positions but was purged in 2012 – he is the son of Bo Yibo, a revolutionary leader and a leading political figure in the 1980s and 1990s.

Another important faction is the so-called "Shanghai clique", made up of politicians from Shanghai. This Chinese economic powerhouse has always had its own interests which may not always be in line with Beijing's vision. The most important figure in the "Shanghai clique" has been former President Jiang Zemin and his allies.

The membership in individual factions is not mutually exclusive, therefore, one can be a princeling and have a career in the Communist Youth League as well. Xi himself, for example, has undoubtedly championed policies that would be seen as populist. Affiliation to factions can often be assessed only based on circumstantial evidence – for example, by who the people they have associated with are. Many important leaders also create their own factions of reliable confidants. For example, many of the officials promoted by Xi Jinping had links with him from the past.[10] Thus, individual factions often arise and disappear together with specific people. In fact, Xi Jinping has managed to centralize power to such extent that the previous divisions into fractions may not be relevant any more after the 20th National Congress.

Retired leaders also retain their influence, despite no longer holding official functions. The incumbent leadership also consults with them on fundamental issues of the Party's direction. The best example is Deng Xiaoping, who retained considerable power practically until his death in 1997. Similarly, Jiang Zemin was seen as a gray eminence for many years after he officially left office. The meeting of the current leadership and senior leaders takes place every summer in the seaside resort of Beidaihe near Beijing. Although no information about the course of the meeting appears in the Chinese media, it is assumed to be one of the most important events of the year in terms of political significance.

The Party of reform

After the collapse of the Soviet Union, many observers expected the Chinese regime to face a similar fate. However, the Communist Party not only maintained its hold on power but even strengthened its position over time. Since the late 1970s, the Party has undergone some fundamental reforms, which have ensured its survival.

One of the most important reforms was the introduction of a mechanism for the regular transfer of power. The change of leadership of the communist parties in the world has never been very successful – just think of the power struggle in the Soviet Union after Stalin's death and how Khrushchev, who emerged victorious in the succession contest, was eventually replaced unceremoniously. The succession struggle inevitably leads to instability and thus threatens the Party itself. Deng Xiaoping was well aware of this and therefore introduced a system of rotation of political generations. After ten years, the Party leaders were to hand over their functions to their followers. So far, the Party has had five generations of leaders: Mao, Deng, Jiang, Hu, and Xi.

The succession reforms entailed the introduction of age limits for the Party and state officials. In this way, the Communist Party was also supposed to avoid another ailment of the communist system – the so-called gerontocracy, i.e., the government by elders. A maximum age limit has been introduced for different Party and state functions. For example, a threshold of 67 years was set for entering the Politburo. However, many of these rules have not been formally established, which allows for some flexibility. In particular, Xi Jinping managed to remain in power after he reached 69 years old (and is expected to stay there indefinitely), meaning he has broken the previously established system of changing the generations designed by Deng.

The second important element of the post-Mao reforms was the introduction of collective decision-making. Deng attributed many of the failures of the Mao era mainly to the excessive concentration of power in one person. That is why Deng initiated the distribution of authority in a larger collective, where decisions are taken jointly by consensus. This model reached its peak during the reign of Hu Jintao, who was considered "the first among equals" and not the uncontested leader. Again, this has significantly changed since Xi Jinping entered office.

The third important reform was the expansion of the CCP membership base and the opening of Party membership to the entrepreneurship class, which has become the most dynamic class in Chinese society. Since the Party was to represent the revolutionary classes, it had long resisted the admission of "capitalists". This changed only after 2000 when Jiang Zemin allowed practically all representatives of Chinese society, including those from private businesses, to join the Party. If Mao Zedong had lived, he would probably have denounced his successors for turning the revolutionary Party of the proletariat into an all-encompassing ruling party with no clear class affiliation. However, through this move, the Party ensured the enlargement of the base of its support.

Today, the Communist Party counts even the richest Chinese entrepreneurs, such as the founder of Alibaba, Jack Ma, among its members. According to one calculation, 153 of the richest people in the NPC and CPPCC are together worth $650 billion.[11]

Some pro-reform politicians, in particular the then General Secretary Zhao Ziyang (more in Chapter 3), went so far as to seek partial separation of the Party from the state in the 1980s. The CCP was supposed to set the strategic direction and not participate directly in the executive power, which was supposed to remain a competence of the state authorities. However, this reform has never been completed, as many (perhaps justifiably) feared that it could eventually endanger the Party's monopoly on power. After the bloody events of 1989, talk of political reforms was silenced, with Zhao himself spending the rest of his life under house arrest.

Through its reforms, CCP has demonstrated a remarkable ability to adapt to the changing circumstances over the past decades; they made the system more predictable and institutionalized and broadened the basis for the Party's popular support, all the while avoiding any serious challenge to its power monopoly. However, a lot of this is in flux right now.

The Party of Xi Jinping

Since 2012, China has been ruled by Xi Jinping, who has brought along some of the most fundamental changes in the country's political direction since Deng Xiaoping. In many areas, it can be argued that Xi has eroded Deng's reforms and set out on a completely new course in China's political development. As early as his first term, Xi built a position of power for himself that China has not seen since Mao Zedong.

The first aspect of Xi Jinping's changes was the reiteration of the Party's dominance over the state. Xi's ideal is to subordinate to the Party all aspects of politics, but also of society and, to a large extent, of the economy. This follows Mao's slogan: "East, West, South, North, Centre, Party, Government, Military, Society and Education – the Party controls Everything". In 2019, in line with this objective, significant institutional changes were initiated, and some state institutions were "absorbed" by the Party authorities.[12] Xi also places emphasis on increasing the number of Party cells in non-partisan organizations and strengthening their powers.

The second aspect of Xi's changes has been the centralization of power and its concentration in his hands. In Xi's view, collective decision-making was too slow and inefficient, the central authority was weakened, and Party officials could often do as they pleased. One of the accompanying phenomena was the growth of corruption.

However, after assuming power, Xi Jinping usurped the dominant position in the Politburo Standing Committee and side-lined Prime Minister Li Keqiang. Xi largely took over the economic agenda, which according to the traditional division of work should be managed by the prime minister. Xi created several new executive bodies, putting himself in their leadership. The number of Xi Jinping's various positions and titles has grown to such an extent that he has earned the nickname "chairman of everything".

The third aspect of Xi's changes is the circumvention of institutional constraints. Xi Jinping has abandoned previous reforms that have introduced a regular change of leadership – he has not identified a successor, and in 2018 he pushed through a constitutional change, according to which nothing prevents him from remaining a president potentially until his death. In autumn 2022, he indeed became for the third time the General Secretary of the CCP, and in spring 2023 he was confirmed as the President for a third term as well. In addition, he has surrounded himself with the most loyal cadres, while pushing aside those perceived as being from other Party fractions, such as Li Keqiang, Hu Chunhua, and Wang Yang.

Xi Jinping seems to be building his own personality cult, which Deng warned against. Xi came up with a new ideological formula of "Xi Jinping's Thought", pushing its inclusion into the Party constitution while still in power, a feat which only Mao Zedong succeeded in during his lifetime. The larger-than-life position of Xi Jinping is also reflected in the Party propaganda. Reports from all the state media focus primarily on Xi Jinping, turning his speeches and instructions into never-ending ideological campaigns. Xi even got the label of a "people's leader" in Chinese propaganda, previously reserved for Mao Zedong.

A new criterion for career growth in the Party has thus become personal devotion to the leader. Party members are falling over each other to be the most ardent in repeating his words, fulfilling his political goals, and expressing absolute devotion. This, of course, weakens the meritocratic aspects of the system – and often reduces the willingness of officials to act on their own out of fear of doing something against the leader's wishes.

How did Xi Jinping manage to push through these epochal changes? Initially, Xi's ascent to power was considered a compromise between the different factions in the CCP. He was allegedly seen as someone who would not stand out too much and would not antagonize any important players. Many observers also expected new liberalization reforms from Xi Jinping – his father Xi Zhongxun was, after all, one of the key figures in economic reforms in Guangdong. However, Xi Jinping surprised everyone and quickly dominated the entire political system after assuming leadership positions.

Xi Jinping's most powerful tool has been the fight against corruption. Virtually immediately after his accession, he announced a massive campaign aimed at strengthening intra-Party discipline and punishing corrupt cadres. This task was entrusted to one of his closest associates in the Politburo Standing Committee, Wang Qishan. Throughout China, the dreaded inspectorate of the Central Disciplinary Commission, headed by Wang, began to operate. Some of the officials who had learned that an inspection had come to their town committed suicide rather than face an investigation.[13]

Xi Jinping used the fight against corruption as a tool against his opponents. In China, one would be hard-pressed to find an official who did not help himself

Figure 6.3 Xi Jinping's book in various languages (source: Robert Barca).

to considerable wealth on account of trading political access for benefits. However, if such an individual were to disobey orders from Beijing or come to cross Xi Jinping, his fate was sealed. The anti-corruption campaign thus led to the downfall of several prominent Party officials and the collapse of competing power centers. The atmosphere of fear has led many to realize that the best way to survive is to be as faithful as possible to the 'Party core'. On the other hand, the campaign was relatively positively received by the wider population, which has perceived corruption as a huge problem in recent decades, and the enthusiastic efforts by the "people's leader", supported by massive propaganda, are sympathetic to many.

Since Xi Jinping is likely going to stay in power for years to come, what can we expect from him? His clinging to power may backfire on the Party. Its survival in recent decades has been based on its institutional capacity to adapt to the changing situation. However, the system of one-man rule is much less flexible. Moreover, the cult of personality that Xi Jinping has built around him, and the requirement of ideological obedience, lead to other problems – the leader gets surrounded by "yes people". Such a situation is a recipe for disaster. It is quite likely that the COVID-19 pandemic spread initially in Wuhan also because of the system reinforced by Xi when local authorities did not want to relay bad news to their superiors. Moreover, if Xi suddenly becomes seriously ill or dies without determining his successor, the country may fall into chaos, with rival factions fighting for power.

Finally, the one-man rule could become a problem for Xi Jinping himself. When everything is under one's control, it is difficult to avoid responsibility for failures. The challenges China will face in the coming years and decades, whether it be a slowing economy, growing social discontent, demographic pressures, or a great power rivalry with the United States, will present a difficult challenge for Xi Jinping. Unable to cope with the challenges, Xi will hardly be able to shift the responsibility to someone else.

Notes

1 K. G. Lieberthal & David M. Lampton, *Bureaucracy, Politics, and Decision Making in Post-Mao China*, Berkeley: University of California Press, 1992.
2 R. McGregor, *The Party: The Secret World of China's' Communist Rulers*, New York: Harper Collins Publishers, 2010.
3 C. Buckley & S. Lee Myers, "China's legislature blesses Xi's indefinite rule. It was 2,958 to 2", *The New York Times*, 11 March 2018.
4 R. W. McMorrow, "Membership in the Communist Party of China: Who is being admitted and how?", *JSTOR Daily*, 19 December 2015.
5 L. S. Sullivan, *Historical Dictionary of the Chinese Communist Party*, Lanham: Scarecrow Press, 2012.
6 H. Wang, P. Nikolov & K. Acker, "The wage premium of Communist Party membership: Evidence from China", IZA Discussion Paper (12874), 2019.
7 N. Grunberg & K. Drinhausen, "The Party leads on everything", *Merics China Monitor*, 24 September 2019.
8 W. W. L. Lam, *Routledge Handbook of the Chinese Communist Party*, London: Routledge, 2018.
9 D. A. Bell, *The China Model: Political Meritocracy and the Limits of Democracy*, Princeton: Princeton University Press, 2015.
10 C. Li, *Chinese Politics in Xi Jinping Era*, Washington, DC: Brookings Institution Press, 2016.
11 S. Wee, "China's parliament is a growing billionaires' club", *The New York Times*, 1 March 2018.
12 Grunberg & Drinhausen, "The Party leads on everything".
13 A. Krishnan, "Why Xi Jinping's corruption crackdown is pushing corrupt officials to suicide", *The Print*, 10 December 2018.

7 Chinese economic miracle

How did an underdeveloped country change into a world leader?

Martin Šebeňa

Over the past 40 years, China has changed beyond recognition. Traditional Chinese architecture has been replaced by skyscrapers, and rice paddies have given way to huge factories. Today, a dense network of highways and high-speed railways cuts through the Chinese landscape. The stunning speed of China's economic growth and its material results have inspired many politicians and economists abroad, who are keen to replicate this economic miracle in their countries. Although the Chinese economy has been gradually liberalizing since 1978, the government still retains a number of tools in its hands. This has created a mixed economic system in which market capitalism is combined with a strong role of the state in the economy. It has come to be known as 'socialism with Chinese characteristics', which is also the official name for the economy of the People's Republic of China. ***But what exactly is the "Chinese model", a term sometimes used to describe the set of political and economic reforms that have led to the country's wealth? How has the Chinese economy developed since 1978, when it started opening up to the world? Does the country owe its success to proper economic planning, or is it a result of improvisation?***

The 1970s: The beginning of reforms

The traditional analysis of China's economic miracle dates its beginning back to December 1978, when Deng Xiaoping announced the reforms and the "Open Door Policy" at a plenary session of the Chinese Communist Party. This date is important because it marks the start of Deng Xiaoping's dominance in the Chinese political system. However, some political and economic reform efforts were underway even before Mao Zedong's death in 1976.

One of the most significant acts at the beginning of the reform process was a secret agreement of a farmers' association in Anhui Province to dissolve a collectively owned cooperative, divide its land among themselves, and keep the crops left after the mandatory levy. As this led to a significant increase in productivity, the chairman of the local branch of the Communist Party supported this idea. The Party chairman in Sichuan Province, Zhao Ziyang, also implemented this method.

DOI: 10.4324/9781003350064-10

Figure 7.1 Fathers of the Chinese economic miracle – Deng Xiaoping and Zhao Ziyang (source: Forrest Anderson/The LIFE).

In 1978, Deng Xiaoping confirmed that economic reform would begin in agriculture. Deng supported the transformation from collective cooperatives to the farming of individual households, in particular by deregulating the prices of agricultural products, thus increasing the incomes of the farming population. Zhao Ziyang became prime minister of China in 1980 and led economic reforms until 1989. As a result of the transition from collective management to a system of urban and rural enterprises, whose lands were owned by townships together with individual farmers, yields increased rapidly and rural incomes grew. Increased revenues generated savings, which have become one of the main sources of investment in the economy.

While the decisions of Deng and Zhao were critical in steering China on the path toward fast economic growth, this would not have been possible without the foundations that had been built in the preceding decades. Mao Zedong's model of economic development, which emphasized SOE-led investment into heavy industry, may have led to an economic standstill in the early 1970s, however, it endowed the country with an educated pool of laborers, low indebtedness, and a bulk of state capital. These laid a foundation for the market reforms carried out by the reformers in the 1980s.[1]

In addition to agriculture, the reforms also focused on building an export industry. To spur the growth of exports, four special economic zones (SEZs) were set up in southern China to attract foreign capital, mainly from ethnic Chinese from Taiwan, Hong Kong, and Southeast Asia. Many companies from these areas moved production to China due to cheaper labor, preferential conditions in SEZs, and appropriate timing – globalization was accelerating and the so-called Asian tigers (Taiwan, South Korea, Hong Kong, and Singapore) were moving away from simple manufacturing and switching to production of more sophisticated products.

The 1980s: Decentralization and experimentation

However, the core feature of economic development in China was the decentralization of state administration and the economy. The state abandoned the policy of strict central planning, price controls, and direct management of state-owned companies. Prices were deregulated and started being determined by market forces, state-owned companies were split into smaller units, and some of them were privatized. After catastrophic experiences with drastic changes in the direction of the economy in the previous period, especially during the Great Leap Forward in the late 1950s, the method of slow and incremental changes, so-called gradualism, was introduced.[2]

The deregulation of prices clearly demonstrates the gradual and experimental nature of macroeconomic policymaking in this period. Rejecting the advice of Western economists to rapidly liberalize prices, Chinese politicians let the market decide the prices only in a piecemeal fashion over more than a decade. In contrast to the economies of Central and Eastern Europe, which introduced market prices in a short period of time across all economies, China avoided larger price shocks and associated decreases in purchasing power for a large part of its population.[3]

Changes in state administration delegated economic competencies primarily to authorities at lower administrative levels. Thus, local or district officials had a lot of space to experiment with new tools to support economic growth. Deng Xiaoping also openly supported the experimentation with the well-known statement that it was necessary to "cross the river by touching the stones" (in Chinese, *mozhe shitou guo he*). If an experiment proved successful, it was gradually implemented in other regions, or even throughout the whole country. If it didn't work out, it was quickly stopped.

Decentralization did not only concern local officials. A number of regulatory authorities were created, private enterprises were tolerated, and state-owned enterprises also had to operate in a competitive environment. A system was created, in which the central government retained the power to decide on the country's economic development, but the specific way in which the plans would be implemented was up to the local officials, who could in some cases even afford to ignore the central government's plans if they considered them inappropriate for their location.

Officials were rewarded and promoted based on a quota system. In the first decade, quotas were scarce and focused mainly on GDP growth targets and the ability to attract foreign direct investment to their localities. This policy has transformed the Chinese administration into a system known as "fragmented authoritarianism" – although the central government is unelected and has considerable power, it performs mainly managerial tasks, coordinating millions of relatively independent local bureaucrats.[4]

This form of governance has generated significant economic growth, as motivated officials did all they could to support the economy in their area. At the same time, the reforms helped to stabilize the country as a whole, as different areas could implement policies that were better suited to their regional specificities. However, the disadvantage of the system was that officials often resorted to corruption, which very quickly reached enormous proportions. The economic boom also raised the rate of inflation, which negatively affected the purchasing power of a large part of the population.

Dissatisfaction with corruption and high inflation, low-income stability during the rapid reform process, and political demands shaped by rising living standards were the main economic factors that strengthened the reform and protest movement in the late 1980s. It ended on 4 June 1989 with the Tiananmen Square massacre in Beijing. Politically, the top victim was Zhao Ziyang, the Party's secretary general, who had steered China's economy in the preceding decade.

The 1990s: Relaunching reforms

Following the bloody crackdown, many countries imposed sanctions on China, inflicting short-term damage on China's export-oriented economy. At the same time, a debate arose in the Communist Party about the continuation of reforms: the conservative wing demanded their cessation, because, according to them, the reforms led to protests, which posed a direct threat to the Party. On the other hand, the reformists maintained that only a rich China could be strong and demanded the continuation of reforms. The debate ended with Deng Xiaoping's famous "journey to the south" in 1992, during which he visited the special economic zones and supported the resumption of capitalist reforms. Deng thus definitively confirmed the dominance of the reform wing and gave impetus to a new wave of economic growth.

Meanwhile, Zhu Rongji took control of the Chinese economy. In the 1980s, Zhu successfully started rapid economic growth in Shanghai, where he attracted the first major Western European investment in China – the German carmaker Volkswagen. As a deputy prime minister and later prime minister, he directed the transformation of the Chinese economy for ten years, culminating in China's accession to the World Trade Organization in 2001.

His most significant contribution to economic development was comprehensive tax reform. In the previous period, state budget revenues fell sharply as state-owned companies reinvested profits instead of paying taxes, in order to achieve the highest possible economic growth. Zhu changed the system so that taxes were first paid to the state, which then decided on their further use. The positive consequence was that more than 50% of all taxes collected reached the central government, and their volume also increased significantly.

On the other hand, local governments remained responsible for investing in the economy and meeting the government's economic goals. As the tax reform dried up their source of income, they ran into deficits. Although they were officially never in deficit, as the central government compensated them with a transfer of funds, in reality, money from Beijing often came with great delays. Local governments, therefore, addressed the lack of resources in three ways: the first was the collection of various fees, often fictitious and illegal, to raise money mainly from ordinary people.

The second way was the privatization of urban housing at the turn of the millennium, which led to an explosion in the real estate market.[5] Since the proceeds from the sale of land (or rather the "sale of land use rights", because in communist China all land is formally state-owned) remain with local governments, they seek to drive up land prices as much as possible and sell as many slots as possible. This often led to the illegal eviction of their inhabitants and the destruction of their homes due to the construction of development projects. Local officials often benefit from these transactions, whether through corruption or through achieving promotion in the state hierarchy as a reward for the economic growth of their area.

The third source of funding for the local administration has been borrowing money. As local governments cannot borrow directly, they have begun to set up special entities, the so-called Local Government Financing Vehicles, to borrow on their behalf. These entities do not fall under the same regulation as other state bodies or private companies, so the degree of local governments' indebtedness is not entirely clear. This is one of the reasons for a general concern that the volume of Chinese local government loans obtained in this way exceeds their ability to repay.[6]

Another important measure introduced by Zhu Rongji in the 1990s was the reform of state-owned companies. In the first phase of the reform period, they pursued a simple strategy for economic growth based on a large volume of investment. These investments, financed mainly through borrowing, often had only a low or negative return because they lacked a thorough economic analysis. With the decline in economic growth, they ran into financial problems that threatened not only them but also the entire economy.

The solution was to reduce the number of state-owned enterprises either by selling them or consolidating them into larger units. However, these new "mammoth conglomerates" only impacted a few strategic sectors, such as energetics, telecommunications, or the construction of large infrastructure projects. The result of the

Figure 7.2 Zhu Rongji in 1999 (source: Wikimedia Commons).

reform was an increase in the profitability of these companies and the stabilization of the economy. However, this had a negative impact on employment, as state-owned companies employed 60% of the workforce before the reform and only a quarter after the reform. For many, working in a Chinese state-owned enterprise meant income stability. It was the famous "iron bowl of rice" that many people were losing in the 1990s. However, due to the rapid economic growth, averaging more than 10% a year, new jobs were generated relatively fast. Those who were made redundant in state-owned enterprises were able to find new jobs in the private sector.

The beginning of the new millennium: The engine of the world economy

The Asian financial crisis, which also affected China in 1997–1998, impacted the country in two ways. Globalizing China had for the first time felt the impact of other countries' economic woes. Its response was to not reduce the value of the yuan, thus indirectly supporting the countries of Southeast Asia, as China did not increase the competitive pressure on their exports during the critical period. The second measure was the introduction of a fiscal stimulus, where the government sought to maintain high growth of its own economy through state investment in infrastructure development.

The Chinese government has long used the opportunity to set interest rates and the exchange rate of its currency, renminbi (literally "people's currency", abbreviated as RMB and with its base unit yuan), to support economic growth. The Chinese government earns most of its revenue for the state treasury by taxing companies and from import duties. Unlike in developed countries, personal income tax accounts for only a small part of budget revenues. The government receives additional income from individuals through so-called financial repression, which occurs when the interest on bank deposits is lower than inflation. Deposits are therefore loss-making, and this loss is perceived as a form of hidden taxation, as the state benefits from them.[7]

To this day, the Chinese government does not allow free international trading of its currency and sets its exchange rate, which has long been undervalued in order to help domestic export-oriented companies. On the other hand, an undervalued currency reduces the purchasing power of the domestic population.[8] The government is also working to internationalize its currency and has achieved the listing of the Chinese yuan as a reserve currency of the International Monetary Fund since 2016. Because most of the world trade is conducted in US dollars, in times of crisis, the government and the central bank do not have effective tools to address it. Therefore, after the financial crisis in 2008, there have been increased efforts to internationalize the yuan. Nevertheless, a paradoxical situation arises, because to achieve its internationalization, the government would have to allow free international trade in yuan, which, however, continues to be restricted by the state. Efforts to internationalize the yuan thus run counter to conflicting efforts to maintain a high degree of control over currency developments.

The government once again deployed a large fiscal stimulus during the global financial crisis in 2008 and 2009. It reached enormous proportions as the government ended up spending about a third of the GDP. The construction of high-speed railways, motorways, and airports has given a significant impetus not only to the Chinese economy but also created a positive impact on countries in Europe and Asia. China has thus become one of the main driving forces of the world economy.

Although China managed to overcome the crisis relatively quickly, the massive investments were largely financed by debt. The Chinese government and its various institutions were already in debt before 2008; however, the global financial crisis meant a significant increase in debt, which according to some estimates reached 300% of GDP in 2019, making it one of the highest in the world.[9]

Consumer-based economic growth

The crisis in 2008 led to a reassessment of China's economic model, which for a long period of time overly depended on exports. A significant step was the effort to change the structure of the economy and support domestic consumption, which is for various reasons lower in China than in other countries. One way to allow the population to spend more was to create a shadow banking system. This term refers to a network of non-banking companies that provide loans and investment financial products to individuals.

Chinese banks mostly focus on servicing companies. Therefore, many individuals have no other choice but to get a loan through the shadow banking system. The positive aspect of shadow banking has been the gradual end of financial repression, as citizens have access to financial products with higher returns than ordinary bank deposits. However, shadow banking also contains a high risk and is difficult to regulate. It has led to a rapid indebtedness of households to such an extent that in 2019 the amount of debt held by an average Chinese household was one-third higher than its income.[10] Therefore, since the end of 2020, the government has tightened regulations and strictly enforces them against companies operating in this area, especially Ant Financial, which is owned by one of the richest Chinese, Jack Ma.

Rapid economic growth over the past four decades has been made possible by the fact that China has benefited from a "demographic dividend" – a vast amount of labor that was highly mobile and willing to relocate for work. Economic development under Deng Xiaoping's motto "it's great to get rich" has also brought about a significant increase in the living standards of the population. Wealth, however, remains very unevenly distributed, and the income disparities between urban and rural populations, and between rich and poor provinces, are abysmal.

At the same time, it should be noted that the growth of wealth held by the population was slower than the growth of GDP which is concentrated disproportionately in industrial production and investment in infrastructure. In an effort to reduce the economy's dependence on foreign demand, the government has set out to "rebalance" the economy (President Xi Jinping renamed it to the policy of "dual circulation"), which means trying to increase the share of domestic consumption in GDP. Therefore, the consumption of Chinese households has risen since 2010, but it is still far below the global average.[11]

Xi Jinping: Striving for self-sufficiency

With the arrival of Xi Jinping as the chairman of the Chinese Communist Party in 2012, the state's economic policy changed. Xi Jinping has focused on an ideological campaign against corruption to control society more closely, and this has also defined his economic policy. On the one hand, it emphasizes the liberalization of certain elements, such as prices or the allocation of capital. To this end, the economy has become more open to the world as foreign investors have been given access to Chinese stock and bond markets. On the other hand, the position of state-owned companies in the economy was strengthened, which has increased state control over the economy.[12]

Under Xi Jinping's reign, there has also been a renewed emphasis on the so-called industrial policy, which aims to support the development of certain sectors – through increased investment, a privileged position, and restrictions on market entry. An industrial policy similar to the current one has been used in China since the 1980s as a tool inspired by the Asian tiger economies, and its first goal was to make China a "factory of the world". Later on, the industrial policy focused on making China a world leader in certain industries. These efforts were successful in areas such as high-speed rail, photovoltaics, and telecommunications accessories. Within selected industry areas, there is an effort to create "industrial champions", i.e., companies that – with the help of state support – will dominate not only the domestic market but will also be able to gain a share of the world market. The best-known example of such a company is the telecommunications giant Huawei.

The current Chinese president is using industrial policy to make China a leader particularly in emerging areas such as artificial intelligence and biotechnology. Strengthening domestic technological capacity is also amplified by the pursuit of self-sufficiency, because since the outbreak of trade wars with the United States in 2018, China has been threatened with restrictions on access to the latest technologies, which could significantly damage the country's economic growth (see Chapter 10).

In 2013, China introduced the Belt and Road Initiative, which – among other strategic goals – aims to support its economic growth and build infrastructure projects connecting China with countries in Africa, Asia, Europe, and Latin America. In addition to increased connectivity with other regions, China is benefiting from these initiatives by being the main lender of financing infrastructural projects, Chinese companies are involved in their construction, and new markets are being created for Chinese industrial production. However, this also leads to conflicts with trading partners as China often benefits much more than its counterparts.

GDP: Closely watched indicator

China has experienced more than four decades of continuous rapid economic growth, which is unprecedented given the size of the country. In recent years, GDP growth has been gradually declining, approaching the rate of 6% per year and even falling further as a result of strict "zero-COVID" policies. There have been, however, concerns about the credibility of Chinese economic statistics for a long time. On the one hand, the statistics have been "adjusted" by junior officials who tried to inflate the economic results in their locality. A curious situation thus arises, in which the sum of the GDP of individual Chinese provinces is higher than the total GDP of China – the central government knows that the authorities do not send reliable figures, so it corrects them. On the other hand, the central government is also interested in achieving the pre-defined GDP goal and thus gets into a conflict of interest. To measure the actual GDP growth, a number of alternative measures have been developed. The best known among them is the so-called "Li Keqiang index", which measures economic activity according to the volume of rail freight, electricity consumption, and the number of bank loans. However, it should be noted that according to academic studies, Chinese data do not show significant anomalies at the national level.[13]

It is undeniable that the Chinese economy outgrew the Japanese economy in 2010 and is currently the second largest national economy in the world measured by the nominal value, while it has already become the largest national economy in the world in 2017 in purchasing power. On the other hand, China's GDP per capita is far below the most developed countries in North America, Western Europe, and East Asia. Still, China has been catching up, and with a GDP per capita of 12,556 USD in 2021 according to the World Bank, it is more than that of EU member Bulgaria.

Future challenges

In recent years, it has become increasingly clear that China's economic growth model based on exports and investments in infrastructure and real estate is being exhausted. World markets are saturated with Chinese products and protectionism is growing in many parts of the world, which is a serious threat to Chinese exports. On the other hand, stimulating the domestic economy through debt-financed infrastructure investments leads to high indebtedness, which reaches dangerously high levels.

The Chinese leadership is aware of these problems and tries to solve them in several ways. The most fundamental of these is the support of domestic consumption, which currently has a much smaller share in GDP than in developed economies. However, in order for Chinese consumers to spend more, they need to earn more. If the Chinese workers earn more, the price of their labor will rise, which will increase the price of the products they produce, and they will be less competitive in the world markets. It is very difficult to find the right balance, which is why China's efforts to change its economic structure have only had partial success in the last decade.

The Chinese government has also invested in the production of increasingly sophisticated products and wants to gain dominance in new industries such as artificial intelligence and biotechnology (see Chapter 10). If the country succeeds in achieving these goals, the productivity and incomes of Chinese workers would increase, which would make it easier for China to change the structure of the economy. However, the road to dominance in new industries will take a long time, and there is no guarantee that China will get there at all.

Notes

1 H. Hung, *China Boom. Why China Will Not Rule the World*, New York: Columbia University Press, 2015.
2 Y. Ang, *How China Escaped the Poverty Trap*, Ithaca: Cornell University Press, 2016.
3 I. Weber, *How China Escaped the Shock Therapy: The Market Reform Debate*, New York: Routledge, 2021.
4 K. Lieberthal & M. Oksenberg, *Policy Making in China: Leaders, Structures, and Processes*, Princeton: Princeton University Press, 1988.
5 "The China economic quarterly: Housing privatization", *Financial Times*, 4 February 2008.
6 B. Naughton, *The Chinese Economy: Transitions and Growth*, Cambridge: MIT Press, 2007.
7 A. R. Kroeber, *China's Economy: What Everyone Needs to Know*, New York: Oxford University Press, 2016.
8 F. J. Contractor, "Is China a 'currency manipulator'?", *ETH Zurich*, 23 August 2019.
9 "China's debt tops 300% of GDP, now 15% of global total: IIF", *Reuters*, 18 July 2019.
10 L. Wright & A. Feng, "COVID-19 and China's household debt dilemma", *Rhodium Group*, 12 May 2020.
11 M. Pettis, "The only five paths China's economy can follow", *Carnegie*, 27 April 2022.
12 S. Heilmann, *Red Swan: How Unorthodox Policy Making Facilitated China's Rise*, Hong Kong: The Chinese University Press, 2018.
13 "Are Chinese GDP statistics reliable?", *Bank of Finland Bulletin*, 13 April 2016.

8 Social control and propaganda

What is "social credit" and how has China handled COVID-19?

Filip Šebok

The most fundamental objective of the Chinese Communist Party is to maintain a monopoly on political power in China. However, this requires more than just control over the policy-making process and the institutional oversight of the political system and social organizations. Repression and violence are neither the only nor the most effective tools for maintaining control over Chinese society, even if the Chinese government does not hesitate to use them when necessary. Instead, Beijing has learned to use "modern" tools of social control in a flexible way, constantly adapting to new challenges posed by rapid socio-economic and technological development. These tools include the vast system of propaganda, Internet management, and even the infamous "social credit" system. With the help of these tools, the Party manages to build and maintain support among the population and prevent challenges to its rule. In the event of an upheaval, Beijing has proved capable of turning a crisis into an opportunity, as evidenced by its response to the COVID-19 coronavirus epidemic. ***How does the Chinese propaganda work? Is there any opposition in China?***

The cycle of tightening and relaxation

After the end of the Mao era in 1976, the Chinese party-state stopped intervening in many aspects of people's daily lives; however, it has managed to hold onto its political monopoly and maintain an exclusive prerogative to set the boundaries of socio-political development. These confines have cyclically narrowed and widened in recent decades.[1] The relative liberalization that characterized the 1980s ended in the bloody suppression of the protests in 1989 and was followed by a return to a more repressive governance model and the freezing of political reforms. The Hu-Wen era in 2002–2012 was again a period of relative political relaxation, with more space for the public to air critical views.

However, with the ascent to power of Xi Jinping in 2012, a period of tightening has returned. Any social movements outside the Communist Party's control are perceived as potential threats, and tolerance for criticism of the regime has shrunk to a minimum. The Party has increased its direct control over the media, universities, and NGOs. The plurality of public debate is severely limited as the Party has

DOI: 10.4324/9781003350064-11

stepped up restrictions on what can be discussed and how. The government has also introduced a drastic policy toward minorities, embodied in efforts to "re-educate" the Uyghur minority (see Chapter 12), the developments in Tibet (see Chapter 13) and Hong Kong (see Chapter 14), and also Inner Mongolia. Few observers now expect the democratization of the Chinese regime or any liberalization reforms in the foreseeable future.

The current atmosphere is well illustrated by an internal document of the Communist Party, the so-called Document No. 9, leaked in 2013. The document lists seven "Western" values dangerous to China – constitutional democracy, universal values, civil society, economic neoliberalism, media freedom, historical nihilism (questioning the official version of history), and examining the policy of reform and opening up.

The cyclical concept of tightening and relaxation is helpful in guiding our thinking about Chinese politics, but there is also a great deal of continuity in Chinese politics. In many areas, Xi has merely continued the policies of his predecessors. In any case, there are no indications that the current cycle of repressions will enter the relaxation phase soon. At the same time, however, it is good to keep in mind that China has often been able to surprise outside observers in the past, as many previous changes have taken place unexpectedly.

The tightening and relaxation cycle is also present on a smaller scale. During "sensitive" periods in the calendar – such as anniversaries of sensitive historical events or important political meetings – the mechanism of social control is significantly strengthened. The state apparatus at all levels strives to avoid any kind of political disturbances. This is especially characteristic of life in Beijing, where the most important political meetings physically take place.

What does it look like in practice? Security checks in public places are suddenly taken more seriously. Internet censorship gets stricter, and the Great Chinese Firewall becomes even more impenetrable, even with the use of VPNs.[2] The number of police patrols increases in the streets, and even military personnel can be seen at important junctions. During sensitive anniversaries such as 4 June, potentially "problematic" activists are often sent on a forced "vacation" away from Beijing to keep them from organizing any public activities. After the end of the sensitive period, things usually return to normal.

Is there an opposition in China?

One of the most frequent questions in international discussions about the Chinese regime is the existence of political opposition. The Chinese dissidents who have openly defied the system and called for democratic changes are usually at the forefront of such debates. Among these was the Nobel Peace Prize laureate Liu Xiaobo, who participated in the 1989 protests and was one of the signatories of Charter 08, which was inspired by Charter 77 from normalization-era Czechoslovakia, and called for the establishment of pluralist democracy and respect for civil rights. Liu Xiaobo was convicted for his role in drafting Charter 08 for "inciting subversion of state power" and eventually died in 2017, shortly after release from

Figure 8.1 Nobel Peace Prize laureate Liu Xiaobo (source: BBC, www.bbc.com/news/world-asia-40403811).

prison due to a terminal illness. There are hundreds to thousands of similar political prisoners in China.[3] Many other activists outside prison are constantly bullied by the authorities, and their freedom (and that of their families) is restricted in various ways.

Nevertheless, the black-and-white view of China, which portrays the authoritarian party-state apparatus on one side and the pro-democracy dissidents on the other, is overly simplistic. Equally unsustainable is the image of Chinese citizens as brainwashed subjects of the regime or, conversely, its impoverished victims. The reality is, as usual, much more complicated.

According to available surveys from renowned international agencies and academic research, Chinese authorities generally enjoy strong support from the population. These results seem largely valid even after taking into account the difficulties of measuring public opinion in authoritarian regimes.[4] There are several reasons for the apparent popularity of the Chinese regime among the Chinese. The most important factor is undoubtedly the economic growth of recent years – Chinese people under 40 have in their lifetime experienced a dynamically growing economy and an improving life quality. China's middle class, often perceived, especially in the West, as a potential driver of political change, largely sees its interests in maintaining the *status quo*.

The Chinese regime has also been able to adapt to emerging developments and implement major reforms. This ensured the regime's responsiveness to the changing demands of the population and its ability to alleviate potential social conflicts in their initial stages. Support for the regime is also, to a large part, linked to nationalism. China's growing power on the international stage bolsters national pride and, consequently, support for the government, which is seen as the protector of China's interests and prestige in the world. Finally, propaganda, a political tool that the Communist Party is constantly perfecting, also plays an important role in ensuring support for the regime and limiting the critical voices.

Nevertheless, many different opinions remain in Chinese society, most of which are far from the uncritical defense of the Party line or the support for the overthrowing of the regime and the establishment of Western-style democracy. Many people do not challenge the basic contours of the Chinese political system but do not shy away from criticizing some specific issues, pushing for a gradual change. On many social issues, if they are not "politically sensitive", there are lively debates in China. To some extent, the CCP accepts the involvement of citizens in issues that it does not consider politically sensitive. These include individual cases of corruption, environmental pollution, or, to a limited extent, the rights of LGBT people.

However, this criticism often hits hard limits – in the end, the Chinese authoritarian regime is at the root of many of the social problems, which cannot be dealt with unless the system itself is challenged. An example is the "rights protection movement" which has involved lawyers from all over China since the beginning of the new millennium. Their movement was motivated by an effort to provide protection to the ordinary people against the arbitrary exercise of power by the authorities or companies in cases of land confiscation, police or mob violence, or environmental damage. The movement for the protection of rights did not oppose the regime as such and fought for the goals formally promoted by the Communist Party. Nevertheless, the Party still saw it as a challenge to its power, and, following a massive crackdown and a wave of arrests in 2015, the movement was practically eliminated.

A harmonious society?

Despite the relative popular satisfaction and an effective system of repression, China is far from the ideal of a "stabilized harmonious society". China has experienced tumultuous societal change in recent decades, with few precedents in other countries around the world. In the 1990s, for example, state-owned enterprises laid off tens of millions of workers, leading to the sudden loss of the "iron bowl" – job security, accommodation, and other benefits associated with employment. These rapid changes led to a steep rise in societal tensions and conflicts, including protests. That is why the former Chinese leader Hu Jintao came up with the term "harmonious society" – not as a description of the present, but as a goal to strive for. Although China's growing defense budget has attracted attention in recent years, China actually spends more on internal security.[5] This demonstrates the fact that the Chinese regime perceives the situation within its own borders as a potentially greater threat than international challenges.

While it may sound surprising, there are tens of thousands of protests in China each year – 2010 figures estimate 180,000 incidents per year; in most cases, these protests were linked to spontaneous local disputes and not "high politics". The most common causes of protests include unpaid wages, disputes over land sales to developers without adequate compensation for the original owners, environmental pollution by local companies, or classic cases of NIMBY (Not in My Backyard) activism.

These protests often result in violence between protesters and local security forces. In disputes, it is often not the police who are involved, but the so-called *chengguan* – the universally hated quasi-police forces designed to enforce administrative orders, such as bans on street hawking. Similar incidents are naturally a problem for social stability and a headache for local officials. However, these protests rarely grow into organized movements. What is more, local authorities are motivated to offer, in addition to repression, active solutions to problems to help ease social tensions. Therefore, protesters often end up achieving their goals, at least partially.[6]

What Beijing is really concerned about are massive, organized protests spanning across regions, involving different social strata and espousing political goals, echoing the 1989 protests. If similar signs emerge, Beijing will intervene uncompromisingly. In 1999, thousands of Falun Gong practitioners protested peacefully in front of the leadership compound at Zhongnanhai in Beijing. At the time, the Communist leaders became fully aware of the spiritual movement's ability to organize at the national level and thus launched a massive and often brutal campaign against the movement.

Social credit

When we talk about social control in China, we cannot help but mention the issue of the so-called "social credit". In 2014, the Chinese government announced that it wanted to put in place a nationwide social credit system by 2020. This topic has attracted a lot of attention in the international media, where it was presented as evidence of the Chinese regime turning into a technological dystopia, comparing it to the Black Mirror series or the 1984 novel by George Orwell.

What exactly is social credit? The answer is by no means a simple one. China has not issued any comprehensive document presenting the system. The available information comes from a set of documents issued by different institutions, from which we can pinpoint certain basic characteristics. In general, we can understand social credit on three levels, which largely operate independently, and are united by the idea of data collection and data centralization. To some extent, social credit is the digitization of the so-called "*dang'an*", the personal files that the Chinese authorities have kept about individuals for decades.[7]

The first part of social credit is a simple credit rating. Its aim is to assess the ability of companies and individuals to repay their loans. As personal banking is not as widespread in China and is relatively new, banks are not able to assess the credit risks of potential clients without any credit history.

The second part of the system is the so-called blacklists and redlists. Failing to comply with court orders or failing to pay a fine can lead to placement on the blacklist. It is not a "low score" that leads to blacklisting, but specific misconduct. In recent years, as part of the creation of a comprehensive system, blacklists have been shared between individual state institutions, which makes it possible to impose restrictions across various areas. For example, a debtor blacklist allows limiting personal expenses – people who find themselves on this list cannot buy first-class tickets on trains or planes, stay in luxury hotels, or send children to study in expensive private schools.[8] A company that has been found to have sanitary deficiencies and has been put on a relevant blacklist may have a problem applying for a loan. On the other hand, redlists record commendable actions. This can lead to various benefits, such as better access to credit for businesses or faster check-in at the airport for individuals.

The third part of social credit concerns social and moral education. This seems to be the main goal of the existing systems at the local level. The CCP is aware of the lack of interpersonal trust in Chinese society. The aim of social credit is, therefore, to spread awareness about issues of personal integrity and honesty, through which the Communist Party often seeks a return to the idealized traditional Confucian values. The system also includes public shaming of perpetrators of various offenses – for example, the public display of jaywalkers on huge outside screens.

At the same time, it is good to stress what social credit is not.[9] In the first place, the social credit is not a full-fledged system. As in many other areas of Chinese policy-making, social credit is undergoing stages of experimentation at the local level. There are currently several independent systems in different parts of China, as well as several financial service pilot programs developed by private companies such as Alibaba. As a next step, the central government is evaluating the experience from respective local experiments to decide whether there is a model that could be implemented at the national level. As this has not yet happened, it is currently difficult to assess what the final system will look like. The central authorities had planned to implement the social credit system by 2020, but the COVID-19 pandemic has brought new dynamics and has seen a universally implemented system of QR health codes that can effectively ban the movement of individuals. Although the system is supposed to evaluate health conditions, there have been instances when authorities have misused it for political purposes – and some observers think that the system may well remain a permanent feature in China.

Perhaps most importantly, social credit is not a single numerical score that would record individuals' behavior. This is probably the most common myth about social credit. One does not find a mention of the numerical score as the goal of the national social credit program in any relevant documents. However, it is true that scoring on different scales exists in individual pilot projects at the local level. While positive scores in these pilot systems lead to various benefits and are to serve as an incentive, low scores generally do not have negative consequences.[10] Overall, the real impact of these scoring mechanisms on people's lives in China is still very limited in the vast majority of cases.

Finally, social credit also does not equal social control employed by Beijing. It is true that China is increasingly using technological tools to track its citizens, whether in the real world through ubiquitous cameras, or in cyberspace. However, social credit does not really bring any new data collection but only integrates the information that the state already has at its disposal while emphasizing better and more intensive data collection. Social credit also does not in itself bring new legal restrictions but instead aims at ensuring more thorough implementation. In any case, the tools for restricting personal freedoms in China require attention. Still, social credit is only part of a broader arsenal of instruments and should not be mistakenly used to describe unrelated processes. For example, developments in Xinjiang, where the Chinese state has built huge machinery to surveil and control the local population, are not directly linked to social credit.

What consequences can social credit bring to China? First and foremost, it can be a tool for the state to increase control over the lives of the population, a clear trend under Xi Jinping's rule. To a significant extent, the Party previously lost control over the citizens with economic reforms and the disintegration of the so-called *danwei* – the work units of employees of state-owned enterprises. Until 2003, for example, workers formally needed consent from their *danwei* for marriage or divorce.[11] However, it seems that social credit aims not to directly intervene in people's lives but instead to incentivize people to engage in the desired behavior.

Figure 8.2 Cameras on Tiananmen Square in Beijing (source: Robert Barca).

It is important to note that social credit is not only aimed at individuals but also at companies and even government bodies (although it is still unclear how this will work). Thus, in addition to the tool of social control, it is also a new tool for shaping the business environment. Here, too, the system aims to lead to companies' self-regulation, which would simplify the work of state regulators. From the Communist Party's point of view, social credit should make the market environment more transparent and predictable and thus help the development of the Chinese economy.

While many things about social credit are still left to be seen, it is clear that a similar tool in the hands of an authoritarian power creates opportunities for abuse and the suppression of citizens' rights. However, the idea of social credit seems to be perceived relatively favorably among Chinese people as a tool to increase social trust and reward honesty.[12] Still, China's social credit has not yet become a significant issue in the domestic debate and is paradoxically discussed more vividly abroad.

The Chinese propaganda behemoth

One of the main pillars of the Communist Party's power is propaganda. It is worth noting that "propaganda" is not a negative concept in China and its meaning in Chinese coincides with the word for "publicity". The Communist Party does not hide the importance of "propaganda work", which, in its view, has a positive impact on informing the population and fostering social harmony. In addition to shaping the political debate, censorship seeks to be an arbiter of morality in public space – so pornography and other "immoral" manifestations are also undesirable. Thus, censorship and propaganda strengthen social stability and maintain support for the regime. For example, interventions against politically sensitive speech are often undertaken under the guise of fighting rumors and creating a "healthy" Internet environment.

The propaganda system in China oversees virtually everything involving the transfer of information – the Internet, print media, television, radio, publishing houses, schools, universities, theaters, galleries, and museums. An extensive propaganda apparatus oversees the content and form of information disseminated. The most authoritative body responsible for propaganda is the Central Leading Group for Propaganda and Ideology, headed by the Politburo Standing Committee members, which confirms the crucial role of propaganda for the CCP. Each central committee of the Communist Party, from major Party bodies to the lowest levels, also has its propaganda department. In recent years, the role of Internet regulators has grown, including through Central Cyberspace Affairs Commission, chaired by Xi Jinping himself.

The propaganda apparatus responds to potentially problematic issues by issuing regular directives on how the media should portray them, what to emphasize, and what to avoid. In an unexpected event requiring political interpretation, the propaganda apparatus often does not react immediately, waiting for the establishment of an official line first. Only when the official media comment on the event and "set the tone" are the other media free to report on the issue.

The most authoritative Chinese media outlets, including the Renmin Ribao (People's Daily) and news agency Xinhua (meaning New China), report directly to the Central Committee of the CCP and the State Council, respectively. What appears in these media can be understood as the Party's official line. These media, first and foremost, focus on the activities of the highest Party leaders and policy announcements. The state media employees are, therefore, a *de facto* part of the system of Party propaganda. In addition to their regular public outputs, much of their work consists of preparing internal reports, intended only for the eyes of the Party leadership.[13] Thus, they can be considered to double as an internal intelligence service. In addition to the official media in China, a dynamic sector of commercialized media with tens of thousands of different outlets has emerged since economic liberalization and focuses primarily on profit maximization.

Despite clear limitations, several media outlets in China have been renowned for their quality journalism, constantly testing the limits of the propaganda system. Respected media include, for example, Caixin, Beijing News, and Southern Weekly, which were established under the auspices of local CCP central committees. Provincial media generally have more freedom in investigative work in other provinces, as local authorities lack direct leverage over them. From the point of view of central authorities, they even sometimes play a valuable role in identifying missteps of local administration. However, engagement in controversial topics can mean a death sentence for the more daring media outlets.

In recent years, the emphasis of the Communist Party's propaganda efforts has shifted from the traditional media to the Internet. The Internet was considered impossible to regulate. In 2000, US President Bill Clinton uttered the now infamous sentence that efforts to control China's Internet are "like trying to nail Jell-O to the wall".[14] However, Beijing has been able to transform this potential threat to its power into a new tool of social control, thus demonstrating its adaptability.

Initially, the Internet was indeed a relatively free space in China. Activists used it to draw attention to the abuse of power by officials or social problems. Yet, the free exchange of information in cyberspace jeopardized the ability of the Communist Party to shape vital social debates. The CCP, therefore, realized very soon that it must dominate this nascent cyber sphere. As early as 1998, China began to build the so-called Great Firewall of China – a system of technological and legal tools designed to prevent Chinese Internet users from accessing foreign sites and communication tools deemed problematic, and to subordinate foreign companies to Chinese "cyber sovereignty". Gradually, China blocked a large number of sites with content that it perceived as politically unacceptable. After the riots in Xinjiang in 2009, China banned Facebook and Twitter. Google could operate in China for some time, submitting to local censorship, but left the Chinese market in 2010. Apart from these sites, Instagram, YouTube, Wikipedia, WhatsApp, and some of the world's most respected media, such as the New York Times, the BBC, and Reuters, are also not accessible in China.

Beijing's main motivation for breaking ties with the global Internet was a concern for the regime's stability. At the same time, however, a by-product of this effort was that the international competition for domestic Internet companies was eliminated, thus emboldening this promising sector of the economy. Chinese Internet companies have been given the chance to develop in a protected environment and capitalize on a market with hundreds of millions of potential users. In this way, China has nurtured its own Internet giants, such as Baidu, Weibo, and WeChat. Chinese companies have since built such a strong position in the domestic market that they had a prime position to expand beyond China's borders. One recent example of a Chinese app that has taken the world by storm is TikTok, which was developed by the Chinese company ByteDance.

Through its efforts, the Party sought not only to reduce its links to the global Internet but also to strengthen control over the one existing inside China's borders. For example, the regime has largely stamped out a particularly problematic aspect of the Internet in its eyes – anonymity. Registration of social accounts has become necessary under one's own name and linked to a phone number so that online behavior can be traced to a specific individual. In 2013, authorities intervened against opinion leaders on Weibo – the so-called big Vs – based on the letter V, which proves that the account is verified. Whenever a new platform or communication tool appears, the Chinese authorities respond by trying to get them under control.

How China managed to "nail the Jell-O to the wall"

The bluntest tool of Chinese propaganda on the Internet is direct censorship, which takes many forms. Controversial comments on social networks or problematic articles are deleted. In the case of adverse reactions to government institutions' posts, all comments are often deleted, and the comment section is closed. Searching for politically sensitive terms, such as the "June 4 incident" (bloody suppression of the Tiananmen protests), will not yield any results. Accounts that have published controversial posts are blocked or banned altogether.

Decisions about what will be censored often don't depend on the content but on its reaction. This is the case, for example, with the documentary "Under the Dome" by the Chinese journalist Chai Jing from 2015. The documentary was first promoted in the official state media because it aligned with the Party's environmental policy. After gathering 300 million views and leading to criticism of the government's policies on the Internet, propaganda authorities suddenly withdrew the documentary.[15] Chinese censorship does not primarily aim to limit critical voices as such, although these are routinely censored; instead, calls for real-world action, such as street protests, are the primary targets.[16] China's censors traditionally step up their efforts during sensitive anniversaries or political meetings – following the mini-cycle of tightening and relaxation. During the Tiananmen crackdown's anniversary, for example, posts that would not otherwise attract censors' attention are routinely deleted.

It is worth emphasizing that much of the censorship is governed by private platforms themselves, such as Weibo and WeChat, which have their own tools and staff for this purpose. Beijing thus delegates the censorship responsibility to individual service providers, which greatly decreases the direct burden on state resources. By deliberate design, the specific red lines about what can and cannot be discussed are rarely explicitly set and Internet platforms are therefore motivated to censor as strictly as possible so as not to attract scrutiny upon themselves. Internet users and independent content creators are also led to self-censorship. Under recent regulations, for example, the administrators of private group chats are responsible for all the content of the discussions in them, which leads them to avoid sensitive topics.

However, censorship is only one side of the coin. Chinese propaganda places an even greater emphasis on "leading" public opinion. The aim of such efforts is to shape the public debate in a way that suits the Communist Party. The Chinese propaganda apparatus employs a huge number of people in Internet discussions who publish pro-government contributions. This army of loyal netizens is called *wumao*, which means 50 cents in Chinese – alluding to a reward they are said to receive for each contribution. One of their tasks is to spread the so-called "positive energy" – sidelining criticism and negative emotions by emphasizing positive messages and strengthening support for the regime through such messaging.

To keep in touch with the population, propaganda tries to adapt its form and content to emerging trends, by using new forms and platforms. Popular celebrities and Internet influencers are also regularly employed for propaganda purposes. Propaganda has also become gamified. At the beginning of 2019, the *Xuexi Qiangguo* mobile application was launched to study Xi Jinping's thinking. Users can take quizzes about the ideology of the Communist Party and gain points.[17] Some Communist Party bodies have ordered Party members to use the application.

Internet control does not mean that the Chinese population completely lacks access to the information behind the Great Firewall. Specialized software, VPNs, allow Chinese netizens to connect to the global Internet and freely browse foreign sites. Such software, which is widely used by the population, is officially used by state-owned enterprises or state institutions that need free access to the Internet. However, China has also restricted VPN access, especially for private citizens. The government has identified several official VPN providers whose services can be used. People who develop or sell their VPNs can now face years in prison.[18]

The censorship apparatus and netizens are engaged in a constant cat-and-mouse struggle to best each other. Instead of written text, for example, netizens post pictures. However, censorship algorithms are becoming more sophisticated and can now easily thwart these creative solutions. For example, WeChat can automatically block a message when sent – the author sees it as delivered, but it does not reach the recipient.[19] Understanding the debates on the Chinese Internet requires the ability to become familiar with various homonyms or rapidly changing Internet slang. For example, deleted posts are referred to as "harmonized", which is a reference to official propaganda about social harmony. Since the word "harmony" sounds like "river crab" in Chinese (both *hexie*, using different characters and different tones in pronunciation), this animal is often used to refer to the system of censorship.

This phenomenon is well illustrated by the Internet debates following the constitutional change of 2018, which allowed Xi Jinping to remain in office indefinitely. At that time, a wave of discontent arose on the Chinese Internet, and direct criticism of this decision was massively blocked. Yet, netizens found all sorts of ways to express their disapproval, despite the limitations. One of the more ingenious ways was posts referring to Yuan Shikai, a Chinese general who proclaimed himself emperor in 1915. However, censorship reacted quickly, and all contributions about this historical figure were blocked – paradoxically proving that the analogy was on point.

The Chinese Internet management system is sometimes presented as a model worth following by other countries.[20] Its proponents argue that the Internet cannot remain unregulated and that spreading extremist and hate speech, fake news, and other phenomena must be countered.

However, this position stems from a misunderstanding of how the Chinese model of Internet governance works. The main goal of China's control over the Internet is to prevent the online space from becoming a hotbed of political activism against the Communist Party. While the censorship apparatus restricts political speech, it creates ample space or even encourages other controversial topics. For example, the Chinese Internet is a thriving space for ultranationalist and xenophobic expressions, calling for the "eradication of Japanese devils", to give just one example. The CCP finds it useful when it can let the population's dissatisfaction be discharged in the form of nationalism, mainly when directed against an external enemy. Due to the tightening of the political system, nationalism is becoming practically the only permitted way of political expression.

Chinese coronavirus propaganda

The Chinese propaganda apparatus's reaction to the coronavirus pandemic is a telling example of its workings in practice. At the end of December 2019, information began to spread among doctors in Wuhan that a new disease resembling SARS had appeared. Doctor Ai Fen was the first one to alert others to the threat. Subsequently, other doctors further shared the information, mainly using group chats. Eight people involved in disseminating the data, including Doctor Li Wenliang, were then reprimanded by local police for allegedly "spreading false news" and "disturbing social order". The state media also reported the incident as the irresponsible spreading of unsubstantiated rumors. Doctor Ai Fen was summoned by the hospital management, which banned her from further spreading the information about the new disease.[21]

What led to the initial concealment of information? Most likely, it was not based on direct instructions of the top Party leadership but a result of the hierarchical structure of the system, which favors maintaining social stability and concealing negative news from reaching the top echelons of leadership. Both the local police and the hospital management were afraid that the information about the virus would cause a stir, which could create trouble with the superiors. Wuhan was at the time amidst the peak of the political season – from 6 to 17 January, the so-called two sessions of Wuhan City and Hubei Province People's Congresses and People's Political Consultative Conferences were held. Thus, according to official data, there was no reported increase in coronavirus cases during the two sessions.

It is still unclear what role the central authorities played. However, according to the available information, the top leadership led by Xi Jinping had information about the person-to-person transmission of the virus (and thus the severity of the situation) as early as 14 January 2020.[22] Nevertheless, they were still considering how to respond at the time. The Party-controlled media initially reported very little about the growing epidemic, and pre-scheduled propaganda campaigns about Xi Jinping's visits to the homes of poor farmers were still on the front pages of newspapers. Xi Jinping himself did not comment on the situation until 20 January. Afterward, the situation developed rapidly. China confirmed the person-to-person transmission, and on 23 January, Wuhan was closed off as the epicenter of the infection.

The spread of the virus was a massive challenge for the CCP. The Chinese population understood that the authorities' initial response was slow and inadequate. Xi Jinping repeatedly identified the need to "guide" public opinion as one of the priorities in the fight against the epidemic. After realizing the seriousness of the problem, the authorities allowed some media to report relatively freely on the situation in Wuhan – almost all the information about the initial lapses of the authorities was reported by the Chinese media, such as Caixin. Later, however, the authorities tightened control. Some so-called "citizen journalists" in Wuhan, such as Chen Qiushi or Li Zehua, were forced to stop reporting on what was happening inside the city. In contrast, others like Zhang Zhan were even jailed for their activities.

As always, censorship was one of the preferred tools for controlling public debate. An extraordinary outburst of public discontent came after Li Wenliang, one of the doctors punished for spreading "rumors", died in February after contracting the illness. After his death, censors were extremely busy. The leaked propaganda instructions told the media to adhere to the following principles when reporting on Li Weliang's death: use only information from official sources, do not add any additional comments or encourage sensation, take down the report from the list of most searched topics, and limit "harmful" comments.[23] In another notable case, after an interview with doctor Ai Fen in the Chinese media, was published, the article was censored after a few hours. However, it continued to spread on the Internet creatively – for example, in Braille, emoticons, or translations into other languages.[24]

At the same time, the Party propaganda sought to flood the public space with "positive energy". The media produced stories of the personal heroism of health workers and other ordinary people, diverting attention from the failure of the system. Ironically, the Party also appropriated Li Wenliang, who was posthumously praised as a model Party member.[25] The propaganda also turned the epidemic into a "people's war", making every Chinese person a foot soldier in a common struggle. Xi Jinping was hailed as the chief commander in the people's war, further strengthening his personal position.

The Party's propaganda had its job made easier because of the mismanagement of the pandemic abroad – this has shown that a democratic government does not automatically lead to better crisis management. Many governments in the West underestimated the situation, and the anti-epidemic measures came late and were often insufficient. This also suddenly made the Chinese government's response look much better in the eyes of the Chinese people. Moreover, Chinese propaganda began to skillfully use supplies of medical material to foreign countries via the so-called "mask diplomacy" and later "vaccine diplomacy" to portray China as a savior.[26] Along with the spread of misinformation about the virus's origin, COVID-19 practically became a foreign problem. In this way, propaganda also strengthened nationalist sentiments in China, presenting the country as an unappreciated overachiever, wrongfully lambasted by Western countries, which have allowed mass death to occur.

At the same time, however, as the rest of the world started going back to normal in 2022, China again began struggling with the virus after two years of relative normalcy. The new variants of COVID-19 (such as Omicron) were much more transmissive, and even China's very strict "zero-COVID" policies could not prevent rising numbers of cases. The prolonged and unpredictable close-downs and restrictions, combined with repeated mismanagement on the side of the authorities, have led to growing popular dissatisfaction. Moreover, strict "zero-COVID" policies have negatively impacted the economy and people's well-being. In the end, the growth of public discontent, amplified by a deadly fire in Urumqi in November 2022, led to unprecedented nationwide protests across China against pandemic restrictions, which, in some cases, spilled into overtly political protests against Xi's governance, the likes of which China had not seen since 1989. While the continued strict pandemic controls were also becoming difficult to maintain due to the strain on economy, the eruption of public discontent was likely one of the factors that led to a sudden end to the zero-COVID policies in late 2022.

This episode demonstrated that while managing the epidemic in terms of propaganda and social control was a remarkable feat for the Party, the rigid political system that Xi Jinping has been building may not be able to react flexibly to future challenges. Considering the slowing economic growth, which can seriously weaken the people's support for the regime, in the long run, there is no reason for the Party to become complacent. We can therefore expect the Communist Party to appeal more and more to nationalism as the source of support – and control – of the population. This can be dangerous for the world and the Party itself if its policies fail to live up to the increasingly bellicose popular expectations.

Notes

1 D. Shambaugh, *China's Future*, Cambridge: Polity, 2016.
2 A virtual private network (VPN) extends a private network across a public network and enables users to send and receive data across shared or public networks as if their computing devices were directly connected to the private network.
3 "List of political prisoners detained or imprisoned as of October 10, 2019 (1,598 cases)", *Congressional-Executive Commission on China*, 10 October 2019.

4 W. Tang, "The 'surprise' of authoritarian resilience in China", *American Affairs* 2(1), 2018, 101–117.
5 A. Zenz, "China's domestic security spending: An analysis of available data", *China Brief* 18(4), 2018.
6 Y. Tong & S. Lei, *Social Protest in Contemporary China, 2003–2010*, Nottingham: Routledge, 2017.
7 J. Daum, "Untrustworthy: Social credit isn't what you think it is", *Verfassungsblog*, 27 June 2019.
8 "Understanding China's social credit system", *Trivium*, 23 September 2019.
9 J. Daum, "Untrustworthy: Social credit isn't what you think it is".
10 D. Lewis, "All carrots and no sticks: A case study on social credit scores in Xiamen and Fuzhou", *Medium*, 4 October 2019.
11 "Danwei people become citizens", *The Economist*, 4 September 2003.
12 G. Kostka, "China's social credit systems and public opinion: Explaining high levels of approval", *New Media & Society* 21(7), 2019, 1565–1593.
13 D. Young, *The Party Line: How the Media Dictates Public Opinion in Modern China*, Singapore: John Wiley & Sons Singapore, 2012.
14 "Clinton's words on China: Trade is the smart thing", *The New York Times*, 9 March 2000.
15 S. Mufson, "This documentary went viral in China. Then it was censored. It won't be forgotten", *Washington Post*, 16 March 2015.
16 G. King, "How censorship in China allows government criticism but silences collective expression", *American Political Science Review* 107(2), 2013, 1–18.
17 Z. Zhuang, "China's most popular app is a propaganda tool teaching Xi Jinping thought", *South China Morning Post*, 14 February 2019.
18 B. Haas, "Man in China, sentenced to five years' jail for running VPN", *The Guardian*, 22 December 2017.
19 L. H. O'Neill, "How WeChat censors private conversations automatically in real time", *Technology Review*, 15 July 2015.
20 J. Goldsmith & A. K. Woods, "Internet speech will never go back to normal", *The Atlantic*, 25 April 2020.
21 L. Kuo, "Coronavirus: Wuhan doctor speaks out against authorities", *The Guardian*, 11 March 2020.
22 "China didn't warn public of likely pandemic for 6 key days", *Associated Press*, 15 April 2020.
23 S. Wade, "Minitrue: Control temperature on death of coronavirus whistleblower", *China Digital Times*, 6 February 2020.
24 J. Li, "Martian language, emoji, and braille: How China is rallying to save a coronavirus story online", *Quartz*, 11 March 2020.
25 "Update: China releases investigation report on issues concerning Dr. Li Wenliang", *Xinhua*, 19 March 2020.
26 B. Wong, "China's mask diplomacy", *The Diplomat*, 25 March 2020.

9 Rule by law

Is there justice in China?

Matej Šimalčík

China is an autocratic regime. This leads to the conclusion that injustice and impunity run rampant in China, which stems from a general awareness of widespread human rights abuses. However, to consider China a lawless state is too simplistic. Despite the apparent shortcomings in protecting human rights, mainly because of state restrictions, China has a relatively well-developed legal system with a tradition dating back to antiquity. This chapter aims to introduce the issue of the development of law in China and its role today. ***What are the philosophical foundations of traditional Chinese law? Do they manifest themselves in the modern legal system? How do Chinese courts under the control of the Communist Party function, and how is the Chinese judicial system adapting to new digital trends?***

Law of ancestors

The discussion of Chinese law must necessarily begin in ancient times. During this period, the philosophical and moral foundations of the Chinese legal tradition were laid. Just as the Roman legal tradition shaped the modern law of European states, the law of the ancient Chinese period has influenced current legal development. Learning about ancient Chinese law is not a mental or historical exercise. Although modern Chinese law is also heavily influenced by Western concepts, ancient Chinese law still manifests itself in its interpretation.[1] Some institutions that existed in ancient times, such as the *hukou* population registration system, still exist in Chinese law today.

Interestingly, while in ancient Rome there was a great emphasis on the development of private law (regulating relations between individuals), the Chinese dynasties focused more on the development of public law (regulating relations between the state/ruler and the population), especially criminal law. While public law developed in progressively more sophisticated codes, private law existed for a long time only in the form of time-honored legal customs. This difference is illustrated by the fact that in the Xia dynasty (2100 BC–1600 BC), the term *xing* was used for the concept of law, but in contemporary Chinese, it means "punishment".

The first efforts to codify the law also date from the Xia dynasty. The first codes from this period – the Code of the Shun Emperor (*Shun Tian*) and the Punishments of the Yu Emperor (*Yu Xing*) – are, like the entire Xia dynasty, shrouded in myth, and we learn about them only indirectly. If, however, their existence and dating to

DOI: 10.4324/9781003350064-12

the early 22nd century BC were proven, they would be a find of similar value to the Ur-namma Codex from the Mesopotamian kingdom of Ur and predate the famous Hammurabi Code from Babylon by nearly half a millennium. We have more detailed information only about the laws of the Shang dynasty (1600 BC–1050 BC), which produced the Punishments of the Tang Emperor (*Tang Xing*), written at about the same time as the Hammurabi Code.

These three ancient codes are linked by the concept of the so-called five punishments, which were used to punish law violations. In the Shang period, these were capital punishment, corporal punishment, imprisonment, banishment, and castration. The concept of the five punishments persisted across dynasties, although their content varied significantly. During the Zhou dynasty (1046 BC–221 BC), the five corporal punishments consisted of facial tattooing, nose cutting, lower limb cutting, castration, and execution.[2] The killing was carried out by dismemberment, boiling, decapitation, strangulation, or tearing off the limbs and head using dragging harnesses.

Later, the so-called "slow death" (*lingchi*) was used. Also known as death by a thousand cuts, small pieces of the convict's body were gradually cut off. The mutilated convict would die for days in immense pain. Although slow death began to be practiced during the Zhou dynasty, the punishment was used essentially until the end of the imperial period. In fact, slow death was not formally banned until 1905 and even afterward remained practiced until the late 1920s. Thanks to French soldiers stationed in Beijing in the early 20th century, several photographs have survived demonstrating this cruel process

A personal testimony to the use of draconian punishments in ancient China was given by the eminent Chinese historian Sima Qian (145 BC–86 BC). Between the 1st and 2nd centuries BC, Sima Qian undertook to write a complete history of China. However, in defending General Li Ling, Sima Qian opposed the emperor in contravention of the norms of the time. For this, he was sentenced to either death or castration. Per the morality of the time, death was considered the more virtuous choice that would not dishonor the ancestors and the entire family. A noble man could not accept the ignominy of corporal punishment, of which castration was considered the most shameful. Sima Qian himself recorded this practice in his Letter to Ren An:

> Surely, a man has but one death. That death may be as heavy as Mount Tai or as light as a goose feather. It is how he uses that death that makes all the difference! Above all, one must not dishonor one's forebears. Next in importance, a man must not allow anyone to insult his person. Next, his appearance and bearing must not be dishonored. Next, his speech or his commands must not be dishonored. Next, one must not submit to the dishonor of having one's body bent or bound, or, even worse, of having one's robes exchanged for prisoner's garb; or, worse still, of being confined in the stocks and flogged. The next worst is the dishonor of having the head shaved and being put in shackles. Further down the scale is the dishonor of having the flesh carved or limbs severed. But the very lowest, the greatest dishonor of all, is castration, the punishment that corrupts the flesh![3]

Figure 9.1 Sima Qian depicted in a Ming dynasty portrait (source: Wikimedia Commons).

The basic premises of Chinese law were based on the interaction of the many philosophical schools that existed in China. Among the most influential are Confucianism, Taoism, Legalism, and Buddhism, which have influenced the idea of justice and legitimate governance.

Confucianism contributed to the development of the Chinese concept of law by teaching about the will and commands of heaven as the natural order of things. Confucian doctrine regards man as inherently good and endowed with four virtues: humanity, justice, decency, and rationality. Crime is not seen as part of human nature but as the result of adverse external influences. Confucianism initially opposed efforts to codify legal norms in writing and insisted that man should be governed by moral customs and not by an artificial legal order.

In almost complete opposition to Confucianism stands the school of Legalism. Man is regarded as inherently evil, breaking the law unless sanctioned by the state, argue Legalist thinkers. Similarly, Legalism took an opposite view of the question of the written codification of law. According to Legalism, the law must always be recorded and published in writing. The recording and publication of the law thus had an essential preventive significance in addition to its educational value because it limited the power of the state (but not of the emperor, whose power is unlimited) and limited the scope for abuse of position by officials. The need for codification and publication of legislation was gradually accepted also by Confucianists.

Taoism, with its emphasis on living in harmony with nature, privileged morality over the law since the law was seen as a human construct. In particular, the Taoist understanding of the doctrine of the dichotomous natural forces of yin and yang was reflected in law. For example, aggravating and mitigating circumstances were judged according to the predominance of the yin and yang elements when imposing punishments for crimes committed.

During the Han dynasty (206 BC–220 AD), Chinese law first came into more considerable contact with outside influences. The ideas of Buddhism had a significant impact on the further development of Chinese law, thanks to its emphasis on the concept of humanism, which mitigated the multiple excesses of Confucianism (human inequality as the natural order of things) and Legalism (punitive cruelty). Thus, thanks to Buddhism, ideas of equality before the law began to spread in China to a larger extent. A significant reform of Chinese criminal law influenced by Buddhism took place during the Sui dynasty when the imposition of five sentences was relaxed, and more emphasis was put on the expedience of the criminal process to reduce legal uncertainty for the accused.

The development of law during the Han dynasty is of equal importance to the origin and evolution of Roman law. In particular, the process of the law's creation, interpretation, and application was clarified during this period. In addition to contact with Buddhism, this period saw the birth of several legal innovations, such as the precedential nature of judicial decisions. The first collections of judicial decisions began to appear. The oft-cited collection of Judgments of the Spring and Autumn Period by Dong Zhongshu is said to contain judicial decisions from this historical stage (775 BC–475 BC), which preceded the Han dynasty by several centuries.

The codification of the Han dynasty was followed by the law of the Sui dynasty (581–618). Perhaps the most significant change in this period was the reform of the system of five punishments, which had lost much of their severity under the influence of Buddhist ideology. The punishments imposed were either blows with a short bamboo stick, blows with a long bamboo stick, lifetime banishment, short-term banishment, or death. At the same time, under the influence of Sui legal thought, legal orders began to emerge in what is now Japan, Vietnam, and the Korean peninsula.

The law underwent more significant changes during the Tang dynasty (618–906) when the state's division of power and administrative division took place. During the Tang dynasty, state authority was divided into three branches: the executive, the inspection, and the examination branches. The executive branch also incorporated the judiciary and legislature. The inspection power was embodied in an institution called the Censorate, a powerful office that monitored compliance with rules by imperial officials. Although the origins of the office date back to the Tang dynasty, it reached its height during the Yuan (1279–1368) and Ming (1368–1644) dynasties. The examination power consisted of preparing future officials for the profession and testing their competence. Preparation for the future bureaucrats consisted of studying the "Four Books" and "Five Classics" of Confucian teaching. The civil service examination itself consisted of demonstrating the ability to recite a memorized text rather than displaying the ability to interpret it and apply it to practical problems.

After the Mongolian Yuan dynasty (1279–1368) took power in China, a law influenced by Lamaism (Tibetan Buddhism) began to take hold, characterized by a dualism of secular and religious law, where Buddhist monks were not subject to the authority of secular institutions. On the other hand, monasteries had the right to exercise judicial power over the lay population, with a jury composed according to a religious-philosophical principle deciding the verdict. The three-member jury had one Lamaist, Confucian, and Taoist juror.

After the fall of the Yuan dynasty and the takeover of power by the Ming dynasty (1368–1644), the concept of legal discontinuity, uncharacteristic of China, came into play (the previous dynasties did not abolish the existing law but rather refined and improved it in line with Confucian demands to pay respect to ancestors). The founder of the Ming dynasty, Emperor Hongwu (1328–1398), decided to remove the legal changes of the Yuan dynasty and reinstate the legal order of the Tang and Song periods. The Ming period saw a fairly intensive development of what we would now call economic and financial law. There was the development of guilds, the banking and credit system, and the first bills of exchange and checks. At the same time, after a period of uncontrolled inflation, the issue of new paper money began to be regulated.

The last Qing dynasty (1644–1912) is mainly associated with the decline of traditional legal culture. In 1740, the last major codification of the traditional law was adopted. However, with its emphasis on preserving ancestral norms, Qing recodification could not keep pace with the increasing commercial interaction between China and the Western powers. Under this external pressure, the influence of the legal systems of Europe and later North America began to grow.

The Opium Wars were an important milestone for further legal development (see Chapter 1). The First Opium War ended with the signing of the Treaty of Nanjing in 1842 between the Qing Empire and the United Kingdom. It was the first of the so-called unequal treaties, which opened five treaty ports (Guangzhou, Xiamen, Fuzhou, Ningbo, and Shanghai) to trade with the UK. A year later, the British signed the Treaty of Bogue with China, which introduced the application of the extraterritoriality principle in favor of the UK. UK citizens gained immunity from prosecution in Chinese courts while applying English law to their activities. Similar privileges were subsequently granted to the United States (under the 1844 Treaty of Wanghia) and France (under the 1844 Treaty of Whampoa). French diplomats negotiating the treaty also achieved the legalization of Christianity in China. Similar treaties were eventually concluded by Russia, Germany, and other European countries.

The growing experience with European law within the treaty ports and later in the territories of the so-called concessions (parts of Chinese territory where foreign law was applied not only to foreigners but also to the Chinese population) accelerated the penetration of Western legal concepts into China.

Chinese law on the brink of modernity

In the early 20th century, the imperial government undertook to prepare a significant reform of Chinese law that was to be influenced by the German and Japanese legal systems. This effort included the preparation of a civil code in a form typical for continental Europe. The Imperial Recodification Commission prepared a proposal, but the code was not adopted before the fall of the Empire. The new government of the early Republic of China rejected the imperial proposal and undertook to prepare its own draft civil code, also significantly influenced by German civil law, which was adopted in 1929.

However, the civil code adopted during the Kuomintang rule was not adopted by Communist China. The People's Republic of China (PRC) did not see its first civil code as the principal law regulating most interpersonal private relations until almost a century later. In fact, the PRC's first civil code was not adopted until May 2020. Therefore, interpersonal relations were essentially governed by a patchwork of partial legislation, which greatly complicated the clarity of the PRC's legal system.

German influence over the modern Chinese legal system leads to it being substantially different than what one might find in common law jurisdictions like the UK or the United States. Chinese law is embedded in the continental tradition based mainly on statutory law, with court judgments not having a binding precedential nature. This is an important departure from traditional Chinese law.[4]

Rule by law

Traditional law was basically applied in China until the end of the imperial period. Since the mid-19th century, however, Chinese law has been intensely influenced by Western powers, whose influence has led to the penetration of Western legal institutions that were unprecedented in China until then. In particular British and German law had a significant influence on further legal developments. After the establishment of the PRC in 1949, further development of the law was also influenced by the Soviet model.

The Marxist-Leninist model of the legal system, adopted from the Soviet Union, where it was based on the leading role of the Communist Party, sees law as a tool to advance the political goals of the ruling political elite. This element also has its tradition within the Old Chinese School of Legalism. The model of "rule by law" (*faguan*) stands in sharp contrast to the concept of the "rule of law" (*fazhi*). While the rule of law is based on limiting the power of the state through legal norms, under the rule-by-law concept, the state stands above the law, through which social relations are controlled for the benefit of the state. The requirement of rule by law is explicitly captured in the statute of the Communist Party of China.[5]

The rule by law manifests in the Chinese Communist Party's (CCP) control of the courts. While the Chinese constitution formally guarantees the independence and impartiality of the judiciary, in practice, there are both formal and informal mechanisms through which the Party can influence the decision-making of the Chinese courts in its favor. This condition, which can be described as one of "judicial dependency", is characterized by the inability of the courts to compel state and Party institutions in an equal or stronger position of power than the courts to comply with the law.[6]

The influence of the government and the CCP on the courts is manifested through three main instruments. Local governments have the power to control court funding and judges' salaries, as well as the appointment and removal of judges, allowing them to exert pressure on judges in sensitive cases. In one survey by China's Supreme Court, as many as 68% of Chinese judges cited local favoritism as the main reason for unfair verdicts.[7]

Another problem is the existence of CCP cells as part of the courts at all levels of the judicial system. The role of these cells is to oversee Party discipline, which, in addition to checking for corrupt behavior, includes checking that judges do not rule against the interests of the CCP. Political-legal commissions, which monitor the work of the courts and law enforcement agencies, perform a similar function. Last but not least, the position of the prosecutor's office is problematic. In addition to its position as a public prosecutor, it also acts as a controlling body that, together with the legislative bodies, has the right to control the courts' decision-making.[8]

The concept of rule by law is also manifested in the existence of separate oversight bodies that assess and punish illegal activities of CCP members. Indeed, cadres' corruption and violations of "Party discipline" are not investigated and prosecuted by the police and other government agencies but by parallel Party institutions. For this purpose, the CCP by-laws establish the so-called Central Commission for Discipline Inspection of the CCP. In 2018, this committee was partially reformed when it was transformed into the National Supervisory Commission, which is no longer a purely Party organ and can use the procedures used by the original committee against Party members and the general population. The investigative process used by the original Central Committee and subsequently the State Control Commission is customarily referred to by the term *shuanggui*. It is characterized by the use of extrajudicial detention, interrogation, and torture of suspects to force confessions from the investigative body.[9]

Although the National Supervisory Commission and its predecessor, the Central Commission for Discipline Inspection, are institutions closely linked conceptually to the communist understanding of the law, certain parallels can be seen with the institutes and institutions of traditional Chinese law. First, Confucian legal philosophy was based on the concept of the immunity of elites from the law. The second parallel that can be pointed to is the institution of the Censorate.

Although the purpose of the oversight bodies is primarily to prosecute corruption, in practice, they often serve to advance the political interests of some Party members in intra-Party power struggles.[10] The drive to prosecute corruption has intensified since Xi Jinping took power, who has promised to prosecute "flies and tigers" for corrupt acts, i.e., both junior officials and high-ranking cadres. Between 2013 and 2018, more than 250 "tigers" were investigated, detained, or convicted for violating Party discipline.[11] Among the prosecuted cadres were several high-ranking officials who could potentially threaten Xi Jinping's position of power. Noteworthy examples include Bo Xilai (Politburo member and Xi's main political rival until 2012), Zhou Yongkang (Politburo Central Committee member and head of the security forces under Hu Jintao), Sun Zhengcai (Politburo member who was initially considered to succeed Xi in 2022), and Xu Caihou (vice-chairman of the Central Military Commission – the top military post – during Hu Jintao's rule). In cases where members of the CCP's top echelons fell to the anti-corruption campaign, lower-ranking Party officials under their patronage were also likely to fall, regardless of their ability to deliver adequate performance.[12]

Chinese courts and regulators have also been known to selectively apply Chinese laws to foreign subjects to achieve domestic and foreign policy goals. Foreign businesses have been known to complain against selective applications of Chinese antitrust laws in order to protect the Chinese domestic industry against overseas competition.[13]

The extent of the CCP's immunity from the judiciary and its influence on the courts' decision-making is well illustrated in the Rule of Law Index. China ranks at the bottom of the regional (13th out of 15) and global rankings in terms of government influence over civil and criminal courts (civil courts – 122nd out of 128; criminal courts – 112th out of 128). Similarly, China ranks at the bottom in limitations on government power by the courts (regional ranking – 14th out of 15; global ranking – 122nd out of 128).[14]

Human rights on paper

Those who take time to read the Chinese constitution will find that many fundamental rights and freedoms are formally guaranteed in China, such as freedom of religion, freedom of expression, the right to information, or the right to privacy. However, these rights essentially exist only on paper and are systematically violated on a large scale. This situation is typical of legal orders of the Leninist type. The problem of non-respect for human rights is mainly due to the fact that there are no independent mechanisms for enforcing them, as the Chinese courts are subordinate to the CCP.

China has signed several international human rights treaties that are based on the concept of human rights universalism. Nevertheless, in practice, it continues to promote the idea of cultural relativism of human rights, which is manifested in emphasizing that each state should define its own human rights priorities.[15] This means that China rejects external pressure to strengthen civil and political rights and is mainly concerned with improving economic and social rights, especially for the majority Han population.

Human Rights Watch, a non-governmental organization that highlights human rights violations around the world, highlighted ten areas of rights abuses in its 2020 State of Human Rights Report on China. These include China's crackdowns in Xinjiang, Hong Kong, and Tibet, persecution of dissidents and activists, violations of freedom of expression, mass surveillance of the population, violations of freedom of religion, violations of the rights of women and girls, violations of the rights of LGBTIQ people, and violations of the rights of refugees (mainly from North Korea).[16]

The state of human rights in China has been under heightened international scrutiny over the allegations of mass abuses in the Xinjiang Uyghur Autonomous Region (see Chapter 12). Human rights watchdogs have been pointing to mass internments, forced labor, and other abuses of Uyghurs, Kazakhs, and other minorities since 2018. A 2022 report by the UN Office of the High Commissioner for Human Rights concluded that the situation in Xinjiang likely constitutes crimes against humanity under international criminal law.[17]

The state of human rights in China is also illustrated by several international rankings that allow for comparisons with other countries. The Economist Intelligence Unit's 2021 Democracy Index ranked China's state of democracy 148th out of 167 countries evaluated (i.e., the 20th worst ranking globally, 5th worst regionally) with the worst score since the index started in 2006.[18] China is also failing in another prominent measurement of liberties by Freedom House. China scored only 9th out of 100 on the overall global freedom scale and 10th out of 100 on the Internet freedom scale in 2022.[19] China ranked 175th out of 180 in Reporters Without Borders' 2022 press freedom rankings.[20] Last but not least, in the World Justice Project's Rule of Law Index, China ranked 95th out of 140 countries assessed, while ranking 137th in fundamental rights and freedoms and 131st in the existence of limits on the exercise of government power. China ranks slightly better in civil and criminal justice, but in both cases, it scores worse than the global and regional averages, with a negative trend in recent years.[21]

In the context of the discussion on human rights in China, it is, of course, impossible to avoid the death penalty issue. While the death penalty is almost non-existent in Europe, 19 Asian countries are known to use capital punishment. In 2019, however, it was only carried out in China, Japan, North Korea, Pakistan, Bangladesh, Singapore, and Vietnam. According to Amnesty International, thousands of people are executed in China annually, estimating that it is more than the rest of the world combined. However, these figures are only estimates, as the statistics on the number of executions are classified. Executions in China are permitted to be carried out in only two ways – by lethal injection or by shooting.[22] Nevertheless, researchers have identified the occurrence of executions via organ harvesting, a highly problematic practice on account of being both illegal and unethical.[23]

While most countries impose the death penalty only for crimes against life, in China, it is also used for drug offenses, property crimes, or corruption. In such cases, however, the so-called suspended death penalty is often used, which turns into a life sentence if no further offenses are committed within two years of conviction.[24] The practice of imposing death sentences for property crimes runs up against international law, which allows the death penalty only for the "most serious crimes", which include neither property nor drug crimes. While the evolutionary trajectory of international law approaches the absolute abolition of the death penalty, a possible change in China's stance on the imposition of the death penalty seems unrealistic for the time being.[25]

Inconsistent practice across courts in sentencing death penalty cases also remains a problem. There is a real possibility that perpetrators would be sentenced to the unconditional death penalty for the same act in one province, while in another region, they would be sentenced to life imprisonment or even imprisonment for a fixed period of time.[26] From the point of view of justice and legal certainty, this is an unsustainable situation.

One country – two systems

Hong Kong and Macao have a special status within the Chinese legal system (see Chapter 14). European countries administered both areas until the late 1990s – Hong Kong by the UK until 1997 and Macao by Portugal until 1999. One of the agreed conditions for China's takeover of the two territories was to guarantee a high degree of autonomy. The requirement was explicitly captured in the international treaties signed with Great Britain and Portugal.[27] In practice, the high degree of autonomy means that the local governments of Hong Kong and Macau should decide on virtually all governance issues except foreign policy and defense. This has been referred to as "one country, two systems".

The two special administrative regions have different legislation than Mainland China. Hong Kong retained its legal system based on English law after its annexation to China, while Macau continued to apply the Portuguese legal system. Therefore, unless the local authorities have adopted new regulations on specific issues after the handover to China, the legal norms adopted in London and Lisbon continue to apply. In Hong Kong, the influence of the English legal tradition has given rise to strong and independent courts compared to the Mainland, which is one of the factors that has made Hong Kong an attractive place for foreign trade.

In both cases, however, the government in Beijing is gradually taking steps to undermine the high degree of autonomy guaranteed by international treaties. On the occasion of the 20th anniversary of the handover of Hong Kong, a Chinese Foreign Ministry spokesman said: "Now that Hong Kong has returned to the motherland for 20 years, the Sino-British Joint Declaration, as a historical document, no longer has any realistic meaning".[28] Subsequent events in Hong Kong during 2019 and 2020 have shown what this interpretation means in practice.

In 2019, the Hong Kong government attempted to pass a law that would provide for extraditions to Mainland China. Given the lack of guarantee of a fair criminal trial and the potential for the law to be abused to persecute critics of the regime through trumped-up charges, a large wave of opposition to the bill rose in Hong Kong, culminating in several months of massive protests. Although the protesters succeeded in getting the proposal withdrawn, the demonstrations continued, and Beijing's efforts to regain control of the city have not abated. In June 2020, the government in Beijing took advantage of a loophole in Hong Kong's mini-constitution to pass the National Security Law, which uses vaguely worded facts to allow for the prosecution of activists and critics of the regime. In addition, the law introduced the possibility to refer prosecutions to Mainland authorities. The law also has an extensive principle of extraterritoriality, which allows anyone (regardless of nationality) to be prosecuted for endangering national security and inciting the secession of Hong Kong, irrespective of whether the act occurred in Hong Kong. Theoretically, a European journalist who publishes an article critical of the government or police in Hong Kong in the European media could be detained and tried by the Chinese courts on their next visit to Hong Kong.

Beijing is also able to exert its influence over Hong Kong and Macau indirectly through the interpretative opinions of the Standing Committee of the National People's Congress interpreting the Basic Law of Hong Kong and the Basic Law of Macau. These opinions are notorious for favoring an interpretation of the two mini-constitutions that are beneficial to the central government in Beijing. This is a controversial power from the perspective of the democratic principle of separation of powers because the final interpretive opinion of the Basic Laws is not given by the Supreme Court in Hong Kong and Macau but by the political organ of the legislature in Beijing, which is supposed to respect the autonomy of the two territories.[29] In 2007, Beijing used this mechanism to prevent the direct election of the Hong Kong Chief Executive. Later, in 2016, the tool was used to strip four opposition MPs of their seats.

China's digital law

For the last few years, the possibility of using digital technologies in the process of making and application of the law, the so-called LegTech, has attracted the attention of legal communities around the world. The professional community expects these technologies to increase the efficiency of judicial decision-making and the provision of legal services through automated processes and improve their quality through better processing of available information on cases and decision-making practices.

While law and justice are some of the most controversial issues in the case of China, China has developed solutions in LegTech, which can inspire other countries in their efforts to digitize justice. However, the adage "the devil is in the detail" applies here too, and solutions that can provide significant benefits to society when used by democratic governments can quite quickly become another tool for population control in the hands of an autocratic government.

In late 2019, China drew attention with the launch of an AI-based virtual court. The Internet Court in the city of Hangzhou, which handles disputes related to Internet commerce and intellectual property protection on the Internet, began piloting the adjudication of disputes using artificial intelligence. In this case, litigants appear before the court only by video conference, and the AI evaluates all the evidence presented and applies relevant legal norms.[30]

In addition to artificial intelligence, blockchain is being used to adjudicate Internet-related disputes as an efficient tool for recording evidence from cyberspace. A typical problem in proving Internet-related disputes is the relatively easy possibility of changing the content of websites and, therefore, the easy destruction of evidence of infringement. For this reason, it is difficult to prove libel or breach of intellectual property claims on the Internet in court. This deficiency is usually overcome with the help of public notaries that certify the existence of Internet content at a particular time. However, this procedure is impractical and potentially time-consuming, and costly. Blockchain offers a way of overcoming this shortcoming because it can quickly and immutably record the content of a web page at a specific point in time.

Blockchain evidence was first accepted in 2018 by the Hangzhou Internet Court, which was adjudicating a copyright infringement dispute related to an online news site. The online media outlet of the plaintiff published an article about a swimming pool accident, which the defendant subsequently published on its website without the plaintiff's consent. Instead of using notary services, the plaintiff used a platform that allows for the immutable capture of a website's content on a blockchain platform. The Court addressed the issue of the admissibility of such evidence in this case. Having satisfied itself with the methodology for capturing and storing the content and the independence of the service provider from the plaintiff, the court held that blockchain evidence was admissible as an alternative to the traditional notarial approach.[31]

Another innovation is the use of social networks as a tool for communication with the courts. Chinese courts allow parties to communicate with the court via WeChat (a popular social networking application that combines the functionalities of Western social networks such as Facebook, Instagram, and WhatsApp). Chinese people can file a lawsuit, participate in the proceedings, present evidence, and listen to the verdict via the app. According to statistics from China's Supreme Court in December 2019, more than three million people have already taken advantage of such online proceedings.[32]

One of the problems that China's justice system has long struggled with is divergent decision-making practices across the country due to poor communication between courts from different provinces. Therefore, two tools have been introduced in China – mandatory publication of judgments and live streaming from courtrooms. Today, anyone can watch a video of almost any court hearing on the Internet and then read nearly every verdict. Certain exceptions apply when streaming from the courtroom is not allowed – for example, where classified information or cases involving juveniles are being heard. Publication of all court decisions in criminal and civil cases across all tiers of the judiciary is relatively rare worldwide. China implemented this tool in 2013, making it one of the pioneers in disclosing information about court proceedings.[33]

Justice with Chinese characteristics?

China's current legal system is primarily inspired by European legal models, particularly the German and Soviet systems. Despite the transplantation of foreign elements, Chinese law has also retained contact with traditional legal concepts that originated in ancient Chinese law. During the development of Chinese civilization, this gradually changed under the influence of the dominant philosophical schools of the time. Traditional law was most influenced by the philosophical schools of Confucianism and Legalism. New elements enriched Chinese philosophy and law as they made contact with the outside world.

The interaction of traditional and modern normative systems has created a situation in China where we cannot speak of the rule of law but instead of the rule by law. Thus, the law does not primarily serve the people as sovereign to set the boundaries for exercising state power and protecting individual rights and freedoms. The primary purpose of legal norms in the Chinese system of rule by law is to protect the ruling Party's interests. In this setup, there is no independent space for the realization of individual rights and freedoms, especially those of political and civil rights.

Digitalization brings new challenges, including for the field of law. With the increasing complexity and volume of litigation, states are trying to make more intensive use of digital tools for more efficient and better adjudication of disputes. In this respect, it can be said that China is succeeding in innovating the judicial process with the help of new technologies such as blockchain.

Notes

1 M. Tomášek, *Právní systémy dálného východu I.* [Legal systems of the Far East I.], Prague: Karolinum, 2016. Subsequent sections of this sub-chapter draw on this book, too.
2 Q. Sima, *Records of the Grand Historian*, New York: Columbia University Press, 2007.
3 Q. Sima, Letter to Ren An. Cited according to S. Durrant et al., *The Letter to Ren An and Sima Qian's Legacy*, Seattle & London: University of Washington Press, 2016.
4 Z. Kopania & I. Szpotakowski, *Chinese Law Research Guide*, Lodz: ArcheaGraph, 2020.
5 I. Castellucci, "Rule of Law with Chinese Characteristics", *Annual Survey of International & Comparative Law* 13(1), 2007, 35–58.
6 L. Li, "The Chinese Communist Party and people's courts: Judicial dependence in China", *The American Journal of Comparative Law* 64(1), 2016, 37–74.
7 Ibid.
8 "Judicial independence in the PRC", Congressional-Executive Commission on China, n.d.
9 C. L. Jones & M. Varrall, "China: The Party, the state, and the new anti-graft body", *The Interpreter*, 2 April 2018.
10 J. Zhu & H. Li, "Elite power competition and corruption investigation in China: A case study", *Modern China* 46(3), 2020, 307–335.
11 "Visualizing China's anti-corruption campaign", *ChinaFile*, 15 August 2018.
12 Y. Y. Ang, *China's Gilded Age*, Cambridge: Cambridge University Press, 2020.
13 A. Zhang, *Chinese Antitrust Exceptionalism: How the Rise of China Challenges Global Regulation*, Oxford: Oxford University Press, 2021.
14 "Rule of law index", World Justice Project, 2020.
15 S. Sceats & S. Breslin, *China and International Human Rights System*, London: Chatham House, 2012.
16 "China: Events of 2019", Human Rights Watch, 2020.
17 United Nations, "OHCHR assessment of human rights concerns in the Xinjiang Uyghur Autonomous Region", *People's Republic of China*, 31 August 2022.
18 "Democracy index 2021: The China challenge", Economist Intelligence Unit, 2022.
19 "Freedom in the world 2022", Freedom House, 2022.
20 "2022 world Press freedom index", Reporters Without Borders, 2022.
21 "Rule of law index".
22 § 212 Criminal Procedure Law of the PRC.
23 M. P. Robertson & J. Lavee, "Execution by organ procurement: Breaching the dead donor rule in China", *American Journal of Transplantation* 22(7), 2022, 1804–1812.
24 "Death sentence and executions 2019, Amnesty International global report", Amnesty International, 2020.

25 *Death Penalty under International Law: A Background Paper to the IBAHRI Resolution on the Abolition of Death Penalty*, London: International Bar Association, 2008.
26 M. Tomášek, *Právní systémy dálného východu II.* [Legal systems of the Far East II.], Prague: Karolinum, 2016.
27 Joint Declaration of the Government of the United Kingdom of Great Britain and Northern Ireland and the Government of the People's Republic of China on the Question of Hong Kong, 1984; and Joint Declaration of the Government of the People's Republic of China and The Government of the Republic of Portugal on the Question of Macao, 1987.
28 J. Ng, "Sino-British joint declaration on Hong Kong 'no longer has any realistic meaning', Chinese Foreign Ministry Says", *South China Morning Post*, 30 June 2017.
29 I. Castellucci, "Legal hybridity in Hong Kong and Macau", *McGill Law Journal* 57(4), 2012, 665–720.
30 "In brave new world of China's digital courts, judges are AI and verdicts come via Chat App", *Japan Times*, 7 December 2019.
31 V. Chan & A. M. Koo, "Blockchain evidence in internet courts in China: The fast track for evidence collection for online disputes", *Lexology*, July 2020.
32 K. Wang, "China using WeChat for a digital justice system", *Asia Times*, 7 December 2019.
33 G. Du & M. Yu, "You can watch trials in Chinese courts on the internet now", *China Justice Observer*, 20 May 2018.

10 Technological power

Can China innovate?

Martin Šebeňa

In the past four decades, two of the major drivers of China's economic growth have been a constant updating of the country's technological capabilities and its large pool of cheap labor. In the early years of China's economic reform, technological upgrading was achieved chiefly via imitation and technology transfers. This method has now largely run its course. China is approaching – or perhaps even behind – the Lewis Turning Point, when the surplus labor in agriculture is fully absorbed into manufacturing and services. In other words, there are no more cheap workers in the countryside that could take on new jobs in the fast-growing cities. Home-grown innovation and technological progress have thus become the most important driver of economic growth in China. The country is undoubtedly a leader in a number of technology sectors; perhaps the most well-known among them are high-speed railways and mobile payments. ***How advanced are other sectors? Can Chinese companies produce the most complex products, or is China still mostly a world factory? Do Chinese engineers know how to push the boundaries of technological progress, or do they just copy inventions from abroad?***

Development of corporate innovation

The initial Chinese approach to innovation after 1979 was imitation. Widespread copying of foreign products, processes, and brand names was accompanied by the effort to produce low-quality and cheap products. For Chinese customers in the 1980s and 1990s, affordability was the most important factor, and therefore they did not mind the lower quality of the local products. The combination of disregard for intellectual property and low quality of products was colloquially called *shanzhai*, or "mountain bandits".

However, in many cases, imitation went hand in hand with incremental innovation. Responding to the market's demands, Chinese companies quickly learned to adjust products to local conditions. This often meant that their products contained only the features that the customers were willing to pay for, and nothing more. In producing such "good enough" products, Chinese firms learned to streamline processes, reduce waste, and strip down unwanted features. Where the products of their Western competitors came with several costly features, the Chinese products only contained those that the local customers were willing to pay for. Such products were not supposed to be viewed as inferior, rather, they were designed to fit for purpose.[1]

DOI: 10.4324/9781003350064-13

In the second stage, since approximately the mid-1990s, more ambitious companies tried to change the paradigm, and instead of seeing innovation as a necessity, they embraced it as a core component of their competitiveness. Instead of being driven by the market, they started to drive the market, and innovation was approached as a matter of choice rather than necessity. The electronic appliances manufacturer Haier and online marketplace Alibaba belonged to the first group of companies that hired a whole cohort of technological talent in their pursuit of innovation.

The third stage of innovation is embedded in the government's efforts to encourage Chinese firms to pursue opportunities overseas. Innovation was not only supposed to be produced locally or brought to China in the form of investments, but it was also supposed to be acquired abroad. Many Chinese firms embarked on a wave of mergers and acquisitions, mostly targeted at purchasing companies producing high-value products and possessing extensive know-how, patents, and state-of-the-art technology.

We can see various companies pursuing different strategies at the same time. While there are Chinese firms delivering top products and pushing the boundaries of technological innovation, there will also be companies engaging in wholesale imitation of their competitors' products. Therefore, accusations of intellectual property theft, as well as news about breakthrough inventions coming from China, can be true at the same time.

The government's role in innovation

Another way of looking at the trajectory of Chinese innovation capacities is by tracking the government's approach. After 1978, the government opted to pursue an open method of innovation, defined as "the use of purposive inflows and outflows of knowledge to accelerate internal innovation and to expand the markets for external use of innovation, respectively".[2] Initially, the support for innovation was subsumed in the efforts to attract foreign direct investment (FDI), which was accompanied by transfers of knowledge and technology. In 2005, China released the 15-year "Medium-to-Long-Term Plan for the Development of Science and Technology", which defined clear goals for the country to evolve from imitator to innovator.[3]

There are three main areas in which governments can shape innovation practices: in the role of a broker, in generating demand, and in stimulating innovation.[4] In articulating demand, the government can set competition policies that shape or create markets. Matt Sheehan noted that a system of semi-protected markets was created in the third millennium's first decade.[5] In certain areas, foreign firms' access was limited to protect domestic startups from being crushed by foreign competition. The state controls access to the market to favor domestic firms, but this does not mean that foreign firms are not allowed to enter the Chinese market: restrictions are limited to areas identified as a priority, and most firms were allowed to compete in the Chinese market before being shut out or outdone by local juggernauts.

In its role as a broker, the Chinese leadership has actively encouraged collaboration and open exchange of ideas, best practices, and operating models between firms, universities, research centers, and laboratories. These practices often involve engaging partners abroad or encouraging talent to return from overseas and bring knowledge back to China. In stimulating innovation, the country "unleashes a wave of resources" – investments and capital, physical infrastructure, bureaucratic apparatus, and engineering talent – in an effort to support the creation of startups and jump-start many new industries.

A thin layer of innovation

At first glance, China's technological achievements may seem glaring. The country is a leader in mobile payments (applications such as Alipay and WeChat Pay have already penetrated all continents) and the consumer internet (such as the internet giants Alibaba and JD), as well as in the construction of infrastructure projects (such as high-speed rail). However, it should be noted that these achievements do not reflect the overall state of Chinese technology. Progress in these specific sectors has often been facilitated by specific factors, particularly the social environment and the regulatory regime.

People in China quickly accepted mobile payments for several reasons. The first is that many Chinese have trouble opening a bank account, so they either do not have one or use the services offered by the shadow banking system. Another reason is the low nominal value of Chinese banknotes. The highest banknote is worth one hundred yuan (equivalent to about 15 US dollars); therefore, carrying a large stack of banknotes for everyday purchases would often be necessary. Thirdly, credit cards are not very common in China. Because of these limitations, which do not exist in Western countries, people in China have adopted mobile payments faster than elsewhere. This process, called leapfrogging – skipping several levels of technological development – has also led to a boom in retail banking and online shopping.

Chinese firms have also achieved global dominance in areas such as high-speed railways or solar power. They are a volume leader – thousands of kilometers of railroads or millions of manufactured solar panels – and they also set the pace in research and development. Success in these two sectors is primarily based on the government's efforts to make these sectors prosperous. The state has poured vast amounts of money into companies operating in these areas, even knowing that many would eventually go bankrupt. However, the government is aware that such an approach would attract many enterprising and skilled people who fiercely compete with each other in the race toward developing new technologies. Even if only one company emerges from this fight, it would be a global leader in its field.

Nevertheless, it is important to note that in most other sectors, Chinese technology does not reach the level of Western countries or Japan. China must source the most advanced technologies from abroad by purchasing specialized firms or by importing them. Much of the cutting-edge technology requires for its operation the most powerful semiconductors, now produced only by US and Taiwanese companies.[6] The fact that China has not yet been able to develop a deeper technological foundation in the field of semiconductors means that the United States can inflict significant damage to large Chinese companies at any time and that even a giant company like Huawei can face enormous difficulties.[7]

China also has a strong position in the production of industrial goods. Several companies have achieved global leadership in steel, solar energy, and telecommunications accessories. However, firms in other sectors will still have a long way to go to match their German, Japanese, Korean, or American competition. Few Chinese companies are among the world's most successful brands, which is also an indication, albeit imperfect, of the status of Chinese technological progress.

Contribution of state-of-the-art technologies

Chinese technological prowess might be measured by analyzing the country's success in new technologies, such as artificial intelligence, quantum computers, biotechnology, hypersonics, and other areas that are currently trending. There is no consensus on China's position in either of these areas but let us consider it realistic that China can become a leader in them. To date, these areas are more at the level of experimental science rather than real commercial sectors where technology benefits the economy or people. Artificial intelligence is mostly a vague product or an added service. It is not easy to realistically estimate total sales across a whole sector, which also applies to other new industries.[8]

An emphasis on experimental technologies diverts attention away from China's weaknesses in industrial sectors at the forefront of technological innovation, such as semiconductors, machine tools, and commercial aviation. Since their commercial use in these industries has long been validated, technological advances in these areas are measured with much clearer technical and commercial parameters. They are significantly more complex than the production of steel and solar panels, and Chinese companies have much worse results in entering these areas.

This leads to one of the defining characteristics of Chinese innovation: the emphasis on the quantification of inputs. Many analyses focus on the growth in the number of patents, the volume of investment in science and research, or the number of publications and citations in academic journals. It is relatively easy to obtain these data, so the measurement of "innovation" is often based on them. While the increase in the number of patents in China is impressive, it does not necessarily correspond to dramatic progress in innovation. In fact, these inputs are mostly irrelevant if they do not produce quality outputs, and it is unclear whether this is happening in China (and elsewhere in the world). While the graphs charting patent registrations or investments in science and research often suggest that Chinese firms will soon surpass the rest of the world, the commercial outputs have not yet been nearly as impressive.

Additionally, the trade wars with the United States and the inability to produce advanced semiconductors indicate that the medium-term outlook does not look overly encouraging for China's technological advances. However, it is different in the long run because these challenges can enhance the strengths of China's technology sector. In addition to the United States, China is the only country that has succeeded in building internet giants, putting the country in a perfect position to continue developing digital technologies. It has created established brands in hardware, such as smartphones or many types of industrial goods. China also produces a large number of high-quality consumer products. However, it lags far behind in global branding, so the Western consumer market does not know about many of them or has a negative opinion of them. In areas that use R&D-intensive technologies, such as the automotive, semiconductor, and aerospace industries, Chinese companies tend to be weak even in the domestic market.

Long-term advantages: Tacit knowledge and a dynamic market

In the long run, Chinese firms meet two conditions that will enable them to reach the technological frontier in all sectors and gradually move forward. First, because China is the world's factory, China's workforce produces an extensive range of products, which means that it also captures the most knowledge needed in the production process. Secondly, China is a vast and dynamic market. Technological learning is critical in industrialization, as it allows countries to move up the value chain. The best empirical examples come from China's neighbors in East Asia: South Korea, Hong Kong, Singapore, and Taiwan, all demonstrating the outcome of the practical application of technological learning. Technological learning can have two forms: it can be either transferred as codified knowledge or acquired as tacit knowledge. Codified knowledge is articulated into formal language and can be transferred via publications, textbooks, or patents. Tacit knowledge can be acquired via personal experience, most of which is not verbally formulable.[9] Although it is difficult to define, it exists and provides value: each business leader would be able to confirm the value of staff with tacit knowledge to the company.

While the determinant for learning codified knowledge is the recipient's mental capacity, the key aspect in acquiring tacit knowledge is time spent gaining experience. To understand the difference between tacit and codified knowledge, consider a cooking recipe: if two people are given the same recipe (codified knowledge), the person with more experience (tacit knowledge) will likely cook a more delicious meal.

As China moves up the value chain, many of its workforce use technologically advanced products. Even if most workers at the assembly lines of large factories will only perform simple tasks, thousands of line engineers are acquiring the knowledge that is turning them into the world's most competent assemblers. As a result, in the electronics industry for instance, the tacit knowledge acquired in the factories assembling products for Apple and other electronics giants was essential in the development of new industries, such as drones or electric scooters, in which China is a global leader. Even in iPhone production, the value added by the Chinese workforce increased from 4% to 25% of the product.[10]

Two additional factors aid the acquisition and practical use of tacit knowledge. Chinese firms are benefiting from the supply networks of their Western competitors.

Staying with the Apple example, the US firm's Chinese suppliers also serve local manufacturers of smartphones, who derive considerable benefits from sourcing high-quality components for their products. Secondly, there is a strong tendency for clustering production. Heavy concentrations of firms from the same industry in production centers facilitate the exchange of knowledge, which shortens production times and accelerates the circulation of information.

Today, China manufactures about a fifth of the world's total production of industrial products because few multinationals have resisted the temptation to move their production there. American, German, and Japanese firms emphasize that they left the most valuable portion of production in their home country. That is more or less true, but these firms believed that the Chinese workforce they train will not learn to absorb and copy foreign technology. Such an idea has long ceased to apply to companies in areas like high-speed railways, shipbuilding, and telecommunications equipment.[11] It can therefore be expected that, as China's economy grows in sophistication, its capacity to absorb and learn new technologies will continue to grow.

The acquisition of technological knowledge through labor works as a supply-side factor that pushes the capabilities of Chinese firms forward. Still, these firms also benefit from the demand-side factor: China's enormous market. The market size can overcome many shortcomings, such as an outdated education system that stifles creativity. Moreover, although consumer internet companies are not strategically important, they buy components directly from developers. They are in a strong position vis-à-vis European or Japanese companies to learn how to make

Figure 10.1 Shenzhen – the capital of hardware (source: CEIAS).

components themselves and to be able to create digital technologies of the future. Today's China has a vast domestic market created by dynamic firms, a capable workforce, and a strong interest in technology.

Focus on domestic knowledge production

Another factor that may move Chinese technological capabilities forward is determination. China has long been dependent on knowledge transfers and exchanges with other countries. However, after the US sanctions hit China's giants, both state-owned and private firms have been much more committed to maintaining uninterrupted access to technology supplies. Some CEOs of Chinese firms compare US sanctions to earthquakes – they are equally unpredictable and have the same impact on supply networks. Every company, therefore, seeks to create non-American, ideally Chinese, alternatives. This has the most substantial impact on the technology sector because the lack of a few critical components can stop the vast system behind the production of smartphones or telecommunication towers.

It is politically unacceptable for China that the United States can harm companies like ZTE or Huawei at any time. It is in the interest of its national security to increase technological capacity in every central area. The Chinese strategic response has thus increased its focus on innovation and support of domestic firms. The nature of the threat and China's response to it resemble the US innovation drive after the Soviet Union launched the first satellite into space in the late 1950s, known as the "Sputnik moment".[12]

The Chinese government does understand that companies need help. Under the "Made in China 2025" plan, it seeks to raise the technological level of the Chinese industry and achieve dominance in certain sectors. Tens of billions of dollars of funding will have been channeled to innovation during the 10-year program. "Made in China 2025" is the most visible proof of the central government's seriousness toward innovation and technological progress.[13] The question is whether a top-down initiative will contribute to a shift in technical boundaries in the country. We know from experience that state-supported research projects have brought many breakthroughs in a number of scientific areas and in various countries. At the same time, however, it should be noted that many such projects ended in failure and loss of money. In addition to these strengths, China also benefits from the country's leadership's acute awareness of the need for innovation and strongly supports the technology sector. On the other hand, setting specific deadlines like 2025 – also highly ambitious – can be counterproductive because technological developments cannot be precisely planned.

China is lagging in specific sectors because it entered them relatively late and needs more time to reach the level of leading countries and firms. While it is difficult to predict whether China will replace the United States as a world leader in technological capabilities and innovation, it is safe to say that China's economy will cope with the current technological handicap vis-à-vis other countries. Domestic firms will learn to create the most complex products, and new technological leaders from China will enter world markets.

Notes

1 G. S. Yip & B. McKern, *China's Next Strategic Advantage: From Imitation to Innovation*, MIT Press, 2016.
2 H. Chesbrough, W. Vanhaverbeke & J. West, *Open Innovation: Researching a New Paradigm*, London: Oxford University Press, 2006.
3 R. P. Appelbaum, C. Cao, X. Han, R. Parker & D. Simon, *Innovation in China*, Oxford University Press, 2006.
4 A. Faber, R. Kemp & G. Van der Veen, "Innovation policy for the environment in the Netherlands and the EU", in C. Nauwelaers & R. Wintjes (Eds.), *Innovation Policy in Europe: Measurement and Strategy*, Cheltenham: Edward Elgar Publishing, 2008.
5 M. Sheehan, "The Chinese way of innovation, what Washington can learn from Beijing about investing in tech", *Foreign Affairs*, 21 April 2022.
6 J. Horowitz, "Why the semiconductor is suddenly at the heart of US-China tech tensions", *Quartz*, 25 July 2018.
7 J. A. Lewis, "Managing semiconductor exports to China", *Center for Strategic and International Studies*, 5 May 2020.
8 J. Lee, H. Davari, J. Singh & V. Pandhare, "Industrial artificial intelligence for industry 4.0-based manufacturing systems", *Manufacturing Letters* 18, 2018, 20–23.
9 X. Fu, *China's Path to Innovation*, Cambridge University Press, 2015.
10 Y. Xing, "How the iPhone widens the US trade deficit with China: The case of the iPhone X", *VoxEu*, 11 November 2019.
11 D. Fickling, "Alstom and Siemens show how not to deal with China", *Bloomberg*, 6 February 2019.
12 D. Wang, "China's Sputnik moment?", *Foreign Affairs*, 29 July 2021.
13 "Made in China 2025: Global ambitions built on local protections", *US Chamber of Commerce*, 5 March 2017.

11 Environment

Does China care about it?

Klára Dubravčíková

For centuries, the environment in China has been under enormous pressure due to the growing population, which has almost tripled in the course of the 20th century alone. Today, China is approaching its population peak of 1.46 billion inhabitants, which, among other things, represents a significant burden on natural resources. Moreover, at the end of the 1970s, a period of unprecedented rapid economic growth started in China, coupled with increased demand for energy supply and natural resources. The process of opening up to the world did not only bring an economic miracle but also catalyzed social and environmental problems. Air pollution, water scarcity, soil contamination, and many other environmental problems gradually became so evident that they could no longer be overlooked. The Communist Party of China (CCP) had to intervene – it was forced by the pressure of its own population and by growing pressure at the international level. Today, the Chinese leadership has to cope with an environmental crisis that is not easy to resolve. On the one hand, there is a vision of a greener future, but on the other, the risk of substantial economic losses exists. Adopting drastic environmental measures could jeopardize the stability of China's industrial regions, cause unemployment, and raise a number of other problems. ***What are the reasons for the current environmental crisis in China, and how serious is the problem? What is the Chinese government doing to improve the situation and how likely is it to succeed?***

Centenary of the increasing population

Ancient China suffered from deforestation and the depletion of fertile land – as the size of the Chinese population grew, new territories were needed for settlements and forests began to disappear. The lack of agricultural land, that was desperately needed, led to the degradation of other parts of the country, which some emperors also tried to stop. In the 18th and 19th centuries, the rulers of the Qing dynasty declared several areas in Mongolia and Manchuria as protected, enacting unique rules that aimed to prevent unauthorized poaching, deforestation, and meadow mowing. Environmental protection was not the only objective, however. Such measures were supposed to protect the "purity" of Manchuria, from which the Qing dynasty rulers originated.

Much changed at the turn of the 19th and 20th centuries – in the northeast of China, foreign capital was used to build railways, coal and gold mines were opened,

DOI: 10.4324/9781003350064-14

and China, pressured by Western powers, became involved in international trade. In the first half of the 19th century, the proportion of forests in the territory of today's China fell to 17%, and at the beginning of the 20th century, forests constituted only about 12% of the territory. The environmental disaster deepened further with Mao Zedong's rise to power.

In 1949, the newly established People's Republic of China had more than 500 million inhabitants. After the end of the civil war, the population grew rapidly, which impacted the environment significantly. Forests continued to disappear, wetlands and lakes dried up due to arable land growth, and agriculture intensified under the pressure of the population boom. Population growth has also resulted in increased water and energy consumption. However, Mao believed that the wealth and strength of the country lay precisely in population growth, and that man must "conquer" nature – thus, unsurprisingly, he did not devote much effort to protecting the environment. Quite the opposite, in 1958, as part of the Great Leap Forward, Mao launched a number of campaigns and mobilized a large proportion of the population to pursue his goals. One such campaign focused on fighting "against four pests," aiming to eradicate all sparrows, rats, flies, and mosquitoes. People shot sparrows and prevented them from landing until they died of exhaustion and within two years, these birds almost disappeared from the Chinese territory. The result was a rapid proliferation of insects.

Another ill-considered initiative by the Chinese leader was to rapidly increase steel production in order to surpass the United States and the United Kingdom. Backyard furnaces were built across the country, in which people melted all their tools and converted them into virtually unusable steel. Up to 10% of the remaining woodland on Chinese territory was used as fuel for this purpose.[1] Also, a large part of the population focused solely on the goals of Mao's campaigns, and agricultural production became secondary. In other words, the share of the population taking care of food production was substantially lowered, and simultaneously, soil quality suffered from inappropriate practices such as the excessive use of fertilizers. The Great Leap Forward did not bring the awaited success; instead, it resulted in one of the greatest famines in human history. Both the population of China and its environment fell victim to Mao's experiments. Yet, Mao's legacy of "man's conquest of nature" persisted in China for decades to come.

An economic miracle at the expense of the environment

The "Great Helmsman" Mao died in 1976, and with Deng Xiaoping rising to supreme power, the era of reforms aimed at improving the living standards of the Chinese people began. China shifted away from the purely socialist style of governance and started a period of opening up to the world. Besides other factors, lax environmental laws and cheap labor made China an attractive destination for relocating the production of multinational corporations. Rapid industrialization began, worsening the already poor ecological situation in the country – in many Chinese cities, the proportion of sulfur dioxide and dust particles in the atmosphere exceeded the standards set by the government; Chinese rivers, lakes, and coastal waters were contaminated with toxic substances, and groundwater was also being polluted. However, since China was enjoying the phenomenal benefits of rapid economic growth, it was in the interest of the Chinese leadership to maintain it at all costs.

The industrial expansion led to a large increase in energy production and consumption, which, combined with mass interregional migration, urbanization, and urban growth, brought about many environmental problems – the state was becoming rich while the environment suffered, even though the Constitution itself has included an article on its protection since the end of the 1970s. The slogan of the time was "pollute first, resolve later" (in Chinese *xian wuran hou zhili*). China became one of the world's largest energy producers and consumers over the last two decades of the 20th century. Energy supplies were inexpensive, which, together with an affordable and large workforce, made China the world's factory.

The world's largest air pollutant

Compared to the United States, China consumed about one-third of its energy in the 1990s. In 2011, China ranked first in energy consumption globally. As more than 70% of energy was produced in coal-fired power plants, air pollution was persistently present. The extensiveness of the pollution can be demonstrated by the example of Guangdong, the most populous and richest province in China, where greenhouse gas emissions increased by almost one-third between 2005 and 2010 as a result of fossil fuel consumption. China produced huge amounts of carbon dioxide emissions, becoming the world's largest air polluter in 2005.

Even though China no longer dominates the bottom rankings of international air quality, pollution is still a very serious issue, posing a high health risk to the Chinese population. At the beginning of the new millennium, the Chinese government began to actively deal with environmental problems and sought to mitigate the intensity of pollution by introducing various regulations. However, their enforcement has met only partial success. In fact, environmental regulations are often violated by local authorities, concerned about their impact on their respective regions' economies. Indeed, in 2015, 90% of cities still had not reached the acceptable pollution levels set by the central government. It is estimated that more than a million people die prematurely each year in China because of poor air quality.[2]

The rapid decrease in air quality was not a consequence of rapid industrialization and enormous energy consumption only. It also resulted from increasing urbanization and the rise of the Chinese middle class. China very quickly became the largest motor vehicle market in the world. In 2016, 28 million cars were sold in the country, which is more than in the United States (over 17 million) and the European Union (about 15 million).[3] The growing number of cars contributed to an increase in the concentration of particulate matter (PM) 2.5 in the air of large cities, including dust, smoke, chemicals, and other impurities resulting from, for example, coal combustion or chemical processes, which are the main source of toxic emissions in the atmosphere. However, air pollution was not the only problem. Growing cities needed more free land for construction, as well as an increasing supply of energy and water, which, however, is severely limited in the country.

Water and its contamination

Around 20% of the world's population lives in China; nonetheless, the country has only around 6% of the world's freshwater reserves. According to World Bank data, there are about 2,000 cubic meters of drinking water per capita per year in China – about one-third of the global average.[4]

There are several reasons why the country suffers from water scarcity. One of them is the uneven distribution of water – the south of China is much richer in water than the north. In Beijing, for example, on average, people can use only about 100 cubic meters of water, which is comparable to Mauritania or Sudan.[5] On the other hand, in the southern metropolis of Guangzhou, it is up to ten times more. For this reason, too, the government approved the construction of a long-planned water canal that would redirect water from the southern provinces to the northern part of the country, thus helping the densely populated regions, which are also important industrial areas, with

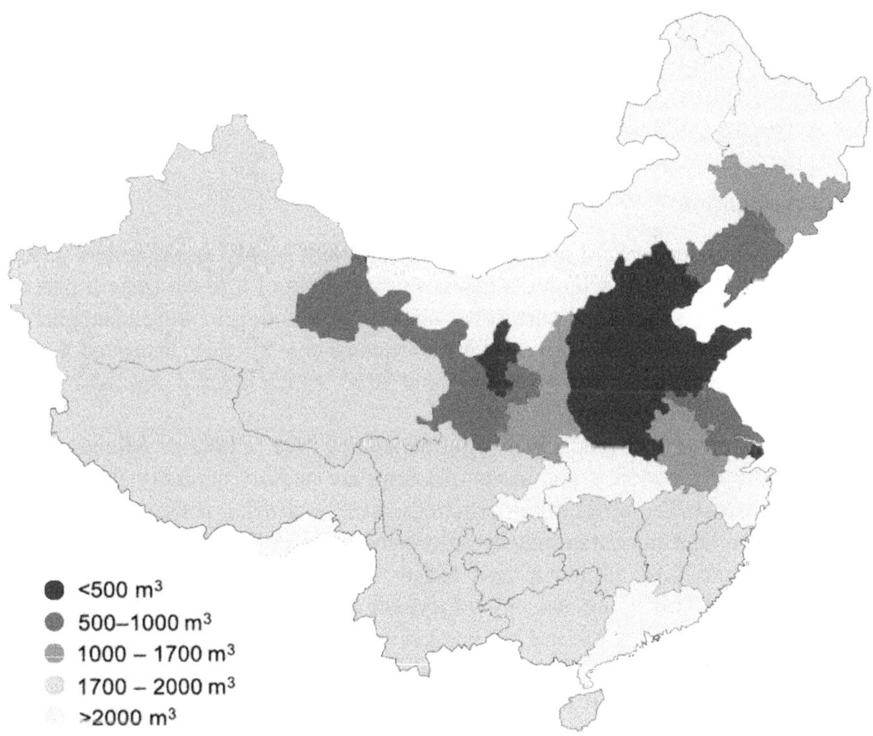

Figure 11.1 Water supply per person for one year (source: CEIAS, adapted from D. Gardner, *Environmental Pollution in China: What Everyone Needs to Know*, New York: Oxford University Press, 2018).

major water shortages. The first phase of this channel was completed in 2014. At the same time, China is also fighting water scarcity via desalination in the Bohai Sea.

Another reason for water scarcity in China is associated with the issue of enormous waste and over-exploitation of resources. This holds true not only for water consumption by individuals but also, and above all, for consumption in industrial sectors. The third reason is the overall degradation of the environment, including the desiccation of wetlands and lakes and the overall pollution of water resources. Deforestation also contributes to the issue.

The process of desiccation is again closely linked to the rapid growth of Chinese cities, as shown by the example of the city of Wuhan in the province of Hubei, where up to 70% of its lakes have dried up since the beginning of the new century due to the expansion of the city.[6] The growth of the urban population has also brought about greater water consumption and a significant deterioration in its quality – according to official data published by the Chinese National Development and Reform Commission, the country produces more than 70 billion tons of sewage every year, some of which does not reach the wastewater filtration system and instead flows back into rivers.[7]

In addition, the construction of water filtration plants cannot keep pace with the rapidly increasing urban population in China. In 2003, nearly 68 billion tons of polluted water were leaked back into the environment, and in 2007 up to 60% of Chinese cities had no water treatment system.[8] Currently, according to data from the Chinese Ministry of Water Resources, 50% of all domestic rivers and 90% of urban waters are polluted.[9]

Soil contamination

The low share of arable land is also a serious problem – only less than 9% of the world's arable land is located on Chinese territory, most of it in the eastern part of the country. At the same time, part of the land suitable for agriculture disappeared under construction. Indeed, urban and infrastructure construction destroyed 8 million hectares of arable land between 2001 and 2013, which today poses risks to the food security of the country.[10]

According to an official study published by the Chinese Ministry for Environmental Protection, some areas of China are heavily contaminated due to mining, unsustainable agricultural practices, and industrial activities.[11] Nearly one-fifth of the land is contaminated – more than one million square kilometers. Moreover, centuries of human impact led to up to one-third of the land being eroded by 2016.[12] This figure is steadily increasing, and it is assumed that up to 1.5 million square kilometers of land are subject to very rapid changes due to deforestation and desertification. Desertification is a very serious problem in China, affecting the capital itself. It is rather common for the citizens of Beijing to face the consequences of desert storms in the Gobi Desert. That is why the government launched a large-scale campaign to plant trees in 1978, hoping to slow the process of desertification down. To this day, about 66 billion trees have been planted on the edge of the desert.

The alarming levels of soil contamination and the growing efforts to attain agricultural self-sufficiency in the production of basic foods have both resulted in increased investment in the prevention and mitigation of soil pollution. At the same time, the government has been searching for land suitable for agricultural production beyond its borders – China's foreign investment in agriculture has risen more than 16 times in the last 20 years, surpassing the United States.[13]

Consequences of consumerism

Pollution and ecological imbalances are also closely linked to the development of consumer society and the increase in the production of solid waste. While in 1976 Beijing generated about 109 kilograms of solid municipal waste per capita, most of which was ash or wood waste, in 2007 it was already 333 kilograms, with 20% constituted by ash and 30% by paper and plastic. Nowadays, every Beijing inhabitant produces less than 380 kilograms of waste per year on average. For comparison, in the United States, every person produces over 740 kilograms of waste per year on average.[14] With the increasing amount of waste that must be processed in some way, the Chinese people's approach to recycling has gradually evolved. In large cities, for example, smart waste-collecting "vending machines" are common, used by the local communities to sort waste. For proper waste sorting, the inhabitants can obtain small financial rewards. In Shanghai, which is one of the largest waste producers in China, waste sorting has even been mandatory since 2019, with strict regulations in force.

The rising consumerism in China does not only affect the situation within its borders. Examples include the demand for ivory, exotic wood furniture, and similar products that are largely obtained through illicit trading. As a result, world populations of elephants, rhinos, tigers, and other endangered animal species are being decimated for profit. Another aspect is the growing consumption of meat, seafood, and other animal products. While the Chinese population consumed less than 10 million tons of meat in the 1970s, in 2012, it was already more than 70 million tons.[15] Compared to other developing countries, this represents a very rapid increase. Overall, China consumes about one-third more meat than the whole of Europe and up to half as much as the United States or other Asian countries combined.[16] In per capita consumption, however, the richer Western countries are still ranking the highest.

Securing the economic prosperity of the Chinese population has become the key guiding principle of the Chinese government. At the same time, it is used for the legitimization of its power. However, the price that China paid for "getting rich" so quickly turned out to be very high in retrospect. The increase in air pollution, the destruction of quality soil, water scarcity, and the contamination of water resources and soil pose significant risks to human health and will lead to further problems.

In China, the incidence of diseases related to environmental degradation, such as cancer or heart and lung diseases, has increased rapidly. Between 1970 and 2004, the country recorded an increase of up to 80% in deaths due to oncological diseases.[17] There are hundreds of so-called "cancer villages" in the Chinese countryside, where an above-average number of people suffer from some form of cancer. This phenomenon is related to the rapid industrialization and growth in the number of factories that were knowingly leaking chemicals and other industrial waste into the local water supplies.

The devastation of the environment and the growing health crisis could no longer be ignored. Indeed, the Chinese population has begun to actively ask the state to change its approach to environmental issues – since the 1990s, the number and intensity of protests motivated by environmental problems have been gradually increasing. In 2003, there were about 58 thousand of them, while in 2008 it was 100 thousand.[18] At the same time, the international community has become aware of the fact that in order to yield at least some success in protecting the environment and mitigating the consequences of climate change, Beijing had to be involved actively in the joint efforts. China has therefore also faced criticism from its peers in the international arena.

The emergence of environmental activism

The year 2008 marked a breakthrough for China – Beijing hosted its first Olympic Games with great pride, and the government spared no expense in its efforts to display China's greatness. Beijing wanted to be perceived as a modern city, but it also wanted to prove to the world that it emphasized sustainable development. Therefore, in the process of preparation for the Games, apart from new roads and metro lines, greenery was also gradually appearing in the city. Moreover, major polluting industries were relocated outside the city and emission standards for vehicles were introduced.

Although air quality was improving, it deteriorated again after the Olympic Games were over. The situation in Beijing in January 2013, when PM 2.5 levels of more than 900 micrograms per cubic meter were referred to as "apocalyptic," became notorious, since the maximum recommended concentration of microparticles in the air was exceeded by about 40 times. Beijing, however, was not the only city facing a similar problem – large cities like Shijiazhuang, Zhengzhou, Luoyang, Changsha, Tianjin, and Chengdu are still facing high concentrations of small particles in the air.

The experience of 2013 was a key moment for China. The alarming data caught the attention of the wider Chinese public, who began to demand clean air, but also access to clean water and safe food, pressuring the Chinese authorities to improve air quality monitoring. At the same time, Chinese citizens were becoming aware of the environmental impacts of large projects, such as the construction of the world's largest dam, Three Gorges. Activism and the fight for a green China have also gained momentum through the expansion of the Internet and better access to a wider range of information. The activities of non-profit organizations, which were heavily involved in the field of environmental issues, have also been contributing significantly to the growing demand for a better environment in China.

Around that time, there was also a wave of investigative journalism focusing on environmental protection in China. Journalists began testing the limit of transparency that Chinese censorship was able to tolerate. The documentary film *Under the Dome*, depicting the impact of air pollution on the human body, can serve as an example. The film by former investigative reporter Chai Jing was published on the Internet in 2015 and was seen by hundreds of millions of people within a few days. The Chinese authorities did not censor the film at first. However, the great interest and debate that it generated eventually resulted in censorship. This happened three years after Chinese leader Hu Jintao spoke to the nation at the end of his term as general secretary of the Communist Party of China, stressing the need for ecological progress and sustainable development, and only one year after the central leadership declared a "war on pollution."

Correcting economic–ecological imbalances

The growing role of the environmental agenda in China can also be observed in the actions of Xi Jinping, who began to emphasize the construction of the so-called "ecological civilization" (in Chinese *shengtai wenming*). Introduced in 2007 by his predecessor, Hu Jintao, as a political commitment to respond to environmental degradation and make necessary steps to move toward a people-oriented economic model, the concept has quickly become a means of power legitimization by the government.

Nevertheless, the decision on how to solve the environmental crisis was up to the new leader to make – Xi Jinping thus faced the challenge of trying to resolve various environmental issues without jeopardizing the country's economic growth. Indeed, going green has not been easy for China. For example, in 2014, the central government decided to close the energy-intensive factories in Hebei province as part of ecological progress; the result was the lowest quarterly growth in the region in 15 years.[19] Again, in 2017, the province practically banned coal heating. However, due to the lack of gas supplies, people were freezing in their homes in the winter months, which produced a wave of outrage, and the government had to relax the ban.

Restricting production and reducing energy consumption would undoubtedly benefit the Chinese environment; however, it is not practically possible due to other non-environmental factors. Moreover, there are other obstacles standing in China's way to becoming "greener." One of them is the government's objective to increase the share of city dwellers and their income. This policy of so-called "hyper-urbanization" essentially entails higher demand for the construction of new buildings and also for cars and energy. The Communist Party is thus facing a great challenge. In previous years, however, it has taken a large number of steps and measures to achieve "ecological harmony," which became one of the main goals of the 13th Five-Year Plan.

In 2012, pressured by the public, the CCP announced that it would start monitoring air quality and publish the collected data. Various restrictions on car traffic and the number of new vehicles registered have also been introduced in large cities over the last decade. The government has also started to actively promote the purchase of electric vehicles and the use of the public transport system. In 2018, half of all electric cars produced globally were sold in China, where, like some Western countries, even limiting the sale of vehicles with internal combustion engines is being considered.

The population has also been active in this regard. Activism and discussions on air, water, and food quality have spread on social networks, and safety has become one of the top priorities for people. For example, demand for organic products has increased in China over the last ten years – today China is the fourth largest consumer of organic products. Food products imported from abroad are also popular among the public, but this is also related to the food scandals of Chinese producers. To this day, for example, the whole nation remembers, when in 2008, infant formula contaminated with melamine entered the market and killed six babies while seriously endangering another 300 thousand. As a result of this scandal, the demand for imported powdered milk in China increased rapidly and confidence in domestic production has not been restored.

Is Xi Jinping a green leader?

In the fight against environmental contamination, China has invested hundreds of billions of US dollars in air pollution control, amended environmental legislation, and begun focusing on renewable resources and reforestation. Today, China is flooded with solar panels that spread over kilometer-long "solar parks," mainly in the eastern coastal areas and in Xinjiang and Ningxia, including one of the largest solar power plants in the world – Tengger – in an area of more than 40 square kilometers. Similarly, it is also the case with wind farms that are concentrated in such a way that they form huge energy bases. By far the largest base is Jiuquan near the Gobi Desert with over 7,000 turbines.

In 2018, less than 38% of Chinese energy came from renewable sources, including hydroelectric power plants, solar panels, and wind power plants. About 60% of the energy was produced in thermal power plants and 2% in nuclear power plants.[20] Thus, in seven years, China has been able to reduce its share of thermal energy by 10% and has become the world's largest producer and exporter of solar panels and wind turbines. At the same time, it has also been one of the largest investors in renewable energy.

Beijing is aware of the seriousness of environmental pollution, not only within its own borders but also on a global scale. At home, the government headed by Xi Jinping is actively dealing with the environmental crisis. In 2016, China committed itself to reducing energy consumption and increasing the share of renewable energy produced, increasing the share of forested land, improving the quality of its water resources, and building wastewater treatment systems. However, economic interests are still a factor that the government does not want and cannot ignore. If the CCP does not want to jeopardize China's economic growth, which has been declining over the last few years and has also been hit hard by the COVID-19 epidemic, it cannot forcibly enforce environmental measures that could unfavorably affect entire economically important sectors.

Even in the international arena, China's leadership, at least in terms of rhetoric, emphasizes a responsible approach to tackling global climate change. China is a signatory to the Paris Agreement on Global Greenhouse Gas Emissions and is seeking to build the "image" of a global "green" leader. For example, in 2020, Xi Jinping announced China's ambition to achieve carbon neutrality by 2060.

However, some Chinese actions contradict these objectives. An example is the construction of thermal power plants financed by the BRI in Africa and Europe, and also in Asian countries. China also remains the world's largest producer of carbon emissions, reaching record-high levels in recent years. However, this is understandable – China is the most populous state in the world and the second largest economy; thus, it is also a big polluter. At the same time, it should be borne in mind that these are absolute values, and when we convert these absolute figures into one person, China is a smaller polluter than even Norway. However, this does not minimize its contribution to the global environmental crisis, and it is necessary for Beijing to support actions that improve the environment because without its involvement in joint global efforts, it will not be possible to tackle climate change at a global level.

Notes

1 D. Gardner, *Environmental Pollution in China: What Everyone Needs to Know*, New York: Oxford University Press, 2018.
2 J. Worland, "9 out of 10 Chinese cities fail pollution test", *Time*, 2 February 2015.
3 P. Kwong, "China 2016 car sales surge at fastest rate in three years", *South China Morning Post*, 12 January 2017.
4 "Renewable internal freshwater resources per capita (cubic meters) – China", The World Bank Group, 2019.
5 Zhongguo zhengfu wang中国政府网, "Nan shui" run Jing jin 5 nian Beijing shou shui yu 52 yi fang, shouyi renkou chao 1200 wan 南水""润京近5年北京收水逾52亿方受益人口超1200万, Zhonghua renmin gongheguo zhongyang renmin zhenfu 中华人民共和国中央人民政府, 16 November 2019.
6 Gardner, *Environmental Pollution in China*.
7 G. Xia夏国才, Gao hao woguo shui ziyuan kaifa liyong de jianyi (er) 搞好我国水资源开发利用的建议（二）, Zhonghua renmin gongheguo guojia fazhan he gaige weiyuanhui, 中华人民共和国国家发展和改革委员会, 28 August 2018.
8 Ibid.
9 S. Wang汪恕诚, "Guanyu 'Zhonghua renmin gongheguo shuifa (xiuding cao 'an)' de shuoming" 关于《中华人民共和国水法（修订草案）》的说明, Quanguo renmin daibiao dahui, 全国人民代表大会29 August 2016.
10 Gardner, *Environmental Pollution in China*.
11 Huanjing baohu bu & Guotu ziyuan bu 环境保护部&国土资源部, "Quanguo turang wuran zhuankuang diaocha gongbao"全国土壤污染状况调查公报, *Zhonghua renmin gongheguo zhongyang renmin zhenfu* 中华人民共和国中央人民政府, 17 April 2014.
12 E. Brunner, *Environmental Activism, Social Media, and Protests in China: Becoming Activists over Wild Public Networks*, London: Lexington Books, 2019.
13 E. Gooch & F. Gale, "China's foreign agriculture investments", United States Department of Agriculture, 2018.
14 "National overview: Facts and figures on materials, wastes and recycling", United States Environmental Protection Agency, 2020.
15 B. Hoffman, "How increased meat consumption in China changes landscapes across the globe", *Forbes*, 26 March 2014.
16 H. J. Godgray et al., "Meat consumption, health, and the environment", *Science* 20, 2018.

17 Brunner, *Environmental Activism, Social Media, and Protests in China*.
18 Ibid.
19 Gardner, *Environmental Pollution in China*.
20 Ziyuan yu huanjing yanjiu zhongxin资源与环境研究中心, "Dianli, meiqi ji shui deng gongyong shiye hangye yanjiu mairu (weichi pingji)" 电力、煤气及水等公用事业行业研究 买入（维持评级）, Guo jin zhengquan, 国金证, 28 January 2020.

12 Xinjiang

Why has China imprisoned more than a million Uyghurs in re-education camps?

Barbara Kelemen

When news of so-called re-education camps in China's largest province (formally "autonomous region"), Xinjiang, began to appear in 2017, the Uyghur question was on the periphery of international events. Today, this issue is an important part of the discussions in international organizations and is emerging as one of the main areas of criticism of China in the sphere of human rights. However, what is the motivation of the Chinese Communist Party behind its policy in Xinjiang? And why is this region so important? Indeed, since early 2021, several countries, including the United States, the United Kingdom, and Lithuania, have declared China's policy toward the Uyghurs to be genocide. In addition, there is concern about a possible replication of the "Uyghur model" of the police state in other parts of China and even its exports to other countries. ***However, will the responses by foreign countries lead to a real change in Beijing's policy?***

Characteristics of Xinjiang

Xinjiang is nominally China's "autonomous region", which is strategically important for China not only in terms of its geographic location but also due to oil and other mineral reserves. In addition, nuclear weapons have been tested here since the late 1950s. Last but not least, the New Silk Road passes through this area (more in Chapter 16). Xinjiang stretches in the northwest of China and has an area of almost 1.6 million square kilometers. It is an ethnically diverse region where the majority of the population subscribes to the Muslim religion, especially the Turkish Uyghur people and, to a lesser extent, the Hui ethnic minority. In the 19th century, the term "Eastern Turkestan" began to appear, but it is rather a vague description of various territories and applies to two different short-term state units that existed for some time in the 1930s and later again in the 1940s. Nevertheless, the state-sponsored migration of the Han population from central and coastal provinces to the area has significantly changed the demographic composition of Xinjiang, and while in the 1940s the Turkish population represented 90% of the population, today it is only about half.

Given the remoteness of the region and its ethnic and religious specifics, the Chinese government tried various strategies to increase its control over the area

DOI: 10.4324/9781003350064-15

during the second half of the 20th century. Instead of integration, however, these have brought about an increase in local nationalism, and the region's population has come under the religious influence of neighboring Afghanistan and Pakistan during the 1980s.[1] The events of 11 September 2001, gave China the opportunity to present a new narrative that depicts Uyghur nationalism in the light of religious extremism and as part of a global jihadist movement.[2] This enabled the central government to present an increasingly authoritarian approach as part of the so-called "fight against separatism and terrorism". State authorities have targeted people from ethnic groups with predominantly Muslim religions, thereby grossly interfering with their privacy through, for example, surveillance or arbitrary detention. Part of this approach is the emergence of detention facilities, where China is estimated to have locked up over a million people for "re-education".

How did Xinjiang become part of China?

In the past, the territory of today's Xinjiang was an inconsistent entity ruled by various rulers or rival groups. The change occurred after the consolidation of Qing dynasty power in the second half of the 18th century, which, after a military victory over the Mongolian tribes in the area, introduced a unified military and later civilian administration. The result was a long-term presence of the Chinese empire in the region and the intensification of trade relations between Xinjiang and the Chinese hinterland. Thanks to the provision of a long-term land lease, many soldiers decided to settle in Xinjiang after a few months of service. Others who moved to the northwest were poor Han farmers with families, as well as members of the Muslim minority from other parts of China – the Hui people.[3]

Many of them came to Xinjiang because of the economic advantages provided by the government. For example, it often covered transport costs and provided cattle, tools, accommodation, or the possibility of a lower levy upon arrival.[4] Even after an increase in the population, the region was unable to pay enough taxes and, at the same time, the Qing dynasty did not have the will or financial means to increase the number of military personnel needed to control the whole region. These reasons caused riots to continue in various parts of the province. In addition to the Kashgar invasion carried out by the Kokandan population, in 1862, the Chinese Muslim population revolted in other Chinese provinces (Shaanxi, Gansu, and Qinghai), followed by the Hui and Turkic Muslims rebellion in Xinjiang in 1864. They managed to temporarily break free from the Qing dynasty, but not for long. In 1865, the kingdom of Kashgar was established in the area, led by the Kokand warrior Yaqub Beg. After his death, the Qing dynasty managed to suppress the uprising in 1884 and formally integrated Xinjiang into the rest of the empire as an official province.

Some Chinese authorities perceived the occupation of the area as a waste of money, but others believed that Xinjiang was an important buffer zone between China and neighboring countries in the west, protecting the Chinese hinterland from possible destabilization from abroad. After the fall of the Qing dynasty in 1912, there was chaos in the territory of Xinjiang. The lack of unified leadership or a comprehensive vision of Xinjiang's independence led to local struggles and various rebellions culminating in the declaration of the first (1933–1934) and later the second (1944–1949) East Turkestan Republic. While some perceive these two republics as the first attempts to establish an Islamic republic in this territory, there are different interpretations in the historiography of the extent to which these state units were based on Islamic teachings. However, other powers, such as the Soviet Union, which directly supported the emergence of the Second Republic, also promoted their interests in the territory during that period. The situation changed after the advent of the Chinese Communist Party government in 1949, which soon consolidated its power across the entire territory of China and launched a campaign against the Uyghur leaders of the former Turkestan republics. The party also implemented new reforms aimed at achieving political, economic, and cultural integration. In the late 1960s, the region became one of the victims of the Cultural Revolution (1966–1976) led by Mao Zedong. Not only did it devastate the already disturbed local economy, but the Red Guard terrorized the local population for several years. This led to the definitive rejection of the Communist Party by the local population in Xinjiang and also encouraged the rise of Uyghur nationalism and separatism.

China's "fight against terrorism" and Uyghur nationalism

Although the violent attacks on civilians in Xinjiang were sporadic in the 1990s, they were usually referred to in China as separatism rather than terrorism.[5] While the line between the two is often blurry, terrorism is of greater political importance, as the designation of a terrorist usually results in the complete delegitimization of a person. The main difference lies mainly in the tactics, which in the case of terrorism are directed against the civilian population with the aim to provoke fear in society. Separatist activities, on the other hand, are concentrated mainly on the territory claiming independence, and violence is directed mainly against the state (police and military units). Separatist groups, however, sometimes use terrorism tactics, which leads to frequent confusion and misuse of terms. China's deliberate confusion of these two concepts allows the state to control the narrative in a way that suits it. For example, the state can ignore the ethnic and social problems that lead to separatism and throw them off the table under the pretext of combating terrorism.

The violent incidents of some Uyghur separatists posed a constant threat from increasingly nationalist-minded groups that China sought to integrate. According to an unpublished study by RAND in 2000, there were 3,000 cases of civil violence in Xinjiang.[6] Following the 2001 attacks on the World Trade Center in New York and the increasingly frequent attacks by Al-Qaeda on the West, the issue of terrorism has come to the forefront globally, and in many cases, this term has become a political instrument that still makes it possible to delegitimize the opposition. At that time, China seized such a chance and embarked on its own "Fight Against Terrorism", which to this day is mainly focused on the Uyghur minority.

Originally, China's counter-terrorism strategy was focused mainly abroad. The geographical proximity between Xinjiang, Pakistan, and Afghanistan has caused many of the ideas associated with jihad and political Islam flourishing in the border areas to affect events in Xinjiang. After the completion of the 1,300-kilometer Karakoram highway between Pakistan and Xinjiang in 1979, Uyghur-Pakistani trade and cultural relations intensified. The fact that the Chinese government allowed the Muslim population to travel to Pakistan for religious education or to use it as a transit country on a Muslim pilgrimage to Mecca has also strengthened cultural influence. Uyghur youth even studied at the universities of Kabul, and some joined local Islamist groups at the time.[7] The influence of Islamic fundamentalism from Pakistan was also helped by the fact that China was materially supporting and even training Afghan Mujahideen in camps near Kashgar and Khotan.[8] That is why China already established contact with groups such as the Taliban or the Islamic Jamathias in the Afghanistan-Pakistan region in the 1990s. Chinese diplomats met several times with Taliban representatives and even established formal trade relations in 1999.[9] A direct flight between Kabul and the capital city of Xinjiang, Urumqi, was also introduced. The main reason for this policy was to ensure that the Uyghur groups that left China to take part in the jihad in Afghanistan did not return to Xinjiang, where they could attack the local population. The Taliban, which lacked finance and was diplomatically isolated from the rest of the world, accepted Chinese cooperation in the form of food and investment support. In return for this, Taliban officials agreed to the condition that they would not allow Afghanistan to become a home for groups intending to attack China.

However, since 2001, China's counter-terrorism strategy has increasingly focused on domestic events in Xinjiang. The daily acts of violence by separatist forces against the civilian population led to a government campaign called the "harsh strike against violent extremism" (in Chinese, *yanli daji baoli kongbu huodong zhuanxiang xingdong*). Mass arrests, extrajudicial executions, or abductions of many men and women of Uyghur origin followed. The process of Hanification continued, i.e., the process of settling the Han population in previously non-Han areas to assimilate the territory more quickly, which began at the end of the 1990s.

Many of the persecuted fled from Xinjiang to neighboring Pakistan, where they joined militant religious groups.[10] China also took advantage of the international horror following the 9/11 attacks and pushed the East Turkestan Islamic Movement into the United Nations sanctions terror list. From then on, the narrative surrounding the violence in Xinjiang was focused specifically on Islamic terrorism and not on separatism.[11] While this government campaign was initially seemingly successful, it later turned out that China had underestimated the ability of groups to mount attacks on the Chinese population. The violent riots in Urumqi in 2009, which claimed more than 140 victims and led to the temporary closure of the area, are now being described as a turning point.[12]

Violence has been among the most intense in the last decade, and attacks have apparently been ethnically motivated, leading to concerns about their impact on wider society. Other organized attacks in 2014 at the Kunming station and in the streets of Urumqi, which claimed 78 victims, caused a sudden change in how the Chinese leadership began to perceive the threat of ethnically diverse Xinjiang. The attack on Tiananmen Square in Beijing in 2013, during which a vehicle crashed into a group of people near the portrait of Mao Zedong and killed five of them, was also very symbolic. All these events led to legislative changes within the framework of the so-called anti-terrorism law and to a change in the definition of terrorism. Indeed, terrorism is now interpreted in China as any activity that threatens society and public order.[13]

These attacks also highlighted the increasing ability of some Uyghur individuals to organize and mount attacks beyond the borders of Xinjiang. The growth of the Islamic State (IS) and its propaganda videos, where IS fighters directly called on the Uyghur population to join them in Syria, also contributed to these concerns. In fact, it was later found out that many people from Xinjiang had actually left and joined the al-Nusra Front in Syria.[14]

The response of China's central government to the fight against domestic extremism would be a new strategy associated with so-called "re-education" camps. According to the Chinese government, camps – also called "re-education centers"– have allegedly the task of preventing the radicalization of the population. In reality, however, the new policy means arbitrary detention, violent indoctrination, and an effort to erase ethnic and religious identity that is not in line with the ideas of the Communist Party. Since the beginning of 2017, when the Chinese authorities approved a regulation on the forced "de-extremism" of their citizens, about one million members of ethnic minorities have been taken to these camps.[15]

Figure 12.1 Kashgar; old and new parts of the city (source: Zdeněk Horníček).

Conversion camps and the role of technology

The Chinese government's activity in Xinjiang has been escalating since 2017, when sophisticated technology was used to track people, including facial recognition camera networks that track, for example, children's expressions during class. The number of police patrols in the region has increased and public space has been militarized, with mandatory legitimacy and security checks (often similar to those at airports) before entering schools, banks, or parks.

However, the most radical change was the introduction of an algorithm that identifies so-called "suspects" on the basis of factors such as religious rituals, clothing, numbers of calls abroad, or even the length of a beard for men. If they do not suit a set of rules approved by Beijing, they are placed in re-education camps, where they are to be educated about their country – China. With accessible documents and testimonies, we now know that this "education", in addition to Chinese language teaching and the ruling party's ideology, includes forced labor and potentially torture.[16] The construction of re-education camps was mapped using satellite images of the East Turkestan National Awakening Movement, based in Washington D.C., and the Australian Strategic Policy Institute.[17] The first organization's annual research has mapped out the existence of 500 such centers. Some reporters even made their way directly to the camps and made videos that are available on the Internet.[18] Some of these camps look more "human", as they were specially prepared to be presented abroad during official excursions organized by China for invited diplomats and journalists. Pictures of the gathered children singing the Chinese anthem have also been released to the public. However, there are also images from camps that are more similar to prisons – they are surrounded by barbed wire and guard towers, and have bars on the windows.

Since the first reports that emerged in 2017, hundreds of thousands of cases of disappearances and deaths of many people of Uyghur and Kazakh origin have been documented, as well as reports of imprisonment of people from other Muslim ethnic groups. Among those imprisoned on charges of "separatism" are prominent personalities such as Uyghur economist Ilham Tohti, former rector of the University of Xinjiang Tashpolat Tiyip, singer Ablajan Awut Ayup, and writer Perhat Tursun, but also ordinary people who have never been members of any terrorist group. One such case is university student Guligeina Tashimaimaiti, who disappeared after returning from Malaysia, where she studied. Guligeina disappeared in December 2017 and was released from the re-education camp only in 2020 after Amnesty International organized an international event to rescue her. This and other similar cases show the inadequacy of the Chinese counter-terrorism strategy, which in practice resembles an attempt at violent assimilation and intimidation.

One of the other problematic aspects of re-education camps is the fact that technology is used in this strategy to *predict* whether someone will commit a crime in the future. Subsequently, these people are identified as dangerous and taken to re-education camps against their will. A document published by Human Rights Watch claims that Chinese authorities in Xinjiang have used databases of DNA and blood group samples collected during annual health checks to track the population.[19]

Figure 12.2 Linxia (Gansu), one of the main religious, cultural, and trade centers of the Chinese Muslim population (source: CEIAS).

In May 2019, evidence also emerged that, since 2016, China has systematically destroyed dozens of religious monuments and temples (mosques, churches, and also Buddhist and Taoist temples and statues).[20]

For some observers, the main problem with China's counter-terrorism strategy is its indiscrimination between two important processes: counter-terrorism itself, and the fight against radicalization. In February 2020, a leaked Chinese document, the so-called Karakax List, was published, which clarifies some of the reasons for the detention.[21] The document has 137 pages and contains a long list with more than 300 names of Uyghur women and men who were sent to correctional camps for "minor religious infection". This document shows that the Chinese government considers the signs of extremism to be, for example, face covering, growing a beard, contacting relatives living abroad, or visiting a foreign website. This is despite the lack of any evidence that they have participated in terrorist activities.

With this in mind, European countries and the United States strongly criticize China's activities in Xinjiang and re-education camps.

What does the rest of the world say?

In October 2018, Beijing confirmed the existence of re-education camps only under increasing pressure from accumulating evidence. But the controversial issue remains of how the rest of the world should approach the issue. From this point of view, the apparent silence of Muslim states, which have taken a neutral position on the Xinjiang issue, is also of the utmost concern. Many countries that criticized the situation in Xinjiang in the past or have been calling out Myanmar for the violations of the rights of the Muslim Rohingya minority remain this time uncritical of China's policies, and some even openly support them.[22]

Another problem is the participation of foreign companies in the forced labor of detainees – whether conscious or unconscious. The findings of February 2020 identified at least 83 international companies as possible customers of Chinese factories that use Uyghur forced labor to produce products.[23] Many of them work in factories that are involved in global brand supply chains such as Samsung, Adidas, Zara, or Apple. This includes imports of cotton by companies such as H&M or IKEA from Xinjiang, where the forced labor of the Uyghur population is most likely used.[24] As a result, many companies are currently facing growing criticism from the civil society of democratic states. But the decision by some companies to stop using Xinjiang's cotton has led to a boycott by Chinese consumers.

In May 2020, the US Congress passed the Uyghur Human Rights Policy Act, which was signed by former President Trump. The law not only condemns China's activities in connection with the establishment of re-education camps but also allows sanctions, blocking of assets, withdrawal of visas, and a ban on entry into the United States for those directly responsible for violence against the Uyghur minority or involved in human rights violations. The law also requires government agencies in the United States to issue an annual report on the situation of the Uyghurs every year. In June 2022, the US government implemented a new Uyghur Forced Labor Prevention Act, creating regulatory challenges for many foreign firms that operate and source their products in China.

The European Union has also been adopting some measures. In 2021, the EU sanctioned four Chinese officials and one state entity for their participation in human rights abuses in Xinjiang. Although the sanctions are largely symbolic and would hardly force China to change its course, they are the first EU sanctions on China since 1989 and thus send the message. In addition, the EU is devising a mechanism that would allow it to block imports that would involve forced labor in their supply chains. While the mechanism will be general, its drafting has been driven by the development in Xinjiang and is likely to be applied to the relevant cases.

While these actions specify China's responsibility for its treatment of the Uyghur minority, they do not yet have the potential to bring about a real change in Beijing's behavior and are more symbolic than substantial. Real change is likely to require active dialogue and increasing pressure combined with positive motivation. At the same time, the situation in Xinjiang also requires concerted action by the international community, not just by some individual countries. However, the lack of direct criticism of Muslim countries that do not want to get into conflict with China significantly weakens the effectiveness of international pressure.

Notes

1 R. Castets, "The Uyghurs in Xinjiang – The malaise grows", *China Perspectives* (49), September-October 2003, 34–48.
2 C. Chung, "China's 'war on terror': September 11 and Uighur separatism", *Foreign Affairs* 81(4), July–August 2002, 8–12.
3 S. Jiménez-Tovar & M. Lavička, "Folklorized politics: How Chinese soft power works in Central Asia", *Asian Ethnicity* 21(2), 2020, 1–25.
4 F. S. Starr, *Xinjiang: China's Muslim Borderland*, London: M. E. Sharpe, 2004.
5 M. Clarke, *Terrorism and Counter-Terrorism in China: Domestic and Foreign Policy Dimensions*, London: C. Hurst & Co., 2018.
6 Starr, *Xinjiang: China's Muslim Borderland.*
7 Ibid.
8 O. Klimeš, *Struggle by the Pen: The Uyghur Discourse of Nation and National Interest, c.1900–1949*, Leiden: Koninklijke Brill, 2015.
9 A. Small, *The China-Pakistan Axis: Asia's New Geopolitics*, London: Oxford University Press, 2004.
10 Clarke, *Terrorism and Counter-Terrorism in China.*
11 Ibid.
12 R. Steenberg & A. Rippa, "Development for all? State schemes, security, and marginalization in Kashgar, Xinjiang", *Critical Asian Studies* 51(2), 2019, 1–22.
13 International Federation for Human Rights, *China's New Counter-terrorism Law: Implications and Dangers for Tibetans and Uyghurs*, November 2016.
14 Clarke, *Terrorism and Counter-Terrorism in China.*
15 S. Nebehay, "1.5 million muslims could be detained in China's Xinjiang: Academic", *Reuters*, 13 March 2019.
16 B. Allen-Ebrahimian, "Exposed: China's operating manuals for mass internment and arrest by algorithm", *International Consortium of Investigative Journalists*, 24 November 2019.
17 N. Russer, "What satellite imagery reveals about Xinjiang's 're-education' camps and coerced labour", *Australian Strategic Policy Institute*, 16 July 2019.
18 "Inside China's 'thought transformation' camps", *BBC*, 17 June 2019.
19 "China: Minority region collects DNA from millions", *Human Rights Watch*, 13 December 2017.
20 L. Kuo, "Revealed: New evidence of China's mission to raze the mosques of Xinjiang", *The Guardian*, 7 May 2019.
21 C. Shepherd & L. Pitel, "The Karakax list: How China targets Uyghurs in Xinjiang", *Financial Times*, 17 February 2020.
22 B. Kelemen & R. Q. Turcsanyi, "It's the politics, stupid: China's relations with muslim countries on the background of Xinjiang crackdown", *Asian Ethnicity* 21(2), 2020, 223–243.
23 V. X. Xu, D. Cave, J. Leibold, K. Munro & N. Ruser, "Uyghurs for sale", *Australian Strategic Policy Institute*, February 2020.
24 E. Batha, "UK urged to stop cotton imports made in Chinese 'prison camps'", *Reuters*, 23 April 2020.

13 Tibet

Why is the mysterious "snowy kingdom" part of China today?[1]

Luboš Bělka

When you say "Tibet", many people think of adjectives such as "mysterious", "inaccessible", and "enigmatic", but also words such as "Dalai Lama", "People's Republic of China", and the "occupation of the Tibetan territory in the early 1950s". Many clichés and stereotypes about Tibet were created in the Western cultural space linked to the myth about the fabled "Shangri-la" valley as a paradise on Earth isolated from the rest of the world. The truth is that the "snowy kingdom" with its capital Lhasa has been hardly accessible to visitors for centuries. Firstly, the journey itself was always physically very difficult, and secondly, it was caused by the policy of isolation toward the rest of the world which the consecutive Dalai Lamas took. This situation persists more or less to this day, with any visit to Tibet being subject to the consent of the authorities, nowadays the Chinese ones. Sometimes the entire Tibet Autonomous Region is closed to people coming from abroad, officially for security and political reasons. Tibet, therefore, remains to some extent isolated from the rest of the world, preserving its mysterious image.

This "mysterious" history, as well as the recent memory of the Chinese occupation and related ongoing human rights violations, make an objective study of Tibet – and especially its relations with China – highly contested. Historical and political interpretations of the Sino-Tibetan relationship are based on different interpretations. The Chinese conception assumes that Tibet has "always" been part of China. However, there is also the opposite view in which Tibet was a sovereign and independent state, subjugated by China at some point in history. In some accounts, Tibet is even seen as having controlled China at one point. It is not our ambition to favor any of these interpretations; we aim to explain the existence of these different interpretations and try to base our conclusions on facts. In the international context, Tibet is often mentioned in regard to its position within China and the level of political rights of the Tibetan minority under the communist regime. Since other chapters in this book deal with human rights issues of different ethnic minorities in contemporary China, due to its complexity, this chapter will focus exclusively on the issue of Tibetan-Chinese relations. ***What are the origins of Tibet, and what were the historical dynamics of Tibet-China relations? How did the Dalai Lamas become the political leaders of Tibet, and how did the system change during the 20th century?***

DOI: 10.4324/9781003350064-16

The origins of Tibet

From a geographical point of view, Tibet is traditionally divided into three large territorial units: U-Tsang, Amdo, and Kham. U-Tsang with its capital Lhasa includes the heartland of Tibet and largely corresponds to what is today the "Tibetan Autonomous Regions" (TAR) of the People's Republic of China (PRC) – the second-largest province of the PRC after Xinjiang, but at the same time, the least inhabited one. The second territorial unit is Amdo, located northeast of U-Tsang. Most of Amdo is now part of Qinghai and Gansu provinces, and its territory has always been inhabited by diverse ethnicities. The same applies to the third territorial unit, Kham, which covers the southeastern part of Tibet. It is currently divided between the Chinese provinces of Sichuan, Qinghai, Yunnan, and TAR.

According to Tibetan traditions, it is unacceptable to penetrate the depths of the Earth and drill downwards, thus it is not surprising that the first major archaeological discoveries in Tibet took place only after the Cultural Revolution of the mid-1970s, and the excavations were led by the Chinese. Thanks to archaeological discoveries, we now know that the first population of Tibet dates back to about 50,000 BC. However, from the period before the introduction of the writing system, we have very little information, all intertwined with legends. Tibetan script has its historically well-known author from the 7th century, Thonmi Sambhota, an

Figure 13.1 Map of Tibet (source: CEIAS).

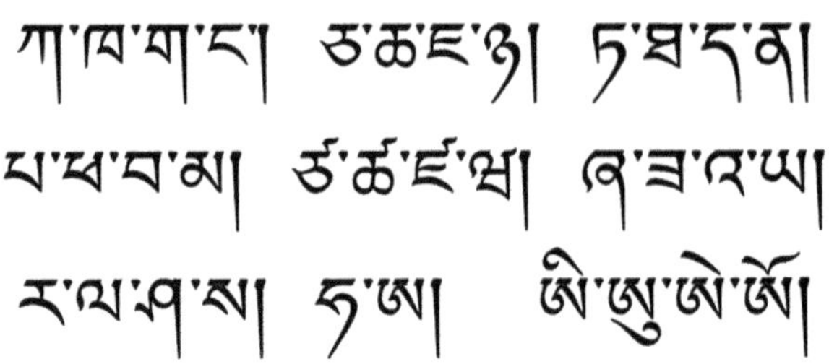

Figure 13.2 The Tibetan alphabet (source: Wikimedia Commons).

educated man from the Tibetan royal court, who was sent to India. There he got acquainted with the spoken and written Sanskrit, and a modified version of the script was established as the Tibetan alphabet.

Written sources about Tibet's distant past date back to the 13th century, when the first Tibetan historiographer Buton Rinchen Drub described primarily the religious history of India and Tibet with a special focus on Buddhism. These sources contain little information about the political history of Tibet. Even if we find some references to socio-political developments, these are often passages taken from Chinese sources, especially the standard history of individual Chinese dynasties. However, Chinese materials represent a one-sided source full of Sinocentric terminology. Nonetheless, Chinese sources are mostly used in the study of Tibetan history due to the lack of other documents. The absence of Tibetan historical sources is to some extent the cause of Tibet's unclear status in relation to China and, consequently, China's claims of Tibetan territory.[2]

The Tibetan Empire

At the end of the 6th century, the power of the Tibetan rulers was significantly strengthened, and the foundations of the future Tibetan Empire were laid in the Yarlung river basin, south of Lhasa. The foundations of the great empire were laid by Namri Songtsen (exact data unknown), according to legends the 32nd Tibetan king, who significantly strengthened the borders of the kingdom. With his son Songtsen Gampo (605–650), who extended the borders, Tibet entered the "great power" scene. The new state had also a new religious dimension. The king himself is considered the first Buddhist ruler of Tibet, as his two wives brought Buddhism to Tibet and introduced it as the state religion. Although Songtsen Gampo was a Buddhist ruler, traditional religion referred to as "Bon" (shamanistic religion) persisted in Tibet.

The legendary wives of Songtsen Gampo played an important role in promoting Buddhism in Tibet. They are both subjects of folk tales, as well as religious and artistic representations. Chinese sources always mention Princess Wencheng Gongzhu, the granddaughter of the Chinese emperor, first, and Princess Bhrikuti Devi, the daughter of the Nepalese king, only second. Tibetan texts, old and new, however, indicate the reverse order, which is an expression of past and present historical and political preferences.

During the reign of Songtsen Gampo, the transfer of the center of power from the valley around the Yarlung River to Lhasa (literally the City of the Gods) took place. Lhasa is home to the most revered and holy Tibetan Buddhist temple "Jokhang", literally the House of Lords (the Lord here is the statue of the great Buddha Shakyamuni).

Songtsen Gampo laid the foundations for the Tibetan Empire, which for more than 250 years was the dominant unit in inner Asia. Tibet flourished economically, militarily, and politically – which was also manifested in the territorial expansion into the surrounding regions, but mainly toward the west.

Another prominent king was Trisong Detsen (755–797), who became famous for consolidating Buddhist positions in not yet entirely Buddhist Tibet. Shamanism and similar teachings were widespread, and interfaith contact was more often violent than peaceful. Supporters of both religions were spread in all social strata, and there was no religious unity in the Tibetan government. It was Trisong Detsen who took a vigorous step in inviting the well-known Indian sage Shantarakshita to spread the Buddha's teachings even in non-Buddhist environments.

His mission was not entirely successful, and before his return to Nepal, he recommended to the monarch that he invite another sage, Padmasambhava. According to Tibetan legends, he was a man endowed with tantra power able to tame evil demons. The integration of local deities of the pre-Buddhist religion into the increasingly expanding Buddhist pantheon has proved to be a very effective way of spreading religion. Padmasambhava became a very popular figure not only in Tibet, where he is called Guru Rinpoche, but also in the surrounding countries where this form of Buddhism is widespread (Ladakh, Sikkim, Bhutan, Mongolia, Buryatia, Kalmykia, and Tuva).

Under foreign influence

In the first half of the 9th century, after a period of great rise, the Tibetan Empire found itself in decline. This period, characterized by the disintegration of state power and foreign domination, lasted until the Dalai Lamas came to power in the 17th century. There were more reasons for the collapse of the Tibetan Empire, but the main factor was internal disputes. An important moment was also the expansion of the Genghis Khan Empire, which dominated not only all of Asia, but its western outcrop reached into the territory of today's Poland. Thus, in Tibetan history, the Mongolian-Sakya government appears to be

> representing the first case of the long-standing involvement of a foreign power in Tibetan affairs, although, over the next three centuries, which represent roughly the time of the Ming Dynasty in China (1368–1644), Tibet remains *de facto* independent, even if it was plagued by domestic internal struggles.[3]

The relationship between Tibet and China during the Ming and Qing dynasties is aptly captured by the current Tibetanist Matthew Kapstein:

> A topic that has been debated at times concerns the actual extent of the Qing dynasty's control over Tibet and the adjacent Tibetan populations during the 19th century. On one extreme are those who argue that Tibet was fully and firmly a part of China under the Manchus, while oppositely some maintain that, except for a small number of forceful interventions, the later Qing had virtually no real authority among Tibetans, whatever nominal powers they may have arrogated to themselves. The truth seems to lie somewhere between these extremes.[4]

In short, Tibet operated more or less autonomously, but at some level recognized the authority of Chinese emperors, similarly to how authorities in Korea, Vietnam, and other countries in the wider Sinocentric system acted at the time. In this context, it must be borne in mind that prior to the 20th century, it is difficult to speak of clearly territorially delimited sovereign states in Asia as we know them today.[5]

The onset of the Dalai Lama

The most famous Tibetan word around the world is *Dalai Lama*, i.e., the title of the highest religious and secular representative of Tibet since the 17th century. However, the word itself is only partially Tibetan, since *Dalai* is the Mongolian term for the ocean or sea, and *Lama* is the Tibetan equivalent of the Sanskrit "guru", that is spiritual leader or teacher. The Dalai Lama is, therefore, "a teacher whose wisdom is as great as the ocean". For the first time, this title was awarded by the Mongolian prince Altan Khan in 1578 to the highest representative of the Tibetan Buddhist religious order called Gelugpa, the third representative of this order Sonam Gyatso. His two predecessors were then awarded the title retrospectively.

The principle of identifying the Dalai Lama in Tibetan Buddhism is very important. It concerns a "reincarnation" of an individual who by their own decision is (re)born to help other people on their way to awakening. In Tibetan terminology, it is called *tulku* (in Sanskrit *Bodhisattva)*, i.e., literally a "being of awakening". Sometimes, the term "living Buddha" is used for such individuals, but this is a misunderstanding of the Bodhisattva institution because Buddha is the one who would *not* be reborn again, thus fundamentally different from the Bodhisattva who *is* reborn again. Thus, every "living Buddha" would have to be the last born in the line, the one who would end this chain of rebirths.

The *modus vivendi* of "priest–patron" relationship between Tibet and China appeared for the first time in the 12th century, when the Western Xia dynasty in northwest China entered into a political–religious partnership with Tibetan high hierarchs. With the Dalai Lama's rise to power, the position of religion in society was strengthened, including from an international perspective, when the relationship between the "spiritual teacher" and "secular protector" was strengthened between the Dalai Lama and the Chinese emperor.

For several centuries, the governance of Dalai Lamas represented a period of "theocracy" – the union of secular and religious power in one person, the ruler. It started with the fifth Dalai Lama. This system is an arrangement in which religious hierarchs hold roles that belong to secular rulers in other systems. The role of the monarch was held by the Dalai Lama (or a regent during his infancy). The reluctance of some regents to hand over power to the newly enthroned Dalai Lama ended in their premature deaths.

The Tibetan system of governance required that monastic hierarchs and officials be directly involved in most governmental institutions. All the authorities except for the Dalai Lama had a dual system, in which each post was occupied simultaneously by two officials – an ordinary person and a monk. After the downfall of the Tibetan government in Lhasa in March 1959, this system also ceased to exist.

Tibet's annexation to China

Soon after the establishment of the PRC in 1949, the Communist government claimed the entire territory of Tibet and began to take steps to move from words to deeds. The occupation of the Tibetan territory began on October 7, 1950, when a major conflict took place between the tiny Tibetan army and the much bigger and more experienced Chinese army near Chamdo. The Tibetan army was defeated and surrendered on October 17, 1950. The advancement from there to Lhasa took a long time – the troops under the command of General Wang Quimei entered the Tibetan capital a year later, on October 9, 1951.

In the meantime, Lhasa requested assistance from the recently established UN (in which the PRC was not represented at the time). However, the effort was in vain, and the Tibetans found themselves in a situation in which no country was willing to stand up for them. Thus, on May 23, 1951, the High Representative of the Tibetan Government signed in Beijing the so-called Seventeen Point Agreement, officially known as the "Agreement between the Central People's Government of the People's Republic of China and the local government of Tibet for the conditions for the peaceful liberation of Tibet".[6]

The situation, in particular the economic one, was gradually deteriorating, especially in eastern Tibet where food supply problems became increasingly frequent. Tibet could not support the large number of new Chinese immigrants who due to the incomplete road network imported only parts of their nourishment, mainly rice. The rest of the food they bought in the places where they were currently located. The food crisis was the cause of unrest, which gained an armed nature and grew into local uprisings. Moreover, in 1956, the Chinese Communist Party was dominated by people who advocated for an accelerated socialization and communization. In Tibet, they introduced reforms that were not contained in the Seventeen Point Agreement.[7] Thousands of Tibetans thus moved from east to west, many to Lhasa, and tensions subsequently increased in U-Tsang.

The whole crisis culminated in mid-March 1959, when Tibetan soldiers set aside their brand-new People's Liberation Army (PLA) uniforms (under the Seventeen Point Agreement, the Tibetan military forces were integrated into the Chinese army) and together with armed civilians from all over Tibet revolted against Chinese domination. Beijing responded by deploying more troops and within a few days suppressed the uprising. After the unsuccessful uprising, the Dalai Lama fled into Indian exile and the victorious Chinese forces established in central Tibet a

> regime, that, as the former Secretary-General of the Chinese Communist Party Hu Yaobang said in 1989, was no different from the colonial regime. The Great Leap Forward and later Cultural Revolution and other absurd campaigns that, from the late 1950s until Mao Zedong died in 1976, hindered the meaningful development of China as a whole, were devastating the traditional Tibetan spiritual values and its fragile economy.[8]

The 1959 uprising was a key event in the history of Tibet – not only because of the departure of the Dalai Lama from the country (before the current 14th Dalai Lama, the 13th Dalai Lama Thubten Gyatso also lived in exile, even twice – in Mongolia and in India), but above all because of radical changes in the country itself. The Dalai Lama's reign ended, Tibet symbolically entered the 20th century, and Chinese influence completely dominated the country. Tibetans have revolted several more times; however, these attempts were always quickly and bloodily repressed. In recent years, a new form of resistance has emerged – public self-immolation of men and women, including clergy. These protests started in 2009 and resulted so far in more than 150 tragic deaths.[9]

Tibet's current situation in the PRC is largely determined by Beijing's religious, security, and economic policies. The decisive factor in determining Tibet's future is Beijing's conviction that Tibet is, and always has been, part of China. Moreover, no other country is realistically able and willing to challenge China's claims.

Tibetan exile in China

As a result of the political developments described above, many Tibetans followed the Dalai Lama and fled to India. The Tibetan exile community began to emerge in the late 1950s and today comprises more than 100,000 people. Other than India, Tibetans also found refuge in the United States and Europe.

While in exile, the current 14th Dalai Lama Tenzin Gyatso undertook significant reforms in the organization of Tibetan society. First, he radically changed the century-old policy of Tibetan isolation when he had to make the decision in the early 1960s whether Tibetan Buddhists and Bonists would open up to the world and meet the strong "demand for exotic Asian religion" in the United States and Europe.[10] An alternative idea was to continue the traditional social, religious, and political isolation – but in the conditions of Indian exile, it was naturally a problem.

The Tibetan exile community first attempted to continue the original notion of rule – the Dalai Lama as the head of the state with its government, the Kashag, composed of ordinary people and monastic ministers. This model proved to be outdated and unfeasible. As a result, the Central Tibetan Administration, as the exile government is called, has started modernizing its system. The most significant manifestation of this effort was when the 14th Dalai Lama relinquished secular power. In March 2011, he resigned from the leadership of the exile government and remained just the Tibetan Buddhist spiritual leader. Lobsang Sangay became the head of the government after the general democratic elections in which exiled Tibetans voted. Theocracy then officially ended.

The exile includes several specific features. One is the existence of the "twin monasteries". Its essence is that exiled Tibetans began to build monasteries with original Tibetan names just after they arrived in India, and their leaders were often the original abbots. Meanwhile, in occupied Tibet, the monasteries, especially during the Cultural Revolution, were destroyed, and so it happened that at some point in time, some Tibetan monasteries existed only in India. Since the 1980s, destroyed monasteries have been restored in Tibet, and there are now many monasteries with the same name in both India and Tibet.

The Tibetan exile government has not been officially recognized by any state. A government that does not have real power over its territory is always in question. For Beijing, the current Dalai Lama is a separatist, nicknamed "wolf in monastic clothing", and Chinese officials refuse to negotiate with him. But the Dalai Lama has abandoned his political powers in the process of democratizing the exile administration and keeps claiming that he only wants the autonomy of Tibet, as defined in the original Seventeen Point Agreement. For his non-violent opposition to the Chinese government, he was awarded the Nobel Peace Prize in 1989, which only added to his popularity in the world – but certainly not in official Chinese circles.

Panchen Lama and the future of the Dalai Lama

The second most prominent figure in Tibetan religious life, directly associated with the institution of the Dalai Lama, is the Panchen Lama, literally "lama, the great scholar". The aforementioned 5th Dalai Lama awarded the title of Panchen Lama to his main teacher Lobsang Chökyi Gyaltsen from the Tashi Lhunpo monastery, thus a student awarding a title to his teacher, a superior and higher-ranking person. Despite the fact, that the Dalai Lama is *de facto* higher than the Panchen Lama, it is the opposite from the religious point of view, because the Panchen Lama is the embodiment of the Buddha Amitabha, while the Dalai Lama is the embodiment of the Avalokiteśvara Bodhisattva, and Buddhas stand higher than Bodhisattvas in this religious system.

Interestingly, if there is a situation in which one of both hierarchs is already enthroned and the other is just recognized as a tulku, the enthroned person has the right to recognize the legitimacy of the other. The adult Dalai Lama thus confirms the child Panchen Lama and vice versa.

The most recent case of the recognition of the Panchen Lama has significant dramatic features and demonstrates the specific relationship between the Chinese Government and the Tibetan religious institutions. When the 10th Panchen Lama Choekyi Gyaltsen died in 1989, his monastery Tashi Lhunpo began the process of looking for and identifying his new incarnation. According to tradition, the 14th Dalai Lama played a key role here, and in 1995 he remotely recognized the six-year-old Gedhun Choekyi Nyima as the 11th Panchen Lama. A strong Chinese reaction followed: the new Panchen Lama disappeared together with his parents and, under the leadership of the Chinese authorities, another boy, Gyaltsen Norbu, was chosen by casting lots from the golden urn in the main temple of Jokhang in Lhasa. In December 1996, without the consent of the 14th Dalai Lama, he was enthroned in Tashi Lhunpo, and the Tibetans call him in a derogatory way the "Chinese Panchen" (even though he is an ethnic Tibetan). This event, well-known in the international context, marks a further development of relations between Beijing and Dharamsala, the Indian seat of the Tibetan government-in-exile.

Generally, the Dalai Lama's inability to achieve progress in dealing with China over the future of Tibet is an issue. The Chinese leadership seems to have concluded that they cannot expect to find accommodation with him and so decided to push ahead with modernization plans in the expectation of his eventual passing. Apparently, they hope that the Panchen Lama they have installed will have achieved wide enough credibility to be able to choose a new Dalai Lama, who will be respected by most in Tibet, if not among the exile community.

The big question, widely discussed, is who will be the next Dalai Lama. As we have already mentioned, according to the Buddhist doctrine, the Dalai Lamas are Bodhisattvas and supposedly decide about their future birth themselves. However, the reality is that people or institutions make the decision. However, there are two antagonistic positions in terms of the way of finding another spiritual representative of Tibetan Buddhism – the exiled Tibetan point of view and the Chinese one.

It seems likely that the reflections and discussions in the Tibetan exile on the future of the Dalai Lama institution will not prevent the Chinese government from selecting their 15th Dalai Lama, just as they did with the Panchen Lama. For the Chinese government, the choice of the Dalai Lama is a key issue that, in their eyes, symbolizes Beijing's sovereignty in Tibet, and is not open to any compromises.[11] We should note that the "Chinese candidate" will be, as in the case of the 11th Panchen Lama, an ethnic Tibetan, but absolutely loyal to the Communist Party. It is doubtful, however, that he will be widely accepted by the Tibetans – and it is probable we will end up with two 15th Dalai Lamas, as the Tibetans in exile will likely select their own.

Notes

1 The work on this paper was supported by the Czech Science Foundation grant No. 23-06406S "Representations and Role of Tibetan Buddhism in Narratives about Tibet from 1950s to Present".
2 M. Slobodník, *Tibet: Krajina, dejiny, ľudia, kultúra* [Tibet: Land, history, people, culture], Bratislava: Fidat, 1996.
3 M. T. Kapstein, *The Tibetans*, Malden: Blackwell Publishing, 2006.
4 Ibid.
5 D. C. Kang, *East Asia Before the West: Five Centuries and Tribute*, Columbia University Press, 2012.
6 T. W. D. Shakabpa, *Tibet: A Political History of Tibet*, New York: Potala Publications, 1984.

7 McKay Alex (ed.), *The History of Tibet: The Modern Period: 1895–1959, the Encounter with Modernity*, RoutledgeCurzon, 2003.
8 I. Bakešová, O. Kučera & M. Lavička, *Dějiny Čínské lidové republiky (1949–2018)* [History of the People's Republic of China (1949–2018)], Prague: Lidové noviny, 2019.
9 K. Buffetrille & F. Robin (eds.), "Self-immolation: Ritual or political protest?", *Revue d'Etudes Tibétaines* 25, 2012.
10 T. W. D. Shakabpa, *One Hundred Thousand Moons. An Advanced Political History of Tibet*, Leiden: Brill, 2010.
11 M. Slobodník, "A difficult rebirth: Tibetan reincarnations in the spotlight of Chinese religious policy", *SOS* 10(1), 2011, 57–80.

14 Hong Kong

How did the "pearl of the Orient" become a city of protests?

Martin Šebeňa

The most common view of Hong Kong presents a forest of glittery skyscrapers whose contours are mirrored in the waters of Victoria Harbour. When looking at a "vertical city," only a few people would guess that Victoria Harbour is a crater of an extinct super volcano that last erupted 140 million years ago, creating today's city shape.[1] *But the bright lights of one of the world's largest commercial and financial centers conceal much more than an old volcano. Behind the dazzling façade, the population's dissatisfaction has been growing for a long time; social, economic, and political conflicts have been intensifying, and a new identity of its citizens has been forming.* ***Why are the citizens of such a wealthy city taking to the streets in enormous numbers, and why are they fighting with the police? What does this have to do with the transition to Chinese rule in 1997 after more than 150 years of British colonial rule? Will the city retain a high degree of autonomy until 2047, as set out in terms of the agreement between the United Kingdom and the People's Republic? Are the British also responsible for the current problems, or do most of the issues arise from the authoritarian government of the current Chinese President Xi Jinping?***

City of myths

Hong Kong's modern history began in 1842 when China was forced to cede Hong Kong Island to Great Britain after losing in the First Opium War. At the same time, the first myths about Hong Kong began to form. One of the oldest is the myth of the "barren rock" Britain is said to have received from China. The myth stems from the statement of the British Foreign Secretary, Lord Palmerston, who was angry that the United Kingdom had only negotiated a "barren rock without a single house on it."[2] Indeed, there was not much at that time in the place where today one of the world's most important financial centers is located. Hong Kong Island is indeed mountainous, and its rocky edges slope steeply down into the sea. Therefore, ever since the colony was established, new land needed to be obtained by pouring sand and rocks into the sea. In the past 170 years, more than 70 square kilometers of new land were reclaimed, where about half of the population lives today.

DOI: 10.4324/9781003350064-17

However, this does not mean that no one lived in Hong Kong when the Brits first arrived. On the island's southern side lived the so-called *boat people*, a non-Chinese ethnic minority related to the Vietnamese population. On the eastern side were the dwellings of the Hakka people, who, while belonging to the ethnic Chinese majority, consider themselves immigrants, as they arrived in southern China in the late Middle Ages from the north and often inhabited peripheral and inhospitable areas. On the opposite side of today's Victoria Harbour, directly facing the British merchants, stood a large fortress of the Chinese army, named Kowloon after the peninsula on which it was located.

Today's territory of Hong Kong was created gradually in three steps. The original colony of 1842 occupied only Hong Kong Island. After the Second Opium War, it was expanded to include a part of the Kowloon Peninsula in 1860. The so-called "New Territories," the largest part of the colony, was added to Hong Kong in 1898. While the United Kingdom acquired the first two territories "permanently," the territory of the New Territories was only rented for 99 years.

The British nurtured the barren rock myth to highlight their merits in creating one of the world's premier trade hubs. Similarly, the local population claims that Cantonese has always been spoken in Hong Kong to enhance the value of their cultural heritage, on which they build their identity. The truth is that the Cantonese-speaking Chinese began moving to Hong Kong only after the first decade of British rule, during which life in the young colony was precarious.[3]

Myths are not limited to the beginnings of Hong Kong. One of the most widespread myths has long been that Hong Kong was the most economically free place

Figure 14.1 Victoria Harbour (source: CEIAS).

globally and ideal for business. This claim has had the backing of a prestigious US think-tank Heritage Foundation, and their annually published "Economic Freedom Index" saw Hong Kong occupying the top spot for 25 consecutive years until 2019.[4] The ranking, however, focuses on factors such as the absence of trade unions, the ease of dismissing employees, or the speed of setting up a company, and ignores massive state interventions in the economy.

While Hong Kong has since its inception been a free port in which ships from all countries could call and trade indiscriminately, local political elites have always strongly intervened in the local economy. In its management of the colonies, London would not provide much economic support for the local administration. Colonial governors had to secure income for their budgets locally, and one of the most common approaches involved land administration. Funds were typically raised through government land sales and auctions, taxing real estate transactions, and regulatory measures. The higher the price of real estate, the more can be collected for the treasury. Hong Kong's governments have always been interested in raising property prices, which they could achieve in two ways. One is to reduce supply, that is, limiting the area on which buildings can be built and slowing down the issuance of building permits. This also incentivizes the construction of ever taller buildings, which is why there are more skyscrapers in Hong Kong today than in any other city in the world. Another way of increasing property prices is to expand demand. The more people need housing, the higher the price of existing properties. Hong Kong has always attracted a high number of immigrants, which helped keep the demand steady. After the transfer of sovereignty to China in 1997, a policy of allowing 150 new immigrants from China to settle in Hong Kong every day helped maintain a relatively steady demand for properties.

The government's interventions have not been limited to the real estate sector, as the administration has actively created monopolies or oligopolies in several industries. This economic management system had gradually developed since the mid-19th century when powerful British trading firms settled in Hong Kong. They became rich mainly in the opium trade, and their enormous wealth guaranteed their political influence. While imports and exports of goods have always remained within the free-market domain and were spared from significant state interventions, wealthy tycoons have generated higher returns by investing in sectors such as energy, public transport, and construction. These areas are still heavily regulated, and only people and companies with excellent contacts with the government can conduct business in them.

During the first 100 years of the colony's existence, monopoly areas were dominated by British firms which originally grew rich through the illicit trade of opium, such as Jardine Matheson, Wheelock, or Swire. However, most of these empires went into financial trouble after World War II. They were often taken over by the new generation of Chinese tycoons, who, like the British, organized themselves into family clans and quickly established close cooperation with the colonial administration.

This cooperation also benefited from broader political circumstances. Since the 1970s, the British began to realize that their rule over Hong Kong was coming to an end and gradually shifted power to the local elites. However, Hong Kong's tycoons had no intention of advancing democracy, as they preferred to keep power in their own hands and only shared a small part of it with the local population. In this system, the interests of citizens were supposedly represented by the economic elites, i.e., the local oligarchy, which maintained a close working relationship with the colonial government, often in exchange for economic benefits. While a number of local people were co-opted into the administration, these were essentially part of the financial elite, and most of the ordinary people had little franchise in their city.

This political and economic system has practically functioned in Hong Kong to this day. When talks were held between the People's Republic of China and the United Kingdom on the future development of the city, the Chinese side had little interest in changing the governmental structure that *de facto* allowed the Chinese Communist Party to maintain control of the city without having to take into account the actual demands of the population. At the same time, it was important for Beijing in the 1980s to maintain good relations with local Hong Kong billionaires because it was mainly them who invested in China's fast-growing economy. While it may sound unbelievable today, as recently as in the 1990s, the GDP of the whole of China was only five times larger than that of Hong Kong, which was therefore very important for China.

City of protests

Although the British bureaucratic apparatus was reluctant to share power and its government was most helpful to billionaire circles, it must be acknowledged that the initially parsimonious colonial administration ultimately did provide substantially for the ordinary people. Especially under Governor Murray MacLehose in the 1970s, huge "new cities" were built, providing tens of thousands of cheap housing units for poorer citizens. The government also built the fundamentals of today's infrastructure, such as the subway system, tunnels connecting Hong Kong Island with the mainland, and water reservoirs. Hong Kong's education and health services have been supported by massive investments, taking them to a world-class level.

But these activities of the colonial government were not based on newly discovered compassion for the poor. They were a response to the violent events of 1967, which shook the character of Hong Kong and forever changed the neighboring Portuguese colony in Macau. Launched in China by Mao Zedong, the Cultural Revolution aimed to destroy old structures and also spread across the border to Hong Kong. At that time, Hong Kong found itself in a minor economic crisis when the post-war economic boom lost pace, and a large part of industrial production shifted to South Korea and Taiwan.

The significant social and economic disparities between the British and local Chinese populations, the weak economic position, and the Cultural Revolution across the border in China created an explosive situation. Massive strikes followed large protests on the first of May. The Communist Party's agitation drove protesters to violent attacks on the police and social figures, during which 15 people died.

The harsh reaction of the Hong Kong police led to 22 casualties among the protesters. The protests ended after a few months due to the response of the colonial police and the order of Chinese Prime Minister Zhou Enlai to stop the violence, but mainly due to events in China, where the situation got out of hand and repelled the people in Hong Kong.[5]

While the British administration stabilized the situation in its colonial possession, the events on the other side of the Pearl River had a different outcome. Although Portugal had deployed an army to quell the protests, it stood no chance against the Chinese-backed protesters. The riots resulted in the *de facto* end of the Portuguese administration in Macau, although it remained nominally under the Portuguese administration for the next three decades. Still, real power passed into the hands of the leader of the local communist revolutionary group that was taking orders from Beijing.[6]

The period after the violent protests of 1967 is marked by a significant social transformation that defines Hong Kong to this day. The administration's significant investments increased the population's well-being and re-started the local economy, which began to focus intensely on financial services. People born in Hong Kong prevailed over immigrants for the first time in the local population. Higher levels of education and resistance to the events of the Cultural Revolution led to the slow formation of local Hong Kong identity.

One of the distinctive features of the emerging identity was cultural expansion. Hong Kong's cinematography and music, known as *cantopop*, began dominating East Asia and became popular in the West during its heyday in the 1980s and 1990s. The professionalization of the state administration was also a source of pride, especially the elimination of corruption from the ranks of the police, which thus gained the hallmark of the best in Asia.

City in transition

The most significant event of the 1980s was the debate about returning Hong Kong to China. Since the early 1970s, the "expiry" of the 99-year-long lease of the New Territories became the center point of policymaking. Interestingly, although the lease did not concern Hong Kong Island or the Kowloon Peninsula, the United Kingdom eventually returned the entire territory of the colony to China. British Prime Minister Margaret Thatcher, encouraged by her country's victory over Argentina in the Falklands War, had initially no interest in returning Hong Kong to China. But China's adamant stance, led by the architect of China's economic miracle Deng Xiaoping and, according to superstitious Chinese observers, her unfortunate fall from the steps of China's parliament, forced her to compromise.[7] The Sino-British Joint Declaration was signed in 1984, in which Hong Kong's return to China was confirmed on the condition that the city would not have the same political and socio-economic system as China for the next 50 years. The population was to be left with the capitalist economic system, the rule of law, and civil rights and freedoms. This principle is known as "one country, two systems."

It is important to note that in the negotiations on the city's future, its citizens were largely left out. As only unelected colonial politicians participated in the negotiations, it was *de facto* a transfer of control over Hong Kong from one colonial power to another. Although local lawyers were invited to the later discussions on the form of the Hong Kong Constitution, it can be said that Hong Kong has never been truly decolonized.[8]

Responses to the agreement on the transition of Hong Kong to the Chinese administration differed. On the one hand, this event was welcomed by many local ethnic Chinese because they symbolically united with the homeland of their ancestors. They also believed that a rich and educated Hong Kong could lead China toward democracy and capitalism. On the other hand, a large part of the population panicked because they feared communist rule. More affluent parts of the population started the first wave of emigration to Western countries, mainly Canada, the United States, and the United Kingdom. The second wave of emigration began in the summer of 1989, after the massacre at Tiananmen Square in Beijing (more in Chapter 3). Hong Kong's citizens strongly supported China's democratic movement; therefore, its bloody suppression shocked the city. Up to a million people – a fifth of the population – took to the streets in protest.

Partial reassurance occurred after the arrival of the last governor, Chris Patten. Shortly after taking office in 1992, he introduced a number of democratic reforms, appointed several local politicians to top positions, and extended the right to vote to broader sections of the population. However, the Chinese government disagreed with most of these measures, describing Patten's measures as a last-minute effort to improve the image of British rule in Hong Kong, and invalidated most of them shortly after Hong Kong came under its administration on 1 July 1997.

City of problems

Although the closely observed transition to the Chinese administration was smooth and generated a wave of pride across China, the first years of Hong Kong Special Autonomous Region, as the new official name of the territory read, were marked by a sequence of adverse events. Between 1997 and 1998, the city was hit by avian influenza H1N1, and the economy was affected by the Asian financial crisis. Hong Kong's economic development was also slowed by China's WTO entry in 2001 since the city lost some of its competitive advantages as the "gateway to China." The most significant impact on the economy and life in the city was the deadly SARS epidemic, which almost stopped all activities for several months in 2002 and 2003 and caused 299 deaths.

In the first years after Hong Kong's return to China, the Chinese government interfered relatively little in the semi-autonomous territory, while civil society became more active. The commemorations of the Tiananmen massacre, held annually on 4 June since 1990, highlighted the anti-communist and pro-democracy efforts. Additionally, every 1 July, on the anniversary of the transition to Chinese rule, protesters marched in the streets to call for attention to the various issues in the territory.

In 2003, the First of July march turned into a massive demonstration when half a million people took to the streets. The first mass protest in Hong Kong under the Chinese administration was in response to the government's efforts to enforce anti-sedition laws, which the citizens perceived as drastic and as China's efforts to suppress the freedoms guaranteed to the city for 50 years after its return to China. The size of the protest surprised the city leadership, which eventually withdrew the bill. The shipbuilding magnate Tung Chee-hwa, the first politician after 1997 to hold the highest political position of the city's "Chief Executive," subsequently abdicated due to low popularity.[9]

The economic recovery after the SARS epidemic was slow due to the Chinese economy's rapid growth toward the end of the first decade of the 21st century. The government has therefore decided to develop the tourism industry. In a few years, the number of tourists, especially from China, multiplied several times, reaching 65 million a year.

Due to the city's socio-economic structure, tycoon families benefited the most from the newly brought wealth, helped by massive infrastructure projects such as the construction of a new airport, a bridge across the Pearl River to Macau, and a high-speed railway. Most of such projects were built by construction companies controlled by the local oligarchy. They aimed to facilitate the arrival of as many tourists as possible, mostly staying in tycoon-owned hotels. Ordinary people shared very few of the benefits of the sprawling tourism industry. At the same time, they faced the downside of overcrowding, which led to the rise of negative attitudes toward mainland Chinese tourists in the city.

The widening gap between the affluent elites and the rest of the population has been exacerbated by the government's long-term policy of raising property prices to collect more taxes. This combination of social inequality, the rising cost of living, reduced public space due to overcrowding by tourists, and the Chinese government's increasingly frequent efforts to interfere in the running of the city have translated into growing frustration and social tensions in the city.[10]

Another open manifestation of civil discontent was the 2012 protests against the government's efforts to introduce patriotic education, which many Hong Kong residents perceived as "brainwashing." A new generation led by high school students from the *Scholarism* group took the initiative, rejected the traditional attempt of pro-democracy politicians to seek a compromise, and promoted a confrontational style. The protests succeeded in forcing the government to withdraw the laws.

The city in flames

Since Chinese President Xi Jinping came to power in 2012, the Chinese government has clearly adopted a more hardline stance toward Hong Kong. China is more directly involved in the city's governance, condemns civil society activities, and, in particular, has changed its legal system (more in Chapter 9) by "interpreting" the Basic Law, i.e., Hong Kong's mini-constitution. One of the most significant interventions was the interpretation of the 2014 Hong Kong Chief Executive's

Elections Act, in which the Chinese government decided that while there would be a universal right to vote in elections – as stipulated in the Basic Law – the candidates would be pre-selected by Beijing. While everyone could vote, only the chosen ones could run for office.

In response to this decision, tens of thousands of people spontaneously took to the streets. The attempt of the police to deploy tear gas to disperse the protesters was unsuccessful, and the protesters occupied the streets in the city center for the next three months. The "umbrella movement" – as the event began to be called when umbrellas were used against tear gas – ended when the protesters did not reach their immediate demands and eventually left the streets voluntarily. But the movement has definitively confirmed the end of the policy of compromise and the use of confrontational tactics by the new generation. During the protests, the police were politicized by the Hong Kong government, thus losing their neutrality and, consequently, their prestige in the eyes of the population.[11]

The Umbrella Revolution has also accelerated the building of local identity. It is based on emphasizing local traditions, which were manifested, for example, in the protests against the removal of historic buildings from the city center. Supporters of "localism" drew the most attention during the so-called "fishball revolution" in 2016, named after the local delicacy the government wanted to ban street hawkers from selling. The movement also supported the right to self-determination; some even began to call for Hong Kong's independence, enraging the Chinese government.

The second pillar in identity-building is the sense of distinction from China. Due to the fact that China and Hong Kong developed separately for one and a half centuries, differences have arisen between them, especially in socio-cultural areas. The most striking difference is in language. While Cantonese is spoken in Hong Kong and traditional characters are used to write the language, the official language in China is standard modern Chinese, sometimes also referred to as "Mandarin Chinese," written in simplified characters. Since the handover in 1997, the Chinese authorities have been trying to enforce teaching and official communication in standard Chinese, which runs counter to a great deal of resistance from the local population.

More than a million people have moved to Hong Kong from China since the transition to Chinese rule, which locals often perceive as colonization. Moreover, unlike previous immigration waves, the "newcomers" refuse to adapt to the local culture. On the contrary, these people often expect the local population to accept their culture, which is most evident in the emphasis on using standard Chinese instead of Cantonese. The anti-Chinese sentiment, which is growing in response to this dynamic, has become a significant part of the local identity. This sentiment, however, sometimes grows into open discrimination against the mainland Chinese, which in turn generates negative perceptions of Hongkongers on the northern side of the border.

After the Umbrella Revolution, the government only took limited steps to address, at least in part, the city's underlying social, political, and economic problems. However, the oligarchic model inherited from the times of the British rulers

Figure 14.2 Protests in Hong Kong in 2018 (source: Wikimedia Commons).

has been taken to the extreme, nearly halting social mobility and critically exacerbating urban inequality.[12] Moreover, in the fight against democratic activists, the government has adopted the so-called "lawfare" tactics, which amounts to the abuse of the legal system. After the 2014 protests, the government not only arrested and tried the protest leaders but also pursued elected members of the local parliament.

A frustrated society exploded again five years after the Umbrella Revolution. In June 2019, millions of people repeatedly took to the streets to protest an extradition law that would allow the Hong Kong government to extradite people to China. Although the government withdrew the laws after several weeks of protests, the demonstrations gained huge popular support, mainly in response to police brutality. The intensity of violence on both sides gradually increased and culminated in violent clashes on university campuses in November. Temporary calming occurred after the local elections in December, in which the anti-government candidates scored an overwhelming victory. The outbreak of the coronavirus epidemic at the end of January 2020 stopped all protest activities.[13]

City of the future?

For a long time, the citizens of Hong Kong enjoyed many political freedoms comparable to those of Western countries, including the freedom of speech, free press, and freedom to protest. However, civil liberties should not be conflated with democracy. Although Hong Kong's society has gradually democratized over the past four decades, during the COVID-19 pandemic, a sudden turn of events took place: pro-democracy parliamentarians were expelled from parliament at the end of 2020, and then in March 2021, the rules were changed to allow only "patriots" to run, which in practice means only people approved by the Chinese government. The local administration called these processes leading to a homogeneous parliament an "effort to stabilize society."

Political theory posits that a political system that provides freedoms without democracy is inherently unstable and either democratizes or people's freedoms are taken away.[14] In the 1990s, in the aftermath of the collapse of the Soviet bloc, there was a belief that democracy would eventually assert itself in China and that Hong Kong would democratize. But with Xi Jinping taking over as the general secretary of the Chinese Communist Party, a second option seems more likely – that Hong Kong's citizens will gradually lose their remaining freedoms. The constrained parliament, the loss of police neutrality, and the undermining of the independence of the judiciary are the most significant steps that indicate that the city is moving in this direction. Civil society has tried hard to halt or at least slow down this trend, but its chances against an increasingly authoritarian China are slim.

In July 2020, China's central government enacted national security laws with the stated goal of punishing an extreme minority of people who it believes seek to undermine Hong Kong's stability and China's sovereignty over it. But the laws have already curtailed many freedoms, including freedom of speech, severely restricting the independence of the judiciary, allowing the Chinese police to move into the city, and are extremely draconian. Moreover, a Beijing-imposed electoral overhaul denied the participation of pro-democratic candidates in the December 2021 elections, resulting in the creation of a rubber-stamp legislature. The national security legislation and electoral changes represent such a significant interference in the city's governance that it is possible to speak of a turning point in which the policy of "one country, two systems" ends and a period of accelerated integration with the Chinese mainland starts.

Notes

1 K. Wong, "Hong Kong formed by rare super volcano eruption", *SCMP*, 31 August 2012.
2 "Speech by FS at Asian Financial Forum cocktail reception", *HKT*, 20 January 2010.
3 C. Munn, *Anglo-China: Chinese People and British Rule in Hong Kong, 1841–1880*, Richmond: Curzon Press, 2001.
4 K. Leung, "Hong Kong loses ranking as world's freest economy due to months of unrest", *SCMP*, 17 March 2020.
5 J. M. Carroll, *A Concise History of Hong Kong*, Hong Kong University Press, 2007.
6 C. A. Mendes, *Portugal, China and the Macau Negotiations, 1986–1999*, Hong Kong University Press, 2013.
7 "China media: Remembering Margaret Thatcher", *BBC*, 9 April 2013.
8 Wir für Hong Kong, "The decolonization of Hong Kong", *Taipei Times*, 26 November 2019.
9 A. Dapiran, *City of Protest: A Recent History of Dissent in Hong Kong*, Australia: Penguin, 2017.

10 T. Summers, *China's Hong Kong*, Agenda Publishing, 2021.
11 H. Fu, "Police and the rule of law", *HKU Legal Scholarship Blog*, 2014.
12 S. Cartledge, *A System Apart: Hong Kong's Political Economy From 1997 Until Now*, Australia: Penguin, 2018.
13 A. Dapiran, *City on Fire: The Fight for Hong Kong*, Australia: Penguin, 2017.
14 "The most likely outcome for HK", *Webb-site Reports*, 3 September 2019.

15 Taiwan

Why does China consider it its own and what does it mean for Taiwan?

Kristina Kironska

Although the People's Republic of China (PRC) is now considered to be China, its predecessor before 1949 was the Republic of China (ROC) under the rule of the Chinese Nationalist Party (Kuomintang, KMT) and President Chiang Kai-shek. After they lost the Civil War with the Communists, the Chiang Kai-shek regime – together with about two million people – withdrew to the island of Taiwan, where the ROC still exists today in an altered form. However, despite the loss of control over the Mainland, the ROC represented China in the UN Security Council until 1971 as one of the victorious states of World War II and as a result of the United States and many other states failing to recognize the Communist government in Beijing as China's legitimate representative. After 1971, however, Taiwan found itself more and more in international isolation – it lost its membership in the UN (and in most other international organizations) and today maintains diplomatic relations with only 14 small states (the largest one being Paraguay). This situation is the result of a complicated relationship with the PRC, which seeks to unite the island with the "motherland".

Taiwan (officially still the Republic of China), de facto independent of China (officially the People's Republic of China), is located southeast of the Chinese Mainland, from which it is separated by a strait 180 km wide. On a relatively small area with an almost uninhabitable mountainous center, the country has more than 23 million inhabitants. This, of course, means a high population density, especially in the west and north of the island. Taiwan has its own government, parliament, currency, army, control over its borders, and relations with other states. In Taiwan, traditional Chinese characters are used, which are different from those in China since the Communist Party in the 1950s introduced simplified characters to support the literacy rate. The Taiwanese passport is also widely recognized – 145 countries grant visa-free entry to Taiwanese citizens, while Chinese citizens have visa-free access in only 79 countries. ***So why does China still insist that Taiwan is one of its provinces? Why did Taiwan never declare*** **de jure** ***independence? How do the people in Taiwan feel about their identity?***

DOI: 10.4324/9781003350064-18

History of the island

The island was originally home to an Austronesian population, which today is in the minority – only one in fifty Taiwanese belongs to it. Today, Taiwan is home to more than 14 indigenous tribes and three major language groups – Atayalic, Tsouic, and Paiwan.[1] You might have heard of Kavalan whiskey – its name is also derived from one of the tribes in Taiwan. This indigenous cultural heritage is important – Taiwan is considered to be the original territory of the Austronesian-speaking people who now inhabit most of the small islands of Oceania and even Madagascar.

In the 16th century, Portuguese seamen named the island *Ilha Formosa*, the Beautiful Island. At the beginning of the 17th century, it was occupied by the Dutch and later for some time by the Spanish. This was followed by an inflow of Hokkien and Hakka people from today's Chinese provinces of Fujian and Guangdong. This gradually changed the demographic structure and connected the island to the Chinese world. Chinese pirate Koxinga (also known as Zheng Chenggong) plays an important role in Taiwan's history – he moved to Taiwan after the Ming dynasty lost control of the Mainland and he expelled European colonizers. After several decades, the Qing dynasty defeated Koxinga's descendants and gained control of the island in the late 17th century. However, the less populated inland remained virtually outside the state administration.

At the end of the 19th century, Taiwan's status within the Chinese empire was elevated to the provincial level, but under the Shimonoseki Treaty which ended the First Sino-Japanese War with a clear victory for Japan, China had to hand over the island to Japan. Therefore, from 1895, Taiwan was under the colonial administration of Imperial Japan. The ceremonial handover of the island took place on board a Japanese vessel due to fears of repression by the island's population. After suppressing the movement against the Japanese occupation and the conquest of the then capital Tainan in the South, Japan introduced significant socio-economic and political reforms to turn the relatively backward island into a showcase colony and thus prove its status to Western powers. Japan's efforts were aimed at improving the economy, and cultural Japanization, and supporting Japanese military aspirations in the Asia-Pacific region, which culminated in World War II.

During the war, Japan committed several war crimes – it was known for its drastic treatment of prisoners and forcibly holding so-called *comfort women* who had to serve the Japanese soldiers as sex slaves. Most of these women came from occupied territories, including Taiwan. The Japanese government has repeatedly apologized for the war crimes it committed and promised compensation to the South Korean survivors but has not yet commented on the Taiwanese ones. In 2020, there were only two women from Taiwan still alive waiting for justice and an official apology from Japan.[2]

Nevertheless, today's view of the Taiwanese population on Japanese domination is rather positive, in contrast to Korea or Mainland China. Japan brought infrastructure and education, and in the last two decades of its rule, Taiwan was considered an integral part of the Japanese Empire, while Korea, for example, was an exploited colony. Many old Taiwanese people today still speak Japanese, and the younger generation is also quite favorable toward Japanese culture.

Figure 15.1 Political map of Taiwan (source: Nationsonline.org).

Transfer of the Republic of China to Taiwan

After the capitulation of Japan in World War II, Taiwan became by the decision of the Allies one of the provinces of the ROC (which was established in 1912 after the overthrow of the emperor). In 1946, the Civil War broke out on the Mainland, in which the ruling KMT was defeated by the Communists. Chiang Kai-shek – still representing the government of the ROC – moved to Taiwan in 1949 and declared Taipei the war capital of the ROC.

With the withdrawal of the ROC to Taiwan and the declaration of the People's Republic of China on the Mainland, there were two entities representing China from 1949 onwards, both originally claiming the same territory. However, since the early 1990s, after the first constitutional reform, Taiwan is only exercising sovereignty over the main island, Taiwan, and the smaller outlying archipelagos of Penghu, Matsu, and Kinmen. However, the official name "Republic of China" remains, and China unequivocally rejects any steps toward a formal declaration and international recognition of its independence.

Since its arrival, the KMT in Taiwan has functioned as a state party (similar to the Communist Party in China), whose government has been characterized by a low level of protection of human rights and civil liberties. This is evidenced by the "Incident 228" of February 28, 1947, when the island population revolted against the authoritarian rule of the KMT. The uprising was violently suppressed, killing thousands. The massacre started the era of the so-called White Terror, during which tens of thousands of people disappeared, were murdered, or ended up behind bars. To deal with this period, the Transition Justice Commission was set up in Taiwan in 2018 tasked with examining the period between 1945 and 1992 (when the so-called mobilization period to suppress the Communists officially ended) and seeking justice in the form of giving recommendations, many of which are passed by the parliament in the form of laws.

Loss of the UN seat and diplomatic isolation

Since the 1950s, the issue of China's representation has appeared on the UN agenda every year, with the ROC and the PRC fighting for the seat representing China, while ensuring continued veto power in the UN Security Council. The gradual decline in international support for Taiwan, which had no control over the Mainland for more than 20 years, culminated with the loss of the UN seat in 1971, shortly after the United States under President Nixon established contact with the PRC.

Crucial to the establishment of relations between the United States and the PRC were three joint statements from 1972, 1979, and 1982, known as the Three Communiqués, in which both sides agreed to respect each other's national sovereignty and develop mutual ties. Moreover, the United States formally acknowledged that "all Chinese on either side of the Taiwan Strait maintain there is but one China" and declared that it would end formal political relations with the Republic of China while preserving economic and cultural ties.[3]

The US Embassy in Taipei was abolished in 1979, and the liaison office in Beijing was upgraded to an embassy. The United States switched recognition to the PRC and severed official diplomatic relations with Taiwan. The US Congress responded to this presidential initiative by adopting the Taiwan Relations Act (TRA). This law is essential, as although the United States does not officially recognize Taiwan as a sovereign state, the absence of official diplomatic relations does not affect the application of US law with respect to Taiwan – the same legal principles apply as if Taiwan were a standard state. Relations with the island take place through the so-called American Institute in Taiwan, which is officially a private non-profit organization. In practice, it serves as a standard embassy.

The United States has been a key international partner for Taiwan. As early as 1950, after the outbreak of the Korean War, the United States prevented Communist troops from invading Taiwan, thus halting the further spread of communism. Over the next two decades, the United States guaranteed Taiwan's security through a bilateral intergovernmental agreement. After 1979, this guarantee is vaguer due to the severance of diplomatic relations. The TRA does not automatically specify the provision of military protection by the United States in the event of an invasion of Taiwan, but it stipulates that it will provide relevant means of defense. In practice, the United States allows the Taiwanese government to purchase military equipment while maintaining the so-called policy of strategic ambiguity regarding supporting Taiwan in the event of military intervention. During the Third Taiwan Strait Crisis in 1996–1997, when China fired ballistic missiles in Taiwan's vicinity, the United States sent an aircraft carrier to Taiwan's waters to signal support. After the Fourth Taiwan Strait Crisis in 2022 (following the visit of the Speaker of the US House of Representatives), however, there were numerous discussions about a potentially changed US stance from ambiguity to an open declaration of military support of Taiwan, as President Joe Biden has repeatedly hinted so in his speeches.

Thanks to American support, Taiwan has maintained *de facto* independence to this day. Gradually, however, Taiwan keeps losing official diplomatic allies to China, and as of 2022, the island has diplomatic ties with only 14 small countries in the world. With China's growing relevance in the international arena, the vast majority of states have decided to maintain diplomatic relations with the PRC, although also preserve unofficial "economic and cultural" contacts with Taiwan (as the One-China Policy – to which countries have signed up by establishing official ties with the PRC – does not allow recognizing both the PRC and Taiwan at the same time).

As for international organizations, Taiwan is a full member of only a few dozen such organizations, typically with an economic focus, which China tolerates. However, it strongly opposes any international activity that would show that Taiwan is an officially recognized sovereign state, i.e., membership in such organizations, where only sovereign states can be members. Taiwan seeks to circumvent this isolation through non-profit organizations supported by the government and its participation in various international fora.

Despite alternative ways of cooperating with the world, diplomatic isolation has an impact on many issues. In 2020, this manifested itself, for example, in connection with the outbreak of COVID-19. Taiwan is not a member of the World Health Organization (WHO) due to China's objections. However, thanks to the consistent approach of the authorities and the discipline of the population, Taiwan managed at the beginning of the pandemic to keep the number of infections low, and it serves as an example of how a democratic regime can deal effectively with a similar problem – even without WHO membership.

Taiwan's economic miracle

The "economic miracle" in Taiwan is considered to be the period when the economy experienced a rapid growth rate, and the country joined the so-called Four Asian Tigers along with Hong Kong, Singapore, and South Korea. Taiwan's gross national product grew by a staggering 360% between 1965 and 1986.[4] While agriculture was the main sector in the 1950s, today the domestic market is dominated by industry and services, and most exports are made up of IT products. Well-known brands include Acer, ASUS, Gigabyte, and HTC.

Key to the island's development was the land reform implemented between 1951 and 1975, effectively ending the unfair land distribution left behind by the Japanese occupation administration, and significantly reducing the gap between the rich and poor. As KMT officials came from the Mainland and had no ties to local landowners, they did not wish to maintain the previous system. The reform thus helped the government to stabilize the situation on the island and gain political support among ordinary people, which was not high after the violence during the period of White Terror. The ultimate goal of the reform was to make the farmers the owners of the fields they cultivated. At the same time, the original landowners did not fare badly either – the government compensated them with bonds or shares in state-owned enterprises. The capital was then used by many of them for creating their own businesses.

In the first phase of the economic reforms, the development plan focused on the transformation from an agricultural to a production-oriented economy. The country first focused on textile production, which is a well-known driver of economic growth in developing countries, as fabric production is the most labor-intensive. Later, Taiwan shifted to consumer electronics, which eventually paved the way for the development of the semiconductor industry, which was another major important driving force. In the late 1980s, the service sector finally became the most dominant sector. During this period, Taiwan applied an export growth strategy, always trying to improve a certain product to such a level that it became internationally competitive. The government subsequently invested the proceeds from the sale of goods on foreign markets in technological improvement, infrastructure, and education.

Throughout the process, the state, same as in Japan, South Korea, and Singapore, has played a significant role in the economy. Although these states practice capitalism, they have not hesitated to interfere significantly in the economy. There is no consensus among economists on the effectiveness of these steps, but these countries have managed in just a few decades to move from the position of poor developing countries to the level of developed Western states.

Democratization

Economic growth and related intra-societal changes gradually began to put pressure on political change. In the 1980s, the KMT ruled Taiwan in an authoritarian fashion with martial law still in place. The growing middle class combined with international diplomatic isolation and also the position of the United States eventually led the government to seek legitimacy in other alternative ways.

The KMT initiated – under domestic and international pressure – the liberalization of the old regime, followed by democratization and the introduction of free elections. Chiang Kai-shek's son – Chiang Ching-kuo began the process, and a major player was Lee Teng-hui who chaired the KMT after Chiang Ching-kuo's death, as his protégé. In 1996 he was elected president in the first direct election. He was the first president to speak publicly about the 228 Incident – until then, speaking of the White Terror was taboo. From a foreign policy perspective, Lee played an important role since he unilaterally ended the official state of war with the Chinese Communist Party and abandoned sovereignty claims to the Mainland. Lee's presidency was significant also because he was the first president born on the island; this strengthened the local Taiwanese identity. After leaving the presidency in 2000, Lee was expelled from the KMT because of his support for Taiwan's independence. However, the processes he started have continued.

Despite its expulsion from the UN, Taiwan has voluntarily acceded to many international agreements. In 2009, Taiwan accepted two major human rights covenants – the International Covenant on Civil and Political Rights (ICCPR) and the International Covenant on Economic, Social, and Cultural Rights (ICESCR),

Figure 15.2 Pride 2022 in Taipei (source: Amnesty International Taiwan).

making them legally binding. Moreover, Taiwan is one of the countries with the highest percentage of women in politics. In 2019, Taiwan became the first country in Asia to allow same-sex marriages. Today, Taiwan presents itself in the world as the only culturally Chinese democracy and one of the most advanced democracies in Asia, along with Japan and South Korea. Despite progressive trends, there are also various human rights violations in the country, such as the use of the death penalty or, until recently, the criminalization of adultery (abolished only in May 2020).

The system of two strong parties and the issue of identity

The biggest domestic rival of the KMT is the Democratic Progressive Party (DPP) which transformed from a protest movement in the 1980s into the main political opponent of the KMT. The DPP came to power for the first time in 2000 when Chen Shui-bian won the presidential race. Among other things, the first DPP president renamed state-owned enterprises which bore the name "China" signaling that while the KMT was originally a Mainland Chinese party, the DPP was a domestic Taiwanese party.[5]

The Taiwan party system is characterized by two strong and several smaller, less important, parties. The KMT is the leader of the "blue" coalition of parties and is considered a pro-Chinese party due to its legacy. The DPP is the leading force in the "green" coalition and stands for limiting Chinese influence in Taiwan. The rise of political opposition in Taiwan led China to side with the KMT – turning four decades of hostilities into cooperation.

Traditionally, northern Taiwan used to be blue and the south green, but this division is slowly disappearing. The blue parties usually conduct their campaigns in Mandarin Chinese while the green parties outside the capital mostly in Taiwanese.[6] The name of the big neighbor is also strongly politicized – the blue proponents use the name "Mainland China" or just "Mainland", and the green people call it simply "China".

The system of two strong parties in Taiwan is closely linked to the question of identity. Descendants of the Chinese who came to the island from southern China prior to the 20th century are considered "locals" (in Chinese, *benshengren*). Their mother tongue is mostly Taiwanese, one of the variants of the Chinese language that evolved from a language spoken in the Chinese province of Fujian (where people call it Hokkien). There are also people in Taiwan who speak Hakka, also one of the Chinese variants. It is quite common in southern Taiwan that the elderly do not speak Mandarin Chinese, which is the country's official language, and speak only Taiwanese. Although the Taiwanese language does not have an official written form, the government is trying to maintain it, and since 2001, it has also been taught in schools as an elective compulsory subject – with every pupil having to choose either Taiwanese, Hakka, or one of the indigenous languages.[7]

The second wave of immigration from China started after the Civil War with Chiang Kai-shek's people arriving on the island. These "newcomers" (in Chinese, *waishengren*) settled mainly in the north of the island and were not Taiwanese or

Hakka speakers, as they came from various parts of China. Today, the vast majority of the people in Taiwan were born on the island, but family origin – local or newcomer – still plays a role.

The issue of identity in Taiwan is fluid, politically sensitive, and is the subject of endless debates. The proportion of those who consider themselves exclusively "Chinese" is gradually declining, with less than 3%, according to a survey from 2020. On the contrary, the proportion of people considered to be exclusively "Taiwanese" has been growing, reaching 67% (compared to only 17.6% in 1992).[8] Overall, a large part of the population considers themselves culturally Chinese and politically Taiwanese. In addition, more than 70% of respondents are currently in favor of removing the word "China" from the English name of the country (*Republic of China*) on the passport to avoid confusion with Communist China. In July 2020, the Taiwanese parliament passed two resolutions calling on the government to emphasize the name "Taiwan" on the passport cover, as well as on the planes of the national "China Airlines" – which is often confused with Chinese airlines.[9]

The last presidential election in Taiwan took place in January 2020. Acting President Tsai Ing-wen (DPP) and Kaohsiung Mayor Han Kuo-yu (KMT) ran for office. The issue of identity was omnipresent in these elections also due to the ongoing protests in Hong Kong – which highlighted the uneven relationship with

Figure 15.3 Gigantic loudspeakers built in 1967 in Kinmen (under Taiwan's control), from which during the Cold War anti-communist propaganda was broadcasted toward Mainland China, 2 km across the sea (source: CEIAS).

China. The older generation does not see an eminent danger in China's growing power – the *status quo* has been maintained in Taiwan for decades, and people have lost their fears of China taking the island by force. Likewise, Taiwanese business circles do not want to lose ties with China – which is by far the largest trading partner, currently with more than 40% of Taiwanese exports and 70% of investments going to China.[10] Many Taiwanese companies produce their goods in China because of the cheaper labor costs. Therefore, the rhetoric of the KMT – having close economic relations with the Mainland, thanks to which Taiwan's economy is growing – is of interest to many people on the island. Thus, many voted for the KMT candidate.

In the end, the incumbent president won the election for a second term, and her opponent was even (unprecedentedly) removed from his post as the mayor of Kaohsiung in a popular vote by the city's residents. Most young people strongly oppose the Chinese Communist authoritarian system, which is why they are more inclined toward the DPP and President Tsai, who is very cautious about Beijing's policies and their long-term intentions. In addition to the situation in Hong Kong, her victory was helped by the growing assertiveness of the Chinese president toward Taiwan, which aroused people's sense of threat and distrust in China's rhetoric of unification based on the formula "One state, two systems". Looking at the fragmentation of freedoms in Hong Kong, more and more people in Taiwan think that something similar would happen to them if they agreed to some form of union with Beijing.

One of the political responses of the DPP and the Tsai administration to problematic relations with China is the *New Southbound Policy* – promoting economic cooperation with South and Southeast Asia and Oceania. The reasons for this policy are the expected rapid economic growth of these regions and, at the same time, the slowdown of China's growth; Taiwan's desire for greater regional participation; and especially difficult relations and deepening economic dependence on China. However, it is questionable whether this will be successful – successive Taiwanese governments have been trying to reduce the dependence on China for a long time.

However, economic relations in the Taiwan Strait developed even before the legalization of trade in the late 1980s (until then, it was illegal in Taiwan to trade with China). In 1994, President Lee Teng-Hui (KMT) called on Taiwanese companies to invest in Southeast Asia, but the Asian financial crisis of 1997 disrupted this plan. In 2002, President Chen Shui-bian (DPP) tried to reintroduce a Southbound Policy, but economic impulses played a stronger role than political preferences, and Taiwanese people continued to invest in China, which was a much more attractive investment destination for them.[11] During the rule of President Ma Ying-jeou (KMT), Southeast Asia was not a priority; on the contrary, connections with the Mainland continued to grow – he allowed, among other things, direct air links between the island and the Mainland (previously people had to fly via Hong Kong). During his rule, Taiwan even accepted a Chinese diplomatic gift (as part of an exchange program) – two pandas named Tuan Tuan and Yuan Yuan, whose names when put together mean "unification".[12] China is a very attractive destination for Taiwanese businesspeople due to the language and similar culture. An example is the company Foxconn, which has built its business model on serving as an intermediary for foreign companies (e.g., Apple) and manages production for them in China.

The future of Taiwan

Taiwan is a very specific player in the international arena, and there are endless discussions about its status and future development. The position of the PRC has not changed since the end of the Civil War – it insists that there is only one China in the world, of which Taiwan is a part. In addition, it considers the issue of Taiwan's status to be an internal Chinese affair and responds irritably to any indication of Taiwan's independence. This applies, for example, to the visits of foreign dignitaries to Taiwan, but also to international companies that present Taiwan on their websites as a territory separated from China. In addition, in 2005, China passed a law legalizing possible military action against the island if it declared *de jure* independence. In China, there are 2,000 ballistic missiles aimed at Taiwan.[13] From China's point of view, it is precisely the military threat that has ensured that Taiwan has not yet declared itself *de jure* independence.

Taiwan's position is complex and has evolved over time. The KMT government in Taipei at first presented itself as China's legitimate representative for many decades and rejected considerations of Taiwan's independence. According to some analysts, the island has missed several chances in the past for declaring *de jure* independence due to ordinary vanity – the KMT leadership refused to abandon the original goal of conquering the Mainland: (1) in 1949, when the Chinese Civil War ended with the defeat of the Chiang Kai-shek, who retreated to Taiwan, and the new Communist government on the Mainland declared the PRC; (2) in 1971, when the UN withdrew the status of China's legitimate representative from the ROC and replaced it with the PRC; and (3) during the Cultural Revolution (1965–1976), when Mainland China was in turmoil.[14] It was not until the 1990s that the island's leaders formally abandoned the idea of re-conquering the Mainland. However, the situation has changed, and China is now blocking any efforts for Taiwan's independence – for example, at the UN, where it vetoes Taiwan's membership efforts.

The two main political parties and the people of Taiwan agree that the regime in Taiwan is sovereign and independent of the PRC. In addition, however, there are divisions over the identity and appropriate form of interaction with China. Taiwan's national consciousness is growing among the younger generation, and they are very angry when their country is described by foreign companies and international organizations as *Taipei and environs*, *Chinese Taipei*, or as a part of China. It can be assumed that they will be more aggressive on the issue of independence in the future. In addition, the "pro-Chinese" KMT has been weakened since the last election, and it is being debated whether revitalization of the party is possible at all.

Of course, the future of the island is not separated from geopolitical realities and China's growing power. According to a recent survey, only 5–10% of Taiwan's population is in favor of the immediate formalization of the status of a sovereign

Figure 15.4 President Tsai Ing-wen during a protest against nuclear energy in Taipei in 2019 (source: CEIAS).

state associated with a possible change in the name of the state and the constitution. This low number is likely related to the Chinese threat of military conflict. In addition, 21% wish to keep the current *status quo* and a declaration of independence in the future. On the other hand, less than 2% of Taiwan's population wants immediate unification with China, and another 9% would like to unite with China sometime in the future. Thus, most Taiwanese people are inclined to maintain the *status quo*.[15]

What is this *status quo?* Can it really be maintained in the long run? On one hand, China is becoming more powerful and, according to the current Chinese leader Xi Jinping, does not intend to wait forever to unite with Taiwan. From a military point of view, the Chinese military would be able to defeat the island, but Taiwan's strategy is to increase the potential cost of such an intervention to a level that is unacceptable to China. In addition, Taiwan relies to a considerable extent on support from the United States. That is why military conflict is unlikely – but not entirely impossible. Chinese power is also manifesting itself in other ways – for example with fewer countries in the world maintaining diplomatic contacts with Taiwan. It is

Figure 15.5 Taiwanese people's perception of cross-strait relations, May–June 2022 (source: Sinophone Borderlands Indo-Pacific Survey (R. Q. Turcsanyi, K. Kironska, A. Gerstl, M. Arnez, J. Čeněk, J. Chen, R. Chen, A. Chubb, P. Gries, T. Wang, "Sinophone Borderlands Indo-Pacific Survey", Palacky University Olomouc, 2022)).

questionable whether and how Taiwan's status would change if it lost all of its diplomatic allies. In addition, China is using its influence to limit non-diplomatic contacts between other states and Taiwan, thus deepening its international isolation. On the other hand, Taiwanese public opinion and political positions have become less in favor of any kind of unification with China over time. It is hard to imagine this long-term trend in Taiwan reversing in the future, leading to growing gaps between the preferences of people in Taiwan and the geopolitical reality of China's power.

Notes

1 J. K. Tse, "Language and a rising new identity in Taiwan", *International Journal of the Sociology of Language* 143, 2000, 151–164.
2 A. Yu, personal communication, Taipei, June 2020.
3 D. P. Chen, *US-China Rivalry and Taiwan's Mainland Policy: Security, Nationalism, and the 1992 Consensus*, New Jersey: Palgrave Macmillan, 2017.

4 J. Kiprop, "What was the Taiwan miracle?", *World Atlas*, 18 May 2018.
5 E. Niou & P. Paolino, "The rise of the opposition party in Taiwan: Explaining Chen Shui-bian's victory in the 2000 presidential election", *Electoral Studies* 22, 2003.
6 G. Schubert & J. Damm, *Taiwanese Identity in the 21st Century: Domestic, Regional and Global Perspectives*, Routledge, 2012.
7 E. Hubbs, "Taiwan language-in-education policy: Social, cultural, and practical implications", *University of Arizona, Working Papers in SLA & Teaching* 20, 2013.
8 "Taiwanese/Chinese identity (1992/06–2020/06)", *Election Study Center, National Chengchi University*, 3 July 2020.
9 K. Everington, "Over 70% favor removing 'China' from Taiwan passport", *Taiwan News*, 30 March 2020.
10 J. Chiang, "Taiwan's new southbound policy and the looming election", *The Diplomat*, 25 October 2019.
11 K. Kironska, "Taiwan-Myanmar relations within the framework of the new southbound policy", *International Journal of Taiwan Studies* 4(2), 2021, 345–375.
12 "Taiwan to accept 'unification' pandas from China", *Reuters*, 14 August 2008.
13 "China on track to aim 2,000 missiles at Taiwan: Report", *Reuters*, 19 July 2010.
14 A. Chun, "Convergences and divergences within the 'new' Greater China", *Current History* 117(800), 2018, 235–240.
15 T. Miu & F. Huang, "Over 27% of Taiwan people support independence: MAC Poll", *Focus Taiwan*, 26 October 2019.

Part III

International relations

16 China in the world

A New Silk Road to world dominance?

Matej Šimalčík

Opening the Chinese economy to the world and adopting reforms initiated by former leader Deng Xiaoping in 1978 led to the rapid growth of gross domestic product (GDP) in the following decades. While the Chinese GDP was less than USD 150 billion in 1978, it was worth USD 13.5 trillion four years later. China has become the world's second-biggest economy, following the United States (or third if the European Union is considered one economic unit). Simultaneously with the economic growth, Chinese defense spending is steadily increasing, and Chinese leaders are becoming more actively involved in the world's politics. China currently has the second-highest defense spending, of USD 237 billion, in the world. High-level government officials during the Xi Jinping era have visited three times as many countries since 2013 as during the 30-year Mao Zedong era.[1]

The noticeable growth of China's power potential since the days of Deng Xiaoping raises many questions about China's interests and intentions in international politics. ***What are the main goals of Chinese foreign policy? Is China trying to achieve global dominance? How does the Belt and Road Initiative relate to the Chinese strategy? Is China a peaceful and benevolent power or an expansive aggressor?***

What is China's deal?

To understand China's behavior in the international arena, it is necessary to first ask the question of what goals China is pursuing. One of the main determinants of China's foreign policy is so-called core interests – a concept developed by Dai Bingguo, a high-level Chinese diplomat during the era of President Hu Jintao. Dai outlined three core interests that should represent fundamental determinants of China's foreign policy: survival of the Chinese Communist Party (CCP) and the preservation of its power monopoly, continuation of China's social and economic growth, and preservation of its sovereignty and territorial integrity.[2]

In addition to motivating Chinese behavior, the core interests are also the red lines of what China sees as acceptable actions by other states. China itself will not act contrary to its core interests, and it will not tolerate the behavior of other states if it should jeopardize China's core interests. However, the content of the three core interests is not entirely explicit, as these are flexible concepts that have not been clearly defined. The malleability of these three interests means that they evolve

DOI: 10.4324/9781003350064-20

dynamically over time. Nevertheless, by studying various official and semi-official documents and statements of Chinese politicians, we can identify their main defining features.

Of the three core interests, the survival of the CCP and preserving the system of government of the so-called socialism with Chinese characteristics are highly important. Therefore, China's core interests are mainly the interests of the CCP. These goals are fulfilled (if we omit repressive measures to suppress dissent) mainly by satisfying the material and immaterial needs of the Chinese population in order to preserve the domestic legitimacy of the CCP. In other words, the Chinese population – or rather the relevant part of it – is satisfied with the CCP government, because it meets their demands for rising living standards and, in their eyes, defends "the Chinese national honor".[3]

At the same time, fulfilling the material needs of the Chinese people is achieved by observing the second core interest – China's continued social and economic development. The essence of this aspect is to maintain China's high economic growth rate. In the last 40 years, it has averaged almost 10% per year, reaching a maximum in 1984, when China's GDP increased by as much as 15%. However, China's economic growth has slowed in recent years, reaching 6.1% in 2019 and further falling as a result of strict "zero-Covid" policies of the Chinese government. To sustain its economic growth, China needs a stable and relatively open international system within which it can develop trade relations with other countries.

The immaterial needs of the Chinese population are inherently linked to the third core interest – preserving China's sovereignty and territorial integrity. In this regard, Chinese media typically discuss several disputes on the Chinese periphery, such as Taiwan, Tibet, the South China Sea, the East China Sea, Xinjiang, and Hong Kong. China does not perceive these issues only in terms of physical territorial integrity but also on a symbolic level. The sovereignty-related core interests can therefore also be seen as the nationalist demands of the Chinese population to strengthen China's power position and its prestige within the international system.

The inclusion of symbolic sovereignty under the concept of core interests helps explain China's asymmetric response to situations that, from our point of view, do not seem very significant. For example, the symbolic dimension of China's foreign policy puts pressure on companies that describe Taiwan, Hong Kong, or Macao as separate entities. Another example happened when the Speaker of the US House of Representatives Nancy Pelosi visited Taiwan in 2022 and met with President Tsai Ing-wen – China interpreted the visit as interfering in its internal affairs and responded with massive military exercises in Taiwan's vicinity. The Chinese people see the issue of symbolic sovereignty as one of China's most critical issues. A 2014 public opinion survey showed that, according to more than half of the Chinese population, territorial conflicts in the South China Sea and East China Sea are among China's most pressing problems. Comparable importance is attached to environmental issues.[4]

Interestingly, although the CCP considers socio-economic development and sovereignty as key issues on which its survival depends, they are often in mutual contradiction. Given that the development of trade relations requires positive relations with other countries, the assertive enforcement of the requirements of symbolic sovereignty tends to undermine efforts to develop trade relations. Therefore, China's foreign policy is largely shaped by an effort to balance existing tensions between the need to build foreign relations and satisfy domestic nationalist needs. Therefore, China often promotes the development of international relations in the long term (e.g., via the Belt and Road Initiative), while in the short term, it takes steps to satisfy the nationalist passions of the Chinese population. In the event of an international crisis, it can also be assumed that the Chinese government will primarily observe the domestic dimension of its foreign policy, and the impact on relations with the rest of the world will bear only secondary considerations.[5]

Is China a peaceful superpower?[6]

China itself likes to claim that its Confucian heritage predisposes it to peaceful behavior, contrary to what China perceives as an aggressive policy of Western countries. Chinese President Xi Jinping also emphasizes this mantra. "The Chinese people have always been peaceful. Our love for peace is firmly rooted in Confucianism", Xi said in a speech to the International Confucian Association in 2014.

In imperial China, Confucianism was the dominant political theory. It was suppressed during the Mao Zedong era, but since Deng Xiaoping came to power, it has gradually become one of the dominant ideological trends in Chinese political thought, including foreign policy thinking and the so-called "Chinese school" of international relations.

Confucian strategic culture (a system of norms and symbols influencing the perception of the world and China's position in it) is based on three main elements: the rejection of violence, preference for defense over offense, and the concept of righteous war.[7] Their interaction subsequently influences China's perception of the use of force in international relations, the perception of potential adversaries, and the choice of appropriate means to neutralize threats.

The preference for non-military instruments, however, does not automatically mean benevolence. The Chinese military thinker Sun Zi had similar thoughts, writing in *The Art of War* that the supreme art of war is to subdue the enemy without fighting. As a result, China tries to influence the preferences of other states to align with Chinese interests through co-optation, positive attraction, and self-example, so that it can win the "hearts and minds" of the local population. Moreover, China often uses non-military means to gain influence over local elites, to manipulate information flows, and to censor uncomfortable opinions to ensure the uncritical spread of China's worldview.[8]

Yet Confucianism also allows several exceptions when the use of force is acceptable. The first exception is the use of force in self-defense.[9] This is even epitomized in Mao Zedong's statement: "If someone doesn't attack us, we won't attack them; however, if someone does attack us, we will definitely [counter] attack."[10] The second exception is the use of force to restore "virtue" (*de* in Chinese) as the basic value of the Confucian normative system. Virtue can be translated into modern language as the moral legitimacy of a government that cares about the common good of society. Confucianism, therefore, demands military intervention where the state's power is not morally legitimate and suppresses the rights of its citizens.

Confucian perceptions of the world and international politics within China's self-reflection can be summarized as pacifist. Due to this self-perceived peacefulness, China has developed a mentality of institutionalized paranoia (the so-called siege mentality), which manifests in a lowered threat perception threshold of Chinese political leaders, diplomatic corps, and military. The perception of its own pacifism means that China commonly perceives the behavior of other states as inherently offensive and interfering with its sovereignty.

However, the siege mentality is not only the result of Confucianism itself but is also influenced by Chinese historical experience, the authoritarian system of government, and the deliberate strengthening of popular nationalism by the Chinese government. Especially the "century of humiliation", when a major part of the Chinese empire came under the control of Western powers (more in Chapter 1), is cited by Chinese leaders as a disaster that cannot occur again.

The issue of institutionalized paranoia can be best illustrated by many of China's territorial conflicts with neighboring states. In the South China Sea (see Chapter 18), neighboring Southeast Asian states have their legitimate claims to parts of the maritime space under the United Nations Convention on the Law of the Sea (UNCLOS). Yet China sees their claims as a violation of its sovereignty allegedly based on historical rights, despite China itself having joined UNCLOS, thereby committing itself to respect its rules. In 2016, an international tribunal decided that Chinese maritime claims had no basis in applicable international law. Nevertheless, China rejects this ruling.

Confucian pacifism, along with other factors, thus leads to hyperbolization of threats, making China paradoxically more prone to using force to defend its interests. The lowered threshold for threat perception means that Chinese leaders subjectively perceive as threats even situations that may not pose a threat in objective terms. The term Chinese "cult of defense" has been used to describe this situation.[11]

Therefore, China itself interprets any military skirmishes in which it has engaged in its modern history as self-defense. Following this line of thinking, China joined the Korean War because it felt threatened by the US-led UN troops approaching the Yalu River border with China as part of an offensive against the North Korean military, although UN troops did not cross the border. Recent events of the "cult of defense" can be well demonstrated by the skirmishes on the Sino–Indian border in June 2020. In this skirmish, China assessed building infrastructure in the Indian-controlled part of the disputed border as an acute threat, therefore engaging in violent conflicts with Indian troops (more in Chapter 18).

The tendency to perceive threats to Chinese sovereignty more sensitively has intensified significantly since President Xi Jinping came to power. "No foreign power can expect China to sell its core interests and swallow the bitter fruit of undermining its sovereignty", Xi Jinping said in 2013. Similarly, in 2018, Xi, in an interview with US Secretary of Defense James Mattis, said: "We cannot lose even one inch of the territory left behind by our ancestors. What is other people's, we do not want at all". However, determining whether any of the peripheral territories belong to China or to one of its neighbors is complicated, as some of the disputed borders are either not adequately defined (as in the case of India), or China claims "historical territory" in contradiction of applicable international law (for example, in the dispute in the South China Sea).

China's growing feeling that its sovereignty is under threat is also evidenced by the growing number of references to the need to protect China's sovereignty, territorial integrity, and maritime rights in Chinese strategic documents. While China's 2010 White Paper on Defense mentioned sovereignty only five times, its 2013 edition refers to sovereignty 12 times, and its 2019 edition as many as 15 times.

China's soft power

The previous section highlighted the self-perceived cultural preference for soft power approaches toward managing relations with other countries. Joseph Nye has famously defined "soft power" as the ability of one country to get other countries to want the same things as it itself wants by relying on the attraction of values rather than economic inducement or military coercion.[12] Nye later calibrated his theory, arguing that to achieve desired policy outcomes, states must skillfully coordinate soft and hard power strategies.

Unlike Nye's original theory, Chinese scholars of soft power (and policymakers) have a broader conception of what constitutes soft power. Beyond the traditional focus on culture and values, Chinese scholars also look at China's development model as a potential source of soft power. This model could be attractive to a host of developing nations as an alternative to the established orthodoxy of the "Washington consensus".

Within Chinese scholarship, the concept of soft power is understood not only as having an external focus but also a domestic one. Under this concept, soft power is targeting domestic audiences as much as foreign ones – a development consistent with the "core interests" theory discussed above. Thus, the motivations to develop soft power in China are both foreign and domestic. Xi Jinping's urge to "tell the China story well" aims to promote a positive image of China and mitigate existing negative perceptions. In turn, improved perceptions of China abroad can turn to CCP's improved domestic legitimacy and create a sense of national pride in China's own culture, thereby shielding the country from perceived Western cultural intrusion.[13]

However, in the practice of authoritarian states such as China, the concept of soft power is regularly distorted beyond its original meaning, by blurring the lines between promotional and coercive measures aimed at influencing its image abroad, both among the public and elites. This led to a push to reconceptualize Chinese power and strategy by new frameworks of analysis such "sharp power", "authoritarian image management", "strategic corruption", or "corrosive capital". While new thinking about Chinese power allows us to grasp current Chinese foreign policy better, this theoretical fragmentation also highlights the challenge posed by China's rise to traditional thinking about international relations.

In practice, Beijing's approach to improving its image abroad and achieving an international environment more conducive to its interests is based on various measures. Chief among them is the promotion of elite relations, spreading of pro-China messaging in foreign media, and establishing relations with academics in the hope they will act as narrative multipliers.

Down the New Silk Road

The issue of Chinese intentions has been highlighted in connection with the Belt and Road Initiative. The official Chinese name for the initiative ("One Belt One Road", *yi dai yi lu*) is relatively confusing for foreign audiences, as counter-intuitively the term "road" refers to maritime routes, and the term "belt" refers to land infrastructure (roads and railways) across the Eurasian continent. This is one of the reasons why the initiative in foreign languages has gradually acquired various names, and to this day there is a wide range of them. In some countries, the name "New Silk Road" is used instead. This chapter uses the internationally accepted term "Belt and Road Initiative" (BRI).

The BRI is currently one of the main pillars of China's foreign policy doctrine under Xi Jinping. It was announced at the beginning of Xi's government in 2013 during his visits to Kazakhstan and Indonesia. While in Kazakhstan, Xi presented the terrestrial part of the BRI entitled "The Economic Belt along the Silk Road":

> To forge closer economic ties, deepen cooperation and expand development space in the Eurasian region, we should take an innovative approach and jointly build an "economic belt along the Silk Road". This will be a great undertaking benefitting the people of all countries along the route. To turn this into a reality, we may start with work in individual areas and link them up over time to cover the whole region."

Later, during a visit to Indonesia, the maritime component of the BRI was presented under the title "21st Century Maritime Silk Road". At the time of the announcement, it was not yet fully known what its content and magnitude would be. However, the BRI's' ambiguity at the time was rather deliberate, as it allowed China to gradually adjust its content to evolving Chinese interests and international reactions. The first official document outlining China's' plans was not published until two years later in 2015, and the first international summit took place only in 2017.

Since the initiative's' announcement in 2013, more than 130 countries have signed up. Among the EU member states, as many as 18 of them signed BRI memoranda of understanding with China. However, the signing of the memorandum itself is only a declarative act, which in principle does not imply any rights and obligations for signatories, let alone preferential access to Chinese investment or the Chinese market. Contrary to common myth, the BRI is not an international organization with membership, structure, or processes. The BRI is perceived by the public mainly in connection with infrastructure construction (railways, motorways, ports, bridges, etc.) and the financing of these projects. However, in Chinese politics, the BRI plays a much more comprehensive role and serves several policy objectives that are strongly linked to China's' core interests.

One of China's' main interests connected to the BRI is to contribute to China's' socio-economic development, especially in the less developed western provinces. China has long struggled with the uneven development of its provinces, where the provinces on the Chinese coast were benefiting from the country's' economic development compared to the inland ones. China's' poorest provinces in the west have nearly five times less GDP per capita than the richest regions in Beijing, Shanghai, and Guangdong.

Other BRI goals are also related to ensuring sustainable economic development. Exporting unused industrial capacity is one of them. In response to the global financial crisis in 2008, China directed economic incentives to develop Chinese infrastructure to improve its economic situation. However, this caused an overproduction of steel, cement, and other commodities. In this context, the BRI may be one way to export this overproduction to the rest of the world, for example through infrastructure projects. Thanks to the construction of infrastructure in Africa, Southeast Asia, and the Balkans, China not only exports surplus steel and cement but also creates space for the realization of Chinese companies. Related to this is another Chinese goal: to help transform Chinese companies operating in the domestic market into global players. However, the question remains whether foreign expansion can help the Chinese economy as much as the strengthening of domestic consumption would do.

These economic goals are not detached from China's' political and security interests. Strengthening the legitimacy of the government of the CCP, which

Figure 16.1 Chinese highways and bridges in Shanghai (source: Robert Barca).

depends on economic development, is primary. The BRI also serves as a source of legitimacy for the CCP based on creating an image of respect by other states for China as a superpower. The Chinese government is using the BRI to formulate a narrative about China's' return to the position of a superpower it occupied before the opium wars and the "century of humiliation"." The fulfillment of this "Chinese dream" is essential precisely for the realization of the main interest of the Chinese Communist Party, its own survival.[14]

By providing finance through the BRI, China is also influencing foreign governments and elites that have a positive view of China and are therefore inclined to accept the rise of Chinese power and the promotion of Chinese interests in the world. The interconnection of economic, political, and security interests is well illustrated by BRI projects in South, Southeast, and Central Asia. China's' economy is heavily dependent on international trade, with nearly 40% of China's' foreign trade being transported through the disputed waters in the South China Sea.[15] In order for ships to travel from the Indian Ocean to the South China Sea, they must cross the 890-kilometer-long Strait of Malacca between Sumatra and the Malay Peninsula. In the event of a military conflict, the strait could be blocked by China's' opponents, putting China under significant pressure and potentially causing domestic instability.

The high degree of economic dependence on a single sea route, which passes through a relatively unstable region, poses an economic and security risk for China, which the Chinese government is trying to minimize by implementing several BRI projects. Perhaps the most ambitious idea in this regard is the canal across

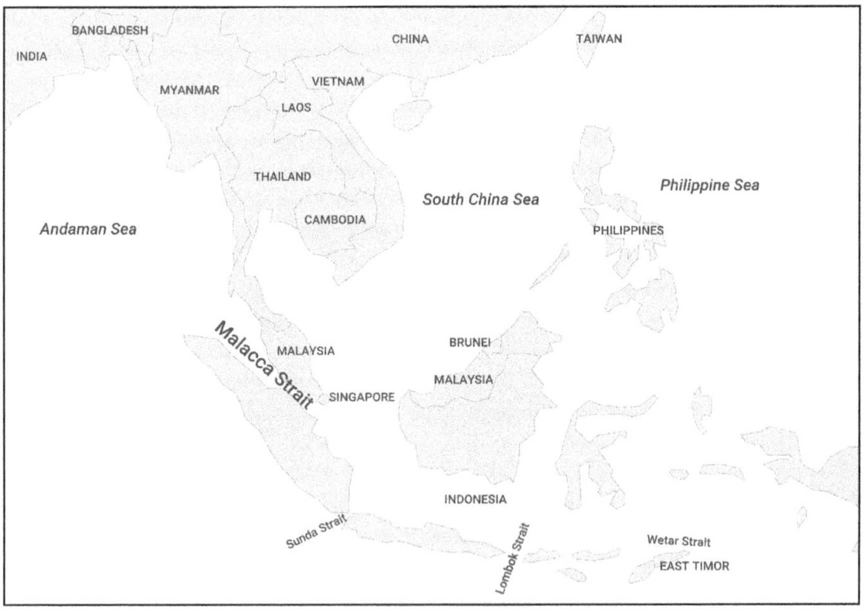

Figure 16.2 Malacca Strait in Southeast Asia (source: CEIAS).

Thailand's Kra Isthmus, which would allow ship transportation (similar to the Panama Canal) across a 128-kilometer strip of Thai territory, allowing Chinese ships to avoid the troublesome Strait of Malacca.

Another important project is the China–Pakistan Economic Corridor. China has funded and conducted the construction of road, rail, and pipeline infrastructure in Pakistan with the aim to connect the western Chinese autonomous region of Xinjiang with the port of Gwadar on the Pakistani coast, which China also operates. This would give Beijing a direct connection to the Arabian Sea, reducing dependence on the South China Sea shipping route. A similar logic is pursued by the construction of transport infrastructure in Southeast Asia. Within the China-Myanmar Economic Corridor (CMEC), China has been funding the construction of oil and gas pipelines, as well as roads and railways, again with the aim of creating an alternative transport route. With the petroleum and gas pipelines from the Myanmar coast to the southern Chinese province of Yunnan, there are, however, doubts about their profitability and impact on China's' energy security.[16]

The construction of new and the purchase of existing ports is not an unusual activity that would only affect Myanmar and Pakistan. In Europe, the purchase of the Greek port of Piraeus near Athens was intensively discussed in 2008, with China taking advantage of the unfortunate economic situation in Greece during the financial crisis. During the summer of 2020, China announced plans to purchase another Greek port in Thessaloniki. Chinese investments in Greek ports are often cited as an example of using investments to enforce political interests. In fact, in 2016, Greece blocked the adoption of a critical EU resolution on Chinese activities in the South China Sea and within the EU is considered to have a more friendly attitude toward China. Chinese state-owned companies partly own a dozen other ports in the EU, for example in Genoa, Valencia, Rotterdam, and Hamburg.

Debt traps on the Silk Road?

When talking of China and ports, we cannot omit the port of Hambantota in Sri Lanka, a construction financed and implemented by China. In 2017, the Sri Lankan government signed an agreement with the Chinese government to lease the Hambantota port for 99 years to a Chinese state company as a way to mitigate the unfavorable financial situation caused also by the loans from China. The Sri Lankan experience has raised international concerns that China is using so-called "debt trap diplomacy" to pursue its goals by providing unsustainably large credits to developing countries, which China will then use to gain control of strategically important infrastructure in case of payment default.

However, rather than China's well-thought-out strategy, the Hambantota case is rather a result of the jointly irresponsible behavior of China as a creditor and Sri Lanka as a debtor. China's irresponsibility regards providing funding for a project that was unprofitable from the start. Sri Lanka repeatedly tried to obtain funding for the construction of the port from other creditors who refused to provide credit precisely because of the project's unfeasibility. The fact that China accounted for only 10% of Sri Lanka's total foreign debt also contradicts the debt trap narrative.

Traditional creditors such as the World Bank or the Asian Development Bank accounted for a larger share of external debt. At the same time, much of the responsibility for the Hambantota case can be attributed to the Sri Lankan government of then President Mahinda Rajapaksa, who insisted on building a port in his hometown, despite the negative opinions of other potential creditors.

It should be emphasized though that China claims to be a responsible power, and its international activities (whether carried out under the BRI or not) represent a "win-win cooperation" (*hezuo gongying* in Chinese). To make this statement a reality, China itself must first adapt its credit practices to international standards and provide financing only for viable projects. Legal research into Chinese lending contracts has shown that China's approach to financing developing country borrowers differs from the standard practices in some key terms. This includes practices like broad confidentiality clauses, unusual security arrangements, or favoritism of Chinese lenders over their overseas counterparts in case of borrower default.[17]

Criticism of unsustainable financing of infrastructure projects under the BRI has not been avoided in Europe either, especially in connection with the provision of a loan to Montenegro for the construction of a highway from the Adriatic coast to Belgrade, Serbia. The story of the Montenegrin highway is essentially similar to the Sri Lankan one. Montenegro has repeatedly unsuccessfully tried to raise funds for highway construction. The two feasibility studies carried out for the project agreed that the highway would never service enough traffic to justify the construction costs. Nevertheless, China financed the project – and it has significantly increased Montenegro's debt. The debt-to-GDP ratio increased from 59% to 79% after the Chinese loan.[18] After Montenegro failed to repay a 1 billion USD Chinese loan in 2021, it was forced to ask for EU help.[19]

Finally, the BRI is also characterized by its approach to the implementation of infrastructure projects. The media – whether Chinese or international – often reports on China's investment abroad. However, in most cases, it is not an *investment* in the true sense of the word, but a *loan* to a foreign government conditioned on hiring a Chinese company to carry out the project, using Chinese labor and Chinese materials. In Africa, China has provided 147 billion USD in loans since 2000, of which up to two-thirds is for transportation, energy, and mining projects, sectors that demand human capital and/or raw materials.[20]

Chinese power and the resignation of the West

The less developed countries' willingness to accept Chinese funding despite its unsustainability raises the question of why they are turning to China. The answer is very prosaic: China is often the only option available to developing countries. The strengthening of China's power position on the periphery of the global West has been largely enabled by the gradual resignation of Western nations (especially the United States and Western Europe) to the role of "public welfare" providers in less developed countries, which is linked to the provision of development aid and is connected to demands for reform of the system of governance, respect for human rights, or the fight against corruption.

At the same time, cooperation with China is attractive to undemocratic regimes, as China's credit is not conditioned on the adoption of reforms to fight corruption, democratization, and respect for human rights. However, this does not mean that Chinese money (whether provided through the BRI or through other sources of cooperation) does not have its own conditionality – besides the requirement to use Chinese companies, labor, and material, there are "silent" demands to refrain criticizing the human rights situation in China. Of the 53 countries that supported Chinese activities restricting Hong Kong's autonomy in the UN Human Rights Council in July 2020, as many as 43 were involved in the BRI. As Herbert Wiesner of the German PEN Center said during a memorial service for the deceased Chinese dissident and Nobel Peace Prize laureate Liu Xiaobo, human rights are "left in the ditches by the sides of the new Silk Road".

Between the core and the periphery: A truly global foreign policy?

It is undeniable that since China began to embark on a journey of economic reforms in the late 1970s, its interests have gradually changed and become more global. However, their purpose has remained essentially the same for decades – Chinese foreign policy is an extended arm of domestic policy and serves the Chinese Communist Party to legitimize it and to guarantee its survival as the ruling political force in China.

Since Xi Jinping came to power, Chinese international activities aimed at promoting national and party interests have come under the framework of the BRI. Despite its misleading name, BRI represents China's pursuit of its own interests on a global scale, particularly through investment, trade, and the provision of financing and development aid for various projects. In 2019, China even became the largest creditor in financing development projects, outrunning institutions such as the World Bank and the International Monetary Fund.[21]

China's activities under the BRI label continue to focus mainly on authoritarian regimes and countries in the Global South. Developed democracies have limited opportunities to benefit from the BRI, and their involvement in the initiative has so far been minimal. Due to growing tensions between China and the West, which the COVID-19 pandemic has further accelerated, the scope for China to pursue its interests through the BRI can be expected to shrink even more in the West. The Chinese political-economic initiative with the intended global reach will thus remain at the level of an instrument for strengthening Chinese power on the "periphery".

Notes

1 R. Q. Turcsanyi, M. Eckert, M. Šimalčík, & N. Majsniarová,, "WHO | WHERE | WHEN – International Travel of the PRC Leaders (1949—2020)", Dataset. Central European Institute of Asian Studies (CEIAS), 2021.
2 B. Dai, "Stick to the path of peaceful development", *China.org.cn*, 13 December 2010.
3 R. Q. Turcsanyi, *Chinese Assertiveness in South China Sea*, Cham: Springer, 2018.

4 A. Chubb, "Exploring China's 'maritime consciousness': Public opinion on the South and East China Sea disputes", Perth US Asia Center, 2014.
5 R. Q. Turcsanyi, "Contradiction of strategic goals as a major constraint of Chinese power in the South China Sea", in E. Fels & T. Vu (eds.) *Power Politics in Asia's Contested Waters: Territorial Disputes in the South China Sea*, Cham: Springer, 2016, 173–196.
6 Adapted from M. Šimalčík, "China and the South China Sea conflict: A case for Confucian strategic culture?", *Journal of Indian and Asian Studies* 1(1), 2020, 1–33.
7 H. Feng, *Chinese Strategic Culture and Foreign Policy Decision Making*, New York: Routledge, 2007.
8 C. Walker & J. Ludwig, "The meaning of sharp power: How authoritarian states project influence", *Foreign Affairs*, 16 November 2017.
9 T. Zhang, "Chinese strategic culture: Traditional and present features", *Comparative Strategy* 21(2), 2002, 73–90.
10 A. Scobell, *China and Strategic Culture*, Carlisle Barracks: Strategic Studies Institute, 2002.
11 A. Scobell, "China's real strategic culture: A Great Wall of the imagination", *Contemporary Security Policy* 35(2), 2014, 211–226.
12 J. S. Nye, "Soft Power", *Foreign Policy* (80), 1990, 153–171; J. S. Nye, *Soft Power: The Means to Success in World Politics*, New York: Public Affairs, 2004.
13 M. Repnikova, *Chinese Soft Power*, Cambridge: Cambridge University Press, 2022.
14 P. Ferdinand, "Westward ho—The China dream and 'One Belt, One Road': Chinese foreign policy under Xi Jinping", *International Affairs* 92(4), 2016, 941–957.
15 "How much trade transits the South China Sea?", *CSIS*, 10 October 2019.
16 J. Garlick, "Deconstructing the China-Pakistan economic corridor: pipe dreams versus geopolitical realities", *Journal of Contemporary China* 27(112), 2018, 519–533.
17 A. Gelpern et al., *How China Lends: A Rare Look into 100 Debt Contracts with Foreign Governments*, Peterson Institute for International Economics, Kiel Institute for the World Economy, Center for Global Development, and AidData at William & Mary. March 2021.
18 N. Barkin & A. Vasovic, "Chinese 'highway to nowhere' haunts Montenegro", *Reuters*, 16 July 2018.
19 S. Jankovic, R. Standish & G. Tuhina, "Montenegro getting European help to refinance its massive China debt", *Radio Free Europe/Radio Liberty*, 23 June 2021.
20 "Chinese loans to Africa database", China Africa Research Initiative at Johns Hopkins School of Advanced International Studies, 2020.
21 R. Dossani, "Demystifying the Belt and Road Initiative", *RAND*, 6 July 2020.

17 China in its immediate neighborhood

A benevolent power or a hegemon?[1]

Alfred Gerstl

The People's Republic of China (PRC) is usually regarded as belonging geographically to Northeast or East Asia, yet at least parts of China's territory, history, and culture link it also to Central Asia, South Asia, and Southeast Asia. In total, the so-called Middle Kingdom shares about 22,800 kilometers of land borders with 14 countries – most of any other country in the world. The longest one is with Mongolia (4,680 km) and the shortest with Afghanistan (76 km). Additionally, China also shares maritime borders with South Korea, Japan, and Southeast Asian countries. China maintains various forms of what it calls "strategic partnerships" with most of its neighbors, reflecting at least a symbolic attempt to build robust relationships among its neighbors.

Due to its economic and military power, the PRC is currently the dominant party in all bilateral relationships with its neighbors. While the relations with the governments of Kazakhstan, Pakistan, and Mongolia are traditionally amicable, Afghanistan and North Korea are more complex partners due to their specific geopolitical and domestic characteristics. Relationships with other neighbors are even more challenging and sometimes openly hostile. India and Vietnam (as well as other Southeast Asian countries) have ongoing territorial disputes with China, which have been escalating in recent years. Sino–Japanese relations are so complex that the territorial disputes in the East China Sea are just one of many thorny issues. Also, despite the "special relationship" with Russia and the common interest in weakening the US-led Western order, there remain issues of contention between Beijing and Moscow which China must take into account (see Chapter 20).

Moreover, China's neighborhood is a place of ongoing geopolitical and geo-economic competition, involving the United States, India, Australia, and other more distant powers, whose interests and policies Beijing needs to consider in the conceptualization and conduct of its neighborhood policy. ***Why are there no detailed guidelines for the conduct of China's neighborhood policy? How does this approach contribute to promoting China's security and socioeconomic development? How do regional and geostrategic dynamics impact China's neighborhood policy?***

DOI: 10.4324/9781003350064-21

Amicable, but also strained relations with the neighbors

Since its economic opening up in 1978, China follows a so-called "good neighbor policy", aiming to develop a more cohesive and integrated policy toward its neighbors.[2] However, besides the objective of establishing amicable relations with its neighbors, China has not defined what exactly this policy entails. A key reason is that the 14 countries are too different. Nevertheless, these countries share a distinct similarity – a border with China. Therefore, Beijing put them in a specific category, not least to demonstrate to the neighbors their political significance for China.[3]

During the reigns of Jiang Zemin and Hu Jintao, China actively sought friendly relations in its periphery, most notably in Southeast and Central Asia. It aimed to portray itself as a responsible, benevolent power interested in promoting bilateral and regional cooperation. Peace, stability, and economic growth in the neighborhood should enable the Chinese regime to focus on domestic reforms and development. The neighborhood policy, however, must be viewed in the larger context of China's foreign policy, which responds to domestic needs as well as regional and global trends. This holds especially true in the era of Xi Jinping. Under his leadership, the Chinese foreign policy became both more ambitious and more assertive.

Some see in Xi a clear departure from the policies of the previous leaders, notably Deng Xiaoping and his famous slogan that the PRC shall "hide its capabilities and bide its time" and Hu Jintao and his "peaceful rise" and "harmonious world" concepts. Others point to more gradual shifts and emphasize continuity or a logical evolution, reflecting China's growing economic might in the last decade.[4] In 2010, then Foreign Minister Yang Jiechi famously stated: "China is a big country and other countries are small countries, and that's just a fact".[5]

Early in his reign, Xi gave various speeches about his foreign policy aims in which he demanded "new great power relations" with the United States – expressing quite openly that he aspired for China to act as America's equal. However, fully in line with his predecessors, he also regularly highlighted the importance of China's relations with its immediate neighbors. In his speech at the Peripheral Diplomacy Work Conference in October 2013, Xi emphasized that Beijing's neighborhood policy is closely related to ensuring China's "great rejuvenation" and further socioeconomic development. It is no coincidence that he introduced the Belt and Road Initiative (BRI) at the same time. Xi emphasized that the neighbors should become more friendly in politics, economically more closely tied to the PRC, and that both security cooperation and people-to-people ties should be intensified.[6] Even though the bonds with countries in Africa or Latin America should be tightened too, the difference is that economic turmoil or deterioration of the security situation in a direct neighboring country impacts China more than in the case of a more distant country.

To preserve stability and peace across its borders, China utilizes economic cooperation – with the BRI being a key tool to bind the neighbors closer in China's regional sphere of influence. The BRI is a complex geostrategic and geo-economic scheme bundling many foreign economic and foreign policy initiatives but has also a strong domestic logic, mainly to promote China's development (see Chapter 16).

China in general prefers to deal with other nations on a bilateral level because that way it is always the stronger party. However, in recent decades, China has also engaged in active forum diplomacy, especially with the countries of the Global South (see Chapter 21). Two multilateral but not deeply cooperating forums that China helped to establish are the regional Shanghai Cooperation Organization (SCO) and the trans-regional BRICS cooperation format consisting of Brazil, Russia, India, China, and South Africa (more in Chapter 20). The main glue for the BRICS members is their opposition to the Western-dominated international political and financial order. Otherwise, they have few overlapping common interests.

The neighborhood policy in a broader theoretical context

"Good neighborliness", "win-win cooperation", or "community of common destiny": many argue that this flowery diplomatic rhetoric behind China's neighborhood policy (and foreign policy in general) deliberately conceals Beijing's sometimes harsh conduct of its foreign policy. To highlight China's strategic ambitions, they point to China's traditional ideological concept of *tianxia*, or "(all) under the heaven" (see Chapter 1). Ancient Chinese political thought views China "as the center of a world that should be unified and peaceful".[7] Accordingly, China's relations in the past with its weaker neighbors followed the logic of unequal, "tributary" relations. Attempts of Chinese intellectuals and politicians in the last two decades to revive *tianxia* as a stepping stone of China's international relations are therefore often raising eyebrows in other countries. Not surprisingly, due to past negative experiences, they are especially rejected in China's immediate neighborhood, notably in Vietnam.

John Mearsheimer builds on *tianxia*, when he argues that the rising China "will attempt to dominate Asia the way the US dominates the Western Hemisphere".[8] Other authors also ask whether Beijing attempts to formulate its own version of the US Monroe Doctrine under the slogan "Asia for Asians" (under Chinese leadership), referring to a speech Xi gave in 2013. Mearsheimer believes that neighboring countries such as India, South Korea, Vietnam, and even Russia are inclined to support Washington in containing Beijing because China's position as a regional hegemon would contradict their national interests. However, this view is contested. First, even though many examples from the past demonstrate that a confrontation between an aspiring great power and the dominant power culminated in a military conflict, a war between the United States and China is not inevitable.[9] Second, notably, Southeast Asia provides evidence that the majority of the countries do not sideline (bandwagon) with the United States to contain China – and neither do they align with China. Rather, they apply a mix of bandwagoning and balancing in their relations with China and the United States, a strategy called hedging.[10]

The debate continues over whether China aspires to become a regional hegemon. It illustrates that China's relations with its neighboring regions and states cannot be fully grasped without taking the interests, strategies, and policies of other great powers into account, particularly of the United States and, albeit to a lesser degree, Russia (notably in Central Asia), India (in South Asia), and Japan (in Northeast and Southeast Asia).

Northeast Asia

China has only three neighbors with a land border in Northeast Asia: Russia, Mongolia, and the Democratic People's Republic of Korea (DPRK – North Korea). However, Japan and South Korea are also important, albeit indirect neighbors. As Sino–Russian relations are covered in Chapter 20, this chapter focuses on the other countries.

China's close relations with North Korea date back to the Korean War (1950–1953), when Beijing supported its Communist partner against the US-backed South. China is the only power that has some leverage on Pyongyang due to its historically close relations with the Kim dynasty and its strong economic influence. Nevertheless, North Korea remains an erratic partner for China. To the annoyance of North Korea, Beijing adheres to the sanctions imposed by the UN. China is concerned about North Korea's nuclear weapons and a collapse of the totalitarian Kim regime. Apart from a potential refugee wave to China, a fear is that the subsequent unification of North and South would follow the model of the German unification in 1991 – the South Korean political and economic system would likely prevail in the whole of Korea. Moreover, China sees the risk that, in the case of unification, Seoul would inherit Pyongyang's nuclear arsenal and US soldiers could be stationed along the Korean–Chinese border. Even more disastrous would be a large-scale war on the Korean Peninsula involving US troops and potentially the use of nuclear weapons.[11] Thus, Beijing pressured Pyongyang to find a diplomatic solution with Washington and viewed Donald Trump's personal meetings with Kim Jong-un positively. China's relations with North Korea must be examined in the broader context of regional politics, notably peace and stability on the Korean Peninsula, and the Sino–US contestation for influence.

Mongolia is a democratic country in need of foreign investments to develop its vast resources and modernize its infrastructure. Locked between China and Russia, its geographic isolation complicates Ulaanbaatar's foreign policy, making it difficult to engage so-called third neighbors in addition to China and Russia to multilateralize its relations. Economically, Mongolia is a beneficiary of the BRI, as it connects Mongolia better to Central Asia and Europe. The connectivity collaboration is broadly defined and involves Russia in the China–Mongolia–Russia Economic Corridor. The BRI became therefore a trigger for viewing China as an economic partner rather than a threat to Mongolia's territorial integrity.[12] The two nations share a long common history, and the ethnic and cultural ties between Mongolia and notably the Chinese Inner Mongolia are deep. Despite these facts, the Mongolian citizens regard Moscow as the more reliable partner, and there is deep-seated Sinophobia among many Mongolians.[13]

Japan is one of the neighbors across the sea. The bilateral economic ties are strong: China is Japan's main trade partner, and Japan is a leading investor in China. In fact, Japanese investments and know-how transfer have been crucial to China's modernization. Nevertheless, there are tensions and a strong geopolitical rivalry between the PRC and Japan. The lack of trust between Beijing and Tokyo was mainly caused by Japan's brutal war against China (1937–1945) and the ongoing refusal of many leading Japanese politicians to unequivocally condemn the Japanese war crimes. In addition, China and Japan have unresolved territorial disputes in the East China Sea, namely the Senkaku/Diaoyu Islands. Chinese vessels regularly sail through the territorial waters of the Senkaku Islands which are administered by Japan. Chinese military planes also increasingly violate Japanese airspace.

Beijing is highly critical of attempts to change the Japanese constitution to enable the strengthening of Japan's military power. So far, however, the constitution has only been reinterpreted, allowing Japan in some instances to participate in collective self-defense missions and in military actions, if one of its allies (usually interpreted as the United States and Taiwan) were to be attacked. Japan is, together with the United States, India, and Australia, a member of the Quadrilateral Security Dialogue (Quad). A key objective is to uphold freedom of maritime trade in Northeast and Southeast Asia. Moreover, Japan became under former long-term Prime Minister Shinzo Abe a pioneer of the free and open Indo-Pacific concept. Tokyo aims at strengthening the rules-based regional order to counter perceived Chinese attempts to undermine international law and norms.[14]

Similar to Japan, South Korea has a mutual defense treaty with Washington, and US soldiers are stationed in both countries. The US alliance system and the strong military presence in Northeast Asia limit the strategic options of China. In 2016, China responded with economic sanctions to the deployment of an advanced US missile defense system in South Korea (THAAD), which is directed against North Korea but could, according to China, spy deeply into Chinese territory. The bilateral relations were hit hard after the incident, and although the diplomatic links have been normalized, China's public image among South Koreans has suffered greatly.

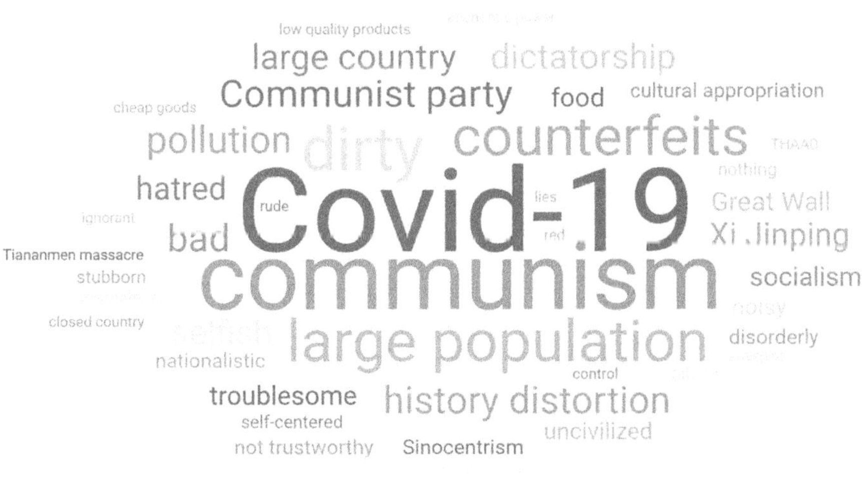

Figure 17.1 South Korean people's perception of China (source: Sinophone Borderlands Indo-Pacific Survey (R. Q. Turcsanyi, K. Kironska, A. Gerstl, M. Arnez, J. Čeněk, J. Chen, R. Chen, A. Chubb, P. Gries, T. Wang, "Sinophone Borderlands Indo-Pacific Survey", Palacky University Olomouc, 2022)).

Southeast Asia

China's relations with Southeast Asia, institutionally represented by the Association of Southeast Asian Nations (ASEAN), have deepened significantly since the end of the Cold War. Up until then, most Southeast Asian governments were skeptical about Communist China. Facing criticism and sanctions from the West after the Tiananmen massacre (see Chapter 3), China moved politically closer to Southeast Asia. It entered into diplomatic relations with Brunei and Singapore and resumed relations with Indonesia, all in 1991. Subsequently, ASEAN was willing to integrate China into the regional multilateral structures, trying to reduce the risk of Chinese unilateralism. Since 1991, the PRC is an ASEAN dialogue partner, and the two parties collaborate closely in economics (e.g., the China–ASEAN Free Trade Area and the Regional Comprehensive Economic Partnership), politics, culture, education, as well as traditional and non-traditional security. Beijing's image improved considerably during the Asian Financial Crisis of 1997/98 when it supported the most affected Southeast Asian nations. Nevertheless, at the same time, many Southeast Asian governments (but also the United States, Japan, and Australia) were suspicious of China's military modernization, reflected in a so-called China threat debate in these countries. The pattern of viewing China as both an economic opportunity and a potential security risk remains valid in Southeast Asia.

Today, China is a member of all ASEAN-led trans-regional structures and endorses ASEAN's centrality in the Indo-Pacific. In 2020, ASEAN became China's main trade partner, ahead of the EU. However, while China is the main trade partner of all Southeast Asian nations, it is not their leading investor. The EU, the United States, and Japan provide usually more investments, and they are also more generous donors of Official Development Assistance (ODA).

Southeast Asia features prominently in the BRI. Except for Singapore, all Southeast Asian nations require large infrastructure investments to facilitate their development. Nonetheless, the BRI investments in the domestic infrastructure are not always viewed positively. Experts and citizens in Southeast Asia alike utter criticism of the costs, the high interest rates, the lack of sustainability, the low quality, the delay of some projects (e.g., the metro in Hanoi), or the use of Chinese rather than local laborers. Corruption and the lack of transparency are further problems for which, however, national politicians must be held primarily responsible.

So far, the BRI has failed to transmit a positive picture of Chinese benevolence toward Southeast Asia.

China enjoys a relatively positive image among the general populations of most of the Southeast Asian countries, except Vietnam.[15] However, the elites are more cautious, not least because of China's assertive behavior in the South China Sea (see Chapter 18). This territorial dispute overshadows the relations with the four Southeast Asian littoral states Brunei, Malaysia, the Philippines, and Vietnam, as well as ASEAN as a whole. Notably the Philippines and Vietnam, but also increasingly Malaysia, deepened in the last years their security and maritime cooperation with the United States. The strong military presence of the United States, together with its allies Japan, Australia, and India, restrict Beijing's strategic leeway. Washington is – similar to the cases of Japan and South Korea – the main security guarantor for most Southeast Asian countries.

Even though Vietnam is, like China, ruled by the Communist Party and has had decades of intense bilateral relations, the government and the citizens alike perceive China with distrust. The Vietnamese stress China's century-long domination of Vietnam, as well as the 1979 border war launched by China and a smaller battle in the South China Sea in 1988. Despite the underlying tensions, the Sino–Vietnamese economic collaboration is very close. Some authors even voice concerns about Hanoi's potential economic dependency on China. On the other hand, Vietnam does benefit from China as a lucrative export destination. Many Western and Japanese companies produce in Vietnam for the Chinese or the global markets, and due to the rising wages in China, many international firms shifted their production plants during the COVID-19 pandemic from China to Vietnam.

In principle, Vietnam's foreign policy is very typical of the respective policies of ASEAN and most of its members – they pursue a so-called hedging strategy. This means they are seeking deep economic relations with China – but also other major actors to counter-balance Beijing's dominance – and close security ties with the United States and other Western and Asian powers. By engaging as many actors as possible in different policy areas, they aim to avoid a dependency on one of the great powers. A key distinction of Vietnam's foreign policy, though, is that it applies the most robust hedging strategy toward China, utilizing more confrontative measures than Brunei, Malaysia, and the Philippines in the South China Sea.[16]

The two direct neighbors, Myanmar and Laos, do not hedge against China. Both the Laotian government and the Myanmar junta see their national interests as better suited by close relations with Beijing. Moreover, they lack potential balancing partners against China, as Western governments criticize the authoritarian nature and human rights violations of these two regimes. China, which itself has a bleak human rights record, has no interest in promoting human rights and democracy in other countries.

Traditionally, China has had close relations with Myanmar. Beijing supported the isolationist and isolated military regime already after the first coup in 1962 and the bloody crackdown on public protests in 1988. Even during Aung San Suu Kyi's civilian rule (2016–2021), the bilateral ties remained strong. Nevertheless, Beijing was concerned about Myanmar's economic and political opening up to the West, as well as the ongoing fights between the Myanmar military and ethnic rebel groups in the borderlands.[17] Nevertheless, Myanmar is an important part of the BRI – inter alia, China built oil and gas pipelines that run from the Bay of Bengal to China. The objective behind these pipelines was to lessen China's dependency on the transit route through the Malacca Strait in the South China Sea.[18]

Laos is, like Cambodia, often supportive of China within ASEAN, undermining a consensus on a stronger stance against Beijing, notably in the South China Sea dispute. The shared Communist ideology facilitates the Sino–Laotian relations.

China is the second largest trade partner (behind Thailand) and a key investor. Laos plays a crucial role in the BRI; however, many investments had already been initiated before 2013. The BRI signature project in Laos is the Vientiane–Boten railway, completed in 2021, leading from the Laotian capital to the Chinese border. Chinese companies control the Boten Special Economic Zone and are also heavily invested in other such zones in Laos, as well as in hydropower, mining, and agriculture projects. China's strong economic engagement in the small neighboring country highlights both positive and negative economic, social, and political impacts – the Vientiane–Boten railway opens new trade opportunities for the landlocked country, as it better connects it with China, and also Thailand in the south. Laos could become a new economic corridor for transport, but also logistics and assembly in Southeast Asia. However, the ambitious railway project in a poor, underdeveloped country of seven million inhabitants has also been criticized, because of high costs and the mostly Chinese workforce.[19]

South Asia

China's relations with its four South Asian neighbors and Afghanistan, but also Sri Lanka, cannot be understood without addressing the strategic rivalry between Beijing and New Delhi, with the small, economically weak nations Bhutan and Nepal increasingly drawn into this regional competition. Another rivalry, which negatively impacts regional stability and economic development in South Asia, is the conflict between India and Pakistan, dating back to the partition of the British Raj into India and Pakistan in 1947. This rivalry also undermines regional cooperation, facilitated by the South Asian Association for Regional Cooperation (SAARC). Compared to ASEAN, SAARC is very weak and loosely institutionalized; China has observer status.

Until the late 1950s, China and India, ruled by the left-oriented Indian National Congress party under Jawaharlal Nehru, had close relations, also cooperating in the global non-alignment movement. Yet, the cordial ties lasted only until 1959, when the Chinese army ended an uprising of Tibetans against the annexation of Tibet, and the Dalai Lama and his government settled in Indian Dharamsala (see Chapter 13). Worse, the border war of 1962 over the disputed border has had a lasting negative impact on the bilateral relations, and skirmishes continue until today (see Chapter 18).[20] Despite these conflicts and the generally competing strategic interests in the Indian Ocean, China and India still work together pragmatically in many policy areas on bi- and multilateral levels. They are partners in the SCO and BRICS, but India has not joined the BRI, of which it is highly critical. However, New Delhi is a founding member of the Asian Infrastructure Investment Bank (AIIB) through which it has some leverage on project financing.

New Delhi fears that Beijing pursues a kind of containment strategy, symbolized in China's "String of Pearls" – a network of harbors leased or used by Chinese companies surrounding India. Key ports are Hambantota (Sri Lanka) and Gwadar (Pakistan), but also involve Bangladesh, Myanmar, and Maldives.

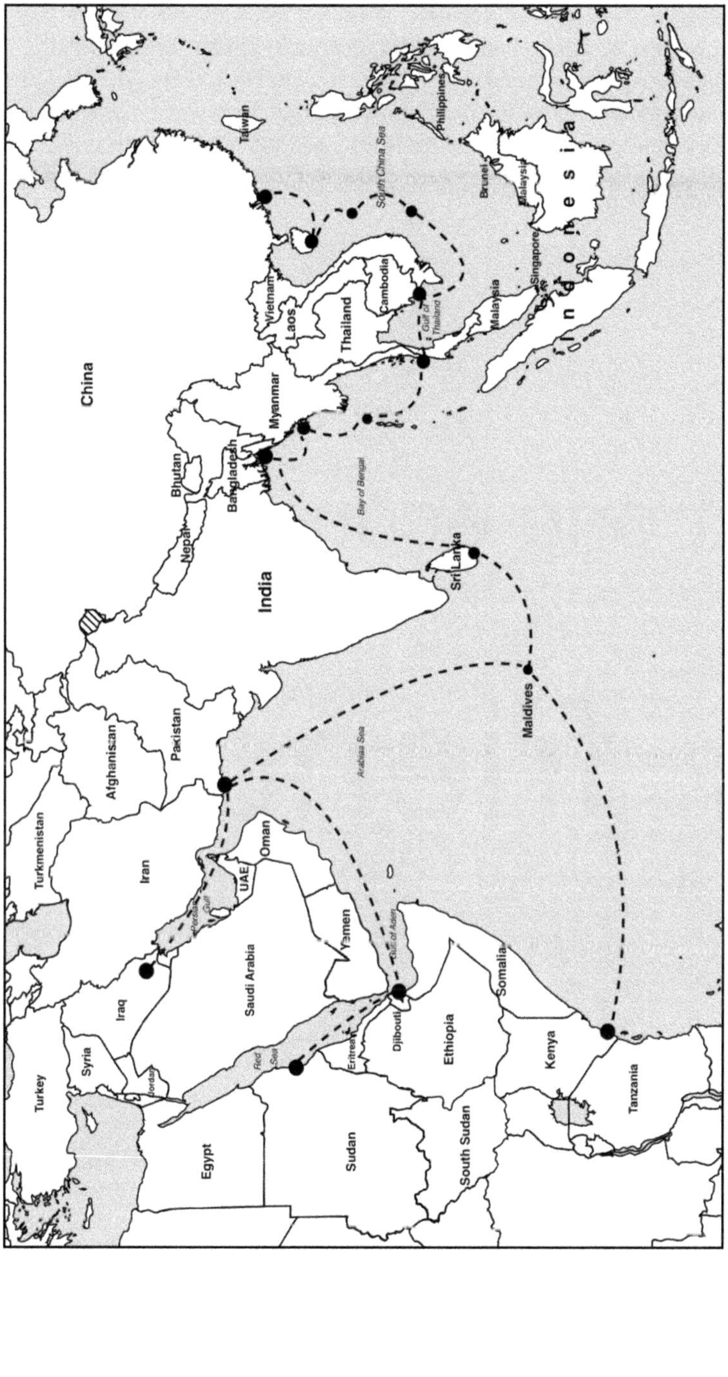

Figure 17.2 String of pearls (source: CEIAS).

China has a strong interest in undermining India's dominance in South Asia – and so has Pakistan. Notwithstanding this shared strategic aim, China and Pakistan are not natural partners – Pakistan has traditionally close ties with the United States, notably in the realm of security, although tensions grew in the last years, especially because of Islamabad's support for the Taliban. Pragmatically, China has strengthened economic bonds with Pakistan in the last years. The BRI provides an additional framework, with the China–Pakistan Economic Corridor (CPEC) being a BRI flagship project. China builds oil and gas pipelines through Pakistan and modernizes the transport and energy infrastructure. However, the costly CPEC raises financial concerns.[21]

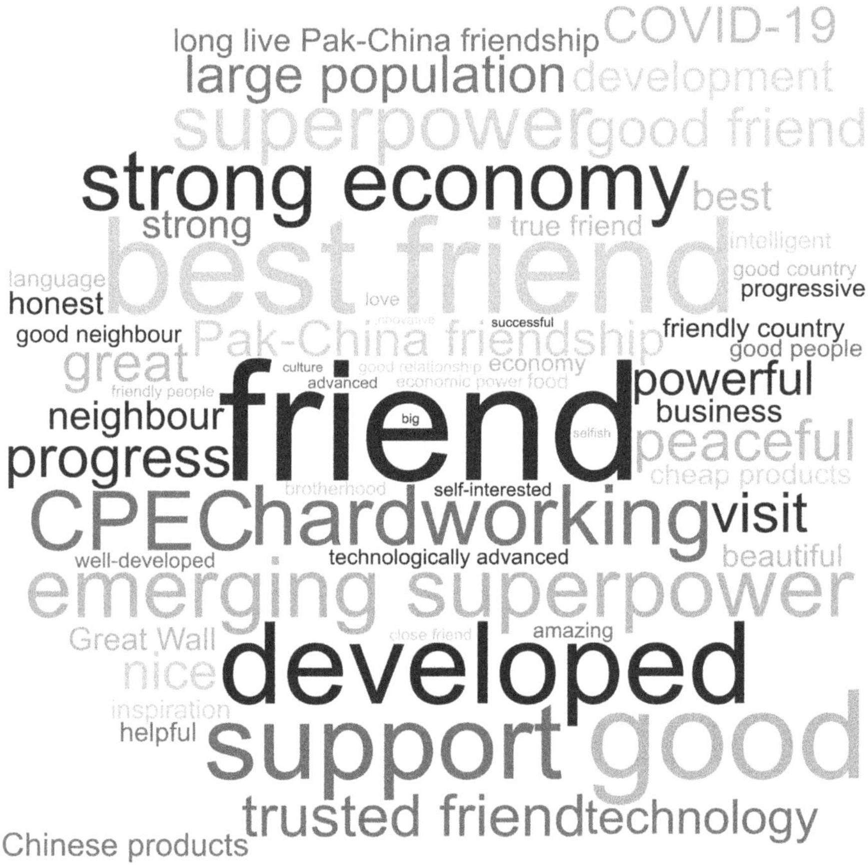

Figure 17.3 Pakistani people's perception of China (source: Sinophone Borderlands Indo-Pacific Survey (R. Q. Turcsanyi, K. Kironska, A. Gerstl, M. Arnez, J. Čeněk, J. Chen, R. Chen, A. Chubb, P. Gries, T. Wang, "Sinophone Borderlands Indo-Pacific Survey", Palacky University Olomouc, 2022)).

Islamabad's considerable influence on the fundamentalist Taliban regime in Afghanistan increases the country's strategic value for the PRC. China's relations with Afghanistan provide an illustration of Beijing's non-ideological foreign policy. Beijing had open discussion channels with all Afghani governments in the last decades while avoiding any military involvement. China's main aim is securing stability in Afghanistan, not least to prevent the spread of terrorism and drug smuggling across the border. Pragmatically, China negotiates with the Taliban about increased trade, investment, and aid, but has not yet diplomatically recognized the government. Security concerns remain an obstacle to including Afghanistan prominently in the BRI.

Thanks to the BRI, China made strong inroads in Nepal and Bhutan – both aim to maintain a balance in their relations with their big neighbors to avoid dependencies, though this is a challenging task.[22] Certain neorealist scholars claim that small nations can have a considerable degree of agency in such a big power rivalry.[23] However, while the foreign policy of small and middle powers can certainly affect China's policies, the impact of China's policies and behavior on their policies is incomparably higher.

Central Asia

After the dissolution of the Soviet Union in 1991, China suddenly had three new neighbors in Central Asia. At this time, Beijing demonstrated considerable goodwill, making territorial and economic concessions to resolve the bilateral border disputes, inherited from the Soviet Union, with Kazakhstan, Kyrgyzstan, and Tajikistan.

Among China's main interests related to Central Asia are securing the stability of Xinjiang, which shares a border with the three Central Asian neighbors, and preventing the spread of the "three evils" (namely terrorism, separatism, and religious extremism) to China. Other priorities are getting access to energy and other resources and improving China's land connection to Eurasia via this strategically important region. Central Asia is often regarded as belonging to Russia's "near abroad". Consequently, Beijing must be skillful to not openly undermine Moscow's key interests, while aiming to shape "Sino-friendly norms and acceptance of a beneficent Chinese presence".[24] Apart from Russia, the United States, the EU, Turkey, and Saudi Arabia are influential players whose policies China must monitor carefully too.

Due to its geographical location, territorial size, and vast energy resources, Kazakhstan is Beijing's key partner in the region. It also plays a major role in the BRI (as it did in the ancient Silk Road), acting as the gateway. Not surprisingly, Xi introduced the land-based Silk Road in a speech in Astana in 2013. Chinese companies have invested heavily in the Kazakh oil and gas industries. The political cooperation is close, too, especially after the two governments resolved their border dispute in 1998. The elites portray cooperation with China very positively, and this has impacted positively also the general sentiment, despite the fact that the rights of ethnic Kazakhs in China's Xinjiang are suppressed and there are many citizens of Kazakhstan who have seen their family members disappeared in the 're-education camps'. Kazakhstan's government, however, has so far not condemned Beijing's treatment of the Uyghur population.

China's two other Central Asian neighbors, Kyrgyzstan and Tajikistan, are much poorer than Kazakhstan. Strongly interested in alternative sources of FDI, they actively participate in the BRI. They benefit from the modernization of their transport infrastructure and better connections to China and Europe. However, the strained political relations between Kyrgyzstan and Tajikistan complicate transnational collaboration. To fight against terrorism and Islamism, the PRC increased in the last years its economic and security collaboration with Tajikistan, which shares a 1,350 km long porous border with Afghanistan.

Having a second strong partner in China is helpful for the Central Asian governments in avoiding dependence on Russia. All Central Asian states pursue a so-called multivector (or omnidirectional) foreign policy, meaning they aim to diversify their political and economic relations.[25] However, unlike Kazakhstan, the weaker Central Asian countries lack both economic and military power, as well as strongly committed partners to adopt a credible hedging strategy toward China and Russia.

Notes

1 This work was supported by the European Regional Development Fund Project "Sinophone Borderlands – Interaction at the Edges" CZ.02.1.01/0.0/0.0/16_019/0000791.
2 S. Zhao, "China's periphery policy and its Asian neighbors", *Security Dialogue* 30(3), 1999, 335–346.
3 E. Kavalski & S. F. Jackson, *China's Regional Relations in Comparative Perspective: From Harmonious Neighbors to Strategic Partners*, London: Routledge, 2018.
4 A. Benvenuti, C. P. Chung, N. Khoo & A. T. H. Tan (eds.), *China's Foreign Policy: The Emergence of a Great Power*, London: Routledge, 2022; A. S. Ding & J. P. Panda (eds.), *Chinese Politics and Foreign Policy under Xi Jinping: The Future Political Trajectory*, London: Routledge, 2021; and A. Goldstein, "China's grand strategy under Xi Jinping: Reassurance, reform, and resistance", *International Security* 45(1), 2020, 164–201.
5 J. Kurlantzick, "The belligerents", *The New Republic*, 27 January 2011, 14–16.
6 W. Song, *China's Approach to Central Asia: The Shanghai Cooperation Organisation*, London: Routledge, 2016.
7 D. A. Bell, "Realizing Tianxia: Traditional values and China's foreign policy", in B. Wang (ed.), *Chinese Visions of World Order. Tianxia, Culture, and World Politics*, London: Duke University Press, 2017, 129–146.
8 J. J. Mearsheimer, "Can China rise peacefully?", *The National Interest*, 2014, 1–40.
9 G. T. Allison, "Destined for war: Can America and China escape Thucydides' trap?", *Scribe*, 2017.
10 A. Gerstl, *Hedging Strategies in Southeast Asia: ASEAN, Malaysia, the Philippines, Vietnam and their Relations with China*, London: Routledge, 2022.
11 O. S. Mastro, "Why China won't rescue North Korea: What to expect if things fall apart", *Foreign Affairs* 97(1), 2018, 58–66.
12 S. K. Soni, "China–Mongolia–Russia economic corridor: Opportunities and challenges", in B. R. Deepak (ed.), *China's Global Rebalancing and the New Silk Road*, Singapore: Springer, 2018, 101–117.
13 F. Bille, *Sinophobia: Anxiety, Violence, and the Making of Mongolian Identity*, University of Hawaii Press, 2014.

14 K. Koga, "Japan's 'Indo-Pacific' question: Countering China or shaping a new regional order?", *International Affairs* 96(1), 2020, 49–73.

15 R. Q. Turcsanyi, K. Kironska, A. Gerstl, M. Arnez, J. Čeněk, J. Chen, R. Chen, A. Chubb, P. Gries, & T. Wang, "Sinophone Borderlands Indo-Pacific Survey", Palacky University Olomouc, 2022.

16 Gerstl, *Hedging Strategies in Southeast Asia.*

17 K. Kironska, "The new era of Sino-Burmese relations: Changes in the bilateral relationship in view of China's rise and Myanmar's reforms", *Journal of Burma Studies* 24(2), 2020, 197–227.

18 M. Lanteigne, *Chinese Foreign Policy: An Introduction*, London: Routledge, 2020.

19 C. C. Kuik, "Laos's enthusiastic embrace of China's Belt and Road Initiative", *Asian Perspective*, 45(4), 2021, 735–759.

20 K. Bajpai, S. Ho, & M. C. Miller, *Routledge Handbook of China–India Relations*, London: Routledge, 2020.

21 J. Garlick, *Reconfiguring the China-Pakistan Economic Corridor*, London: Routledge, 2021.

22 H. B. Jha, "Nepal-China relations under the shadow of geopolitics", Observer Research Foundation, 2022.

23 T. V. Paul, "When balance of power meets globalization: China, India and the small states of South Asia", *Politics* 39(1), 2019, 50–63.

24 G. Shakhanova & J. Garlick, "China's faltering normative power drive in Kazakhstan", in A. Gerstl and U. Wallenböck (eds.), *China's Belt and Road Initiative: Strategic and Economic Impacts on Central Asia, Southeast Asia, and Central Eastern Europe*, London: Routledge, 2021.

25 A. Kazantsev, S. Medvedeva, & I. Safranchuk, "Between Russia and China: Central Asia in greater Eurasia", *Journal of Eurasian Studies* 12(1), 2021, 57–71.

18 Territorial disputes

Will China go to war?

Denisa Hilbertová

Territorial disputes are one of the major flashpoints in international relations in the Indo-Pacific – and China is at the center of almost all of them. Today, China is highly sensitive about its sovereignty and territorial integrity, but in the past, its various dynasties did not have clearly defined borders with the neighbors. In fact, the historical relations between China and its present neighbors were governed by very different rules to those of today's international system – its main feature being formally hierarchical relations with acceptance of the Chinese emperor as the unique figure. Complex territorial disputes are one of the legacies of this past.

This chapter focuses on two long-term territorial disputes in which China has been engaged and where a potential military escalation is possible, if not likely – the South China Sea and the border conflict with India. In the past, China has chosen to descale some territorial conflicts in times of significant internal upheaval. On the other hand, when China feels an outside threat, it can opt to prove its strength through armed forces. China has become the leading player in the region and effectively the second most powerful state actor in the world after the United States. For the stability of the international community, it is crucial how the Chinese government decides to deal with these conflicts. ***Based on the People's Republic of China's (PRC) historical behavior and current strategic approach, can we assess the likelihood of a military escalation in the future? Are there any signs or circumstances that can warn us of upcoming Chinese military involvement?***

China's territorial disputes

The People's Republic of China (PRC) has the longest land border of any country in the world (22,116 kilometers). In total, China has 14 neighbors on land and another eight at sea – which is also the most compared to any other country. The PRC has been involved in 23 border territorial conflicts since its establishment in 1949. Out of these, 17 have already been resolved, including those with Pakistan, Afghanistan, Kazakhstan, Kyrgyzstan, Tajikistan, Russia, North Korea, Mongolia, Nepal, Myanmar, and Laos. Likewise, the PRC has also closed the issues of the land border with Vietnam and the maritime border in the Gulf of Tonkin. In these disputes, China generally offered significant concessions, in the form of more than 50% of the disputed territory, and gave up potential claims to other territories that were part of Chinese states in the past (for example in the case of Russia).[1]

DOI: 10.4324/9781003350064-22

China often opted for compromise solutions in periods of great internal turmoil, such as during the Tibetan uprising in the late 1950s (see Chapter 13) or after the Tiananmen Square massacre in 1989 (see Chapter 3). The settlement of these disputes subsequently helped stabilize the international situation in the region, and China has respected these agreements ever since.

However, six territorial disputes remain open, and China has used military means in most of them. China is in dispute over border issues with India and Bhutan, the sovereignty of land features in the South China and East China Seas, and the status of Taiwan (see Chapter 15). These disputes can potentially escalate to an open military conflict even with the participation of major powers, such as the United States.

In general, China's willingness to use military solutions depends on its overall security and territorial strategy.[2] American political scientist M. Taylor Fravel highlighted the fact that China, despite its impressive economic growth, did not become more aggressive until about 2007.[3] Afterwards, however, it is possible to observe changes in China's foreign policy behavior, especially in connection with territorial disputes.[4]

China's sensitivity to the issues of national sovereignty seems to have increased since the COVID-19 pandemic. The Chinese Communist Party (CCP) is being challenged and responds by trying to demonstrate power, unity, and uncompromising stances domestically as well as internationally. At home, the CCP was pushing for a zero-COVID policy at huge economic, social, and human rights costs. On the international scene, the CCP is projecting its resolve through numerous actions, such as a military escalation on the Sino–Indian border in the summer of 2020, consolidation of the China–Russia partnership, frequent disturbances over the Taiwan Straits, or sharpening of anti-Western narratives. It is possible that the CCP leaders fear that a calm and measured approach to territorial problems could send an undesirable signal that it is a sign of weakness rather than prudence.

Sino–Indian border dispute

In the early evening of 15 June 2020, Chinese and Indian military forces clashed in a border skirmish in the remote Galwan Valley in the Himalayas, which is part of the vast territory that China and India are disputing. Twenty Indian and four Chinese soldiers died as a result of fistfights using sticks, stones, and clubs wrapped in barbed wire. It was the first encounter that resulted in the loss of life on the Sino–Indian border in half a century. Although Beijing and New Delhi are trying to calm the situation and held numerous rounds of military and diplomatic talks, the world's two most populous countries are still watching each other with considerable suspicion and are taking steps to advance their military positions for the future. What is at stake on the Sino–Indian border, and what preceded the current escalation?

The border conflict between China and India can be traced back at least to 1914, when representatives of the United Kingdom, the newly formed Republic of China, and Tibet met in the north Indian city of Simla. The purpose of the meeting was to

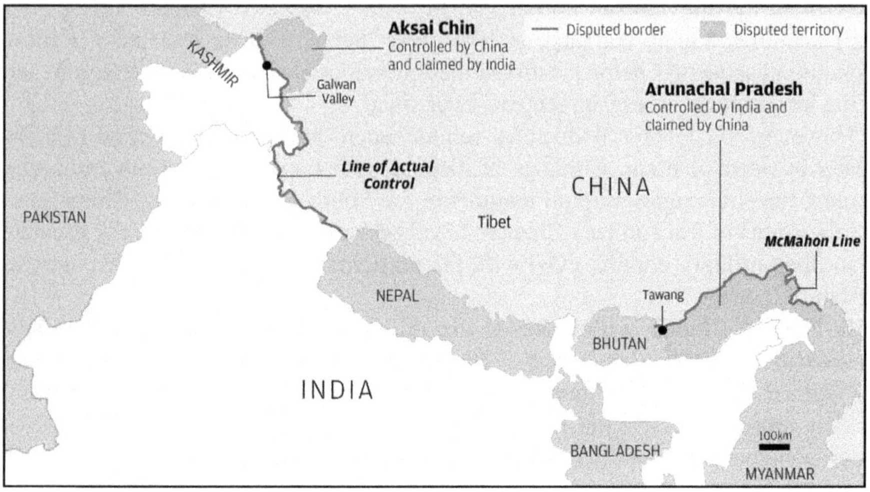

Figure 18.1 Sino–Indian border (source: CEIAS).

discuss the status of Tibet and to agree on the border between then-British India and China. The Chinese side disagreed with a proposed passage that would have guaranteed Tibet's autonomy and refused to sign the agreement. However, Britain and Tibet signed the agreement and accepted the so-called McMahon Line as the border between the two countries. To this day, India maintains the nearly 900-kilometer-long line that runs through the inhospitable Himalayan region as its official border.

However, China has never accepted this delineation, and the result is a disputed area between China and India covering a staggering 125,000 square kilometers – larger than the entire territory of North Korea. The dispute can be divided into three separate parts: the western, central, and eastern sectors. The western sector, also known as Aksai Chin (approximately 33,000 square kilometers), is under the control of the PRC. The eastern sector (approximately 90,000 square kilometers) includes the Indian state of Arunachal Pradesh which is under the control of India. The central sector (approximately 2,000 square kilometers) is located to the west of Nepal and the control is split between the PRC and India. Moreover, along the entire length of the disputed territories, the so-called Line of Actual Control (LAC) is not even clearly defined, which increases the possibility of accidental escalation.

In 1947, India announced independence from the British, and two years later Mao Zedong declared the establishment of the PRC. Almost immediately, the world's two most populous states found themselves in a complicated border situation. This was despite the efforts of India's first prime minister, Jawaharlal Nehru, who believed that India and China could work together and therefore accepted Chinese sovereignty over Tibet. However, tensions escalated during the 1950s when China gradually brought Tibet under its full control, insisting that it was never an independent country and therefore legally unable to sign an international border agreement. Efforts for a peaceful solution to the border conflict led nowhere, partly also because China wanted to gain control of the key road linking Xinjiang with Tibet, which passes through the disputed territory of Aksai Chin. The Sino–Indian relations became even more challenging in 1959 when the Dalai Lama fled Tibet for India, where he would remain in exile ever since (see more in Chapter 13). The Tibetan uprising of 1959 – though unsuccessful – showed how vulnerable the PRC was in its border areas, especially the borders populated by ethnic minorities. After the Dalai Lama left Tibet, the local border dispute turned into a question of the territorial integrity of the whole of China.

In 1962, Mao Zedong decided to launch a military attack on India. China viewed India's long-term efforts to build a network of supportive border bases as changes to a *status quo* putting China in a more difficult situation. Interestingly, however, Mao's goal was not to achieve a final resolution to the conflict but to improve China's position for further negotiations with India, as well as with other rivals. Chinese troops crossed the McMahon Line and took positions in Indian territory to control key positions. The war lasted one month and claimed more than 1,000 casualties on the Indian side, while more than 3,000 of their soldiers were captured. China lost less than 800 troops. The fighting was particularly brutal under extreme conditions, as the battles took place at an altitude of 4,000 meters above sea level. In November of the same year, Chinese Prime Minister Zhou Enlai declared a ceasefire, thus unofficially rewriting the effective boundary between the two states. The Chinese troops remained close to the territory they had gained control of in the previous weeks, creating the factual LAC.

The unstable situation between the two countries escalated again five years later, in 1967. Skirmishes broke out when Indian soldiers laid barbed wire in places that India recognized as its side of the border. More than 150 Indians and 340 Chinese were victims of the border clashes that were later named the Second Sino–Indian War. The result of this collision was the destruction of the Chinese fortifications and the expulsion of Chinese troops back into their territory near the Cho La Pass. These border clashes have shown how different the two countries' ideas about the exact position of LAC were. At the same, those were the last casualties on the Sino–Indian border before the 2020 clashes.

However, that does not mean the situation was calm in the time in between. In 1987, the Indian army conducted exercises to test how long it would take to move troops to the LAC. The movement of large numbers of troops and war material on the Indian side surprised the Chinese military command, which responded by moving troops into what China considered to be the LAC. However, both sides quickly assessed the danger of an escalation and averted the crisis without shedding blood. In the years that followed, both countries tested their adversary with various advances or destruction of the other side's infrastructure (such as roads). None of these maneuvers escalated into an open conflict, but nevertheless, permanent instability prevailed in the region.

Both sides consider the *de facto* state border to be the LAC. An agreement on mutual acceptance of the LAC concept itself was signed in 1993, but it does not clarify the actual route of the LAC. There are at least 13 points on which the two countries disagree.[5] The length of the LAC itself shows that the situation is far from final. India considers the LAC to be 3,488 kilometers long, while China considers it to be only about 2,000 kilometers long.[6] India accuses China of having created its LAC through points connected by a direct line or by aggressively pushing it deep into Indian territory. China, on the other hand, is anxiously watching India's efforts to strengthen its position in the border regions.

Easy access to the border is crucial for more effective control of the territory around the LAC. India is therefore gradually building strategic military routes and local airports along the LAC, with the purpose of undermining China's military superiority in the border region, especially in the western sector.[7] Just within the last five years, India built over 2,000 km of roads along LAC.[8] From this perspective, the skirmishes in the Galwan Valley in 2020 may have been an effort by the PRC to disrupt the completion of road projects on the Indian side of the LAC, as China sees India's road works as an attempt to change the status quo around LAC.[9] Meanwhile, China is also expanding and upgrading its transport network along the LAC.

After numerous rounds of diplomatic meetings, the current two-year border tension which began in 2020 is easing off, but bitterness remains. China agreed to withdraw from the border point in the Gogra-Hot Springs region in eastern Ladakh in exchange for almost 1,000 square kilometers.[10] Therefore, some on the Indian side claim the Chinese move can hardly be called a withdrawal. Chinese soldiers managed to advance toward what India claims as its territory in the last two years in many critical border areas, and China generally refuses to resort to the *status quo* of April 2020. It is clear that the Sino–Indian border conflict will not be fully resolved in any near future – certainly not to mutual content.

The question remains: how probable is another military escalation in this context? The CCP could choose to escalate the conflict as it did in 1962 if China fears that it is losing its position and that other states perceive Beijing as weak. China faces many internal and external challenges such as the COVID-19 pandemic, economic slowdown, Xi Jinping's unprecedented third presidential term, intense situations in Hong Kong and Xinjiang, and delicate relationship with Russia after its invasion of Ukraine – all in the context of the worst relations with the United States and the West in a long time. There is an option that Beijing could use a military conflict to rally the nationalist sentiments and/or divert attention from these and other issues it is struggling to cope with.

South China Sea conflicts

Perhaps the most internationally visible Chinese territorial conflict in recent years has been the issue of disputed sovereignty of land features and maritime boundaries in the South China Sea. Six actors with territorial claims to the disputed area are directly involved – apart from the PRC, it is also Taiwan (based on identical claims to the PRC), Vietnam, the Philippines, Malaysia, and Brunei, while the seventh actor – Indonesia – is only partially involved due to possible overlapping maritime claims around its Natuna archipelago.

The conflicts in the South China Sea have direct impacts on the stability of the international system and global maritime trade since the world's busiest trade routes pass through the area. The strategic interests of China and other regional and global powers meet here, as whoever gains control of the area would have the ability to paralyze global shipping routes and could project military power toward the Indian and Pacific Oceans. In addition, oil and gas reserves were discovered in the South China Sea in the 1960s, leading to littoral states making their claims more actively. Another important factor is fishing, as the South China Sea is an important source of food and income for fishing communities in the surrounding countries. Overall, the South China Sea may be regarded as one of the most watched and most frequently analyzed conflicts today.

For China, the southeast coast has always been considered the primary area of interest and a potential security risk. Indeed, the major population centers are concentrated there, and they are the economic heart of the country. To protect these assets, China has been intensively strengthening its naval military forces and has invested in the ability to operate as far as possible from its shores to meet a potential threat before it comes too close. Moreover, the dispute over Taiwan, which is closely related to the question of Chinese identity, nationalism, and the legitimacy of the Chinese Communist Party (see also Chapter 15), is also a factor here, as increasing influence and control over the South China Sea also serve the functions of strengthening positions vis-à-vis Taiwan.

The conflicts in the South China Sea can be divided into disputes over the sovereignty of the land territories on the one hand, and the maritime rights and borders on the other. These two disputes are to some extent interconnected but are by no means identical. Under the United Nations Convention on the Law of the Sea (UNCLOS), coastal states have exclusive rights over natural resources within 200 nautical miles of the coast, the so-called Exclusive Economic Zone (EEZ). Importantly, only the mainland or an island can generate the EEZs, but not reefs. This makes the land features in the middle of the South China Sea of potential importance – if they were to be considered islands and would generate the EEZs, their owner would be able to claim rights and control much of the sea.

However, it is crucial from this perspective that in 2016 The Permanent Court of Arbitration at The Hague ruled that none of the formations in the so-called Spratly Islands are "islands" under UNCLOS and thus cannot generate EEZs. This decision significantly weakened the claims of China and Taiwan, which assert their maritime rights based on control of the alleged islands, while other actors demand maritime rights based on distance from their coasts. In other words, the Tribunal ruled that under UNCLOS law, even the sovereignty over the land territories in the South China Sea does not allow a country to create a large-scale EEZ around them.

The PRC, however, ignores the Tribunal's decision and seeks to affirm its claims on the basis of "historical rights". According to China, the PRC has the right to the South China Sea based on the so-called "nine-dash line", which the Kuomintang government drew onto its maps in 1947. This line encircles virtually the entire sea, spanning a territory of approximately two million square kilometers, with the furthest part up to 2,000 kilometers away from the Chinese coast. The problem with these Chinese claims, however, is that UNCLOS does not recognize the concept of historic rights, and the Tribunal's 2016 decision rejected the nine-dash line under international law.

Compared to the border conflict with India, China considers the South China Sea to be its priority, and for this reason, it is also taking a more active role there. Since 2009, China has strengthened its position through a series of steps. In 2009, it opposed a joint proposal by Malaysia and Vietnam on the delineation of their EEZs by submitting for the first time officially the map with the nine-dash line. At the same time, the presence of Chinese ships in the area has been on a steady rise since the end of the 2000s. Similarly, the number of incidents where Chinese ships have encountered vessels from other states has also increased, mainly from Vietnam but also from the Philippines, Malaysia, and Indonesia. China has also sabotaged the efforts of Vietnam and the Philippines to survey the seabed for energy resources.

The most controversial Chinese activity, however, has been the massive construction of artificial islands and their gradual transformation into military bases,

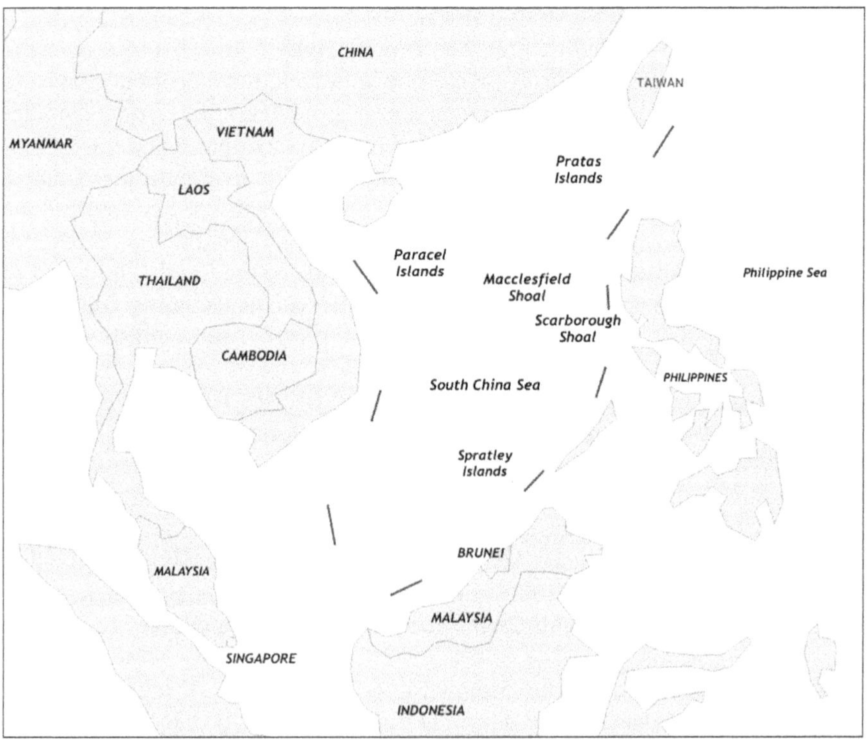

Figure 18.2 Chinese claims in South China Sea (source: CEIAS).

which have fundamentally changed the distribution of military power in the region. Since 2014, China has built seven such artificial islands in the Spratly Islands and constructed full-scale airfields capable of accommodating the largest aircraft on three of them. These artificial islands can also serve as ports for Chinese ships and submarines. The importance of these military footholds cannot be overstated, as they provide strategic naval and air military support and allow China to effectively control the region. In the event of an armed conflict, China has an undeniable advantage over its rivals, as these bases allow it to monitor the movements of other actors, reconnoiter the seabed, and, above all, have an immediate and decisive military presence. China has not yet resorted to a direct confrontation nonetheless, but there are frequent encounters with other actors or even with the United States, which does not want to accept Chinese dominance over a strategically key area.

The situation in the South China Sea has not changed much since the outbreak of COVID-19. China continued to adhere to its long-term strategy of gradually increasing its control over the whole area. As in the case of India, China's assessment of the situation is that if it were to ease up on its pressure for a while, it could be interpreted as a weakness. The difference from the Sino–Indian border region is that the United States is much more likely to become involved in a potential conflict in the South China Sea, which could then quickly expand the conflict to other international areas. Therefore, de-escalation of a potential military conflict would be more complicated here than with India. Indeed, there is the possibility that a minor naval skirmish or accident could escalate into a full-scale military engagement involving China, other claimants, and even great powers from outside of the region, including the United States.

Diplomacy or war?

In general, China treats the use of military means as one of many options for managing and resolving disputes. It resorts to them when it feels it has exhausted other options to gain the upper hand – whether economically, diplomatically, by building a favorable historical narrative, making intimidating statements, or demonstrating its military power. At the same time, it must be stressed that the PRC has resolved most of its territorial disputes over the past decades through peaceful agreements and extensive concessions. Importantly, China has respected those treaties.

In all the remaining unresolved territorial conflicts, China has a lot at stake, whether from a strategic, material, or nationalist-symbolic point of view. Along with its growing power, China's self-confidence is also growing, and in recent years it has used much tougher rhetoric in connection with the remaining disputes, backed up by specific actions. President Xi Jinping stated in 2018 that "not a single piece of territory inherited from our ancestors shall be lost". The Communist Party is reducing the chances for future compromises by making such propaganda statements because it could be then criticized by its own nationalist population. China's growing power and low willingness to compromise in the remaining disputes create a dilemma for China's opponents that is difficult to resolve.

Notes

1 M. T. Fravel, *Strong Borders, Secure Nation: Cooperation and Conflict in China's Territorial Disputes*, Princeton: Princeton University Press, 2009.
2 Ibid.
3 M. T. Fravel, "Power shifts and escalation: Explaining China's use of force in territorial disputes", *International Security* 32(3), 2007/2008, 44-83.
4 R. Q. Turcsanyi, *Chinese Assertiveness in the South China Sea*, Cham: Springer, 2018.
5 S. Menon, *Choices: Inside the Making of India's Foreign Policy*, Washington: Brookings Institution Press, 2016.
6 S. Singh, "Line of actual control: Where it is located, and where India and China differ", *Indian Express*, 18 June 2020.
7 R. Sen, "New Doklam roads set to alter India, China military dynamics", *Hindustan Times*, 3 October 2019.
8 "BRO built 3,595km of roads along LAC in 5 years: Govt", *The Times of India*, 26 July 2022.
9 M. T. Fravel, "Why are China and India skirmishing at their border?", *Washington Post*, 2 June 2020.
10 B. Hussain, "China border resolution leaves some in India unhappy", *VOA*, 25 October 2022.

19 Relations with the United States

Are the two great powers headed for a collision?

Richard Q. Turcsanyi

China's relationship with the United States is often referred to as the most important bilateral relationship in the world, as they are currently the two largest economies and the most powerful states in the international system. The United States has dominated world politics and the economy (at least) since the end of World War II, and, after the collapse of the Soviet Union, has remained uncontested as the only superpower. The debate about the weakening of the US position is not new and has been going on at least since the 1980s when many assumed that Japan would catch up with the United States. From today's point of view, this may be difficult to fully grasp – nonetheless, this is also a reason why it is good to maintain a certain degree of skepticism even in the case of claims about China's future world domination. But China is not Japan, and the fact remains that Beijing has been catching up with the United States. Still, it remains questionable whether its economy or military strength would ever surpass the United States.

US–China relations fell into a deep crisis during Donald Trump's administration, and they have not substantially improved under Joe Biden, either. After 50 years of cooperation and growing economic, political, military, and interpersonal contacts, the trend has reversed. Now, "decoupling" is the program of the day, where both sides are trying to reduce their dependence on each other. There are even voices that warn against military escalation. Indeed, the exchange in the positions of the most powerful actor in the international system has in the past been accompanied by a huge military conflict. According to this logic, the conflict between China and the United States is inevitable, based simply on the fact that China is gradually catching up with the United States in power.[1] Another reason for this pessimism is that relations between the United States and China are politically highly sensitive for both sides, which is based on their historical heritage, but also on persistent ideological and political differences.[2] ***What historical legacy is the current US–China relationship built on? Is there a threat of military conflict between the two great powers? Will China become the most powerful country in the world?***

DOI: 10.4324/9781003350064-23

Heritage of the 19th century: An imperialist or an ally?

Relations between China and the United States date several centuries back. Even at the emergence of the independent United States, China played an interesting role: the War of Independence with Great Britain began with the so-called Boston Tea Party, when American colonies rebelled against the monopoly of the British East India Company over trade with China, especially with tea, which became a popular commodity and from which colonies were to pay taxes to London. It is, therefore, no coincidence, that shortly after the Declaration of Independence, the young state established direct trade relations with China, and in 1785 a ship, the *Empress of China*, was sent to exchange American ginseng, fur, and silver for Chinese porcelain and tea. Trade with China then became an important source of income for the newly created state, and it helped the United States emerge from the international isolation of Great Britain and build the wealth of the cities of New York, Boston, and Philadelphia. It has also contributed to the development of the West Coast of the United States, which has progressively developed trans-Pacific contacts with China and other Asian countries.[3]

Today, many Chinese perceive the activities of the United States in China during the 19th and early 20th centuries in a negative light, similar to those of European empires and Japan. American business circles were indeed involved in the lucrative opium trade on which a large part of the Chinese population became addicted, and which contributed significantly to the crippling of Chinese society and the state. The US military also played an important role during the military intervention of eight powers in China during the Boxing Uprising from 1898 to 1901. Military intervention was aimed at rescuing besieged foreigners in Beijing's diplomatic district, but the operation itself was accompanied by murder, rape, destruction, and theft of historical cultural artifacts, which then went to Western museums and collections. Even though it is difficult to determine the share of blame of individual foreign powers in these events (and America's probably belongs to the smaller ones), these events are perceived as some of the darkest chapters of the "century of humiliation" in today's China (see Chapter 1).[4]

At the same time, however, the United States also played a positive historical role from a Chinese perspective when it was not interested in dividing China into "spheres of influence," and acted against the efforts of Europe (and Japan) to divide China's territory into separate colonies. Their "open door" policy sought to make the whole of China accessible to all foreign actors, and they succeeded in doing so to a large extent, even though Japan and Russia did not fully respect it. In addition to free trade, the approach of the United States to China was motivated by a "missionary" vision. This, of course, primarily consisted of the activity of American missions spreading Christianity in China but also led to the spread of education and modern technologies. The first Chinese universities, which are still rated as the top ones, were founded in cooperation with the United States – including, for example, the two most famous universities in China – Tsinghua and Beijing Universities. In addition, since the late 19th century, the new Chinese elite has studied directly at American universities.[5]

These contacts have, among other things, fostered the growth of Chinese emigration to the United States. Chinese immigrants (overwhelmingly male) were initially employed in building railways, mines, fishing, agriculture, or other manual labor. Specifically, the "gold rush" in California increased the prevalence of the Chinese in San Francisco and other parts of the west and south of the United States, and, to a lesser extent, also on the northeast coast. But as the numbers grew, so did the xenophobic sentiment among the local white population, who perceived Chinese immigration as a threat not only because of their different traditions but also because they provided cheap labor. Chinese migrants were also seen as carriers of various diseases. In 1875, immigration of Chinese women was practically banned to control the size of the Chinese community, and later in 1882, Chinese immigration was completely outlawed. This unique racist law remained in force until 1943 when the Republic of China had already been an important military ally against imperial Japan for several years. The second wave of Chinese immigration to the United States did not begin until the 1960s, when the Chinese became equal, received the opportunity to acquire citizenship, and marry the white population.

In today's United States, citizens of Chinese ethnicity (from mainland China, but also Taiwan, Hong Kong, or Southeast Asia) represent about 1% of the total population and often hold important political, economic, or other functions. In recent decades, the number of students from China has grown rapidly. But there are still anti-Chinese xenophobic sentiments in part of American society, which became more visible during the COVID-19 pandemic and as US–China relations worsened.

World War II and the Cold War: Enemies or allies?

It is shocking how fundamentally US–China relations have changed over the course of the 20th century – and more than once. These changes are even more visible if we include Japan in the discussion. The beginning of the 20th century caught the Chinese in an unenviable subordinate position to the world powers; the United States viewed China as a culturally, economically, and politically backward country. On the contrary, Japan was perceived as an Asian country that was able to modernize and rank among the "civilized" (Western) powers. This changed after the outbreak of World War II, when Japan became an "inhumane" enemy, while China suddenly became a key ally in Asia.

An interesting role in this process of rapprochement was played by Song Meiling, the wife of Chinese President Chiang Kai-shek, who had studied in the United States and during the war successfully lobbied for China. Another symbol of the alliance was American pilots who flew under Chinese colors (so-called "flying tigers"), or the American effort to keep supplying China's government via a difficult path from India through Burma. Paradoxically, when Chinese Americans began to finally acquire rights in the United States, Japanese Americans were interned in camps as a potential threat during the war.[6]

After the victory over Japan, the United States was interested in China being invited to the most important table and winning one of the five permanent seats

Figure 19.1 Eleanor Roosevelt and Song Meiling in front of the White House (source: Wikimedia Commons).

among the newly formed members of the UN Security Council, along with the right of veto. The United States continued its assistance to Chiang Kai-shek's regime during its civil war against the communists. But even large-scale American aid did not save China's nationalist regime, and in 1949 Mao Zedong declared the emergence of the People's Republic of China (PRC), while the leadership of the Republic of China (ROC), led by Chiang Kai-shek, along with approximately two million Chinese people, fled to Taiwan (more in Chapter 15). Initially, the Americans had no interest in maintaining aid for Chiang Kai-shek's Kuomintang Party, which they came to perceive as corrupt. But America's hope that relations with the newly formed communist regime could develop positively ended with China's intervention in the Korean War, where more than a million Chinese "volunteers" fought the US-led UN troops.

Relations between the Chinese communist regime and the United States were to remain frozen for another 20 years. Meanwhile, after the start of the Korean War, the United States also reassessed its attitude toward the ROC in Taiwan, and for the next 20 years diplomatically recognized the regime in Taipei as China's representative. For the United States, Chiang Kai-shek once again became a strategic ally both for Taiwan's geopolitical position and because his regime still controlled China's veto power in the Security Council. As a matter of fact, the UN was able to militarily respond in Korea thanks to Chiang Kai-shek's support: had China, with its communist regime, been a UN Security Council member, it would have vetoed the resolution. What is even more interesting is that the vote was not vetoed by the Soviet Union, which at that time boycotted the Security Council precisely to protest that the PRC was not a member.

During the 1950s and 1960s, the United States and the PRC mainly maintained communication through their embassies in Warsaw, but there was no shift in their relations. On the contrary, the two great powers stood on the brink of another war during the first and second Taiwan crises of 1954–1955 and 1958, when, after military provocations by Mao Zedong, battles broke out over the smaller islands in the Taiwan Strait, which remained under the control of Chiang Kai-shek's regime. Another conflict that has seen the US and Chinese armies facing each other was the Vietnam War; however, Chinese support was less significant in this case, and both sides tried to avoid direct military clashes.[7]

The war in Vietnam eventually led to a revolutionary change in US–Chinese relations. During the 1960s, both actors experienced a difficult period. China was living in domestic turmoil after the famines caused by the Great Leap Forward and later by the Cultural Revolution. In foreign policy, Mao Zedong's regime remained in an isolated position, as its alliance with the Soviet Union fell apart in the late 1950s. In the late 1960s, several military skirmishes erupted on the borders of China and the Soviet Union, and there was a possibility that the world's two largest communist nuclear-weapon states would wage an open war with each other. Moreover, in 1962, China fought a border war with India (more in Chapter 17), and their relations remained problematic. Mao Zedong was therefore in dire need of international allies. The United States was not in the best shape either, after the unrest associated with the Afro-American struggle for equality, the assassination of President Kennedy, and the fiasco of the failed invasion of Cuba which was supposed to overthrow the newly formed communist regime. But the main problem for the United States began to be the war in Vietnam in the late 1960s, where the positions of the United States and its allies in South Vietnam were gradually unsustainable. In the United States, which eventually lost more than 50,000 people in the war, the public opposition to military participation gradually grew, among others, because of the medialization of the massacres of the local population by American troops.

The international and domestic issues in China and the United States led to something that only few could imagine: the largest democratic and capitalist state with a dedicated anti-communist as the president began communicating with the largest (by population) communist state at the time when Mao Zedong's massive ideological campaign of the Cultural Revolution was just taking place. Eventually, the complicated communication through intermediaries and the secret trip of the US Presidential Security Advisor Henry Kissinger to Beijing resulted in President Richard Nixon's official visit to China in 1972, which triggered an international shock. Sino–American relations during the next 20 years could be characterized as an informal alliance and a classic example of rapprochement based on a mantra of "the enemy of my enemy is my friend." Despite huge ideological, political, economic, and other differences, the United States and China managed to ally themselves against the Soviet Union, which they both viewed as a security threat.[8]

One of the biggest obstacles to normalizing relations between the United States and the PRC was the issue of Taiwan (see Chapter 15). In 1971, the PRC joined the UN (leading to the withdrawal of the ROC), and in 1979 the United States diplomatically recognized the PRC, which also meant that the United States ended diplomatic relations with the ROC in Taiwan, as both Beijing and Taipei insisted, at that time, that they represented the whole of China. Washington and Beijing addressed the issue of Taiwan during several negotiations in the 1970s and 1980s, resulting in three diplomatic communiqués. However, they did not result in a common position, as the two great powers differed significantly in the interpretation of the signed documents. The PRC assumed that the United States would give up any support for Taiwan after the establishment of diplomatic relations with Beijing – as President Nixon had promised, but this was only supposed to happen at a late stage (and has never happened so far). On the contrary, the United States later pointed out that it did not claim that it "recognized" Taiwan as part of China, but simply "acknowledged" that this was the position of the regimes on both sides of the Taiwan Strait. There have also been major disagreements about US arms supplies. While the United States committed to an "eventual" cessation of supply, it later stressed that this would only happen if the security threat to Taiwan ended. Elsewhere, the text of the communiqué calls for a "gradual" reduction in arms supplies, but in practice, both sides disagreed on how the scale of military support would be measured. The United States has thus further supported Taiwan and argued that this is not a contradiction of previous statements.[9]

The situation concerning Taiwan also changed with the US Congress passing the Taiwan Relations Act (TRA) – an immediate response to the diplomatic recognition of the PRC in 1979. Congress requested the US government to maintain relations with the island despite the absence of its diplomatic recognition. While the law does not explicitly state that the United States would intervene in the event of a military conflict, it demands a policy designed to ensure the security of the island. Since the enactment of the law, the position of the United States vis-à-vis Taiwan has remained essentially unchanged and can be characterized as a "strategic ambiguity" of the nature of military intervention, should a conflict arise between Beijing and Taipei. This position is intended to discourage Beijing from a military attack, but also Taipei from a formal declaration of independence. President Biden has, however, indicated a move away from the ambiguity, as he has publicly stated a few times that the United States would, indeed, defend Taiwan.

Ultimately, Taiwan's issue remains sensitive to this day. Beijing's position regarding Taiwan as a part of China has not changed, and from the PRC's viewpoint, had it not been for the United States, Taiwan would have been united with the PRC long ago. The United States, in turn, continues to support the regime in Taiwan and insists that the final solution must be peaceful and consider the opinion of the people in Taiwan. Beijing perceives these demands as interfering, and Chinese officials feel that the United States has not respected the previous agreements.

Tiananmen: Another shock

From a certain point of view, we can argue that the informal alliance between the United States and China ended the Cold War in Asia 20 years earlier than in Europe. Another view may say that the Cold War in Asia is not over to this day – three of the world's four communist regimes are in Asia, while the Cold War divisions persist in the cases of Korea and China. Finally, one might also say that Asia has never experienced a Cold War – unlike Europe, there has been an open "hot" conflict between opposition blocs several times. Whichever view we choose, China–US relations have been the decisive element behind these historic events. To this day they define not only the international situation in Asia, but – with the growing importance of China – they have become a crucial determinant of the nature of international relations on a global scale.

The "golden age" of the 1980s ended with two events – the Tiananmen Square massacre in Beijing (see Chapter 3) and the collapse of the Soviet Union. The gradual improvement of relations between the United States and the Soviet Union, and also between China and the Soviet Union, meant that China and the United States were losing the main reason for their pragmatic relations. This trend was not so visible until 1989, as Chinese leaders led by Deng Xiaoping, Hu Yaobang, and Zhao Ziyang continued to ease the regime. It is worth mentioning that during this period, China was among the least repressive communist regimes, and there was general optimism about further developments in China. The bloody suppression of protests in Tiananmen Square, however, changed the way China was perceived. While European communist regimes collapsed and embarked on the path of democratization, China chose the opposite path: the liberalizing country suddenly became a communist dictatorship (again) that attacked its people. In the context of the absence of a common enemy and China's growing power, the allies quickly became major rivals.

After the events in Tiananmen Square, relations between the United States and China developed in a contradictory way. On one hand, fundamental differences between Washington and Beijing in political, value, and (particularly) human rights arenas have come to the fore. On the other hand, the economic relationship was deepening, which suited both countries. At first, the United States argued that economic cooperation with China didn't mean preferring trade over human rights: the argument was that cooperation with foreign countries and the economic well-being of the people in China are the best ways to support the liberalization of the Chinese communist regime.[10] This view (in addition to the United States' own economic interests) was behind America's support for China's membership of the World Trade Organization (WTO), which China joined in 2001 after tough negotiations. Subsequently, membership in this organization strongly supported China's economic growth – thanks to favorable access to most markets, it became the "factory of the world." During this period, China became the country that benefited significantly from globalization and the liberal international system (more in Chapter 9).

Ten years after the Tiananmen Square massacre, relations between the two great powers were relatively stable. The United States was preoccupied with developments in the Middle East after the terrorist attacks of 9/11 and didn't perceive China as an acute threat. In some ways, China became a partner for George Bush's counter-terrorism policy. In 2006, the US military took the view that cooperation with Chinese partners made sense and could reduce the potential for conflict. In the election to the US Senate, neither candidate used a "Chinese card," and American businesses oriented themselves toward a fast-growing market in which they saw an opportunity. US Secretary of State Robert Zoellick expressed prevailing sentiment when he argued that China "is not a threat because it does not seek to propagate a radical anti-American ideology, does not reject capitalism, and has no interest in the collapse of the international system." At the same time, however, Zoellick required China to be more involved in global governance.[11]

Cold War 2.0?

More visible cracks have started to appear in relatively stable relations between China and the United States since 2008. At first glance, the global crisis highlighted the difference between the United States as the "declining" superpower and China as an aspiring superpower. While the crisis spread from the United States, China's economic growth slowed only slightly, returning to its previous trajectory after a short period of time. The divergent impact on the US and Chinese economies resulted in a significant shortening of the prediction of when China's economy would overtake the American one. Meanwhile, the crisis boosted China's self-confidence. While in the 20 years since the Tiananmen Square massacre China behaved relatively moderately in foreign policy in line with Deng Xiaoping's doctrine, after 2010, China's policy has become "more assertive."[12]

This trend only intensified after 2012, when Xi Jinping became China's leader. Xi did not conceal his glorious ambitions to achieve a "national revival" and put China back at the center of the world as a respected superpower. In domestic politics, the level of repression has risen again. In the economy, the policy of protecting the domestic market and supporting Chinese companies abroad continued. These developments increased frustration in the United States, as many expected further easing of the political regime and liberalization of the economy. Overall, China's willingness to compromise on various conflicts with foreign actors declined, and the number of incidents with neighboring states began to rise. Moreover, Xi Jinping began to oppose the United States more openly and publicly presented his vision that only Asian countries should play strategic roles in Asia. This has openly signaled the intention to exclude the United States from the region, in which it has maintained its position as a hegemon since the end of World War II and has long been a security guarantor for several Asian countries.[13]

Partly motivated by these developments, US President Barack Obama began the so-called "Pivot to Asia," which was supposed to signal a shift of major foreign-policy interest from the Middle East to the East Asia-Pacific region, which was identified as the new strategic priority for the United States. China was the key factor in this strategic doctrine – it was Chinese activity and growing nervousness on the part of America's partners in China's neighborhood that led the United

States to increase its presence in the region, thereby counterbalancing the growth of China's influence.

Even though the US administration emphasized that "pivot" is not an anti-Chinese policy, China perceived recurrent American activity in the region in principle as an attempt to limit its growth and thus as a direct challenge. For a long time, various ideological camps in China have debated America's strategic intentions toward China. Traditional perceptions of Chinese strategic culture assume that while Asian cultures are pacifist, the West is aggressive and expansive. The orthodox Marxist teachings likewise set the capitalist United States against the (nominally) communist China.[14] In addition, John Mearsheimer's theory of offensive realism has become a popular explanation of America's strategic approach, according to which the United States, as the world's hegemon, will put up a resistance against China as a growing superpower that could one day threaten America's dominant position.[15]

Thus, the Chinese communist regime has long felt threatened by the United States, and the announcement of the "pivot" in the eyes of most Chinese observers confirmed what they had long thought. According to this perception, the United States is trying to strategically encircle China, prevent China's geopolitical and economic growth, and finally orchestrate the regime change. This somewhat paranoid perception has long been supported by the US military presence in the region (South Korea, Japan, Guam) and the existence of US partnerships that surround China. The events of the Arab Spring also supported the threat perception.

Donald Trump's rise to the US presidency further escalated these trends. President Trump placed the main emphasis on the deepening of the trade deficit, Chinese protectionism, and the relocation of production to China, which he said were robbing US citizens of their jobs and the United States of their money. Other representatives of the Trump administration, in turn, stressed Chinese state policies that, in their opinion, unfairly favored Chinese companies, whether that were monetary manipulation, state initiatives such as "Made in China 2025" or the Belt and Road Initiative (Chapter 16). A separate topic is the allegations of theft of intellectual property and (economic) espionage (see Chapter 10).

Frustration with Chinese economic and other practices was not a specificity of Trump's administration, but gradually secured a dominant position in recent years also in the EU and other Western countries. At the same time, there is no consensus on an effective solution, and Trump's actions were perceived as controversial and many, especially in Europe, but also in American democratic circles, saw them as counterproductive. Trump took several tough measures against China. One of the most visible ones was the so-called "trade war," in which the administration declared tariffs on Chinese products to offset America's trade deficit. However, the situation escalated when both parties started introducing "retaliatory" tariffs on an increasing range of products. Meanwhile, negotiations were opened between the representatives of both parties, leading only to partial agreements at the beginning of 2020, which did not address the key issues of disputes. President Biden has retained the duties on Chinese products since his election, and they are still valid as this book goes to print in the summer of 2023.

In addition to the "trade war," the Trump administration competed with China in many other areas. Perhaps the most visible symbol has been the refusal of Huawei's (and ZTE's) participation in the construction of 5G networks, where the United States has put great pressure on its allies and partners to exclude the Chinese companies. The overall atmosphere in the United States turned strongly against Chinese investments, which became perceived primarily as a security risk. Technological cooperation with Chinese companies became problematic, as did the research cooperation, while risks of espionage or theft of intellectual property started to be emphasized. In a stark reversal of the situation from ten years ago, American leaders now call China a major threat to the United States – and the world – and do not consider cooperation to be appropriate or even possible.

Paradoxically, while the United States began to address rivalry with China as a priority during the Trump administration, many of America's concrete actions helped China. Right at the beginning of his office, Trump withdrew from the forthcoming TPP (Trans-Pacific Partnership) free trade agreement, which was to support the economic presence and position of the United States in the Asia-Pacific region. At the same time, the agreement was supposed to establish high standards of international economic cooperation, which were in the interest of the United States and which were supposed to link the region to the United States economically. On the contrary, following Trump's withdrawal from the economic agreement, the Asian states, together with China (which was not supposed to be part of the TPP), agreed to accelerate the alternative RCEP (Regional Comprehensive Economic Partnership) free trade agreement, which is closer to Chinese preferences on traditional trade agreements.

Another consequence of Trump's actions was the weakening of relations with American allies and partners. While Trump focused on unilateral strengthening of American military readiness by increasing the military budget, American power in the region and in the world largely depends on good relations. Militarily, China is gradually becoming a relevant US opponent, especially in its vicinity, and it was the cooperation with China's neighbors that constituted the aspect by which the United States maintained a significant power lead. Therefore, from the US perspective, the decline in confidence in the wider East Asian region is a major strategic setback that cannot be replaced by an increase in military spending. Even though with President Biden, the international image of the United States has risen, America's partners around the world know that sooner or later, US policy may change significantly again, depending on the outcome of the presidential election. Many therefore consider the extent to which they can rely on cooperation with the United States.

The exchange in the position of president of the United States has brought some changes. President Biden is a "more traditional" politician who immediately after being elected began closer cooperation with American allies and international organizations. But Biden has not brought about any improvement in relations with China. Indeed, frustration with China has spread in American society, which is one of the few things on which there is consensus in both major political parties today. The business community, which until recently saw China as an opportunity, has largely lost its optimism and is now demanding a more vigorous US policy too. Intra-political developments in China play an important role – the growing persecution of religious minorities (especially in Xinjiang), the escalation of the situation in Hong Kong, and the further centralization of power by Chinese President Xi Jinping, in turn, highlight the authoritarian aspect of China. Overall, there is a growing perception in the United States that competition with China is an ideological dispute between the "free world" and a communist dictatorship.

Back to the future

American political scientist Robert Sutter described the three fundamental strategic interests of the United States in Asia as preventing an enemy superpower from becoming a regional hegemon, ensuring free economic access for the United States to regional markets, and spreading liberal values such as democracy and human rights.[16] In contrast, Xi Jinping envisions Asia without a US presence, so China could take the lead role. Based on these visions, it is easily understood that the interests of the United States and China are in many ways contradictory – the CCP regime's sense of threat from the United States is built on a somewhat realistic basis and the United States will view a growing China as a threat to its interests.

Relations between the United States and China can be described by the concept of a "security dilemma," where both sides feel threatened by the other side and interpret each step as a threat to their own security in a context of mutual distrust. This triggers a spiral where the action of one side leads to the reaction of the other side. Thus, in the 21st century, is the world threatened by a war between the two most powerful states – the current superpower and potentially a future one – as has happened several times in history? If we think of a conflict like World War I or World War II, the positive news may be that there is a low chance that "World War III" would look similar. One reason is the US military superiority over China, but, in general, also the existence of weapons with such devastating potential that both sides are "deterred" from entering a full-scale bloody conflict. This does not rule out the possibility of an accident or misunderstanding that could escalate into conflict, but there is still little chance that the two powers would use full military force against each other.

To avoid this scenario, it is necessary to maintain communication and have crisis scenarios in place that, in the event of various unexpected incidents, allow de-escalation in a politically acceptable way for both parties. We are more likely to experience a "Cold War 2.0," but it will also have its specifics. While the United States and the Soviet Union were virtually isolated from each other, and a large part of the world was clearly in the bloc of either superpower, today's China and the United States are interconnected, and the rest of the world wants to maintain a certain level of contact with both sides. But, at the same time, US–China relations tend to compete universally on all imaginary fronts, representing different ideological camps, which bears resemblance to the Cold War. An increasing number of contacts and exchanges are perceived on both sides as a security threat. The "arms race" is only part of this competition, which will increasingly take place in cyberspace, in space, in efforts to gain technological secrecy from the other side, to control its critical infrastructure, and, overall, to achieve information superiority. Much of this is already a reality – thus the question of whether this represents a new Cold War may already be more suited for academic discussion.

What are the chances that China will emerge from this rivalry as the world hegemon? If we mean the dominant position that the United States has held in recent decades, then China is unlikely to succeed. It is true that China has got relatively close to the United States in terms of GDP, and that China's military power, technological level, and influence on international institutions have grown. China, after enormous growth, has been put in a position where it is the second most powerful state player in the international system. But the gap between China and the United States is still significant, and with sensible policies, the United States may be able to maintain its intrepid position even in the distant future. The United States maintains a hard-to-reach lead in military power and economic maturity and technology. A very important source of American power is the alliances and partnerships that the United States can lean on around the world. By contrast, China has very few international partners who are willing to take its side – and these are usually "troubled" states like North Korea, Venezuela, Cuba, and Iran – although Russia could be a real asset. Still, the power and influence of the United States are also rooted in the essence of the international institutions that were created under American patronage after World War II, which, in their "DNA," have normative elements, such as liberalism, democracy, or human rights, and the principles of international law in general. China would continue to face an uphill struggle in competing with the United States. Finally, domestic demographic dynamics is another area in which China will increasingly face challenges which may slow down its future rise of power (see also Chapter 5).

Notes

1 G. Alison, *Destined for War: Can America and China Escape Thucydides's Trap?*, Boston: Houghton Mifflin Harcourt, 2017.
2 A. L. Friedberg, "Ripe for rivalry: Prospects for peace in a multipolar Asia", *International Security* 18(3), 1993, 5–33.
3 E. J. Dolin, *When America First Met China: An Exotic History of Tea, Drugs, and Money in the Age of Sail*, New York: Liveright, 2013.
4 Z. Wang, *Never Forget National Humiliation: Historical Memory in Chinese Politics and Foreign Relations*, New York: Columbia University Press, 2014.
5 J. Pomfret, *The Beautiful Country and the Middle Kingdom: America and China, 1776 to the Present*, New York: Henry Holt and Co., 2016.
6 P. H. Gries, *The Politics of American Foreign Policy. How Ideology Divides Liberals and Conservatives Over Foreign Affairs*, Stanford: Stanford University Press, 2014.
7 J. W. Garver, *China's Quest. The History of the Foreign Relations of the People's Republic of China*, New York: Oxford University Press, 2016.
8 H. Kissinger, *On China*, New York: Penguin Books, 2011.
9 A. J. Nathan & A. Scobell, *China's Search for Security*, New York: Columbia University Press, 2012.
10 D. Kang, *China Rising: Peace, Power, and Order in East Asia*, New York: Columbia University Press, 2007.

11 D. Shambaugh, *China Goes Global: The Partial Power*, New York: Oxford University Press, 2013.
12 R. Q. Turcsanyi, *Chinese Assertiveness in the South China Sea*, Cham: Springer, 2018.
13 "China president speaks out on security ties in Asia", *BBC*, 21 May 2014.
14 Nathan & Scobell, *China's Search for Security*.
15 J. J. Mearsheimer, "The gathering storm: China's challenge to US power in Asia", *The Chinese Journal of International Politics* 3(4), 2010, 381–396.
16 D. Shambaugh, *China and the World*, New York: Oxford University Press, 2020.

20 Relations with Europe and Russia

Partners or competitors?

Richard Q. Turcsanyi

China and Europe are key international players, and the EU–China relationship can be seen as the most important economic relationship in the world: the two sides are each other's largest trade partners. Investment exchanges between China and the EU are also intense, and their importance is increased by the fact that they are often tied to key sectors in terms of technology, exports, or infrastructure. Europe is one of the most important sources of technology for China, which is essential for China's further economic development and thus for the Chinese Communist Party's (CCP) political agenda. Contacts between China and the EU have some parallels with those with the United States, but at the same time, they differ in certain important aspects so one cannot simply speak of the "West" as a single actor in relations with China – although especially during the Biden administration, the trans-Atlantic cooperation on China has become more active. Even though China and the EU increasingly disagree on many issues, both sides still want to preserve a functional partnership, which makes the EU–China relationship different from the US–China relationship.

For Russia, China is not only the most important economic but also a strategic partner – and its importance has dramatically increased after Russia started a full-fledged war on Ukraine in February 2022. However, although Russia and China share the strategic goal of weakening the West, and the United States in particular, China has also benefited greatly from the globalized liberal international system in recent decades. Therefore, China still is less willing to enter an open conflict with the West, as Russia has done. China's ambiguity vis-à-vis the Russia–Ukraine war documents this balancing position.

Paradoxically, both the EU and Russia perceive China within a similar framework of opportunity vs threats. For Russia, in recent years, the threat perceptions of China have minimalized, as China provided the opportunity to balance the collapse in relations with the West. For the EU, it has developed in the opposite direction, and China is increasingly being seen as a "rival" and a "challenge", and sometimes openly as a threat. For China, the EU and Russia are key international actors with whom it seeks to develop cooperation in ways that would contribute to China's strategic interests, primarily in terms of balancing the power of the United States and establishing the multipolar international order. ***How are the EU, Russia, and China navigating the relationship with each other – and how***

DOI: 10.4324/9781003350064-24

does the US factor impact their choices? What are the historical legacies on which the current relationships are based? Will China and Russia get closer? Will EU–China relations more resemble the current stage of US–China relations in the future?

A problematic historical heritage

While Chinese and European civilizations were at opposite ends of the vast Eurasian continent, there were already contacts between Chinese dynasties and Europe in ancient times – whether during ancient Greece and Rome or later during the Middle Ages and the Renaissance. China's luxury products such as silk, porcelain, and tea, which were transported along the historic "Silk Road", were sought-after commodities among the European elite.[1] This civilization framework is still relevant, also because it is elevated in China today: in recent years, we have observed that the Chinese leadership refers to "civilizational" relations not only with the EU as a whole but also with Greece, Italy, and other states that are so-called "continuers of ancient civilizations" – such as Iran, Iraq, Egypt, Peru, Bolivia, and Armenia.[2]

But a more important historical legacy for today's Sino–European relations is the so-called "century of humiliation". Throughout the 19th century, the European powers (along with the United States and Japan) gradually gained an influential position in imperial China, which therefore came to the brink of complete disintegration. In today's China, this historical episode also feeds on the intense propaganda of the Communist Party, which uses nationalist anti-Western sentiments to legitimize itself among its own population.

However, this negative perception does not apply to Russia, which has been in intense contact with China since the 17th century at the latest.[3] Russia was formally present in Beijing before other European countries, and during the 19th century acquired vast territories through the so-called "unequal treaties", such as around Lake Baikal or the city of Vladivostok. These territories are still part of the Russian Federation, and, despite friendly relations, this issue sometimes appears in the Chinese debates on the Internet, although it is not officially raised.[4]

The European powers became important actors in Chinese development during the 19th century and maintained their positions basically until the communist victory in the Chinese Civil War. Europe acquired this status after repeated military victories that forced a weakened Chinese government to sign the "unequal treaties". In the First Opium War (1839–1842), the United Kingdom acquired the island of Hong Kong, and several other Chinese ports were finally opened up for international trade (see Chapter 16). The Second Opium War (1856–1860) also included France, and the joint Franco–British troops undertook a military campaign in Beijing, during which they destroyed the old summer imperial palace. This act was already strongly criticized by some European intellectuals of the time, such as Victor Hugo. The ruins of the old Summer Palace (in Chinese, *Yuanming yuan*) still stand in Beijing today and are a popular tourist attraction.[5] Subsequently, eight nations participated in the major military intervention to suppress the anti-Western

Boxer uprising – in addition to the United Kingdom and France – the United States, Japan, Russia, Germany, Italy, and Austria-Hungary – whose troops, after liberating the diplomatic quarter besieged by the Boxers, occupied Beijing in 1900 and 1901.

One of the consequences of these military interventions is the collection of ancient Chinese artifacts, which were stolen and transported mainly to museums in London and Paris. To this day, they are a sensitive political issue, as China demands their return. Portugal, Spain, Belgium, the Netherlands, and the United Kingdom of Sweden and Norway have also signed unequal treaties with China. Since the middle of the 19th century, foreign powers have gradually acquired a number of rights in China, controlled its foreign trade, and administered large territories and major rivers, and their citizens could not be judged on the basis of Chinese law, while in "concessions", even the Chinese population had to comply with European laws.

The newly established communist regime rejected from the very beginning all previously enforced contractual obligations, which it declared invalid. The new regime's policy was to create conditions so unpleasant that foreign entities would leave China without having to be directly expelled. Indeed, this policy succeeded, and within a short period of time, foreign influence almost disappeared from China. Long-term benefits for foreigners were abolished, and religious missions and enterprises were not allowed under the communist regime to continue their activities freely. A mass "exodus" led to almost no foreigners remaining in China after the beginning of the Korean War in 1950.[6]

Relations with communist countries were an important exception: European communist states were among the first to diplomatically recognize the People's Republic of China (PRC) as early as a few days after its announcement on October 1, 1949. The importance of relations within the communist bloc can also be seen from the fact that Mao Zedong traveled abroad only twice during his life, always to Moscow – for the first time already at the end of 1949. During his first trip, Mao met Stalin and, after difficult negotiations, managed to achieve his goal to conclude an alliance relationship with the Soviet Union. This strategic step marked the leaning of the PRC to the side of the Soviet Union at the onset of the Cold War and constituted an important security guarantee for the PRC against the United States, which was at the time perceived as the main security threat.

The Soviet Union and, to a lesser extent, Europe's other communist countries played an important role in China's development during the 1950s, which can be referred to as the "golden age" of their relations. Less-developed China began to copy Soviet economic practices, and there were thousands of "advisers" from communist states in China helping it to industrialize and develop. After its inception, the Chinese communist regime was internationally isolated by Western states – and even more so after the outbreak of the Korean War. Therefore, the communist states constituted an important (and basically the only available) source of much-needed technology.[7]

Meanwhile, relations between China and Western European countries have remained frozen, even as China gradually established diplomatic relations with some of them – as early as 1950, for example, with Switzerland, the United Kingdom, Sweden, and other Nordic countries. France joined in 1964, Italy in 1970, and Austria in 1971. Subsequently, China was accepted as a member of the UN, and most of the countries of the world changed their diplomatic recognition from the regime in Taipei to that in Beijing.

Meanwhile, China's relations with the communist states ran into trouble. After Stalin's death in 1953 and the advent of new Soviet leadership, ideological and other disagreements began to emerge. These eventually resulted in the entire withdrawal of Soviet advisers from China in 1960, as well as advisers from other European communist states (except for Yugoslavia, Romania, and Albania, which maintained greater independence from Moscow). Relations between the two largest communist countries subsequently deteriorated to such an extent that in 1969 military clashes broke out between them, and the two nuclear powers were preparing for a potential open conflict even with the use of nuclear weapons. Beijing, for example, during this period, built a large-scale underground city system, which was planned to serve as a shelter for almost half of the capital's population in the event of a nuclear attack.[8]

Another change in relations with Europe came after the advent of Deng Xiaoping, who began reforming and opening up China to the world in the late 1970s. In the following years, international trade began to develop, and foreign investment – including from Europe – began to flow to China, especially with the vision of a huge market and a virtually unlimited amount of cheap labor. After Gorbachev's arrival, relations with the Soviet Union and then with Soviet satellites in Eastern Europe also improved in the second half of the 1980s.

This positive period for China when it enjoyed positive relations with most foreign countries ended with the 1989 massacre in Tiananmen Square (see Chapter 3). In the same year, the European communist regimes collapsed, followed by the Soviet Union's dissolution in 1991. Communist China thus found itself in a problematic international position, once again. After a short time, however, the Chinese leadership succeeded in restoring functional relations with European countries. However, relations with Central and Eastern Europe are still influenced by the events of 1989, as post-communist regimes derive their legitimacy precisely from the rejection of communism, and many of them see China in a negative light as the surviving communist country.[9] In the case of Sino–Russian relations, however, the unsuccessful Russian transformation of the 1990s, and the growing anti-Western sentiments, played an important role in turning the complex historical legacy around.

EU–China: Partners, competitors, and rivals

In March 2019, the European Commission issued a paper analyzing strategic relations with China.[10] In this document, China is referred to as a *partner* in the debate on global issues, with which the EU needs to find a balance of interests, an economic *competitor* in technological development, and a systemic *rival* that promotes an alternative model of governance. This partner–competitor–rival triangle is the basis for understanding the approach of the EU institutions and most of its member states toward China in recent years. While, on the one hand, the EU explicitly identifies China as a "rival" with different value frameworks and international goals for the first time, it stresses that China is also a "partner" to cooperate with. However, the EU does not seek cooperation with China at all costs – on the contrary, it clearly recognizes the existence of differences, yet argues that it is necessary to seek agreement and compromise where possible.

For a relatively long time, member states and the EU institutions treated China predominantly as an economic opportunity. Although the human rights situation in China has always been perceived negatively, it has been, to some extent, overlooked in the past as the EU and its member states sought to develop economic relations. While this was in the economic interest of European states, the human rights criticism was also pushed back by arguing that China's economic development and its links with Western countries were the most effective way of promoting liberalization reforms in China (similarly to the United States). Since 2003, the EU and China have started to call their relationship a "strategic partnership", and the following years were its "golden age", also due to the shared opposition to the foreign policy of US President George W. Bush, especially regarding his military intervention in Iraq.

Over time, however, EU–China relations have cooled. China was dissatisfied that the EU had not lifted the military embargo and granted it the market economy status, which it saw not only as the EU's inability to break free from US influence but also as a failure to honor its World Trade Organization (WTO) obligations and as a disrespectful political gesture. The EU, on the other hand, has not been satisfied with the economic results of relations that did not meet its expectations, as well as with China's unwillingness to open its market to European firms, while access to the European market for Chinese firms is significantly easier. In addition, some aspects of human rights problems in China have come to the fore in connection with the 2008 Beijing Olympics and, in particular, the protests in Tibet. Yet there was no fundamental shift in the EU's approach to China. Moreover, following the announcement of the New Silk Road project by Chinese President Xi Jinping in 2013 (more in Chapter 16), European economic expectations and perceptions of the opportunity temporarily increased again.

A shift toward a more assertive EU position vis-à-vis China can be observed from about 2017. The EU has been increasingly critical of domestic developments in China but also of some Chinese foreign policy actions, such as in the South China Sea. During the first Belt and Road Forum in Beijing in 2017, for example, the EU countries did not join the Final Statement, and instead, European leaders began to stress the need for free trade and fair competition, thus indicating quite clearly that they were critical of the initiative.[11]

One of Europe's key demands – and sources of frustration – is the lack of reciprocity in market access and fair conditions for economic competition between Chinese and European businesses. Chinese companies, in general, can compete and invest in the European single market, and, as for companies from any other country, they can participate in tenders for public projects. In 2018, for example, the Chinese company China Road and Bridge Corporation won a tender for the construction of the Pelješac Bridge in Croatia, which is financed by the EU and Croatian public funds. Chinese firms own shares in key economic sectors and critical infrastructure in Europe, including ports, energy, and telecommunications. In 2016, for example, a Chinese company bought the German robotic company Kuka, and Swedish Volvo has a Chinese owner as well.

The problem is that European firms generally do not have similarly free access to the Chinese market. Many sectors in China are directly closed to foreign investment, and it is bureaucratically very difficult to enter the open ones. In the technology sectors, European companies often complain about practices that lead to involuntary transfers of intellectual property – or even its open theft. The EU assumed that business conditions in China would gradually improve with its development, but there has been frustration among businesses about the persistence of Chinese protectionism. From the EU's point of view, the conditions for China's accession to the WTO in 2001 have not been met, which is why the EU still refuses to grant China "market economy" status.

Despite the increase in skepticism about China, the EU's approach differs from that of the United States. In June 2020 (while President Trump was still in office), the EU High Representative for Foreign Policy, Josep Borrell, referred to escalating US–China relations, for which he blamed both China's problematic foreign policy and domestic actions during Xi Jinping's reign, and the US policy of economic "decoupling" from China. In this context, Borrell argued that the EU must create its own position, which, while closer to that of the United States, will differ in several respects.

According to Borrell, in addition to the value framework, the EU and the United States largely agree on the definition of China-related problems, whether it concerns national repressive policies, assertive actions against neighboring states, or state interference in the economy, which unduly favors Chinese enterprises and thus prevents fair competition. However, the EU does not share the view with Washington on how to deal with this situation. During President Trump's reign, the United States launched a policy of general strategic "containment of China", and President Biden has not adjusted the approach much.

The EU disagreed with Trump's unilateral foreign policy, the frequent use of tariffs and sanctions (including against the EU), the withdrawal from the nuclear agreement with Iran, and the negotiations on climate change. Despite its frustration and lack of patience with China, the EU is of the opinion that it still needs to be engaged on these and many other major global issues, such as the pandemics. At the same time, however, Borrell added that cooperation with China must not threaten European interests and values.

Nonetheless, the EU relations with China continued to deteriorate at the end of 2020 and early 2021, highlighting aspects of different interests and values. A few days before the end of 2020 – and before the end of the German EU Presidency – a political agreement, after eight years of negotiations, was announced on a bilateral investment agreement between China and the EU. Even if European companies were to gain further access and rights on the Chinese market under the agreement, many critical voices asked whether the EU really wanted to deepen economic relations with China's increasingly authoritarian regime – and whether it trusted that it would honor its commitments.

What is more, the agreement still had to be ratified by the European Parliament (EP). Meanwhile, in March 2021, the EP declared sanctions against four Chinese officials and one entity, which it saw as responsible for the repression of the Uyghurs in Xinjiang (see Chapter 13). China reacted with retaliatory sanctions, but included a larger number of Europeans and entities, including independent researchers and European MPs, causing significant resentment. Against this background, the EP decided to suspend the process of ratification of the agreement until the Chinese sanctions are put down.

Chinese leaders often talk about their preference for a multipolar world, an arrangement where the United States would not be the dominant global player but several major powers would balance each other in international politics. Of course, China fits into the role of one of these powers, and the EU should supposedly be the third of the key poles. That is why China reiterates that its aim is to promote European integration and that it has no interest in fragmenting and weakening the EU.

At the same time, China's ideas that the EU could be one of the independent "poles" in international politics have remained unfulfilled, and China is frustrated by Europe's inability to act strategically – or to be more precise, not to take a similar position as the United States. In particular, on critical issues such as embargoes or sanctions, China perceives the EU as leaning toward the United States, interpreting this as succumbing to US pressure. That is why China often focuses on its relations with the member states in its negotiations with Europe, even though it also develops relations with the EU institutions. This Chinese approach is sometimes referred to as the "divide and rule" policy application and has been frequently mentioned in recent years in the context of Central and Eastern Europe (CEE) and the 17+1 platform's diplomatic initiative. However, although initially many CEE countries were interested in engaging China for economic reasons, their willingness has been decreasing as the benefits have not materialized. Eventually, China's tacit backing of Russia over the war in Ukraine has poisoned relations with most of the CEE countries.[12]

In general, the Russian full-scale invasion of Ukraine in 2022 has presented a new issue of friction between the EU and China. As Russia has come to be seen as an unequivocal aggressor waging offensive war in the EU's immediate vicinity, it is impossible for the EU to overlook the "friendship with no limits" announced by President Xi and President Putin just days before the war began in February 2022. Although China has tried to position itself as not supporting the war – for instance, by abstaining in various votes within the UN – the EU does not find it sufficient and wants China to apply pressure on its "friend" Russia to stop the war. In this context, it is unlikely that the EU will "move on" and that EU–China relations will improve any time soon. In fact, the general mood is that while the triangle of partner–competitor–rival is still valid, more emphasis is being put on the "rival" part. On the other hand, the EU by and large still sticks to its position that China is a necessary partner one needs to talk to: the official visits to China by the EU leaders, including new German Chancellor Scholz and the French President Macron, in Autumn 2022 and Spring 2023 reflect these complicated dynamics. China, for its part, can be expected to play along and preserve a relatively functional relationship with the EU and its main members.

Russia and China: On the road to an alliance?

Russia and China are often presented as two authoritarian powers that are similar in many ways and pose a threat to the West. Indeed, China and Russia have become each other's closest strategic partner over the past three decades.

When a coup against Gorbachev took place in the Soviet Union in 1991, the Chinese Communist Party supported the conservative communist regime. After the coup was suppressed, the Soviet Union disintegrated within a few months, and Boris Yeltsin came to power with his transformation program. At that time, it was not clear for a moment what direction the relations between the newly formed Russian Federation – which had just rejected communism – and communist China would take. On the one hand, the collapse of the Soviet Union was a positive event for China because the immediate military threat from the Soviet Union on the northern border had disappeared. Indeed, it was the communist Soviet Union – and not the capitalist and democratic countries – that had been the main security threat to the PRC since the 1960s.

On the other hand, the collapse of the Soviet Union confronted China's communist leadership with several fundamental problems. The collapse of the historically first communist regime meant a significant loss of credibility for the communist ideology. China's communist leadership has spent a lot of time and effort studying why the Soviet Union fell apart and how to prevent a repeat of a similar scenario in China. To this day, the Chinese leadership is trying to "learn" from the case of Eastern European communist regimes and avoid the actions that led to their collapse.[13] Thus from a global policy perspective, communist China suddenly found itself in international isolation as one of the few surviving communist regimes.

The collapse of the Soviet Union also meant that a unipolar international system was established in which the United States had a dominant role as the global hegemon. This dominance was reflected, among other things, in the fact that ideas and models coming from the West influenced the whole world and for some time there was practically no alternative to them. Development financing, for example, was conditional on the so-called Washington Consensus, which was based on democratic values and neoliberal views of an unrestricted free market, private property, deregulation, and minimizing state interference in the economy. Furthermore, humanitarian military interventions led by the United States to promote democratic values and protect human rights were an even greater threat to authoritarian China. In the years since the end of the Cold War, the United States has shown its military ability and the will to intervene virtually anywhere in the world.

In this international context, criticism of the Western "preaching" approach began to spread very quickly in Russia. The Russian economy collapsed sharply when many businesses were unable to compete with foreign products, neither abroad nor at home. Oligarchic structures have gained a strong influence over further developments in the country, and a political and economic transformation, similar to that in Central Europe, came to a halt in Russia. At this point, China seemed to be a viable alternative for Russia's new elite, whether in political or economic terms. Despite political differences, Boris Yeltsin began to develop relations with China almost immediately, right where Gorbachev had left off.

During the 1990s, China became the major customer of Russia's arms industry.[14] This cooperation was mutually beneficial – for China, it was a source of relatively high-quality military material and technology after the West imposed an arms embargo on China in 1989. Russia, in turn, saw China as an important economic partner for Russian industrial exports, which largely failed elsewhere in international competition and lacked sufficient domestic demand after the collapse of the Soviet Union.

This mutual pragmatically beneficial cooperation during the 1990s was supported by converging political positions. From an international perspective, it was mainly an effort to balance the influence of the United States and the West and to establish a multipolar international system in which the power of the United States would be limited by the power of other states, such as China and Russia. The UN was an important platform for these efforts, and China and Russia prevented the United States from taking several important decisions, such as resolutions allowing military action against Serbia, Iraq, and later Syria, based on their rights of veto in the Security Council. China and Russia have become the main advocates of the unrestricted concept of state sovereignty and non-interference in states' internal affairs. According to the Russian and Chinese views, these principles take precedence over other issues, including human rights.

Relations between Russia and China continued to improve after Vladimir Putin came to power on New Year's Eve in 1999. In 2001, the two countries signed a 20-year amicable relationship agreement that brought their relations to a new level. After Xi Jinping came to power in 2012 and started similar policies (including the abolition of the term limit for his leadership), both regimes moved further toward shared values. The importance both countries pay to each other is well visible from the fact that the first official foreign trip of both Hu Jintao and Xi Jinping in the presidential office led to Russia.

Meanwhile, the countries were experimenting with various forms of cooperation. In the late 1990s, they initiated the so-called Shanghai Process, which later transformed into an international organization called the "Shanghai Cooperation Organization" (SCO). The SCO membership base was first limited to the post-Soviet states of Central Asia, apart from China and Russia. It aimed at increasing mutual trust in addressing territorial issues and security cooperation in addressing the problems of separatism, terrorism, extremism, illegal cross-border trade, and migration. In 2017, India and Pakistan joined the organization, making the SCO one of the most important non-Western international organizations. The SCO is sometimes even presented as a counterweight to NATO, but this comparison is

Figure 20.1 Vladimir Putin and Xi Jinping (source: Wikimedia Commons).

inaccurate – the SCO is not a military alliance, but rather a platform for negotiation and cooperation, often between states that have different interests in many ways.

Another international project of Russia and China is BRICS, which brings together the fast-growing developing countries of the world – Brazil, Russia, India, China, and South Africa. Like the SCO, the BRICS balances Western influence, to some extent, by seeking to promote cooperation between developing countries in the "Global South". But the BRICS does not function as a fully-fledged international organization and is more of an informal club for policy coordination – similar to the G7, to which it creates a counterweight. Moreover, as in the SCO, there are fundamental differences of opinion between the participating states within the BRICS, and it is therefore incorrect to view this association as a coherent alliance.

Looking at Russia's close friendship with China in 2023, the question arises as to whether these two powers can form an alliance, including a public commitment to military assistance in the event of a conflict. Most experts still think that this is unlikely – and there are even assumptions that their relationship may deteriorate in the future. This skeptical view is based primarily on the geopolitical assumption that Russia and China may be "natural" enemies to each other – which is why they have come into conflict with each other in the past. Even a common ideological framework during the Cold War failed to prevent the two communist regimes from reaching the brink of an open war.

As already mentioned, Russia is the only country that still controls the vast territories that it acquired from China during the 19th century through "unequal treaties". In recent decades, these territories have been depopulated, as a large part of Russia's population moved to the European part of the country. There are concerns among the Russian population and in some political circles that China may at one point want to reclaim "lost territories". That is why Chinese migration and the growing influence in the Russian Far East are perceived sensitively.

Another problematic aspect stems from the nature of economic exchange. While Russia supplied China with technologically demanding products during the 1990s, reaching a surplus in bilateral trade, the situation gradually changed. Today, Russia exports mainly minerals and energy resources to China and imports back a wide range of industrial products – and increasingly also technology. Russia is economically significantly more dependent on China than vice versa. China's growing power also manifests itself in limiting Russian influence in areas that Russia perceives as its traditional spheres of influence, such as post-Soviet Central Asia. In recent decades, China has become the dominant economic partner for the countries of the region at the expense of Russia.

The last reason for the possible future problems in Sino–Russian relations is that close and friendly relations are largely confined to the political elites of the current regimes.[15] Although opinion polls show that the populations of both countries perceive the other side positively, these perceptions seem superficially driven by the dominant official narratives, while the people-to-people exchanges are underdeveloped.[16] The friendly and close relationship between Russia and China in recent decades is largely the result of pragmatic decisions by the political elites in both countries and is based on three fundamental pillars. First, Xi Jinping and Vladimir Putin share an interest in supporting normative alternatives to Western liberal democracies – thus, Russian and Chinese authoritarian regimes legitimize and normalize each other. Second, from a geopolitical and strategic point of view, Russia and China are each other's alternatives to the United States, the EU, and the West in general. This shift was clearly visible in Russia after the annexation of Crimea in 2014 and in China after the advent of Xi Jinping. In both cases, Russia and China responded to the deteriorating relationship with the West by seeking to deepen their partnership. Third, from an economic point of view, Russia and China are complementary partners, with Russia willing to provide the vast Chinese economy with the energy and other natural resources it needs, and China selling the final products and technologies to Russia.

The future of relations between Russia and China will depend to a large extent on how the two sides deal with the West. Indeed, in the event of a further worsening of both Russia's and China's relations with the West, they would likely respond by getting even closer to each other. But the great unknown for the future of Sino–Russian relations is the question of President Putin's succession. It is possible that substantial domestic political changes will take place in Russia after his definitive departure. Since the current quality of relations between Russia and China depends precisely on Putin's authoritarian anti-Western regime, any political change in Russia could bring about strategic changes not only in relations with China but also in the nature of global political relations. Of course, domestic political developments in China are also a factor that is difficult to predict and could play an important role.

Notes

1 P. Frankopan, *The Silk Roads: A New History of the World*, London: Vintage Books, 2017.
2 Ancient Civilizations Forum, April 2017.
3 S. Namsaraeva, "Sino-Russian cross-border distrust in the longue durée", *CEIAS*, 6 June 2019.
4 S. Shekhar, "Russia's Vladivostok celebration irks Chinese diplomat, says 'in the past it was our Haishenwai'", *Times Now News*, July 3, 2020.
5 Z. Wang, *Never Forget National Humiliation: Historical Memory in Chinese Politics and Foreign Relations*, New York: Columbia University Press, 2014.
6 J. W. Garver, *China's Quest: The History of the Foreign Relations of the People's Republic*, New York: Oxford University Press, 2016.
7 J. M. Schaufelbuehl, M. Wyss & V. Zanier, *Europe and China in the Cold War: Exchanges Beyond the Bloc Logic and the Sino-Soviet Split*, Leiden: Brill, 2018.
8 Z. Wang, "Beijing's underground city", *China.org.cn*, 15 April 2005.
9 R. Q. Turcsanyi & R. Qiaoan, "Friends or foes? How diverging views of Communist past undermine the China-CEE '16+1 Platform'", *Asia Europe Journal* 18, 2020, 397–412.
10 "EU-China – A strategic outlook", *European Commission*, 12 March 2019.
11 R. Q. Turcsanyi & E. Kachlíkova, "The BRI and China's soft power in Europe: Why Chinese narratives (initially) won?", *Journal of Current Chinese Affairs*, 49(1), 2020, 58–81.
12 R. Q. Turcsanyi, "China and the frustrated region: Central and Eastern Europe's repeating troubles with great powers", *China Report* 56(1), 2020, 60–77.
13 A. J. Nathan & A. Scobell, *China's Search for Security*, New York: Columbia University Press, 2012.
14 R. Sutter, *Chinese Foreign Relations: Power and Policy since the Cold War*, Plymouth: Rowman & Littlefield, 2016.
15 U. A. Bērziņa-Čerenkova, "Sino-Russian narratives of cooperation and what it means for the Baltics", Foreign Policy Research Institute, 2020.
16 R. Q. Turcsanyi et al., "Chinese views of the world at the time of the Russia-Ukraine war", Palacky University Olomouc and CEIAS 2022.

21 China's relations with the Global South

On the rise or past their peak?

Joshua Eisenman and Eric Heginbotham

Over the last two decades, developing countries have become central to China's increasingly ambitious foreign policy. This trend accelerated after the 2009 global financial crisis when China's leaders concluded that US hegemony was declining and that developing states were becoming increasingly important partners in an increasingly multipolar world. China now paints itself as both a developing country and a major power, a self-portrait that attracts like-minded partner countries while insulating Beijing from international leadership on issues unrelated to its strategic priorities. In 2018, Xi Jinping reaffirmed that developing states are "naturally allied" with China and called for strengthening relations with newly emerging powers and more pragmatic cooperation and strategic coordination with the BRICS countries.

This chapter explains China's conceptualization of the Global South (a.k.a., the developing world), its increasing importance in Beijing's ambitious geostrategy, and China's evolving methods and objectives toward developing countries. It identifies the three main characteristics of China's approach: asymmetry, comprehensiveness, and its interlocking structure, and elucidates the various economic, political, and security policy tools that comprise China's comprehensive engagement with countries in the Global South. ***Are Beijing's primary objectives – regime survival and advancing China's position vis-à-vis the United States – sufficient to engender widespread support among most developing countries for a China-led world order?***

Developing countries in China's strategic thought

The Chinese Communist Party (CCP) seeks to build an international coalition of l ike-minded partners who help further its "core national interests." While there ar e various interpretations of this term, all assume three basic overlapping objectives : to ensure the CCP will continue to rule China, to maintain and defend China's sov ereignty and territorial integrity, and to promote a stable international enviro nment conducive to enhancing China's comprehensive national strength.[1] China especially prioritizes developing countries' support for its "territorial integrity," most notably Taiwan (see Chapter 15) and its maritime claims (see Chapter 18). Internationally, China sees itself as both a major power and the leader of a coalition of developing states working to "democratize" international institutions in

DOI: 10.4324/9781003350064-25

ways that would give them greater representation.[2] To advance common political interests, Beijing has engaged major developing states to help balance Western, particularly US, dominance.[3]

China's foreign policymakers have long differentiated international relations based on the characteristics of partner states: specifically, relations with major powers (*daguo*), peripheral states (*zhoubian guojia*), developing countries (*fazhanzhong guojia*), and, since the 18th Party Congress in 2012, multilateral (*doubian*) international forums.[4] The boundaries between these categories are somewhat ambiguous, and many states traverse two or more of them. While there is no definitive list of major developing states, they appear to include several large, more politically influential states such as the developing members of the G-20 – Argentina, Brazil, Mexico, South Africa, India, Indonesia, Saudi Arabia, Turkey, Iran, and Thailand.

Part of the Global South falls within China's traditional "strategic periphery," which constitutes a geographic belt around China that is of particular importance for Beijing. Under Xi Jinping, China's conception of what constitutes the "greater periphery" has grown apace with its power and influence to include the Middle East, the South Pacific, and parts of East Africa. This expanded definition reflects China's widened economic interests and increasingly tense relations with the United States, Europe, Japan, and India.[5]

Characteristics of China's relations with developing countries

Asymmetry is the first and most enduring characteristic of China's relations with developing countries, and Beijing's calls for "brotherhood" and "equality" are efforts to downplay it and mitigate any ill will it might engender. Disproportionate power is more a statement of fact than strategy, but because lopsided resources and information flows give China significant advantages in negotiating with smaller partners, it also influences both sides' objectives and tactics.

The second characteristic of Beijing's relations with the Global South is their *comprehensiveness*. China's relations with developing countries had generally prioritized economics, however, in recent years, political and security relations have become increasingly important. While financial incentives are generally the most persuasive element in Beijing's toolkit, China's comprehensive engagement goes beyond economics and aims to build stable, multifaceted, and mutually beneficial relationships with political elites as well as those serving in the military and police departments. Chinese educational institutions, the United Front Work Department, and the Ministry of Propaganda have built extensive people-to-people networks with thought leaders in universities, think tanks, NGOs, and media outlets throughout the developing world.

The third characteristic of China's engagement is its *interlocking* structure. As former vice foreign minister He Yafei explained, China's foreign policy involves "multi-centric, multi-layered and multi-pivotal sub-networks of regional and international cooperation that are interconnected and interwoven."[6] This dense overlapping latticework binds all four levels of China's relations with developing countries – bilateral, sub-regional, regional, and global – and creates a stable and mutually reinforcing structure to build interpersonal relationships that advance Beijing's interests.[7]

China's bilateral ties with developing states remain the foundation of its relational network. Across the developing world, Beijing has deepened its relationships with and within states and maintains strategic partnerships with some 67 countries.[8] Within each region, Beijing places considerable emphasis on its relations with large and important hub states where circumstances of geography, politics, or economics make relations with China particularly propitious. In East Asia, these include Indonesia and Thailand; in South Asia – Pakistan and India; in Central Asia – Kazakhstan; in Africa – South Africa, Egypt, and Ethiopia; in the Middle East – Iran; and in Latin America – Brazil and Argentina. This list is not definitive and has and will continue to evolve over time. Other states, like Venezuela under Hugo Chavez and Nicolas Maduro, may receive special attention due to a particular (and sometimes temporary) political alignment. Small, but strategically located states, like Djibouti and Cambodia, seem to be more susceptible to China's influence; the former now hosts a People's Liberation Army (PLA) base, while the latter has become a valuable "nail-house" vote in consensus-governed ASEAN.

China's regional-level interaction with the developing world can be traced back to 1996, with the establishment of the ASEAN+1 framework with Southeast Asian nations, and the Shanghai Five regional grouping with Central Asian nations. Since then, Beijing has gone on to create similar frameworks to structure relations with nearly every developing region, including the Forum on China–Africa Cooperation (FOCAC) in 2000, the China–Arab States Cooperation Forum in 2004, the 16+1 Cooperation between China and Central and Eastern European Countries in 2012, and the China–Community of Latin American and Caribbean (CELAC) States Forum in 2014. China's relations with sub-regional African organizations (e.g., the Economic Community of West African States and the East African Community) have come to constitute a distinct level of China's foreign relations that is unique to the continent.[9]

At the global level, China is shaping international relations among nations to suit its interests and those of its partners. Beijing regularly affirms its "UN-centered diplomacy," calls on all states to observe the UN Charter, and contributes thousands of peacekeepers to UN forces. Still, China continues to resist any impingement of its sovereignty and has pushed back hard when international institutions have made decisions that run contrary to its interests, such as the 2016 UN Permanent Court of Arbitration's ruling against China's claims in the South China Sea. In September 2022, China lambasted another UN report – this one describing torture, sexual assault, and forced labor in Xinjiang – as "wholly illegal and invalid" and "manufactured firsthand by the US and some Western forces."[10]

Methods of China's engagement with the developing world

Economics

When China's top leaders hold meetings overseas, they often travel with large business delegations and signed memoranda of understanding (MoUs) worth hundreds of millions, if not billions, of dollars. Reports of the trade, FDI, and debt financing deals that come from these meetings are regularly lauded in China's official media.

Between 1980 and 2021, China's GDP grew by a real compound annual growth rate of about 9.2% while the average annual growth rate of trade increased by 12.8% per year.[11] Thanks to large and sustained trade surpluses, by 1999 China had amassed about $155 billion in foreign reserves and was looking to gain higher yields and open new markets, especially in the extractive and construction sectors. In response, then-General Secretary Jiang Zemin launched the so-called "going out strategy" to encourage Chinese firms to identify international trade and investment opportunities.[12] Under the strategy, Chinese firms' collective outbound FDI ballooned from $1 billion in 2000 to a peak of $196 billion in 2016.[13] In 2020, China had the largest outbound FDI in the world with $133 billion invested and was the fourth largest investor in Africa behind France, the United States, and the United Kingdom.

Emerging markets, which offer both greater potential returns and risks, became central to China's "going out strategy." In 1990, developing countries represented only 15% of China's total foreign trade, but by 2010 they accounted for 31%, and by 2020, they accounted for 37%.[14] In 2020, trade with developing Asia make up 16% of China's total trade, Eastern Europe represented 4%, the Middle East represented 7%, Sub-Saharan Africa represented 3%, and developing countries in the Americas represented 7%.[15]

Meanwhile, Beijing has sought to expand its role in international financial institutions and has long pushed to change quotas and vote shares in the World Bank, International Monetary Fund (IMF), and Asian Development Bank (ADB). Impatient with the pace of IMF reform, in 2014 Beijing helped establish the Shanghai-based New Development Bank (NDB), a.k.a. the BRICS bank, with $100 billion in initial funding. In 2016, the Asian Infrastructure Investment Bank (AIIB) was founded in Beijing, and by 2020 it had over 100 member countries. During its first years of operation, however, the AIIB loaned far less than expected, and the quality of its loans has not matched that of other multilateral banks. In 2019, Jin Liqun, the bank's president, said "to improve its asset quality" the bank would push the cap on lending for infrastructure projects in China up from 3% to 10% of the bank's total loan portfolio.[16] According to its website as of June 2022, 7.5% of approved AIIB projects were in China and accounted for $3.29 billion in credit.

When the Belt and Road Initiative was announced in 2013 (see Chapter 16), it created a political narrative and policy architecture to support China's policy banks' unprecedented expansion of financing for developing countries. By 2016, the China Development Bank (CDB) and China Export-Import Bank (China Ex-Im) had become go-to lenders for developing countries, and Chinese infrastructure and telecoms firms were building railroads, dams, airports, highways, and fiber optic networks at a frenzied pace in dozens of countries. That year, the outstanding loan portfolio of CDB and China Ex-Im Bank exceeded $700 billion, more than the combined total from all six Western-backed multilateral banks. But by 2022, this approach appeared exhausted, beset by a combination of poorly or non-performing loans and China's sluggish growth amid its zero-COVID lockdowns and real estate crisis.

China also uses regional forums to ink deals. FOCAC has become China's primary conduit for providing resources to African countries. At the 2018 and 2021 FOCAC meetings, China pledged a combined $100 billion in financing for Africa.[17] And Beijing has contributed substantially to the African Union, including funding and building its $200 million headquarters in 2012. In Latin America, the first China-CELAC Forum concluded with the 2015–2019 Cooperation Plan, under which China pledged to invest $250 billion in Latin America over the next decade.[18] The subsequent two plans, covering 2019–2021 and 2022–2024, did not attach monetary targets but sought to advance cooperation in a range of areas from cyber security to agriculture to science and technology.

Foreign aid has emerged as another important policy tool, and Beijing released White Papers on the topic in 2011, 2014, and 2021. China's foreign assistance has grown rapidly, partially because unlike Western countries and institutions, which often place conditions on aid related to transparency and governance, China's aid does not require such assessments. China's aid disbursements totaled $14.4 billion between 2009 and 2012, or about a third of the total value of Beijing's aid in the nearly 60 years from 1950 to 2008.[19] In 2019, China provided roughly $5.9 billion in foreign aid, mostly to Africa.[20]

Until 2018, the Ministry of Commerce and the Ministry of Foreign Affairs jointly handled foreign aid in a somewhat piecemeal fashion and did not provide year-on-year tracking, effectively prohibiting systematic evaluation. That year, however, as part of a sweeping overhaul of State Council and Central Committee organs, Beijing created an international development cooperation agency to oversee and coordinate foreign aid disbursements. Still, according to at least one assessment, the new agency has not adequately coordinated the management of foreign aid, mitigated inter-ministerial rivalry, or increased transparency in allocation.[21]

Politics

China's prioritization of state sovereignty and non-intervention is replete in its diplomacy, party-to-party relations, military–military exchanges, and party propaganda with developing countries. The country's leaders use broad principles and unifying political narratives to promote Chinese interests and expand its leadership among developing countries in regional and global institutions. These principles help shield China from international condemnation, sanctions, and intervention related to its human rights abuses and harsh policies toward dissidents and minorities in Tibet and Xinjiang (see Chapters 12 and 13). Beijing has vetoed UN resolutions that it claims violate the principle of state sovereignty, and it generally votes with regional partners whose interests are directly affected.[22]

Still, Beijing's cooperative approach cannot fully alleviate its political risk in turbulent developing countries. In Libya, Sudan, South Sudan, and Venezuela, for instance, Chinese investors lost billions during violent, long-lasting political transitions. To mitigate the possibility of power transitions, China has publicly supported and provided largesse to friendly leaders and political parties during elections in Sierra Leone, Zambia, and Zimbabwe.[23]

To become a "major cultural power" China has stepped up its external propaganda programs. Since Xi Jinping's accession to power in 2012, he has spoken repeatedly on the need to increase China's soft power by, among other things, creating a compelling Chinese narrative and strengthening Beijing's capacity to convey its message overseas.[24] Beijing wants to improve younger generations' perceptions to counter what it sees as Western efforts to portray China in an unfavorable light. In 2004, the Ministry of Education's Centre for Language Education and Cooperation created the Confucius Institute program to promote the study of Chinese language and culture abroad. In 2021, there were 541 institutes around the world, and despite concerns in the United States and Europe, most developing countries have welcomed them. In 2022 China hosted the 5th Forum on China–Africa Media Cooperation in Beijing including more than 240 media professionals from more than 40 African countries.

Two key aspects of China's public diplomacy during the COVID-19 pandemic have been its mask and vaccine diplomacy. However, while China's propaganda has portrayed these actions as humanitarian gifts to developing countries, more than 99% of personal protective equipment and around 96% of Chinese vaccines were sold, not donated.[25] Although these exports generated substantial goodwill in some countries, some recipients were upset because unscrupulous Chinese suppliers cut corners on quality in order to speed up production and maximize profits.

Outreach by the International Department of the Central Committee of the CCP (ID-CCP) is a historical and ongoing feature of China's foreign policy and supplements the diplomacy conducted by the Ministry of Foreign Affairs and military cooperation led by the PLA. Party cadre training is organized by the ID-CCP and conducted by CCP academies, party schools, and other relevant training institutions. In 2022, Chinese construction firms completed the Julius Nyerere Leadership School in Tanzania. Built with CCP financing, the new academy is now training cadres from ruling parties in Tanzania, South Africa, Mozambique, Angola, Namibia, and Zimbabwe. In 2022, it hosted its first seminar for youth cadres of former liberation movements of Southern Africa.

Security

Although in the 1980s and 1990s China paid scant attention to military diplomacy, it has emerged as an integral part of China's larger outreach to the Global South. The policy origins of China's expanded military engagement can be found in the 1998 National Defense White Paper, which presented China's "new security concept" and contained the first official use of the term "military diplomacy."[26]

China's security footprint in the developing world remains small relative to its economic heft, but it has grown over the last decade apace with Chinese interests and the PLA's capabilities. China dispatched its first anti-piracy detachment to the Gulf of Aden in 2008, and although the piracy threat has long since abated, Beijing sent many more task forces with warships, helicopters, and resupply vessels. In 2017, the PLA opened its first overseas base in Djibouti, adjacent to military outposts operated by several other countries including the United States. PLA warships and large cargo aircraft are increasingly being deployed, and combat aircraft and aerial refueling tankers are likely to follow, suggesting that China's military deployments will continue to expand in the foreseeable future.

China's most institutionalized security relationships, those including defense and security consultation mechanisms, are with Southeast Asian states and South Asian states, although Beijing also conducts regular security dialogues with more distant major developing states such as South Africa, Egypt, and Turkey. In 2015, China committed $100 million in military assistance to the African Union, and in 2018 hosted the first China–Africa Defense and Security Forum in Beijing, including senior military leaders from 50 African states.

China is now among the top contributors of UN peacekeeping personnel and the largest among the permanent Security Council members. By 2019, the PLA had committed more than 8,000 troops to the UN peacekeeping standby force, roughly 20% of the total, and as of 2022, 2,237 Chinese peacekeeping personnel were serving in UN peacekeeping operations.[27]

In 2022, a leaked secret agreement between the Solomon Islands revealed an expansive, but ambiguously defined set of rights, under which Chinese security forces could intervene in local security affairs under a range of circumstances. That year a US Coast Guard vessel was denied permission to dock there, raising further questions. The unprecedented agreement has prompted a political backlash among some more Western-leaning island states that ultimately scuttled China's efforts to push through a collective security agreement with ten Pacific Island nations.[28]

China's 2013 Defense White Paper discussed protecting overseas interests and stipulated that "vessel protection at sea, evacuation of Chinese nationals overseas, and emergency rescue have become important ways and means for the PLA to safeguard national interests."[29] There have been calls both within the PLA and among the public to strengthen the military's capability to rescue Chinese nationals under threat abroad, a topic popularized by China's most viewed film, *Wolf Warrior 2*.

During the Mao era, China provided weapons to revolutionary groups or communist partner states. Today, China is again a sizable arms supplier – moving up from the world's sixth largest during 2002–2011 to the fourth during 2012–2021.[30] Although some buyers, like Turkey and Venezuela, may purchase Chinese arms to send a political message to Washington, the weaponry's main attraction is its combination of low price, high capability, and reasonable durability.

Looking forward: Leaning into headwinds

To help create a world where the CCP is safe from both internal and external threats, Beijing's economic, political, and military engagement is aimed at cultivating its leadership of a like-minded, if loosely affiliated and sometimes fractious, coalition of developing states. To achieve this, China preaches non-intervention, actively engages governments of all political ideological stripes, and works to enhance the voice of developing countries in international institutions. But China's efforts to unseat US hegemony are facing growing challenges that have damaged the country's image in many capitals. Even as Xi Jinping offers developing countries a "China Option," Beijing continues to suffer from self-inflicted wounds such as its support for Russia's war in Ukraine, a sharp downturn in economic growth catalyzed by its draconian COVID-19 measures, and emerging debt crises both at home and among many of its closest partners from Ethiopia to Venezuela.

Moscow's attack on Ukraine created a new and stark division between China and numerous developing countries. China's willingness to stand with Moscow has sullied its reputation in some regions, particularly Eastern Europe, where Lithuania, Latvia, and Estonia have already left its 16+1 cooperation framework. Most developing countries joined the UN vote to oppose Russia, although the majority of abstentions on the resolution came from African countries and five Latin American states – Bolivia, Cuba, El Salvador, Nicaragua, and Venezuela.[31] This split in the developing countries' views of Russia's invasion has placed China in a difficult position, because, as the *Economist* noted in April 2022: "Each new Russian atrocity in Ukraine prompts a question about China."[32]

In this way, Russia's war in Ukraine is driving a wedge between developing states and challenging China's efforts to unite the Global South behind its anti-US agenda. Meanwhile, the cohesiveness of the Western response to Moscow's invasion has demonstrated to Beijing that it too could face such a coalition if it uses military force against Taiwan or in the South China Sea.

China's domestic development, particularly the reduction of extreme poverty, has won the admiration of leaders across the Global South. Throughout 2020 and 2021, Beijing touted its ability to hold the COVID-19 virus in abeyance as proof of the superiority of its political system, with Xi declaring: "The pandemic once again proves the superiority of the socialist system with Chinese characteristics."[33] However, in 2022 the rise of the highly transmissible Omicron variant produced widespread lockdowns in Shanghai, Xian, Chengdu, and other cities, which damaged China's reputation for effective governance. The massive economic impact of the lockdowns coupled with enhanced oversight of private businesses has been devastating: the IMF cut China's 2022 GDP growth estimate to 4.4%, and tens of thousands of students from around the developing countries were forced to abandon their studies in China.

According to the World Bank, COVID-19 has hit poorer economies harder than richer ones. Beijing has already begun to reschedule significant portions of debt, a process that looks likely to continue as politically friendly countries like Zambia, Ethiopia, Zimbabwe, Sri Lanka, and Venezuela face stiff challenges in repaying debts to China. Still, even amid an economic downturn, there is little appetite for meaningful loan forgiveness in Beijing, let alone making new risky loans. Taken together, China's more restrictive economic and travel policies and the resulting GDP slowdown pose a serious challenge to building Chinese influence in the developing world. Ultimately, the fate of China's ambitions will depend primarily on whether its policymakers can resolve the structural problems dogging its economy and mitigate, rather than exacerbate, the effects of its rivalry with the United States on relations with countries in the Global South.

Notes

1 The State Council of the People's Republic of China, "China's peaceful development", 6 September 2011.
2 J. Eisenman and E. Heginbotham, "Building a more 'democratic' and 'multipolar' world: China's strategic engagement with developing countries", *The China Review* 19(4), 2019, 55–84.
3 Z. Feng and J. Huang, "China's strategic partnership diplomacy: Engaging with a changing world", *European Strategic Partnership Observatory Working Paper* 8, 29 June 2014.
4 L. Lin, "Sibada Zhihou de Zhongguo Waijiao Xin Jumian 十八大之后的中国外交新局面", *Sina News* 新闻中心, 9 January 2014.
5 X. Chen, "Zhongguo Tuijin 'Dazhoubian Zhanlue' Zhengdangshi 陈向阳:中国推进"大周边战略"正当时", *cfisnet.com*, 16 January 2015.
6 Y. He, "China's major-country diplomacy progresses on all fronts", *China.org.cn*, 23 March 2016.
7 J. Eisenman, "Locating Africa in China's community of shared future for mankind: A relational approach", *Journal of International Development* 35(1), 2022, 65–78.
8 Feng and Huang, "China's strategic partnership diplomacy".
9 D. Shinn and J. Eisenman, *China's Relations with Africa: A New Era of Strategic Engagement*, New York: Columbia University Press, 2023.
10 "China slams UN report alleging litany of rights abuses in Xinjiang", *Channel News Asia*, 1 September 2022.
11 Data from IMF World Economic Outlook Database, October 2021.
12 Z. Jiang, "Genghao de Shishi 'Zouchuqu' Zhanlue 更好地实施"走出去"战略", Central People's Government of the People's Republic of China website 中华人民共和国中央人民政府, 15 March 2006.
13 M. Yu and T. Zhong, "China's opening-up policies: Achievements and prospects", in D. Dollar, Y. Huang, and Y. Yao (eds.), *China 2049: Economic Challenges of a Rising Global Power*, Washington, DC: Brookings Institution Press, 2020.
14 These figures are the percentage of China's total world trade accounted for by "emerging and developing economies" in the IMF Direction of Trade Statistics, viewed 8 June 2022.
15 Direction of Trade Statistics, IMF.
16 "AIIB President suggests taking on more Chinese projects to improve asset quality", *China Knowledge*, 1 February 2019.
17 Y. Sun, "FOCAC 2021: China's retrenchment from Africa?", *Brookings Institution*, 6 December 2021.
18 "Cooperation plan (2015–2019)", *China-CELAC Forum*, 23 January 2015.
19 J. T. Areddy, "China touts $14.4 billion in foreign aid, half of which went to Africa", *Wall Street Journal*, 10 July 2014.
20 N. Kitano and Y. Miyabayashi, "Estimating China's foreign aid: 2019–2020 preliminary figures", *JICA Ogata Sadako Research Institute for Peace and Development*, 14 December 2020.
21 Y. Wu and M. Zhang, "China International Development Cooperation Agency: Establishment, improvement, and limitations", *Journal of Global and Area Studies* 5(1), 2021, 63–83.
22 R. Mu, "China's non-intervention policy in UNSC sanctions in the 21st century: The cases of Libya, North Korea, and Zimbabwe", *Ritsumeikan International Affairs* 12, 2014, 101–134.
23 C. Inveen and R. Maclean, "China's influence looms as Sierra Leone goes to the polls", *The Guardian*, 7 March 2018.
24 W. Feng (ed.), "Xi Jinping Tan Guojia Wenhua Ruan Shili: Zengqiang Zuo Zhongguoren de Guqi he Diqi习近平对国防和军队改革研讨会作出重要指示", *Xinhua* 新华, 25 June 2015.

25 B. Lin, M. P. Funaiole, B. Hart, and H. Price, "China is exploiting the pandemic to advance its interests, with mixed results", *CSIS*, 30 September 2021.
26 C. Jin and B. Wang, "Youguan Zhongguo Tese Junshi Waijiao de Lilun Sikao有关中国特色军事外交的理论思考", *Taipingyang Xuebao* 太平洋学报23 (5), May 2015.
27 United Nations, "Contributors to United Nations Peacekeeping Operations as of 31.03.22", n.d.
28 K. Hille, "Pacific Islanders snub China by rejecting security pact", *Financial Times*, 30 May 2022.
29 "The diversified employment of China's armed forces", *Xinhua*, 16 April 2013.
30 "SIPRI arms transfer database", www.sipri.org/databases/armstransfers, n.d.
31 "The world's response to the war in Ukraine: A 27-country global advisor survey", Ipsos, April 2022.
32 "Don't underestimate Xi Jinping's bond with Vladimir Putin", *The Economist*, 9 April 2022.
33 "Xi confers medals for virus fight at victory ceremony in Great Hall", *The Sydney Morning Herald*, 8 September 2020.

Index

Page numbers in **bold** denote Tables; page numbers in *italics* denote Figures.

4:2:1 family model (4:2:1 problem) 64
16+1 platform; 17+1 platform 246, 251n9, 254, 259

Africa 2, 96, 145, 199, 202, 204n20, 206–7, 249, 253–8, 260n7, 260n9, 260n17, 260n19
air pollution 9, 136, 138, 141, 143–4
all under heaven, tianxia 18, 20, 207, 216n7
anti-terrorist policy (counter-terrorism strategy) 148–51, 152–3, 155n5, 155n10, 155n13–14, 215–16, 234, 248
Asia-Pacific 178, 234, 236
Association of Southeast Asian Nations (ASEAN) 210–12, 216n10, 254

Beijing Olympics 244
Belt and Road Initiative (BRI); A New Silk Road; One Belt One Road; yi dai yi lu 10, 96, 145, 193, 195, 198–200, 202–3, 204n14, 204n21, 206, 208, 210–12, 214–16, 217n19, 217n24, 235, 251n11, 255
Biden, Joe 181, 227
BRICS 207, 212, 249, 252, 255
Buddhism 7, 18, 48, 50, 52–4, 57n18, 116–18, 158–60, 164
Bush, George W. 45, 234, 244

censorship 34, 45, 48, 100, 106–11, 113n16, 143
Central and Eastern Europe (CEE) 40, 46, 91, 243, 246, 251n9, 251n12, 254
Central Asia 10, 18, 23, 115n3, 184, 200, 205–8, 215–16, 216n6, 217n24–5, 248, 250, 254
century of humiliation 20
Chen Shui-bian 184, 186, 190n5
Chiang Ching-kuo 183
Chiang Kai-shek 5, 30–1, 177, 180, 183–4, 187, 229–31
China as the factory of the world 58, 96, 233
China's economic growth 1, 58, 89, 97, 128, 144, 194, 233–4
China's political system 8, 73, 78–9, 86, 90, 100, 102, 110, 112, 175, 259
China's power 2–3, 189, 193–4, 202
China–Community of Latin American and Caribbean (CELAC) 254, 256, 260n18
China–Myanmar Economic Corridor (CMEC) 201
China–Pakistan Economic Corridor 201, 204n16, 214, 217n21
Chinese civilization 3, 6–7, 15–16, 18–21, 48, 125, 143, 241, 251n2
Chinese Communist Party (CCP) 2, 9, 15, 20, 25–6, 29–31, 34, 40–1, 43–4, 48, 51–3, 55, 56n14, 61–2, 66, 73, 76, 77, 78–81, 84–6, 88n5, 88n8, 89, 96, 99, 102, 104, 106–7, 110–11, 119–21, 126n6, 136, 143–4, 147, 149, 161–2, 169, 175, 183, 193, 194, 197, 199–200, 203, 219, 222–3, 237, 240, 247, 252, 257–8
Chinese dynasties 17, 18, **22**, 114, 158, 241
Chinese history 7, 15–17, 19, 25
Chinese national identity (Chinese identity) 16, 18, 55, 190n8, 222,
Chinese People's Political Consultative Conference (CPPCC) 76, 78–80
Christianity 7, 48, 51, 53, 118, 228,
Clinton, Bill 107, 113n14,
communist revolution 30, 170,
COVID-19 9, 61, 87, 97, 98n10, 99, 104, 112, 144, 175, 182, 194, 203, 211, 219, 222, 225, 229, 255, 257, 259
Cultural Revolution 25, 29, 32–8, 54, 55, 81, 149, 157, 162–3, 169–70, 187, 231
cultural values 58

Dalai Lama 156, 159–64, 212, 221
Democratic Progressive Party (DPP) 184–6
Deng Xiaoping 9, 32–3, 36, 41, 43–4, 46, 55, 77, 82–5, 89, *90*–1, 137, 170, 193, 195, 206, 233, 243

East Asia 19, 97, 132, 164n5, 170, 205, 234, 238n10, 254
environmental activism 46n10, 142, 145n12, 146n17
ethnic minorities 58, 67–8, 74, 79, 147, 151, 156, 167, 221
economic miracle 89–*90*, 136–7, 170, 182
Exclusive Economic Zone (EEZ) 223–4
economic development 1, 10–11, 32, 34, 38, 43, 68, 90–2, 95, 171, 194, 199–200, 212, 240, 244
EU–China relations 240–1, 243–4, 246, 251n10
European Union (EU) 1–2, 11n5, 45, 61, 97, 135n4, 138, 154, 193, 198, 201–2, 210, 215, 235, 240–1, 243–7, 250, 251n10
environment 2, 9–10, 36, 62, 67, 74, 91, 106, 108, 130, 135n4, 136, 137–8, 140, 142–43, 145n16, 198, 252

Falun Gong 45, 51–2, *53*, 103
foreign direct investment (FDI) 91, 129, 216, 255
foreign oppression 15
Forum on China–Africa Cooperation (FOCAC) 254, 256, 260n17

G7 249
gender 64–6, 68,69n21, 252–3
Global South; developing world 11, 11n5, 46, 203, 207, 249, 252–4, 257, 259
good neighbor policy 206
Great Leap Forward 29, 32–3, 35, 38, 91, 137, 162, 231
Guangzhou 61, 118, 139

Han 6–7, 18–19, **22**, 47, 54, 63, 67, 117, 121, 135n3, 147–8, 150
Hong Kong 4–6, 8, 22–3, 26, 45, 65, 74–5, 77, 79, 90, 98n12, 100, 121, 123–4, 127n27–9, 132, 166–74, 175n1, 175n3–6, 175n8, 176n10, 176n12–13, 182, 185–6, 194, 203, 222, 229, 237, 241
Hu Jintao 8, 36, 78, 83–4, 102, 121, 143, 193, 206, 248
Hu Yaobang 40, 43, 162, 233
Hua Guofeng 33
human rights abuse and violation 6, 53, 114, 121, 154, 156, 184, 211, 256

India 3, 7, 10, 18, 21, 53, 62, 69n10, 158–9, 162–4, 196–7, 200, 204n6, 205, 207, 209, 211–12, 214, 217n20, 217n23, 218–19, *220*–5, 226n5–10, 228–9, 231, 248–9, 253–4
innovations 117, 125, 128–31, 134, 135n1–5, 135n9
investments 42, 90–7, 129–31, 141, 145n13, 149, 169, 170, 186, 198, 201–3, 208, 210, 212, 215, 236, 241, 243, 245, 255
Islam 7, 48, 51, 53, 149–51, 214–6

Japan 2, 7, 10, 19–20, 23–4, 27n8, 29–31, 47, 54, 117, 122, 127n30, 130, 178, 180, 182, 184, 205, 207–11, 227–9, 235, 241–2, 253
Jiang Zemin 8, 35, 78, 82–4, 206, 255

Kennedy, John F. 231
Kissinger, Henry 231, 238n8
Kuomintang (KMT) 5, 24, 27, 29–31, 119, 177, 180, 182–7, 223, 230

Lee Teng-hui 183, 186
LGBTIQ 67, 102, 121
Li Keqiang 83, 85–6, 97
Line of Actual Control (LAC) 220–2, 226n6
Liu Shaoqi 33–4

Ma Ying-jeou 186
Macao 74–5, 77, 123, 127n27, 194
Malacca Strait 200–1
Mao Zedong 5, 8–9, 25, 29, *30*, 31, 33–5, 37–8, 39n4, 42–3, 50, 54–5, 62, 66, 78, 84–6, 149, 151, 162, 169, 194–5, 220–1, 230–1, 242
May Fourth Movement 24, 27
Middle East 7, 234, 253–5
military: conflict 5, 11, 188, 200, 207, 219, 222, 225, 227, 232; force 21, 237, 259; in Central Military Commission 76–8, 121

National People's Congress (NPC) 76, 78–9, 85, 124
neo-Maoism 35
nine-dash line 223–4

Nixon, Richard 231
North Korea 2, 8, 10, 44, 65, 121–2, 196, 205, 208–9, 216n11, 218, 220, 238, 260n22

Obama, Barack 234
one country, two systems 6, 75, 123, 170, 175, 197
one-child policy 63–6, 68
Open Door Policy 54, 89
orientalism 20, 27n10

Panchen Lama 163–4
Pearl River 170, 172
People's Liberation Army (PLA) 33, 76, 78–9, 161, 254, 257–8
population control 62–4, 124
population growth 58, 62–4, 68, 136–7
pragmatism 48
propaganda 9, 17, 19, 26, 30, 38, 55, 86–7, 99, 102–3, 105–12, 113n17, 151, *185*, 225, 241, 253, 256–7
Putin, Vladimir 112, 219, 246, 248–50, 261n32

re-education camps 6, 33, 147, 151–2, 154, 155n17
religion 6–8, 47–55, 56n1–3, 56n5–6, 121, 147–8, 158–60, 162, 164n1
Republic of China (ROC) 5, 7, 19, **22**, 24, 27, 31, 52, 119, 177, 180, 185, 187, 219, 229–30, 232
rule by law 119–20, 126
Russia 2, 10–11, 23, 26, 118, 205, 207–8, 215–6, 216n12, 217n25, 218–19, 222, 228, 238, 240–2, 246–50, 251n16, 259
Russia–China relations 208, 243, 250, 251n3, 251n15

Shanghai 29, *30*, 58, 61, 74, 76, 82–3, 92, 118, 141, *199*, 207, 216, 248, 254–5, 259
Shanghai Cooperation Organization (SCO) 207, 212, 248, 248–9
Sino–Indian border 196, 219, *220*, 221–2, 225–6
social control 99–101, 103–4, 106–7, 112
social credit 9, 99, 103–6, 113n7–10, 113n12
social issues 31, 58, 102
socialism with Chinese characteristics 43, 55, 89, 194
soft power 155, 155n3, 197, 204n12, 204n13, 251n11, 257
soil contamination 136, 140–1
South Asian Association for Regional Cooperation (SAARC) 212
South China Sea 7, 10, 194, 196–7, 200–1, 203n3, 203n5–6, 204n15, 210–11, 218, 222–*4*, 225, 226n4, 239n12, 244, 254, 259
South Korea 2, 10, 20, 90, 132, 169, 178, 182, 184, 205, 207, 208, *209*, 211, 235
Southeast Asia 5, 7, 10, 90, 94, 186, 196, 199, *200*, 201, 205, 207, 209–12, 216n10, 217n16, 217n24, 229, 254, 258
special economic zones (SEZ), jingji tequ 58, 90, 92, 212

Taiwan 4–6, 17, 19–20, **22**, 23–4, 26, 31, 51–2, *53*, 54, 68n1, 74, 90, 132, 169, 177–8, *179*, 180–8, 189n1, 189n3, 190n4–5, 190n7–13, 190n15, 194, 209, 219, 222, 223, 229–32, 252, 259
Taiwan Relations Act (TRA) 181, 232
Taiwan Strait; Cross-Strait relations 180–1, 186, 219, 231–2
Taoism 7, 47–8, 53–5, 116–7
territorial disputes 7, 204n5, 205, 209, 218–19, 225, 226n1–2
Tiananmen 1989 events 8–9, 25, 27n18, 31, 34, 38, 40–6, 46n2–6, 46n8, 46n11, 46n13, 52, 78, 82, 85, 92, 99–100, 103, 108, 112, 151, 154, 162, 171, 210, 219, 233–4, 243
Tibet 6–7, 17–19, 23, 26, 56n10, 56n13, 63, 67, 74–5, 100, 118, 121, 155n13, 156, *157–8* , 159–63, 164n2–3, 165n6–7, 165n9–11, 194, 212, 219, 220–1, 244, 256
Tibetan exile 162–4, 221
trade war 96, 131, 235–6
Trump, Donald 154, 235–6, 245
Tsai Ing-wen 185, 188, 194

Ukraine 222, 240, 246, 251n16, 259, 261n31
United Nations Convention on the Law of the Sea (UNCLOS) 196, 223–4
United States 1–3, 10–11, 16, 23, 36, 45, 46, 88, 96, 118–19, 131–2, 134, 137–8, 141, 145n13, 145n14, 147, 154, 162, 171, 177, 180–1, 183, 188, 193, 202, 205–7, 209–11, 214–15, 218–19, 222, 225, 227–38, 240–2, 244–8, 250, 252–3, 255, 257, 259
US–China relations 5, 11n5, 135n6, 189n3, 227, 229, 237, 240–1, 245
Uyghurs 6, 53, 63, 67–8, 74, 100, 122, 126n17, 147–54, 155n8, 216

Vietnam 8, 10, 19, 23, 54, 65, 117, 122, 160, 167, 205, 207, 210–11, 216n10, 218, 222, 224, 231

Wen Jiabao 36, 37
West 2, 6, 11, 18, 20, 23, 29, 42, 45–6, 49–50, 54, 61, 85, 101, 112, 135n2, 148–9, 159, 161, 164n5, 170, 177, 199, 202–3, 210–11, 220, 222, 228, 229, 235, 240, 247–8, 250, 254

Xi Jinping 8, 25, 33, 37, 46, 55, 66, 68, 73, 76–8, 80, 82–6, *87*, 88n10, 95, 96, 99, 106, 110–12, 113n17, 120, 143–5, 166, 172, 175, 188, 193, 195–6, 198, 203, 204n14, 216n4, 225, 234, 237, 244, 248, *249*, 250, 252–3, 259, 260n24
Xinjiang 6–7, 17–18, 23, 53, 67–8, 74–5, 105, 107, 121–2, 126n17, 144, 147-54, 155n1, 115n4, 155n6, 155n12, 155n15, 155n17, 155n20–2, 157, 194, 201, 215, 221–2, 237, 246, 254, 256, 260n10

Zhao Ziyang 43–4, 46n9, 85, 89–*90*, 92, 233
Zhou Enlai 170, 221
Zhu Rongji 92, *93*

For Product Safety Concerns and Information please contact our EU representative GPSR@taylorandfrancis.com
Taylor & Francis Verlag GmbH, Kaufingerstraße 24, 80331 München, Germany

www.ingramcontent.com/pod-product-compliance
Ingram Content Group UK Ltd.
Pitfield, Milton Keynes, MK11 3LW, UK
UKHW020013200926
475702UK00014B/1864

* 9 7 8 1 0 3 2 3 9 5 0 8 1 *